Mirror

HISTORY THAT TIME FORGOT

100 front pages and the
stories behind them

First published in 2014

A catalogue record for this book is available from the British Library

ISBN: 978-0-85733-727-6

Published by Haynes Publishing, Sparkford, Yeovil,
Somerset BA22 7JJ, UK
Tel: 01963 442030 Fax: 01963 440001
Int. tel: +44 1963 442030 Int. fax: +44 1963 440001
E-mail: sales@haynes.co.uk
Website: www.haynes.co.uk

Haynes North America Inc., 861 Lawrence Drive,
Newbury Park, California 91320, USA

Images © Mirrorpix

Creative Director: Kevin Gardner
Designed for Haynes by BrainWave

Printed and bound in the US

Mirror

HISTORY THAT TIME FORGOT

100 front pages and the
stories behind them

Adam Powley

CONTENTS

The *Daily Mirror* newsroom in 1971.

The first front page of the first *Daily Mirror* – though it wasn't *actually* the front page; that was initially reserved for advertisements.

INTRODUCTION

There's a familiar saying that everyone can remember where they were when President Kennedy was shot. More recently, the same could be said about the death of Princess Diana or the day of the terrorist attacks in New York in 2001. These are among the defining moments of the age that no one who lived through them will ever forget.

Such extraordinary stories grab the headlines and become the biggest news items not just on the day of when they happened, but they are seared into our collective consciousness for decades afterwards. Think of the moon landings and other remarkable human achievements. Recall the terrible disasters and political earthquakes; the dramatic incidents, famous escapades, and the often bizarre events and colourful characters central to them. Together they become part of history itself, snapshots of time that live well beyond their initial impact.

There are other stories, however, that do not stay quite so long in the memory. They grab people's attention at the time but then fade away until they are all but forgotten, usually left to be remembered only by those involved or directly affected. These are the stories that history forgot.

This book rediscovers and presents just some of those stories. There are thousands of them to choose from: the news items that quite rightfully made the front pages at the time but which, for a variety of reasons, have disappeared in the intervening years. What follows here is a selection of those headline-makers, brought to our attention once more.

Drawn from the pages of the *Daily Mirror*, they tell a series of remarkable tales about big events and the people central to them that have subsequently been neglected. They run across a whole range of subjects, from wars to murders, high-profile court cases and sensational scandals to human tragedies, triumphs and outrageous, often comical, capers and adventures. Reading them now it frequently seems incredible that many have been all but forgotten. But they are a reminder of how the world moves quickly on, leaving the past behind.

All life is here, revealed in superb journalistic style by the nation's most enduringly popular newspaper. These are stories that don't just give the bare facts but paint a colourful and engaging picture of time and place, expressing in vivid style the sheer drama and compelling interest of each event.

Over a century ago, when the *Daily Mirror* first hit the news-stands, it was launched as a publication intended to be bought by middle-class female readers. Yet it quickly became a mass-market newspaper with a rapidly rising circulation. As the paper evolved, so too did its approach and its unique style of popular journalism, making it at one stage Europe's biggest-selling daily newspaper.

The *Mirror* had, and still has, a reach and influence that makes it central to our daily lives and how we record them, covering not just the big stories at home, nor simply those involving the powerful, famous and infamous, but the news around the world as lived by everyone, whoever they may be. The *Mirror* may have a deserved reputation as a campaigning paper, but it has based its success fundamentally on its day-to-day reporting. Successive editors and journalists have taken pride in that reputation.

As a consequence the paper has had a distinctive way of bringing the world to life and showing what takes place both at home and abroad. Whether it has been in the shape of history-defining events, or the small, individual stories that often lie behind them, the coverage of sudden breaking news or the sagas that developed over time, the *Mirror* has been on hand to bring it to the attention of its millions of readers – even if that attention was fleeting, as with these oft-neglected tales.

Many of the reporters who told them are themselves now largely forgotten. Famous in their day, they now live on in their articles, accompanied by some of the best ever headlines devised by the smartest of sub-editors.

As masters of the craft, the *Mirror*'s reporters did an outstanding job in writing news pieces. This book is, in large part, a tribute to their skill and expertise in creating engaging, lively, informative and entertaining journalism.

These stories are told not just by words alone but by some of the finest newspaper photography in the business (not forgetting some outstanding illustrators who would compose beautiful sketches of events in the days before wires that could send photos in an instant, ready for publication the same day).

Naturally not all the content is worthy, nor wholly admirable. Not everything that made the various editions was entirely true or truly representative of what actually happened. The enquiry and intrusion into the lives of ordinary people making them famous figures for a day, willingly or otherwise, shows that the modern demand for sensation and gossip is nothing new.

Instead the reader then and now is left to judge how responsibly and fairly each subject was handled. What cannot be doubted is the fascinating insight into past times that these stories provide.

And there are a host of truly incredible tales. Here are the exciting reports of long-forgotten battles, such as in the bitter conflict between Russia and Japan in 1904–05. Dramatic political events get the full banner headline treatment, major crimes emerge as an enduring fascination, while shocking exposés reveal the devastating truth that had previously remained hidden.

There are some often hilarious stories of various moral misdemeanours and scandals, usually involving high-society figures or naughty "respectable" individuals. It's intriguing to see how the *Mirror*'s attitudes towards sex evolved, becoming more daring and explicit as society itself changed.

There are also, sadly, several reports of both natural and man-made disasters. Decades on, these awful events still have the power to move, even if the suffering they caused has been more or less consigned to the past. But, like all the headline pages featured here, they create a portrait of a world that may have been largely forgotten – but one that is still fascinating to look at, all these years later.

<u>Note:</u> Dates are for the day the report appeared in the *Daily Mirror*, not the date on which the actual event occurred. Not all reports featured as front pages. Factual information relates to what the paper reported at the time (for example numbers killed in disasters, not necessarily the actual figures).

CHAPTER ONE

EVERY MAN FOR HIMSELF!

The Glen Cinema in Paisley, scene of one of the worst and most heartbreaking disasters in British history (see page 50) – but one in which some displayed incredible bravery.

TO-DAY'S WEATHER.

Our special forecast for to-day is: Keen easterly breezes and frosty weather; cloudy, with slight snow at times.

Lighting-up time, 5.0 p.m.

SEA PASSAGES.

English Channel, rather rough to moderate; North Sea, rather rough; Irish Channel, moderate.

The Daily Mirror.

1st Day of Year. Friday, Jan. 1, 1904. 365 days to Dec. 31.

PAGE 3.

1904.	January.					
Sun.	...	3	10	17	24	31
Mon.	...	4	11	18	25	...
Tues.	...	5	12	19	26	...
Wed.	...	6	13	20	27	...
Thurs.	...	7	14	21	28	...
Fri.	1	8	15	22	29	...
Sat.	2	9	16	23	30	...

To-day's News at a Glance.

Home.

. . . "And the New Year's coming up. . ." It is a Leap Year.

The Lord Chamberlain has issued an official notice regarding the series of Courts to be held at Buckingham Palace during the season.—See page 7.

A son and heir has been born to Lady Sybil Grant, and Lord Rosebery is now a grandfather.

London was a little colder yesterday; the temperature dropped to 31 degrees. A little snow or sleet fell throughout the southern counties.

Emily Bailey, a nurse at Beechwood House, Pembury-road, Tunbridge Wells, was watching a workman felling a tree yesterday when a falling bough fell on her and killed her.

A woman knelt down beside the railway track at Hoddesdon (Herts) yesterday, and placing her neck upon the rail was decapitated by a passing train.

The police have not yet effected any arrest for the murder of Mrs. Dora Kiernicke, in Whitfield-street, Tottenham-court-road.

After forty-seven years' service, Mr. T. J. Allen, the chief traffic superintendent of the Great Western Railway, retired yesterday from office.

Stockbrokers gladly said "good-bye" yesterday to the poorest year on 'Change they have experienced.—See page 5.

The campaign fund now being raised by the National Free Church Council to fight the Education Acts has reached £9,000.

Three lads were drowned while skating yesterday—two in Monmouthshire, and the third, the son of Mr. Arthur Shepherd, bank manager, at Woking.

Foreign.

The condition of Princess Mathilde has undergone a decided change for the worse. Her Imperial Highness is extremely weak.

Fêtes are being organised in Spain, with Government support, to commemorate the tercentenary of the writing of "Don Quixote."

Officialism at Hamburg has issued a public notice, calling upon a woman, born in 1765, and of whom nothing has been heard since 1826, to report herself to the registrar, "failing which, she will be entered as dead."

Fourteen cars have entered for the Gordon-Bennett-Auto Cup Race next summer, the entries closing yesterday.

The Pope has confirmed the decision of the Propaganda rejecting the candidates selected by the Chapter of Southwark for the Bishopric of that diocese.

Colonial.

Mr. Bosanquet has injured his right hand while practising at the nets, and will be unable to play in the Test cricket match which begins to-day at Melbourne.

"Bradstreet's Review of Canada" for the year 1903 states that the Dominion has completed the most successful year in its history.

TO-DAY'S ARRANGEMENTS.

General.

Dinner to Mr. T. Skewes-Cox, M.P., at Richmond.
Second Test Match begins at Melbourne.
New Year's Day Concert, Queen's Hall, 3.
Concert, Albert Hall, "Messiah," at 8.

Racing.

Manchester.

Sales.

Redmayne and Co., 19, 20, New Bond-street, W.; costumes, tea-gowns, furs, lace, &c.

Theatres.

*Adelphi, "Little Hans Andersen," 2; "The Earl and the Girl," 8.15.
Apollo, "Madame Sherry," 8.
Avenue, "All Fletcher's Fault," 9.
Comedy, "The Girl from Kay's," 8.
*Court, "Brer Fox and Brer Rabbit," and "Snowdrop," 2.
Criterion, "Billy's Little Love Affair," 9.
Daly's, "A Country Girl," 8.
*Drury Lane, "Humpty Dumpty," 1.30 and 7.30.
Duke of York's, "Letty," 8.
Gaiety, "The Orchid," 8.
*Garrick, "Water Babies," 2.15; "The Cricket on the Hearth," 8.15.
Haymarket, "Cousin Kate," 9.
His Majesty's "The Darling of the Gods," 8.
Imperial, "Monsieur Beaucaire," 8.30.
Lyric, "The Duchess of Dantzic," 8.
*New, "Alice Through the Looking-glass," 2.30 and 8.15.
Prince of Wales's, "The School Girl," 8.
Royalty, "Kyritz-Pyritz," 8.15.
St. James's, "The Professor's Love Story," 8.30.
Strand, "A Chinese Honeymoon," 8.
Terry's, "My Lady Molly," 8.15.
*Vaudeville, "The Cherry Girl," 2 and 8.
Wyndham's, "Little Mary," 9.
Alhambra, "Carmen," doors open 7.45.
Empire, "Vineland," doors open 7.45.
*Hippodrome, "The Elephant Hunters," 2 and 8.
Palace, New Bioscope Pictures, 8.

*Matinees are on the day of performance indicated by an asterisk.

THEATRE DEATH-TRAP.

Tragedy that has Desolated Chicago.

NEARLY 600 DEAD.

Women and Children Struggle for Life.

PATHETIC INCIDENTS.

Millionaires Searching for Dead Relatives.

The theatre is the newest and finest in Chicago, . . . and was supposed to have all the latest devices for safeguarding human life.—"Times" correspondent.

This is the most startling fact revealed in connection with Wednesday afternoon's appalling catastrophe at the Iroquois Theatre, which has filled Chicago with dismay. An electric spark started flames in the wings—a fire so slight that it might have been promptly subdued; some of the "latest devices for safeguarding human life" failed; discipline vanished behind the proscenium; panic seized the house; all the artists, numbering 240, effected their safety in flight; almost one-half of the audience perished.

The number of persons in the auditorium was 1,700; the dead bodies recovered number 564, and 314 persons are still reported missing. Fully fifty of the injured will die.

The suave qui peut struggle for escape caused the greatest sacrifice of life; with forty exits available it has been established the terror-stricken people sought flight only through the few doors they best knew.

STORY OF THE DISASTER.

Compiled from the Narratives of Survivors.

There were 1,700 people in the great theatre. It was a matinée, and mothers had brought their children to see the pantomime of "Bluebeard" from Drury Lane.

The first act and part of the second had passed in merry jest and tuneful song, and the peals of childish laughter had just died away in preparation for one of the prettiest items of the whole piece.

It is a part song called "In the Pale Moonlight," sung by a double octette. The lights are lowered, for there is a moonlight effect that can only be seen at its best in darkness.

A Ribbon of Flame.

Suddenly there appears on the stage, tricked out with a wealth of scenery, a tiny ribbon of blue flame, that shoots up into the air, and then curls round the scene like a sinister fiery snake. The children's eyes open wide with surprise; one would think in their innocence they saw in this a new and startling effect devised for their pleasure.

But some of the elders in the balconies rise in alarm, and crowd forward. An actor steps to the curtain and asks them to keep their seats. Then there is a cry, a shrill feminine shriek of terror—"Fire!" It is a signal for panic and "sauve qui peut." The whole of the vast audience rises, with deadly terror at the heart and the pallor of panic on their faces.

Terror on the Stage.

The people on the stage seem frozen with affright. When the flame first appears, fire-extinguishers are turned upon it, but without the least effect. Fear seems to paralyse efficiency. The flames gain every moment. Then the heavy asbestos curtain is lowered to shut off the stage from the house.

Half-way down it jams, and remains immovable, showing the glow of fire behind it. The stage hands' fright is complete; they lose their heads and fly. The half-lowered curtain acts as a great flue. It sucks the flames like a tornado over to the balcony—the dress circle of a London theatre.

But the horror is not yet complete. In a moment comes an explosion of the gas reservoirs, lifting the roof and spreading deadly asphyxiating fumes throughout the building.

Then the flaming curtain falls outward on the plush seats, and sets them on fire, causing clouds of suffocating smoke.

The madness of terror seizes the audience. Chivalry, modesty, shame—every human feeling is lost in the blind, overpowering instinct of self-preservation. There are "forty ample exits," but the people know it not, and only fight fiercely for the three or four they see.

Down the tiers of seats in the balconies sweep men, women, and children in one confused mass. Some in their frenzy leap over the rails into the pit below. But the great majority struggle for the doors.

A Rush for Life.

There are few men, but some of them forget all manhood. They fight with fists, they push, they tear the clothes of the women in their rush for life. Mothers, with their little children, battle with clenched hands, with other women in similar case competing with them for safety.

Over this struggling mass the flames play fiercely. Some are mercifully killed at once by the blast of combined flame and gas. Whole rows of women, dead, their heads hanging over their breasts, are seen in the balcony chairs.

But the panic is more terrible even than the fire-torrent. The aisles of the balconies are quickly piled with corpses three and four deep. Children fall under foot, and the adults rush heedless over their bodies. Near the exit the scene is indescribably horrible. The mass of bodies soon reaches within two feet of the ceiling—crushed and mangled women and children overcome while crawling over the bodies of those who have already died.

The Rescuers.

Some are with closed fists, still clenching fragments of clothing torn from others in the wild fight for existence.

The faces of some are trampled so that no semblance of the human remains. One man's body is actually beheaded, and crushed into pulp. The dead near the main exit are so jammed that the firemen, when they come, cannot lift them singly; it is necessary to seize a limb and pull the body out by sheer force.

Men who have seen bloody battlefields are overcome by horror; they have never seen a sight so gruesome in war.

And all this dreadful business has taken but ten minutes in the doing; a quarter of an hour ago all was gaiety in the "safest theatre" of Chicago!

The work of rescue commences; firemen crawl up the stairs leading to the balcony. When the door is reached one man turns round to his comrades, and exclaims, "Good God! don't walk on their faces." They find a pile of bodies of women higher than themselves—with faces that tell of the agony of their death.

A strange uniformity is observed. In nearly every case the victim's left arm is held stiff and close to the body, while the right is stretched out as if warding off the peril.

Frenzied Relatives.

There is a maddening scene outside—frenzied relatives demanding that they shall at least come near the scene of the holocaust.

The rescue goes on as well as can be expected.

A Roman Catholic Bishop, who happens to pass, takes a prominent part. With the spirit of the ancient fathers he climbs to the gallery, and in the midst of hard, practical work gives absolution to the dying and injured. So long as any remain alive the brave Bishop refuses to leave.

Falls to Death.

Even after fire-escapes arrive many people are killed; the crush is so great that they are hurled to the ground. At one of the emergency exits, only half finished, is a scene of horror. It is fifty feet over a stone-paved alley, and there is no ladder to reach the ground.

Crowds of women are here, and one after another is pushed over to meet her death on the pitiless flags, the next rank being in turn doomed to destruction. At last a bridge is formed to an adjoining building, but there are twenty victims before this avenue of safety is found.

The Actors Escape.

The stage company, numbering 240, have escaped lightly. They had rushed out of the theatre in their grotesque make-up, and only one, Miss Annabella Moore, is mortally injured.

The chorus girls were driven into the bitter cold in their tights, but Miss Violet McDonald, one of the most beautiful, declined to leave in this dress, and returned to her room to put on ordinary clothes. There she was pinned in until the firemen hauled her through a coal-hole. Over fifty more were rescued through coal-holes, as the dressing-rooms were in the basement.

Heroes of the Fire.

Great credit is given (says Reuter) to the comedian Eddie Foy for the coolness with which he tried to calm the audience while the fire was raging round him.

The well-known baseball player, Mr. Houseman, was a spectator, and after getting out his own family, worked nobly in rescuing others. One terrified woman appealed to him from a window in the upper gallery, and, shrieking "Catch me," jumped. Mr. Houseman caught her in his arms, broke her fall, and she walked away uninjured.

The Cause.

The managers' explanation is that the fire was caused by the explosion of a calcium light. Reuter states that the underwriters' inspection revealed that a wire on which the Queen of the Aerial Ballet was to fly out over the audience in the second act prevented the curtain being lowered.

Two English Victims.

It is feared that two English chorus girls, the daughters of Mr. Long, of Warwick, have perished.

The Funeral—King Edward's Sympathy.

The general burial of the victims will probably take place to-morrow, and the Mayor of Chicago suggests the closing of all business premises, as well as the quiet observance of New Year.

The King and Queen have sent a telegram of sympathy through Lord Lansdowne.

The Mayor of Chicago yesterday received the following message from President Roosevelt: "In common with all our people throughout this land, I extend to you and to the people of Chicago my deepest sympathy in the terrible catastrophe which has befallen them."

The following message was sent by the Lord Mayor of London to Mr. Choate, the American Ambassador:—"The citizens of London offer their deep sympathy and sincere condolences with the American people on the awful loss of life through the fire at Chicago."

AFTER THE FIRE.

Scenes in the Sepulchre of Pleasure-Seekers.

The theatre, become the sepulchre of so many hundreds of hapless pleasure seekers, now presents (says Reuter, telegraphing last night) a spectacle of indescribable ruin and confusion. The marble staircases are littered with bits of scorched clothing and fragments of charred remains, while from the upper galleries the auditorium looks like the crater of a burnt-out volcano.

The various garments—cloaks, furs, and the like—which were gathered after the fire was extinguished, are piled up in a saloon close by, and five bushel-baskets are filled with purses, gloves, handkerchiefs, and such miscellaneous articles, abandoned by the terrified women and children in their attempts to escape. There are also two barrels filled with shoes and overshoes picked up in the building.

Heartrending Scenes.

The various improvised morgues are still haunted by thousands of sorrow-stricken relatives of the victims, searching for their dead.

Mr. Ludwick Wolfe, a millionaire, has searched in vain for his little daughter. One father identified his headless boy by his watch.

Mr. William Hoyt, president of an important grocery concern, found his daughter had escaped, but all his grandchildren are still missing, except one boy, who has been identified by his handkerchief. The friends of Mrs. Van Ingen, who is among the injured, found the body of one of her sons, and her other four children are also believed to have perished.

Mr. Crane, a millionaire, searched in vain all night for two of his nieces.

Tragic Surprise.

A telegraphic operator, who transmitted a long account of the fire, was unaware that his own wife was among the victims.

Many remarkable escapes are announced. One little girl who sat on the ground floor managed, unassisted, to climb over the heads of the terror-stricken fugitives who were between her and the only means of escape. Her clothing was in shreds.

Among the first to escape were two children, seated sixteen rows from the stage. Four women fainted near them, and others, dazed, remained where they sat. The children, however, got up, kicked the door open, and escaped.

The livery stable drivers on strike unanimously voted a ten days' truce to help bury the dead.

1st January 1904

THEATRE DEATH-TRAP

Tragedy that has Desolated Chicago

NEARLY 600 DEAD

Women and Children Struggle for Life

PATHETIC INCIDENTS

The theatre is the newest and finest in Chicago ... and was supposed to have all the latest devices for safeguarding human life.

– "Times" correspondent

This is the most startling fact revealed in connection with Wednesday afternoon's appalling catastrophe at the Iroquois Theatre, which has filled Chicago with dismay. An electric spark started flames in the wings – a fire so slight that it might have been promptly subdued; some of the "latest devices for safeguarding human life" failed; discipline vanished behind the proscenium; panic seized the house; all the artists, numbering 240, effected their safety in flight; almost one-half of the audience perished.

The number of persons in the auditorium was 1,700; the dead bodies recovered number 564, and 314 persons are still reported missing. Fully fifty of the injured will die.

The sauve qui peut struggle for escape caused the greatest sacrifice of life; with forty exits available it has been established the terror-stricken people sought flight only through the few doors they best knew.

STORY OF THE DISASTER

Compiled from the Narratives of Survivors

There were 1,700 people in the great theatre. It was a matinee, and mothers had brought their children to see the pantomime of "Bluebeard" from Drury Lane.

The first act and part of the second had passed in merry jest and tuneful song, and the peals of childish laughter had just died away in preparation for one of the prettiest items of the whole piece.

It is a part song called "In the Pale Moonlight," sung by a double octette. The lights are lowered, for there is a moonlight effect that can only be seen at its best in darkness.

A Ribbon of Flame

Suddenly there appears on the stage, tricked out with a wealth of scenery, a tiny ribbon of blue flame, that shoots up into the air, and then curls round the scene like a sinister fiery snake. The children's eyes open wide with surprise; one would think in their innocence they saw in this a new and startling effect devised for their pleasure.

But some of the elders in the balconies rise in alarm, and crowd forward. An actor steps to the curtain and asks them to keep their seats. Then there is a cry, a shrill feminine shriek of terror. "Fire!" It is a signal for panic and "sauve qui peut." The whole of the vast audience rises, with deadly terror at the heart and the pallor of panic on their faces.

Terror on the Stage

The people on the stage seem frozen with affright. When the flame first appears, fire-extinguishers are turned upon it, but without the least effect. Fear seems to paralyse efficiency. The flames gain every moment. Then the heavy asbestos curtain is lowered to shut off the stage from the house.

Half-way down it jams, and remains immovable, showing the glow of fire behind it. The stage hands' fright is complete; they lose their heads and fly. The half-lowered curtain acts as a great flue. It sucks the flames like a tornado over to the balcony – the dress circle of a London theatre.

But the horror is not yet complete. In a moment comes an explosion of the gas reservoirs, lifting the roof and spreading deadly asphyxiating fumes throughout the building.

Then the flaming curtain falls outward on the plush seats, and sets them on fire, causing clouds of suffocating smoke. The madness of terror seizes the audience. Chivalry, modesty, shame – every human feeling is lost in the blind, overpowering instinct of self-preservation. There are "forty ample exits," but the people know it not, and only fight fiercely for the three or four they see.

A Rush for Life

There are few men, but some of them forget all manhood. They fight with fists, they push, they tear the clothes of the women in their rush for life. Mothers, with their little children, battle with clenched hands, with other women in similar case competing with them for safety.

Over this struggling mass the flames play fiercely. Some are mercifully killed at once by the blast of combined flame and gas. Whole rows of women, dead, their heads hanging over their breasts, are seen in the balcony chairs.

But the panic is more terrible even than the fire-torrent. The aisles of the balconies are quickly piled with corpses three and four deep. Children fall under foot, and the adults rush heedless over their bodies. Near the exit the scene is indescribably horrible. The mass of bodies soon reaches within two feet of the ceiling – crushed and mangled women and children overcome while crawling over the bodies of those who have already died.

The Rescuers

Some are with closed fists, still clenching fragments of clothing torn from others in the wild fight for existence.

The faces of some are trampled so that no semblance of the human remains. One man's body is actually beheaded, and crushed into pulp. The dead near the main exit are so jammed that the firemen, when they come, cannot lift them singly; it is necessary to seize a limb and pull the body out by sheer force.

Men who have seen bloody battlefields are overcome by horror; they have never seen a sight so gruesome in war.

And all this dreadful business has taken but ten minutes in the doing; a quarter of an hour ago all was gaiety in the "safest theatre" of Chicago!

BACKSTORY

The *Daily Mirror's* report on the Iroquois Theatre fire, reflected the mannered but gripping journalistic style of the day. As a publication originally catering for a readership of middle-class women, the newspaper naturally highlighted the desperate suffering of mothers and children in the disaster – and the apparent cowardice of some of the men in the audience. "Sauve qui peut" translates as "every man for himself".

The final death toll was estimated at 602, making it the worst single-building fire in US history.

The Daily ILLUSTRATED Mirror.

½d.   **½d.**   **½d.**

A Paper for Men and Women.

No. 83.   Registered at the G. P. O. as a Newspaper.   MONDAY, FEBRUARY 8, 1904.   One Halfpenny.

WAR!

Japan says "No More Negotiations," and Recalls Her Minister in St. Petersburg.

FIGHTING EXPECTED ANY MOMENT.

Tsar Goes to Moscow to Pray for Russian Success.

The long diplomatic struggle between Japan and Russia is at an end; it remains for the questions at issue to be decided by the arbitrament of the sword.

Japan, according to an official message from St. Petersburg, has broken off negotiations, and the Legations in both countries have been ordered to withdraw. This can only be interpreted as the precursor of war, and news that hostilities have actually broken out in the Far East may be expected at any moment; probably the hostile fleets are within a day's steam of each other.

It has been quite evident to well-informed and intelligent observers for some time past that war was the logical and inevitable ending of the negotiations, which have lasted since last October. But the continual delays led the man in the street to believe nothing serious was likely to ensue.

Russia, it will be observed, attempts, as had been expected, to throw the responsibility on to Japan; but those who have watched the weary diplomatic battle must admire the patience with which our ally has acted throughout. It is certain that this final step has not been taken rashly. It has been adopted only because Japan was convinced that her enemy meant war in the long run, and was only playing a game to give time for the completion of war preparations.

THE FIRST NEWS.

Russia Declares that the Responsibility Lies on Japan.

The news of the rupture of negotiations came in a Reuter's telegram from St. Petersburg, and reached the London newspaper offices at seven minutes past eleven yesterday morning. The message is given below:—

The "Official Messenger" to-day (Sunday) publishes the following circular telegram, dated February 6, sent by the Russian Minister for Foreign Affairs to the Russian representatives abroad:—

"Acting on instructions from his Government the Japanese Minister at the Imperial Court has presented a Note which informs the Imperial Government of the decision of Japan to break off further negotiations and recall its Minister and the whole staff of the Legation from St. Petersburg.

"In consequence of this his Imperial Majesty has been pleased to order that the Russian Minister at Tokio, with the whole staff of the Imperial Mission, shall leave the capital of Japan without delay.

"Such a procedure on the part of the Tokio Government, which has not yet even awaited the arrival of the answer of the Imperial Government which was sent off during the last few days, throws the whole responsibility for the consequences which may arise from the rupture of diplomatic negotiations between the two Empires on Japan."

TSAR LEAVES FOR MOSCOW.

A St. Petersburg telegram yesterday afternoon stated:—

"The Tsar is leaving here to-day for Moscow in order to attend a religious service at the cathedral there. This is in accordance with custom on the outbreak of war."

MINISTERS LEAVING.

Baron Rosen, the Russian Minister in Tokio, is expected to leave in a few days, and preparations are already in progress at the Legation.

It is believed that M. Kurino, Japan's representative at St. Petersburg, and the Legation staff will leave for Berlin to-day. The British Embassy at St. Petersburg will take charge of Japanese interests.

Continued on page 2.

READY TO FIRE THE FIRST SHOT.

The Japanese sailors on their fast-steaming torpedo-boat destroyers are scouting over the Eastern seas in search of the enemy's ships.

8ᵗʰ February 1904

WAR!

Japan says "No More Negotiations," and Recalls Her Minister in St. Petersburg

FIGHTING EXPECTED ANY MOMENT

Tsar Goes to Moscow to Pray for Russian Success

The long diplomatic struggle between Japan and Russia is at an end; it remains for the questions at issue to be decided by the arbitrament of the sword.

Japan, according to an official message from St. Petersburg, has broken off negotiations, and the Legations in both countries have been ordered to withdraw. This can only be interpreted as the precursor of war, and news that hostilities have actually broken out in the Far East may be expected at any moment; probably the hostile fleets are within a day's steam of each other.

It has been quite evident to well-informed and intelligent observers for some time past that war was the logical and inevitable ending of the negotiations, which have lasted since last October. But the continual delays led the man in the street to believe nothing serious was likely to ensue.

Russia, it will be observed, attempts, as had been expected, to throw the responsibility on to Japan; but those who have watched the weary diplomatic battle must admire the patience with which our ally has acted throughout. It is certain that this final step has not been taken rashly. It has been adopted only because Japan was convinced that her enemy meant war in the long run, and was only playing a game to give time for the completion of war preparations.

THE FIRST NEWS

Russia Declares that the Responsibility Lies on Japan

The news of the rupture of negotiations came in a Reuter's telegram from St. Petersburg, and reached the London newspaper offices at seven minutes past eleven yesterday morning. The message is given as follows –

"The 'Official Messenger' to-day (Sunday) publishes the following circular telegram, dated February 6, sent by the Russian Minister for Foreign Affairs to the Russian representatives abroad: –

"Acting on instructions from his Government the Japanese Minister at the Imperial Court has presented a Note which informs the Imperial Government of the decision of Japan to break off further negotiations and recall its Minister and the whole staff of the Legation from St. Petersburg.

"In consequence of this his Imperial Majesty has been pleased to order that the Russian Minister at Tokio, with the whole staff of the Imperial Mission, shall leave the capital of Japan without delay.

"Such a procedure on the part of the Tokio Government, which has not yet even awaited the arrival of the answer of the Imperial Government which was sent off during the last few days, throws the whole responsibility for the consequences which may arise from the rupture of diplomatic negotiations between the two Empires on Japan."

Tsar Leaves for Moscow

A St. Petersburg telegram yesterday afternoon stated: –

"The Tsar is leaving here to-day for Moscow in order to attend a religious service at the cathedral there. This is in accordance with custom on the outbreak of war."

Ministers Leaving

Baron Rosen, the Russian Minister in Tokio, is expected to leave in a few days, and preparations are already in progress at the Legation.

It is believed that M. Kurino, Japan's representative at St. Petersburg, and the Legation staff will leave for Berlin to-day. The British Embassy at St. Petersburg will take charge of Japanese interests.

BACKSTORY

The Russia–Japan War of 1904 has been somewhat overshadowed by later wars in the 20ᵗʰ century, but it was a major conflict of global significance. It pitted an old and outdated European power against an emerging young empire in the East, as the two nations struggled to gain strategic control and influence over Manchuria, the Korean peninsula and the surrounding waters.

While the war was relatively short-lived, it was brutal and intense, and produced battles of vicious ferocity. The course of the fighting provided newspapers with astonishing stories of combat and immense suffering. The Siege of Port Arthur, the great land battle at Mukden and the decisive naval showdown at the Battle of Tsushima that handed the Japanese ultimate victory, revealed what 20ᵗʰ-century warfare was like – and provided a sombre foretaste of what was to come in the First World War.

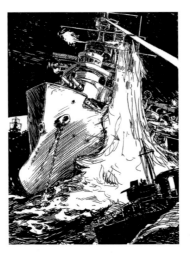

➤ The *Daily Mirror* provided detailed, day-by-day updates on the war, including (clockwise from top left) graphic portrayals of the first shots, the power of modern artillery and the scene of devastation following the Battle of Mukden, which resulted in over 160,000 casualties in a month.

WE FIND MRS. MAYBRICK—Full Story and Photographs on Pages I, 5 & 9.

The Daily ILLUSTRATED Mirror.

½d. ½d. ½d.

A Paper for Men and Women.

No. 89.   Registered at the G. P. O. as a Newspaper.   MONDAY, FEBRUARY 15, 1904.   One Halfpenny.

MRS. MAYBRICK FOUND BY THE "MIRROR."

She is Living as a "Visitor" in the Church of England Sisterhood of the Epiphany, at Truro, Cornwall, Under the Name of Mrs. G——. Transferred from Aylesbury Prison to the Sisterhood Through the Influence of Adeline, Duchess of Bedford.

Mrs. Maybrick, who was released from Aylesbury Prison two weeks ago under the most mysterious circumstances, and whose whereabouts the Government announced would be kept a profound secret, is living in the Church of England Sisterhood of the Epiphany at Truro, Cornwall.

Under an assumed name, her identity is completely hidden from all but the Superior of the institution. In Sanctuary she has at last found rest and comparative freedom.

The few remaining months of Mrs. Maybrick's life sentence are being served out under special licence in a simple cloister that overlooks the cathedral town of Truro. The rigour of prison discipline is changed to the devotional routine that attends a strict Church of England sisterhood. Though guarded as zealously from the outside world as when she wore the convict garb at Aylesbury Prison, Mrs. Maybrick is looked upon as a free woman. She is still beautiful, and the breezes that sweep up from the Cornish moors and coast are bringing back the colour to her cheeks.

The agony of the death sentence, the strain of over fourteen years in penal servitude, have scarcely left their mark: only a careworn look betrays the ordeal which few gentlewomen could have survived.

Though the unnecessary mystery with which the Home Office unctuously clothed its action in this case is now solved by the *Daily Illustrated Mirror*, the Epiphany Sisters and the servants of the Truro Sisterhood have no idea that Mrs. G—— is really Mrs. Maybrick. (We refrain from mentioning the name under which Mrs. Maybrick conceals her identity.—Ed.) She is known as a "visitor."

The transfer of Mrs. Maybrick from the penal prison at Aylesbury to the delightful home of the Epiphany sisters in Truro appears to have been due to Adeline, Duchess of Bedford. In her capacity of visitor to Aylesbury Prison the Duchess, for a long time past, has taken acute interest in Mrs. Maybrick. Eventually she succeeded in persuading the authorities to allow Mrs. Maybrick to serve the last few months of her sentence under less severe discipline. Having been interested in the Truro home of the Sisters of the Epiphany, it was only natural that the Dowager Duchess of Bedford should send Mrs. Maybrick there. The removal of the prisoner from Aylesbury occurred three weeks ago. Since then Mrs. Maybrick's whereabouts have been the subject of much surmise and unfounded report.

From the illustration it will be seen that Mrs. Maybrick's religious prison is a long building, in Tudor style. Formerly it was one of the best private residences in this part

(Continued on page 5. Photographs illustrating the news about Mrs. Maybrick on page 9.)

MRS. MAYBRICK AS SHE APPEARS NOW.

A sketch made by our special artist, showing how little prison life has told upon her.

ANOTHER FATAL BLOW.

Three More Russian Warships Destroyed, Raising the Total of Her Week's Losses to Eleven.

RUSSIAN SUCCESS ON LAND.

The Russian Vladivostok squadron is no longer in existence. Three of the four vessels were blown up while attempting to pass through the Tsugaru Straits on Saturday night.

Shortly after leaving Vladivostok, the Russian squadron attacked two small Japanese trading steamers; one was sunk, but the other escaped.

Another Russian vessel, the Yenesei, a torpedo transport, was blown up in Port Arthur on Thursday by a submarine mine; 96 lives were lost.

Land fighting has broken out along the course of the Yalu River, and the Russian forces are said to have taken eighty prisoners.

The main forces of the Japanese are moving north from Seoul towards the Yalu River, on the banks of which the Russian troops are in position.

In a reported landing at Dalny, near Port Arthur, it is said that the Japanese were repulsed with heavy loss.

Japan has struck another blow at the Russian Navy, and has practically destroyed the Vladi-

vostok squadron. The four cruisers of which the squadron consisted can hardly be said to have done their country much service. After escaping from its icebound harbour the squadron made an attack on two small merchant vessels. One of these was sunk; the other escaped. They then attempted the passage of the Tsugaru Straits, between Yezo and the main island of Japan. The short telegram which announces their fate merely states that three vessels were blown up. It would be strange if the Japanese had not taken the precaution of mining the Straits.

The outbreak of fighting along the Yalu River is in accordance with what was to be expected. The Russian army has been massing in that part for some time past, and the Japanese have hurried forward troops to act as outposts. Some small

Continued on page 2.

RUSSIA LOSES THREE MORE SHIPS.

Three of the four Russian warships which sailed out of Vladivostok last week have been blown up by the Japanese in Tsugaru Straits between the main island of Japan and the island of Yezo. These vessels were the hope of the Russians and were expected to join forces with the ships at Port Arthur. Turn to our map on page 3, on which the narrow strait of Tsugaru is clearly marked.

15ᵗʰ February 1904

MRS. MAYBRICK FOUND BY THE "MIRROR"

She is living as a "Visitor" in the Church of England Sisterhood of the Epiphany, at Truro, Cornwall, Under the name of Mrs. G–. Transferred from Aylesbury Prison to the Sisterhood Through the Influence of Adeline, Duchess of Bedford.

Mrs. Maybrick, who was released from Aylesbury Prison two weeks ago under the most mysterious circumstances, and whose whereabouts the Government announced would be kept a profound secret, is living in the Church of England Sisterhood of the Epiphany at Truro, Cornwall.

Under an assumed name, her identity is completely hidden from all but the Superior of the institution. In sanctuary she has at last found rest and comparative freedom.

The few remaining months of Mrs. Maybrick's life sentence are being served out under special licence in a simple cloister that overlooks the cathedral town of Truro. The rigour of prison discipline is changed to the devotional routine that attends a strict Church of England sisterhood.

Though guarded as zealously from the outside world as when she wore the convict garb at Aylesbury Prison, Mrs. Maybrick is looked upon as a free woman. She is still beautiful, and the breezes that sweep up from the Cornish moors and coast are bringing back the colour to her cheeks.

The agony of the death sentence, the strain of over fourteen years in penal servitude, have scarcely left their mark: only a careworn look betrays the ordeal – which few gentlewomen could have survived. Though the unnecessary mystery with which the Home Office unctuously clothed its action in this case is now solved by the Daily Illustrated Mirror, the Epiphany Sisters and the servants of the Truro Sisterhood have no idea that Mrs. G– is really Mrs. Maybrick. (We refrain from mentioning the name under which Mrs. Maybrick conceals her identity.–Ed.). She is known as a "visitor."

The transfer of Mrs. Maybrick from the penal prison at Aylesbury to the delightful home of the Epiphany Sisters in Truro appears to have been due to Adeline, Duchess of Bedford. In her capacity of visitor to Aylesbury Prison the Duchess, for a long time past, has taken acute interest in Mrs. Maybrick.

Eventually she succeeded in persuading the authorities to allow Mrs. Maybrick to serve the last few months of her sentence under less severe discipline. Having been interested in the Truro home of the Sisters of the Epiphany, it was only natural that the Dowager Duchess of Bedford should send Mrs. Maybrick there. The removal of the prisoner from Aylesbury occurred three weeks ago. Since then Mrs. Maybrick's whereabouts have been the subject of much surmise and unfounded report.

⬥ Florence Maybrick, cause célèbre – and wife of Jack the Ripper?

BACKSTORY

The murder trial and conviction of Florence Maybrick was a sensation in the late 19ᵗʰ century. It had all the elements of a Victorian melodrama: a beautiful young woman married to a domineering and philandering husband much older than her, the whiff of sexual scandal, a mysterious fatal poisoning – and over a century on, a grisly link to one of the most infamous series of crimes in history.

Mrs Maybrick was an 18-year-old American who met James Maybrick, a Liverpool cotton trader 23 years her senior, en route to England. Maybrick, a hypochondriac who took regular doses of poisons as "tonics", had numerous affairs. But when his wife was accused of having an affair with a businessman, Alfred Brierley, local society was scandalized. Maybrick beat his wife and threatened divorce.

The Mirror reported Florence's death in 1941, and summed up her remarkable story:

A FAMOUS murder trial of fifty years ago, known all the world over as the "arsenic from flypaper" case, is recalled by the death in the United States, at the age of 80, of Mrs. Florence Elizabeth Maybrick.

In 1889 Mrs. Maybrick was found guilty of the murder of her husband, James Maybrick, and sentenced to death by Mr. Justice Stephen. There was a murmur of disapproval in court at the verdict and as the Judge drove away the crowd hissed and hooted him and stones were thrown. Mrs. Maybrick was reprieved just before the date fixed for her execution, and released from prison in 1904 after serving fifteen years.

Florence Elizabeth Chandler was 18 when she married James Maybrick and settled at Aigburth, Liverpool. A son and daughter were born. In the spring of 1889, Mr. Maybrick complained of numbness in the knees. He died on May 11. The following day his wife was arrested on suspicion of having caused his death.

The prosecution relied on evidence that Mrs. Maybrick had been carrying on an illicit intercourse with a friend, that she had written a letter to her lover while her husband was ill saying, "he is sick unto death," that she had bought a number of flypapers from which she had otained asenic.

Florence spent the last few months of her 14-year sentence at the Church of England Sisterhood of the Epiphany in Truro before being released. She eventually returned to America and lived out her life there.

But the saga took a remarkable twist when it was alleged in 1992 that James Maybrick was Jack the Ripper. It was claimed that a diary had been found at his former home, Battlecrease House. The diary purported to contain a confession to the horrific murders that had taken place in London's East End in the late 1880s. Ripper experts have since cast serious doubts over the authenticity of the diaries.

½d. # Daily Mirror

For **2/6**—
IF you cut out
the Coupon
on page 2.

No. 209. | Registered at the G. P. O. as a Newspaper. | TUESDAY, JULY 5, 1904. | One Halfpenny.

700 LIVES LOST OFF THE BRITISH COAST

The details of the loss of the Danish emigrant steamer Norge, wrecked on Rockall, a single isolated granite pile 290 miles from the Scottish coast, become more terrible now that the survivors' stories are told. Over 800 men, women, and children were on board at the moment of the disaster. As boats were lowered they were dashed against the ship and broken, till the sea was strown with bodies and lifebelts.—(Drawn from a description furnished by a survivor of the disaster.)

5th July 1904

OVER 600 DROWNED

Grim Story of the Lost Emigrant Ship

CAPTAIN GONDELLE SAVED

Survivors Describe the Horrors of the Wreck

AGONISED WOMEN

Try in Vain to Save Their Little Children

Latest details of the wreck of the Norge show that it was one of the most appalling of modern times.

Loaded with emigrants from various parts of Europe, the America-bound vessel struck a reef in the Atlantic about 180 miles west of the coast of Scotland, and foundered in a few minutes. There was a terrible panic, and heart-rending scenes. Women and children were drowned literally by the hundred.

There were 694 passengers and a crew of 71, making a total of 765. Of these only 128 are known to have been saved.

Among the seventy survivors picked up in the lifeboat by the steamer Energie was Captain Gondelle.

There is a possibility that some of the passengers and crew of the Norge managed to reach St. Kilda and Flannan Islands in boats, and the Lighthouse Commissioners have been asked to send a steamer to search these and other islands in the Hebrides.

STORY OF THE TRAGEDY

(from our own correspondent)

Grimsby, Monday Night

That awful tragedy of the sea – the sinking of the Danish emigrant ship Norge, and the drowning of over six hundred men, women, and children – can now be told in detail.

From the lips of survivors, some of whom were still half-mazed by the horror of their terrible fight for life, I have heard it. By men and women it was told me, in Danish, Swedish, Russian, and Polish, and more than one interpreter was necessary.

The Norge, commanded by Captain Gondelle, belonging to the Copenhagen Ltd. Steamship Co., left Copenhagen on June 22. She touched at Christiania and Christiansund, and with 694 emigrants, men, women, and children, and a crew of seventy, started for New York. She carried 296 Norwegians, 236 Russians and Poles, and a number of Danes, Swedes, and Finns.

At half past seven in the morning on Tuesday, June 28, with a heavy sea running, she was travelling steadily through a fog some 180 miles west of the west coast of Scotland. Some of the passengers were in their bunks, a few had risen for breakfast. All was quiet, and there was no thought of danger.

Then, without the slightest warning, there was a shock, followed immediately by a terrible, grinding crash! The Norge had struck on the reef surrounding the Rockall, a lonely, inhospitable crag, seventy-five feet high that stands up from the Atlantic.

SCENE OF TERROR

In an instant all was wild confusion. There were loud shouts from those in command, and the vessel was backed off, grinding over the reefs back into deep water.

A horde of many-tongued, frantically screaming emigrants, men, women, and children, some half-dressed, some in their night gear, rushed up on deck. The port bow was stove in, all the ship's plates were started, and she began to sink rapidly. The frenzied, fear-maddened mob made a wild rush for the boats, which the crew at once endeavoured to launch.

It was impossible to keep any order in that pandemonium. Directly the first boat was lowered there was a mad rush to get into her. She was overcrowded in a moment, a heavy sea dashed her against the side of the ship and overturned her, and her load of struggling humanity was thrown into the water to drown – for none could give thought to rescuing them.

A second boat was launched, filled, and sank, in just the same manner.

By now the ship's decks were awash, and many of the maddened, screaming, struggling horde on her, rendered insane by fear, leapt overboard.

Then three other boats were launched and, filled to the uttermost, managed to get away from the wreck. Even amid the confusion which reigned there were noble deeds of self-sacrifice and heroism. One lad of seventeen, seeing there was only room for one more in a boat, threw his sister into it.

An officer of the ship, finding the boat he was in overladen with women and children, leapt overboard to give them a chance of escaping.

But the sea was now strewn with a struggling mass of people, and these made wild clutches at the boats as they passed. And those in the boats, to save themselves, beat the drowning wretches off with stretchers and oars.

Soon after these boats had got clear of her, the Norge, her nose already under water, took a great plunge forward. For a moment her stern was high in the air. Then, with a sudden rush of escaping air and a chorus of yells from the hapless folk left on board, she sank.

And these horrors, from the time the ship struck to the time she sank, are said to have occurred in but a little over twelve minutes.

After twenty-four hours' drifting and baling in misery one boatload of twenty-seven was picked up by the fishing boat Salvia and brought into Grimsby, where they arrived on Sunday night. Another boatload of thirty-two was picked up by the Dundee steamer Cervona, and landed at Stornoway yesterday. And the lifeboat, with sixty-nine half-starved and nearly-naked souls on board, was sighted by the steamer Energie, which took them into Stornoway. On this boat was the body of a child which had died from exposure.

BACKSTORY

Losses at sea, with all the drama, heroism and human tragedy they entailed, were inevitable headline news. As an island nation, Britain and the surrounding waters provided a depressingly regular succession of stories about sunken ships. Sadly, the huge loss of life on the *Norge* would seem small compared to the sinking of the *Titanic* less than a decade later.

The Daily Mirror

THE MORNING JOURNAL WITH THE SECOND LARGEST NET SALE.

No. 762. | Registered at the G. P. O. as a Newspaper. | WEDNESDAY, APRIL 11, 1906. | One Halfpenny.

RIVERS OF MOLTEN LAVA BURNING VESUVIAN TOWNS.

Striking photograph, taken by night, of Vesuvius in eruption, with the burning streams of lava pouring down the sides of the mountain. Already the town of Bosco Trecase has been engulfed, whilst the inhabitants of all the neighbouring towns have fled to Naples. There, under the weight of sand and ashes from Vesuvius, the roof of the great central market gave way, burying at least 250 people in the wreckage. Many were killed and a still larger number seriously injured.

WRECKED OFF FLAMBOROUGH HEAD.

The steam trawler Royallieu, lying partially submerged on the rocks off Flamborough Head. On the left can be seen the cliffs, which tower to a height of 300 feet.

TERRIFIC GALE AT REDCAR.

During the recent gales which have been raging round the coast of the United Kingdom Redcar has experienced storms which have never been equalled during the past quarter of a century. The photograph shows the tremendous seas running.

11th April **1906**

250 BURIED ALIVE AT NAPLES

Catastrophe Caused by the Vesuvius Eruption

RENEWED PANIC

Lava Again Pours From Crater and Thick Dust Falls on Naples

Scarcely had the lava ceased to pour out from Vesuvius, and the panic in Naples been allayed, than a terrible catastrophe occurred in the city, the roof of the Monte Oliveto market collapsing under the weight of ashes and sand from the volcano on the busy crowd yesterday.

Twelve persons were killed, and two fatally, twenty-four severely, and 100 slightly injured. There were about 250 people in the market.

Lava is again pouring from Vesuvius, a dense shower of sulphur is falling on tile desolated towns, and reddish sand is descending on Naples. Panic has seized the people.

It is estimated that more than 500 persons lost their lives in the district between Ottaviano and San Giuseppe.

King Victor and Queen Elena, who returned to Rome yesterday, have placed £4,000 at the disposal of the Premier for the relief of the victims of the eruption.

TERRIBLE SCENES AT DISASTER

Naples, Tuesday – Monte Oliveto market here has been completely destroyed by the fall of the roof. The place is a heap of ruins.

It appears to have been definitely ascertained that in the collapse twelve persons were killed, two were so injured that they cannot recover, twenty-four were severely injured, and about 100 received less serious hurts.

The disaster was caused by the weight of ashes and sand from Vesuvius which had fallen upon the roof.

The populace seems to be distraught. The collapsed building is surrounded by thousands of despairing people.

Women are tearing their hair, cursing, and screaming out: "My husband is there!" and "Bring out my child!" and similar ejaculations. They are trying with their own hands to lift the beams imprisoning their friends and relatives.

Rescuers Sob at Work
The groans of the wounded and their cries for help are so heartrending that the rescuers sob aloud at their work.

The distressed relatives find that the work of rescue is progressing too slowly. But the extrication of victims is attended with some difficulties, as the removal of the debris may cause a fresh collapse, killing those who are now buried, but still alive.

Many priests are assisting in the work, consoling the dying and administering the last sacrament.

So far eleven bodies have been recovered, while about a hundred persons are known to have been injured. A fireman and policeman were injured in the salvage work.

The crowd collected around the scene of the disaster is kept back with difficulty by cordons of Carabinieri. Doctors, Carabinieri, firemen, municipal guards, policemen, and workmen from the dockyard are co-operating in the salvage operations.

The houses in the neighbourhood are being vacated, owing to fears that they may also collapse. – Reuter

BECAME A "VERITABLE INFERNO"

Naples, Tuesday – The terrible roof collapse occurred at a moment when the whole city was gay and bright with sunshine.

Suddenly a tremendous crack was heard and a terrific roar of rending and tearing of wood. The roof of the market completely collapsed, burying all beneath it. It is estimated that those buried in the wreckage numbered at least 250.

In a moment the scene near the market became a veritable inferno as the terrorised populace surged round the building while the injured screamed and shouted for help.

The bodies which have been extricated from the ruins are frightfully mutilated, some being crushed almost beyond recognition. – Exchange

HOW DEATH CAUGHT NUMBERS

Naples, Tuesday – Ottaviano is completely destroyed.

The Naples correspondent of the "Tribuna" telegraphs that more than 500 persons lost their lives in the district between Ottaviano and San Giuseppe. – Reuter

Naples, Tuesday – The loss of life at Ottaviano is uncertain. Eye-witnesses speak of hundreds of deaths.

The scenes when the first victims were unearthed were of the most terrible description. The position of the bodies showed that they had suffered great fear before death, the faces still retaining a distinct look of terror.

Three bodies were found in a confessional at one of the churches, and two others under the high altar, one holding convulsively to the crucifix as though he hoped for a miracle.

An old woman was found kneeling with her hands raised as if to ward off the advancing danger.

A little girl was discovered curled up like a dog, with her arm raised across her face, apparently to protect herself against the ashes. – Reuter's Special

---

BACKSTORY

Vesuvius (above) has loomed large in history from ancient times, with its most famous eruption destroying the city of Pompeii, Herculaneum and other towns and villages in AD 79. But there have been many more eruptions since then, and few more dreadful than the otherwise neglected 1906 eruption.

Over nearly three weeks, the mountain spewed rivers of lava and dense clouds of ash, resulting in the terrible disaster at Ottaviano, the Monte Oliveto market and other sites, while threatening the whole of Naples itself. Today, this vast and crowded city still bustles under the summit of the mighty volcano – largely dormant since 1944 but an ever-present threat.

The Daily Mirror

THE MORNING JOURNAL WITH THE SECOND LARGEST NET SALE.

No. 1,266. | Registered at the G. P. O. as a Newspaper. | WEDNESDAY, NOVEMBER 20, 1907. | One Halfpenny.

THREE KINGS AND FIVE QUEENS PHOTOGRAPHED AT ONCE: HISTORIC GROUP AT WINDSOR CASTLE.

Never before have three kings and five queens posed for the same photograph, as they did at Windsor Castle last Sunday. After luncheon in the State Dining-room the King and Queen of England, the Kaiser and Kaiserin of Germany, the King and Queen of Spain, and the Queens of Portugal and Norway adjourned to the Crimson Drawing-room, where Mr. William Downey, who has been Court photographer for forty-four years, photographed the group reproduced above by means of a 10,000-candle power arc lamp. Queen Alexandra is standing in the centre, the Kaiser and King Alfonso standing on her right, the Kaiserin sitting directly in front of the Kaiser, and the Queen of Norway in front of the King of Spain. King Edward, who is also standing at the back, has the Queen of Portugal sitting on his right-hand side, and the Queen of Spain on his left. Afterwards the larger group, which is reproduced on pages 8 and 9, was taken.—(W. and D. Downey.)

18ᵗʰ November 1907

GREAT ROYAL GATHERING

Three Kings and Five Queens at Windsor

HISTORIC SCENE

German Emperor and the King of Spain Meet at Luncheon

Three Kings and five Queens sat down to luncheon at Windsor Castle yesterday. In all its long history, dating back to William the Conqueror, the Castle has never seen a more notable gathering.

The party comprised – King Edward and Queen Alexandra, The German Emperor and Empress, The King and Queen of Spain, The Queen of Norway, The Queen of Portugal with the Grand Duke and Duchess Vladimir of Russia, the Infanta Isabella of Spain, Prince and Princess Johann-Georg of Saxony, the Duchess d'Aosta, the Prince and Princess of Wales, the Princess Royal and the Duke of Fife, Princess Victoria, the Duke and Duchess of Connaught, Prince Arthur of Connaught, Princess Victoria, Patricia of Connaught, and Princess Henry of Battenberg.

This unique party of twenty-four sat down together in the beautiful state dining-room. The occasion was all the more interesting because of the meeting of the Kaiser and King Alfonso.

Immediately after luncheon some very interesting photographs were taken in the Crimson Drawing Room by means of a special arc-lamp of 10,000 candle-power . . .

The King and Queen of Spain, the Queen of Portugal, and Princess Henry of Battenberg arrived at the Castle shortly before one o'clock in motor-cars from London, and thousands of people assembled on Castle Hill to watch their arrival.

Two hours before little Prince Olaf had marched out of the Grand Quadrangle clad all in scarlet, with a miniature toy rifle at his shoulder. He had come out to see the Grenadiers relieve guard, and as the Guards, preceded by their band, marched up the hill the little Prince saluted, but few of the people about knew it was Prince Olaf . . .

At noon the King and Queen, the Kaiser and Kaiserin, the Queen of Norway, and other members of the Royal Family attended divine service in the private chapel at the Castle, and for thirty-five minutes were held by a magnificent sermon preached by the Bishop of Ripon, Dr. Boyd Carpenter. It was a sermon to kings, the text being, 'How does Jehovah stand?' and dealt with the prosperity of nations, and what made them prosperous. The King and the Kaiser were both very deeply interested.

What made King and Kaiser both "deeply interested" in a sermon on the prosperity of nations? It was likely to be the growing rivalry between their two great powers, which culminated in the First World War.

At a time of widespread economic, political and social upheaval, coupled with a grab for empire and prestige abroad, the world faced an uncertain and dangerous future.

Yet while it may seem extraordinary now, the gathering of Europe's royal clans at Windsor in 1907 was a sign of how closely tied the families were. They were part of an interrelated royal clan, bonded by blood but destined to be broken by conflict. Kaiser Wilhelm II was a cousin of King Edward VII. Even as late as May 1913, they met again at a wedding in Berlin. A little over a year later their two countries were at war.

WHY DID THE KAISER BUILD DREADNOUGHTS?

Even as the Kaiser and King Edward were posing for photographs in 1907, their countries were lining up to oppose each other. Germany published plans that month for the build-up of her navy, as part of a deadly arms race. This was mocked in the *Mirror* on 25ᵗʰ September 1913.

By the time the First World War was entering its third year, the Kaiser – seen here strategizing with Field Marshal Paul von Hindenburg, (left) and General Erich von Ludendorff (right) – was a despised figure in Britain.

With Germany defeated in 1918, the Kaiser was deposed and forced into exile, living out his days in bitter resentment in Holland.

NEW LICENSING BILL CLOSES 32,000 HOUSES.

Drastic Proposals in Mr. Asquith's New Measure.

THE TRADE TO PAY.

Question of Sale to Children to Rest with Local Justices.

14 YEARS' TIME LIMIT.

Clubs To Be Placed Under Supervision of Plain-Clothes Police.

ARE BARMAIDS DOOMED?

To a packed and profoundly interested House Mr. Asquith, the Chancellor of the Exchequer, outlined the provisions of the eagerly-awaited Licensing Bill in the Commons yesterday.

The measure is of sensational magnitude. These are the principal features, in the order in which they were sketched by the Chancellor:—

Compulsory reduction of "on" licences to the proportion of one for every 750 people in towns and one for every 400 people in country districts. (The present ratio is about one for every 350 as a whole.)

Estimated suppression by Government scheme of 30,000 to 32,000 licences, or one-third of the total number.

Every licensing authority compelled to prepare scheme for carrying out the statutory reduction.

Such scheme to be submitted to a Central Licensing Commission of three persons, with whom compensation fund will be vested.

OPTIONAL REDUCTION.

Local licensing authority to select licences to be extinguished with power of "optional reduction"—i.e., power to reduce licences still further after the above statutory reduction "if they think fit."

Should the local authority fail to prepare or to carry out the scheme, Licensing Commission to act in its place.

Compensation to be paid out of the same sources as in Mr. Balfour's Act of 1904—viz., a levy on the trade.

Time limit of fourteen years, at the expiration of which period the State recovers "complete dominion over licences."

Local option for Wales for additional reduction of licences.

Local option for parochial electors in England to determine whether new "on" or "off" licences should be granted. A simple majority to decide the issue.

Clubs to apply for renewal of registration annually, and to be subject to objections. Clubs of rich and poor to be placed on the same level in this respect.

POLICE SUPERVISION OF CLUBS.

No clubs to be closed on the ground of "redundancy." This merely affects public-houses.

Plain-clothes police to have power to enter all clubs.

Hours of opening on Sundays to be shortened. No change in London, but outside the metropolis no public-house to open on Sundays for more than one hour in the middle of the day or more than two hours in the evening.

"Bona fide" travellers' limit during prohibited hours to be six miles, instead of three.

Local Justices to have power to say:—

(1) Whether any children shall be allowed in a bar.

(2) What the age limit of a "child" for this purpose shall be.

(3) Whether there shall be any barmaids.

(4) Whether public-houses shall be closed on polling days and various other occasions.

(5) To punish any breach of these regulations by *extinguishing licences without compensation.*

"A RATHER LONG SPEECH."

Bishops, brewers, publicans, and well-known temperance advocates thronged the Strangers' Gallery, and when Mr. Asquith, pale and slightly nervous, rose at a quarter to four he faced an unusually crowded and expectant House.

The Chancellor's speech—a model of lucidity and conciseness—lasted an hour and a half.

Diving, during the roar of Ministerial welcome, into the depths of his dispatch-box, he drew forth his crumpled notes, and when the cheers had died away he grimly warned the House that the speech was going to be a rather long one.

"An effective reform of the licensing laws is long overdue," was his opening proposition, and he proceeded to indicate the *general scope* of his scheme.

By effective reform he meant:—

(1) An immediate and progressive reduction in the facilities for the retail sale of intoxicants.

(2) The gradual and complete recovery by the State, with due regard to existing interests, of its dominion over the monopoly which has been improvidently allowed to slip out of its control.

Members, packed shoulder to shoulder, leaned eagerly forward when Mr. Asquith passed to the compulsory suppression of "on" licences.

The Government, he explained, had taken "density" of population as a basis for the number of licences.

"Where there are two persons or fewer per acre there will be one licence per 400 persons."

Between 2 and 25 per acre one for every 500.
Between 25 and 50 one for 600.
Between 50 and 75 one for 700.
Between 75 and 100 one for 800.
Between 100 and 200 one for 900.
Over 200 per acre one for every 1,000.

There were shouts of laughter, mingled with *expressions of surprise,* when Mr. Asquith explained how the scale would work.

"I find it will mean in a certain area in Birmingham the suppression of 141 out of 158 licences, and in a certain area of Nottingham sixty-nine out of seventy."

The general result, roughly speaking, was, he said, that the scale would lead to the suppression of from 30,000 to 32,000 "on" licences, or one-third of the whole.

With the keenest attention members listened to the Chancellor's important statement of the time-limit, and there was a bitter party laugh when he caustically observed that, whatever the proposal was, he would be told to-morrow morning that there had been "confiscation."

TERM OF FOURTEEN YEARS.

Having regard to the legal situation on the one side and to the *expectations of licence-holders* on the other, the time-limit should, he urged, be long enough to suffice for the prudent trader, who carried on his business with due regard to its special character and its peculiar risks, to make adequate provision against the disturbance, at the close, of the profits which were attributed to the monopoly value of the licence.

"After much consideration the Government think these will be satisfied by a term of fourteen years."

There were cries of delight from the Liberal benches, and indignant "Oh's" from the Unionists.

But the greatest demonstration of Radical and *Socialist joy came when the Chancellor dealt with* the equality of treatment to be meted out to the clubs.

PALL MALL NOT EXCEPTED.

"To enforce the law as to these institutions, power will be given to the chief constable, inspector, or superintendent of police, or officer of superior rank to inspect club premises, including those in Pall Mall or St. James's."

Amid general laughter Mr. Asquith mentioned that these officers of the law "need not be in uniform," and there was a further burst of merriment at the decision of the Government to make bona-fide travellers go "six" miles instead of three to get Sunday refreshment.

Finally, he said, the Bill was not conceived in a spirit of vindictive hostility to any particular class. It was not put forward as incapable of amendment, and criticism upon it was invited.

DEBATE ON THE BILL.

Mr. Balfour was on his feet before the cheers which marked the close of Mr. Asquith's speech had died away.

"With no great moral object in view and no prospect of any enormous improvement in the morals of the people, we are going to commit a gross injustice on a part of the community," was his contention.

"*The time-limit is a grotesque proposal,*" cried the ex-Premier, in shrill denunciation of this portion of the Bill.

"In the name of insurance we are going to make the owner of a public-house deprive himself of his annual income—so that bankruptcy may stare him in the face.

"It is no use calling Bishops in support of such a proposal"—a hit at Mr. Asquith's recital of certain Prelates' utterances which moved Unionists to laughter.

"You call it insurance! It is robbery," exclaimed Mr. Balfour, pointing an accusing finger at the Government. The Unionists yelled approval.

"The Bill violates the fundamental equities which should govern our legislative proposals, and the only *compensating advantage you offer* is the transfer of the consumption of alcoholic liquor from premises over which magistrates have control to premises over which there is no such control.

"That, surely, will not conduce to temperance. The Bill is neither honest as regards the property of licence-holders nor effective in the great cause for which it is introduced.

Sir Thomas Whittaker, one of the leaders of the Temperance Party, expressed satisfaction with the Bill as a whole.

The leader of the Labour Party, Mr. Henderson, pressed the Chancellor of the Exchequer to consider seriously a restriction of the *hours during which* clubs might remain open.

There was an amusing incident when Mr. Bottomley rose.

Producing a large roll and holding it up to the inspection of the House, he said he had extracted from the Joint-Stock register the names of ministers of religion who had invested their hard-earned savings in licensed and brewery properties.

"Read! Read!" demanded members.

"There are 1,280 names and addresses," said Mr. Bottomley, "and if any hon. member wishes to know the position of his own particular clergyman on this question—well, the roll is open to his inspection.

"The Chancellor is simply pulling the legs of members when he tells them that the right of entry by police will apply to the clubs of Pall Mall.

"The proposals of the Bill are a monstrous *interference with the liberty of the subject.*"

"LITTLE VICTIMS PLAYING."

Mr. F. E. Smith declared that the Government was really doing nothing respecting clubs. "A more futile attempt to deal with those institutions has never been put forward."

Mr. Smith quoted the poet Gray to describe the conduct of the Government:—

Alas! regardless of their doom
The little victims play!
No sense have they of ills to come,
Nor care beyond to-day.

For political reasons, he proclaimed, the Government were permitting the survival of clubs where drink could be obtained with the same freedom as in the public-houses which they were suppressing throughout the country.

APOLOGY TO CONSUL.

British Warship Trains Guns on to Haytian President's House.

NEW YORK, Thursday.—*The correspondent of* the "New York Herald" at Port au Prince, the capital of Hayti, telegraphs that yesterday, while leaving the residence of President Alexis, a stone was thrown at the British aide-de-camp.

The official informed the British Consul, Mr. Arthur G. Vansittart, who complained to the President. He did not receive any satisfaction, and thereupon reported the incident to the captain of H.M.S. Indefatigable, a second-class cruiser, which was anchored outside the harbour.

The British captain immediately demanded an apology, and, pending a reply from President *Alexis, he manœuvred his ship so as to bring her* guns to bear upon the President's residence.

General Alexis tendered a personal apology.—Central News.

TO-DAY'S WEATHER

Our special weather forecast for to-day is:—Cold and very squally north-westerly winds; changeable, short, fine periods; occasional snow or hail.

Lighting-up time, 6.34 p.m.

Sea passages will be stormy.

NEW BISHOP ENTHRONED AT CHICHESTER.

Dr. C. J. Ridgeway (in the centre) knocking at the door of Chichester Cathedral yesterday before his enthronement as the Bishop of Chichester. The small photograph is a portrait of Dr. C. J. Ridgeway.—("Daily Mirror" photographs.)

THE KING HONOURS TWO BRAVE MEN.

Gallant Miners Receive Edward Medal from His Majesty.

MODEST HEROES.

The King personally invested two brave miners—Mr. Francis Chandler, of Barnsley, and Mr. Everson, of Hengoed, South Wales—with the Edward Medal at Buckingham Palace yesterday.

The Edward Medal is a sort of miners' V.C., being only conferred for extreme gallantry in coal mines, and the gracious act of his Majesty in making yesterday's investitures a personal matter will certainly give an additional lustre to this decoration.

The two heroes first visited the Home Office, where they were met by friends, including the M.P.s for their districts.

CAB TO PALACE.

It was the King's wish that they should proceed unaccompanied to the Palace, and, accordingly, Chandler and Everson were *placed in charge of* one of the King's Home Service messengers, and were accompanied by him in a four-wheeled cab to the Palace, with ringing cheers for a send-off.

The daily change of the guard was in progress when the miners reached the Palace, and they were not a little interested by the sight.

The interview with his Majesty was timed for 11.15, and the twenty-odd minutes to elapse before that hour were pleasantly spent in looking over the Palace.

In the meantime the Home Secretary, Mr. Herbert Gladstone, had arrived and was privately received by his Majesty.

The reception took place in the room which the King generally uses for the Privy Council meetings. The two miners were presented to his Majesty by the Master of the Household. The King received them cordially, and quickly dispersed *all feelings of nervousness.*

WHAT THE KING SAID.

Mr. Gladstone then read to the King a record of the gallantry of the men which had won for them the high honour about to be conferred on them, and the King then handed to each of the men one of his medals, known as the Edward Medal. In bestowing the decoration his Majesty said:—

"I am glad to receive you brave men, and I congratulate each of you on your gallant deeds, and have great pleasure in handing you these medals in recognition. I hope you will live for *many years to enjoy the wearing of them.*" The King further expressed great pleasure on learning that Chandler was a Norfolk man, being a member of a Lynn family.

Before retiring his Majesty shook hands cordially with Chandler and Everson, and bade them good-bye. The proud recipients of the medals were subsequently entertained to lunch at the Palace.

Interviewed afterwards, Mr. Chandler said he felt very nervous when he was presented to the King.

"But," he continued, with a smile, "his Majesty put us at ease almost immediately by the cordiality of his greeting and the graciousness of his reception.

"I was frightfully nervous," said Mr. Everson, "but when the King gave me a hearty shake of the hand and spoke to me all that disappeared. *After that I felt quite at home.* Everyone seemed to be doing all they could for us. We were treated like lords," he added, with a laugh.

TWO TALES OF HEROISM.

It was in November last that Francis Chandler, aged and hearty—he has spent thirty-six years in mines—was in charge of a gang of men at Hoyland Silkstone Colliery.

Suddenly a girder collapsed, bursting a boiler and extinguishing the lights.

Knowing that two men were *imprisoned under* the debris in the scalding steam, Chandler, groping his way in the darkness, succeeded in dragging one of them to safety. Though badly burned, he returned for the other, but his further effort was unavailing.

Harry Emerson, a mechanic in the Penallton Colliery, and a native of Hengoed, Rhymney Valley, on September 12 last witnessed the fall of two men 40ft. down a shaft, where they were guiding a huge barrel into water below. The only means of reaching them was by a narrow pipe, and at great risk he dragged one to a place of safety. The other was drowned.

(Photographs on page 1.)

MEDAL FOR HERO'S SISTER.

The Lord Mayor of Newcastle yesterday presented to Miss Lamb the King Edward medal awarded to her brother George, who lost his life in trying to save four men in a burning mine at Alberta, Canada. The Lord Mayor said that it was the King's wish that Miss Lamb should herself wear the medal.

MIDNIGHT TELEGRAMS.

In the Chamber at Rome yesterday the Socialists' motion proposing the complete abolition of religious teaching in the schools was rejected by 339 against 102.

NEW YORK, Thursday.—A grand jury has to-day indicted the millionaire brothers, F. R. and O. F. Thomas, for irregularities in their administration of the affairs of the Provident Life Insurance Company.—Exchange.

28th February 1908

NEW LICENSING BILL CLOSES 32,000 HOUSES

THE TRADE TO PAY

Question of Sale to Children to Rest with Local Justices

14 YEARS' TIME LIMIT

Clubs To Be Placed Under Supervision of Plain-Clothes Police

ARE BARMAIDS DOOMED?

To a packed and profoundly interested House Mr. Asquith, the Chancellor of the Exchequer, outlined the provisions of the eagerly-awaited Licensing Bill in the Commons yesterday.

The measure is of sensational magnitude. These are the principal features, in the order in which they were sketched by the Chancellor –

Compulsory reduction of "on" licences to the proportion of one for every 750 people in towns and one for every 400 people in country districts. (The present ratio, is about one for every 350 as a whole.)

Estimated suppression by Government scheme of 30,000 to 32,000 licences, or one-third of the total number.

Every licensing Authority compelled to prepare scheme for carrying out the statutory reduction.

Such scheme to be submitted to a Central Licensing Commission of three persons, with whom compensation fund will be vested . . .

No clubs to be closed on the ground of "redundancy." This merely affects public-houses.

Plain-clothes police to have power to enter all clubs.

Hours of opening on Sundays to be shortened. No change in London, but outside the metropolis no public-house to open on Sundays for more than one hour in the middle of the day or more than two hours in the evening . . .

Local Justices to have power to say –

1 Whether any children shall be allowed in a bar.
2 What the age limit of a "child" for this purpose shall be.
3 Whether there shall be any barmaids.
4 Whether public-houses shall be closed on polling days and various other occasions.
5 To punish any breach of these regulations by extinguishing licences without compensation.

"A Rather Long Speech"

Bishops, brewers, publicans, and well-known temperance advocates thronged the Strangers' Gallery, and when Mr. Asquith, pale and slightly nervous, rose at a quarter to four he faced an unusually crowded and expectant House.

The Chancellor's speech – a model of lucidity and conciseness – lasted an hour and a half.

By effective reform he meant –

1 An immediate and progressive reduction in the facilities for the retail sale of intoxicants.
2 The gradual and complete recovery by the State, with due regard to existing interests, of its dominion over the monopoly which has been improvidently allowed to slip out of its control.

Members, packed shoulder to shoulder, leaned eagerly forward when Mr. Asquith passed to the compulsory suppression of 65 on "licences."

The Government, he explained, had taken "density" of population as a basis for the number of licences,

"Where there are two persons or fewer per acre there will be one licence per 400 persons."

Between 2 and 25 per acre one for every 500.

Between 25 and 50 one for 600.

There were shouts of laughter, mingled with expressions of surprise, when Mr. Asquith explained how the scale would work.

"I find it will mean in a certain area in Birmingham the suppression of 141 out of 153 licences, and in a certain area of Nottingham sixty-nine out of seventy."

The general result, roughly speaking, was, he said, that the scale would lead to the suppression of from 30,000 to 32,000 "on" licences, or one-third of the whole.

With the keenest attention members listened to the Chancellor's important statement of the time limit, and there was a bitter party laugh when he caustically observed that, whatever the proposal was, he would be told tomorrow morning that there had been "confiscation."

PALL MALL NOT EXCEPTED

"To enforce the law as to these institutions, power will be given to the chief constable, inspector or superintendent of police, or officer of superior rank to inspect club premises, including those in Pall Mall or St. James's."

Amid general laughter, Mr. Asquith mentioned that these officers of the law "need not be in uniform."

BACKSTORY

Herbert Asquith was no stranger to a tipple or two, but as far as the pub and brewing industries were concerned, he had declared war on their trade with the 1908 Licensing Bill. Drawn up by the Liberal government, backed by the temperance movement and with an eye on "doing a favour" for some business leaders, the bill was designed to raise productivity and put the industry under state control.

In the event, the barmaids and pub-goers of Britain could rest easy. After mass protests, including a 250,000-strong demonstration in Hyde Park, the Bill was defeated. While some restrictions were put in place at the onset of the First World War, barmaids would remain a fundamental part of the great British pub experience (left).

The Daily Mirror

20 Pages

THE MORNING JOURNAL WITH THE SECOND LARGEST NET SALE.

No. 3,113. | Registered at the G.P.O. as a Newspaper. | WEDNESDAY, OCTOBER 15, 1913 | One Halfpenny.

TRAPPED IN A BLAZING MINE: "WORST DISASTER IN THE HISTORY OF THE WELSH COALFIELDS."

A terrible mine disaster, which will probably prove the most serious in the history of the Welsh coalfields, occurred yesterday at the Universal Mine, Senghenydd. A terrific explosion, which was heard at Cardiff, occurred while work was in full swing, and this was followed by fire, cutting off all escape for the unfortunate miners. (1) A view of the pithead, showing the crowd waiting for news. There were heartrending scenes, the fierceness of the explosion apparently causing the women to despair of the safety of their loved ones. (2) Colliers watching rescue operations. Note the debris.—(*Daily Mirror* photographs.)

24

393 MINERS ENTOMBED IN BLAZING COLLIERY IN SOUTH WALES

Fire Follows Explosion in Pit Disaster near Cardiff

A RAY OF HOPE

21 Men Found Alive After 20 Hours' Imprisonment

510 SAVED OF 935

Rescuing Parties Labour Heroically, Themselves in Dire Peril

WIVES' ALL-NIGHT VIGIL

Women in Agonies of Fear Wait for News at Pithead

32 KNOWN DEAD

Hard on the heels of the disaster to the Volturno in the mid-Atlantic comes the news of a disaster which may prove to be even more appalling – "the worst on record in the Welsh coalfields."

Yesterday morning in the mine at Senghenydd, near Cardiff, where 935 men were at work, two explosions occurred in quick succession. Shortly afterwards fire broke out.

Of the 935 below, 489 were rescued alive, 27 were brought up dead, three were killed on the pit bank, and two died in hospital.

In the mine remained 414 men. That all had perished from suffocation or fire was feared to be beyond doubt.

But in the early hours of this morning – after nearly twenty hours imprisonment – twenty-one of the entombed miners were found alive. They were beyond a fall, and were in a weak state.

A man named Evan Moore was first found shortly after one o'clock, and this gave hope to the rescuers.

It is hoped that during the night the rescuers will be able to make fair progress.

"I cannot offer you any information as to the state of the workings," he added, "and we shall really know nothing till the morning."

Mr. Reeves and Mr. Shaw, the general manager, are forming the rescue parties, and there is always one of them down the pit.

In the blackness of night the wives and children of these imprisoned miners are waiting patiently, silently, but almost hopelessly, for tidings.

"My Ben is down there," said one woman to me. She was holding a tiny baby in her arms. The baby was sleeping peacefully.

The mother's eyes were dry. Her voice was clear. "He'll come up all right," she said. Hope was not killed in her.

No Word of Complaint

It is the same, with nearly all the women. They are brave in the presence of death and never utter a single word of complaint or of sadness.

They know the heroic members of the Rhymney Valley Rescue Brigade are doing all they can for the menfolk down in the fiery pit, and they speak with a quiet confidence which is inexpressibly painful to those who know the truth.

The explosion occurred to the west of the downcast. To the east of this shaft is another ventilating shaft, called the upcast. The pit is about 650 yards deep, and the workings radiate from the bottom of the two shafts in various directions.

All the men rescued were working on the east of the downcast. Those poor victims of gas and fire and explosion were on the west side, and they are penned in by the fire, which prevented them from reaching their only means of escape – the downcast.

What gallant efforts have been made to reach those poor imprisoned souls all day long! Rescue parties have been down fighting the flames. Many brave men have fainted with the heat and poisonous air, and have themselves had to be rescued and sent above.

But many of these volunteered to go down again after recovery.

The rescue parties consist of miners who hurried from all parts of Glamorgan to the aid of their unfortunate comrades.

AGONISING SCENES AT PITHEAD – COLLIER REACHES SURFACE ONLY TO FALL DEAD

MOTHERS' DESPAIR

Terrible scenes of anguish and agony occurred all the afternoon and evening at the pithead.

Corpses and injured men were brought up at intervals.

One burly collier reached the surface, and, gripping a water-bottle handed by a comrade, emptied it, then spun slowly round and fell dead.

➤ Crowds lined the streets as a funeral cortège made its solemn progress.

Against the raging flames below the patent fire extinguishers, which urgent telephone calls had brought from all parts of the district, were of little avail, despite the fact that scores were sent up by special train from Cardiff, and every colliery and building in the district had been denuded.

Neither was the patent apparatus of the rescue parties who had hurried to the scene of any avail, and as evening drew on despair deepened.

The little post office was crowded with people, among them many weeping women, dispatching telegrams to friends and relatives in other parts of the country.

Many, of course, were able to send off the joyful tidings of rescue, but it was pathetic to note that where the telegrams concerned men still in the pit they generally wrote: "All hope abandoned."

One woman who has lost her husband, four sons and three brothers was found yesterday evening beating her head against the doorpost, which is but fifty yards distant from the colliery.

Aged women and young girls were bemoaning together the absence of news of their beloved ones, and here and there strong men and women fell upon the necks of those dear to them as they came up from the depths below.

BACKSTORY

The Senghenydd colliery explosion was the worst mining disaster in British history. Four-hundred-and-thirty-nine miners and a rescuer were killed. Caused by a build-up of methane gas, or 'fire damp', and a chain reaction that caused clouds of coal dust to combust, the fire trapped hundreds of doomed men deep underground.

It was not the first time the mine had been hit by an explosion. Eighty-one died in 1901; it appeared the lessons had not been heeded, with pit bosses failing to implement safety measures. Miraculously, 18 miners were rescued two weeks after the 1913 explosion.

➤ One-hundred years after the incident, the Welsh National Mining Memorial was unveiled at the site of the 1913 disaster.

➤ A temporary mortuary was set up at the Universal pit in Senghenydd.

The Daily Mirror
THE MORNING JOURNAL WITH THE SECOND LARGEST SALE.

No. 530.   FRIDAY, JULY 14, 1905.   One Halfpenny.

RECOVERING THE VICTIMS OF THE COLLIERY DISASTER YESTERDAY.

The scene outside the gates of the colliery as one after another of the bodies recovered from the mine was brought out. There was a dead silence, only broken now and again by a stifled moan as the sad little processions passed through the crowd.

At the pit-head in the colliery yard. The scene as the bodies brought to the bank were identified by friends and relatives was painful beyond description.

The number of stretchers ready in the colliery yard for their grim burdens bore eloquent testimony to the magnitude of the disaster. Altogether one hundred and twenty-one lives were lost. There is only one survivor of the men in the pit at the time of the explosion.

Relatives and friends of the dead miners waiting for the bodies to be brought up from the mine

A terribly familiar spectacle in Wattstown during the past two days. One of the victims of the explosion being carried to his home.

Daily Mirror
THE DAILY PICTURE NEWSPAPER WITH THE LARGEST NET SALE.

No. 9,926   SATURDAY, SEPTEMBER 21, 1935   One Penny

Broadcasting—Page 20

DUCE'S "NO" TO BRITAIN AND FRANCE
—Page 3

Amusements : Page 16

ROYAL WEDDING DATE

DYING MINER'S FAREWELL NOTE

Abbey Ceremony for Duke on November 6

IT was officially announced from Balmoral Castle last night that the wedding of the Duke of Gloucester and Lady Alice Montagu-Douglas-Scott will take place at Westminster Abbey on Wednesday, November 6.

Duke of Gloucester.

This date is slightly earlier than had been generally anticipated.

Preparations for the ceremony will be pressed forward at once by the Lord Chamberlain and the other high Court officials.

When the King returns to Buckingham Palace next Saturday a Privy Council will be summoned so that he may give his formal consent, under the Great Seal of England, to the marriage.

Westminster Abbey authorities have been informed of the date, and preliminary outlines of the ceremonial are already under discussion.

The ceremony, it is expected, will follow closely that for the wedding of the Duke and Duchess of Kent at the Abbey last year, but no details have yet been decided.

Primate to Officiate

It is not yet settled who will conduct the service, but it is probable that the Archbishop of Canterbury and the Dean of Westminster will be among the officiating clergy.

The wedding date was decided, it is understood, after consultation with the Duke and his fiancée and the King and Queen.

It is in, or near, Camberley that the newly married couple may have their first home.

Lady Alice Montagu-Douglas-Scott, the royal bride-elect.

'INDECENT' BOOKS IN LIBRARY

Official Replies to Attack

"Absolutely indecent and unsuitable, especially for young girls."

THIS criticism of two books obtainable at Wood Green Public Library, was made by a member at a meeting of the local ratepayers' association.

The borough librarian at Wood Green told the "Daily Mirror" last night that the two books complained of are recognised as of outstanding literary merit.

"The complaint," he said, "is the only one we have received concerning those or any other books in the library for the last two years.

"We take every care to eliminate books of an undesirable type, and each new book is read by members of a panel appointed for that purpose."

Mystery of Big Earthquake Shock

IN Britain, Japan, Australia, and in France yesterday, seismographs recorded earthquake shocks.

All reports agreed that the shocks were ever more severe than those recorded during the New Zealand disaster in 1931.

The epicentre was placed in somewhere in New Guinea.

But the only actual news of any "quake removed to London was a six-second shock at Boux, in Algeria, which destroyed two homes and cracked several others.

CHALKED NOTE TO WIFE IN DEATH PIT

A TREASURED stone lies in the home of one of the victims of the North Gawber Colliery disaster. It bears his farewell to his wife.

An official touring the underground area, where the full force of the explosion was felt, noticed a large piece of stone in the wall on which was clearly chalked—

"Farewell, Fanny, old pet x x x x"

The writing was found to be that of Albert Ibberson, of Allendale-terrace, Mapplewell. As he lay in the pit terribly burned and in great agony, realising that he was dying, he scrawled his pathetic last message to his wife, Mrs. Fanny Ibberson.

The stone was removed and taken to the dead man's home. Ibberson, who was fifty-three, was married only four years ago. His widow is left with a baby.

Says He Was "Executed" as a Spy

Carernow, Friday.

A MAN who claims to be an "executed" spy is causing a good deal of controversy in South Africa.

The man, living at Bloemfontein, says he is Commandant Oldoni Scheepers, a notorious Boer spy, who was said to have been executed by the British at Graaf Reinet.

According to his story he was led out at dawn to be executed, but a friendly sergeant distributed blank cartridges, and allowed him to escape after he had simulated death.

It is known that Scheepers' "grave" was opened by a Commission of Inquiry after the Boer War, and that it was found to be empty. However, Wilfred Harrison, formerly of the Clamforces Guards, who swears that he saw Scheepers shot through t helmet, now the doctor certify him to be dead, and then anointed at the burial.

Harrison explains that the reason the body of Scheepers was not found when the grave was opened was that the southerlies did not dig deep enough.

On the other hand, many of those who have examined the man's story are inclined to believe that it may be true.—British United Press.

150 NAZIS ARRESTED

ANOTHER "Inquisition" has been launched against Nazis in Vienna.

Police last night made a secret raid on an office in the Hernals suburb and arrested 150 Nazis (says Reuter).

It is expected that other police swoops are due.

BACKSTORY

Mining accidents and disasters made an all-too-common appearance in the *Daily Mirror*. Death or injury was an occupational hazard from dangerous work in appalling conditions, yet the individual stories never failed to move.

Here are some reports on the Wattstown disaster of 1905 that killed over 120:

TOGETHER IN DEATH
Father and Son Found Clasped in Each Other's Embrace

PIT DISASTER SCENES

The death-toll of the Wattstown colliery disaster is now returned at 119, it having been ascertained that 120, and not 121, men were in the ill-fated pit at the time of the explosion.

The explorers recount a pathetic discovery they made. They came across the body of Benjamin Lewis, aged fifty-three, of Wattstown, and held close to his breast, wrapped in his coat, was the body of his son, the father having evidently made a heroic effort to save the little lad from the effects of the blast.

A singular circumstance is related in reference to John Rees, another of the victims. Formerly Rees was employed at Tylerstown, but after one of his sons had been killed at that place he could not remain there, and consequently removed to Wattstown. Here another son worked with him, and at the time of the explosion they were together, and both were killed.

A Merciful Absence

A boy named Davies was one of those who attended at the pit-mouth on Tuesday morning in readiness to descend. After waiting until seven o'clock, however, finding his "butty" did not arrive, he was obliged to return home.

Within a few hours the explosion occurred. Congratulated upon his remarkable escape, Davies burst out crying, and turned away, with the words: "But my brother Johnny was in."

Later in 1935 came a heartrending image of one miner's last note of love to his wife:

CHALKED NOTE TO WIFE IN DEATH PIT

A TREASURED stone lies in the home of one of the victims of the North Gawber Colliery disaster. It bears his farewell to his wife.

An official touring the underground area, where the full force of the explosion was felt, noticed a large piece of stone in the wall on which was clearly chalked –

"Farewell, Fanny, old pet x x x x"

The writing was found to be that of Albert Ibberson, of Allendale-terrace, Mapplewell. As he lay in the pit terribly burned and in great agony, realising that he was dying, he scrawled his pathetic last message to his wife, Mrs. Fanny Ibberson.

The stone was removed and taken to the dead man's home. Ibberson, who was fifty-three, was married only four years ago. His widow is left with a baby.

BRITISH BATTLESHIP BULWARK BLOWN UP: TRAGIC LOSS OF LIFE

The Daily Mirror

CERTIFIED CIRCULATION LARGER THAN ANY OTHER DAILY NEWSPAPER IN THE WORLD

No. 3,462.   Registered at the G.P.O. as a Newspaper.   FRIDAY, NOVEMBER 27, 1914   One Halfpenny.

HOW H.M.S. BULWARK WENT DOWN: BATTLESHIP BLOWN UP OFF SHEERNESS WHILE BAND PLAYED: TERRIFIC EXPLOSION.

The band of H.M.S. Bulwark, a British battleship, with 800 men on board, was silenced yesterday morning by a thunderous explosion.

The next moment the vessel was enveloped.

She was lost utterly with her precious lives.

"And the smoke of their torment went upward."

The battleship Bulwark was blown up at Sheerness Harbour early yesterday morning. At the time of the explosion the band of the battleship was playing. Only twelve men were saved out of a crew which numbered between 700 and 800. All the officers perished. The vice and rear admirals who were at Sheerness have reported their conviction that it was an internal magazine explosion which rent the ship asunder.

The ship had entirely disappeared when the smoke cleared away. An inquiry will be held to-day, which may possibly throw more light on the occurrence. The photographs below that of H.M.S. Bulwark illustrate the three views of a mighty vessel destroyed by explosion at sea. They are practically instantaneous. There was not three seconds' difference between the three photographs.

BATTLESHIP BLOWN UP AT SHEERNESS WITH LOSS OF OVER 700 LIVES

H.M.S. Bulwark Rent Asunder by Explosion of Internal Magazine

SHIP'S BAND PLAYING JUST BEFORE EXPLOSION

It is with grief that we have to announce the loss at Sheerness yesterday of the battleship Bulwark.

There were between 700 and 800 men on board, but only twelve, it is believed, have been saved.

Mr. Churchill, in announcing "the bad news" to the House of Commons yesterday after-noon, stated that an internal magazine explosion occurred in the Bulwark at 7.53 a.m. yesterday.

The ship was rent asunder, and when the smoke had cleared away the Ship had "entirely disappeared."

An inquiry, the First Lord stated, will be held to-day, which may throw more light on the cause of the explosion.

The Bulwark was an old battleship, built in 1899 at a cost of just under £1,000,000.

A poignant incident is that just before the battleship was blown to pieces the ship's band on board was playing merrily.

So tremendous was the force of the explosion that debris, it is stated, was blown to the Essex coast on the other side of the Thames Estuary.

HOW FIRST LORD BROKE BAD NEWS TO THE HOUSE

There was deep sorrow in the House of Commons yesterday afternoon when Mr. Churchill announced the loss of the Bulwark in the following words –

"I regret to say I have bad news for the House.

"The Bulwark battleship, lying off Sheerness, blew up at 7.53 a.m. to-day.

"The Vice and Rear Admirals who were present have reported their conviction that it was an internal magazine explosion which rent the ship asunder. There was apparently no upheaval of water.

"The loss of the ship does not sensibly affect the military position, but I regret to say the loss of life is very severe.

"Only twelve men are saved, and all the officers and the rest of the crew, which, I suppose, amount to 700 or 800 persons, have perished.

"I think the House would wish me to express on their behalf the deep sympathy and sorrow with which the House has heard the news, and the sympathy they feel with those who have lost their relatives and friends."

SHIP'S BAND PLAYING

The explosion of the Bulwark, says a Sheerness correspondent, was so terrific that it shook all the buildings of Sheerness to their foundations.

Dense clouds of smoke and flames shot up and the battleship went down immediately.

The Bulwark, a Portsmouth manned ship, was lying in the Medway about two or three miles from Chatham.

It is stated that the battleship had been, or was, taking in ammunition, and that the explosion occurred in the fore magazine.

Everything pointed to it being an explosion in the ship and not to any external agency.

Boats from vessels in the Medway at once put off to rescue survivors, who were taken to Chatham Dockyard.

It is believed at Chatham that many men have been wounded and that all the ship's company were not killed (sic).

An eye-witness of the disaster who was on a ship within a short distance of the Bulwark gave the following account –

"I was at breakfast when I heard an explosion, and I went on deck.

"My first impression was that the report was produced by the firing of a salute by one of the ships but the noise was quite exceptional.

"When I got on dock I saw that something awful had happened.

"The water and sky were obscured by dense volumes of smoke.

"We were at once ordered to the scene of the disaster to render what assistance we could.

"At first we could see nothing but when the smoke cleared a bit we were horrified to find that the battleship Bulwark had gone.

"She seemed to have vanished from sight entirely but a little later we saw a portion of the huge battleship showing about four feet above water.

"We kept a vigilant look-out for survivors, but only saw two men. I don't know whether other boats rescued any. One of the men we saw was dead."

The concussion from the explosion was actually felt at Southend, and dense clouds of smoke could be seen rising across the estuary of the Thames.

An incident which stands out poignantly in connection with the catastrophe is that at the time of the explosion the band on board the Bulwark was playing.

Debris Thrown to Essex Coast

So tremendous was the explosion that some of the debris was thrown six miles over on to the Essex coast.

The district in the neighbourhood of the explosion presented a scene almost too terrible to describe, being strewn with an enormous amount of wreckage.

Amongst the debris recovered is an affectionate letter from the wife of a seaman on board the Bulwark, giving an account of how she was looking after the children, and adding, "I am longing to see you again. Your loving wife till death do us part."

BACKSTORY

Loss of life in the First World War was bad enough: loss of life due to accident and not enemy action had a grim tragedy all of its own. HMS *Bulwark* was an ageing battleship in contrast to the Dreadnoughts with which the Royal Navy was still determined to rule the waves, but her sinking was devastating news. Out of a complement of 750, only 12 seamen survived.

The likely cause of the explosion was overheating cordite charges, or a shell that became live.

Among the ship's former captains was Robert Falcon Scott of Antarctic exploration fame, who commanded *Bulwark* in 1908.

ITALY DECLARES WAR AGAINST AUSTRIA.

The Daily Mirror

CERTIFIED CIRCULATION LARGER THAN ANY OTHER PICTURE PAPER IN THE WORLD

No. 3,613. | Registered at the G.P.O. as a Newspaper. | MONDAY, MAY 24, 1915 | 16 PAGES | One Halfpenny.

THREE TRAINS WRECKED IN THE TERRIBLE ACCIDENT NEAR CARLISLE: HEAVY DEATH ROLL AMONG THE SOLDIERS.

One of the express engines on top of the wreckage of the troop train. The tender, which is being raised by crane, was thrown down a bank.

Burning coach. Inside the compartments are masses of flames.

The Carlisle firemen worked heroically to overcome the flames.

What is probably the worst disaster in the history of British railways occurred on Saturday between Carlisle and Gretna Green, of romantic memory. Three trains were involved. First of all a troop train from Larbert, near Falkirk, collided with a local, but horror was piled upon horror's head when an express from London crashed into the debris, piling engines and carriages in indescribable confusion. Fire broke out and claimed many victims, chiefly among the soldiers.

24th May 1915

BRITISH SOLDIERS HEROISM AMID BURNING TRAIN WRECKAGE

Eager to Give Life to Save Comrades from Death of Agony by Fire

160 DEAD 175 INJURED

Brave Commander Who Perished In Attempt to Save Private from Burning Coach

Killed........................... 160
Injured......................... 175

Such is the heartbreaking outcome of the railway disaster near Gretna Green, the most terrible in the history of the British railways.

A troop train from Scotland, carrying 500 soldiers, first collided with a local train that had been shunted to allow the Scottish express from Euston to pass.

Scarcely had those who were able to extricate themselves from the wreckage begun to move when round a curve came the express hurling itself to death and destruction amid the wreckage.

The horror of this appalling catastrophe is relieved only by the patient courage of its victims and the splendid heroism of those who risked life and limb to save the sufferers from an agonising death by fire.

The fire of furnace heat that broke out among the debris of the shattered trains was powerless to destroy the splendid courage of the British soldier.

The dying faced death fearlessly. There is the instance of one soldier who while the lapping flames slowly advanced, remained absolutely calm and conversed with his rescuers.

Another man, pinned beneath the wreckage, thought only of his chum and begged that the latter should be saved first.

Equally splendid courage was shown by the soldier survivors. They worked might and main to extricate their comrades, and one, Commander Oliphant, sacrificed his life in his attempts to rescue a private.

Nobody had any thought of self, least of all the doctors. The palm of bravery probably goes to Dr. Edward, who crawled underneath the burning wreckage and while the hose played on the leaping flames, amputated the leg of a man who was still pinned beneath the debris.

All of the injured, with a few exceptions, are doing well.

The disaster happened shortly before seven o'clock on Saturday morning, near Quintin's Hill (sic), two miles from Gretna Green, of romantic memory, and 9½ miles north of Carlisle. Three trains were wrecked –

1. A troop train, conveying 600 officers and men of the Royal Scots, southwards from Lambert, near Falkirk.
2. The midnight Scottish express from Euston.
3. A local Carlisle train.

WAVING HAND SIGNAL

Vivid stories of the disaster, describing terrible incidents that will never fade from the memory of those who saw them, were told by survivors.

"It was the most awful scene I have ever witnessed" said Private Gilchrist, of the Scots Guards.

"The cries of the injured people who were among piles of wreckage were heart rending.

"Many of them had to remain where they were for a large time and it was a ghastly sight.

"I managed to clamber out of the wreckage myself and saw a hand waving from beneath the debris. A voice, half cried out, 'Can you see me?'

"It was one of our officers, and when I called to him, 'Yes, sir!' he shouted in reply 'Then for God's sake get me out somehow.'

"A few of us at once set to work on the wreckage. The flames were already leaping around it but we succeeded in hauling the officer out.

"We had no sooner done so when up rushed another man and entreated us to help to save his wife and child.

"Then we rescued a private nearby. After that it was nothing but dead and mangled bodies. They were lying everywhere."

BACKSTORY

Quintinshill was the most devastating of all British rail disasters. In total, 226 people were killed and 246 injured.

The crash was caused by two signalmen forgetting about the northbound passenger train from Carlisle which had backed, as scheduled, onto the Caledonian Railway's southbound mainline from Glasgow to Carlisle. Tragically, they let a southbound troop train proceed at speed along the same track, causing a head-on collision.

The express ran into the wreckage, adding to the devastation as the elderly wooden, gas-lit troop train coaches ignited and the flames also engulfed two goods trains which were stationary in adjacent loop lines.

It is believed that some of the injured men trapped in the flaming wreckage were shot to save them from being burned to death.

The signalmen were jailed for three years and 18 months respectively. Out of the 500 men from the 1st Battalion of the 7th Royal Scots Guards, only 60 attended roll call the next day. The troops had been bound for Gallipoli, itself one of the worst military disasters of the war.

The scene of devastation.

VEDRINES' DARING FEAT: LANDS ON ROOF

The Daily Mirror

CERTIFIED CIRCULATION LARGER THAN THAT OF ANY OTHER DAILY PICTURE PAPER

No. 4,753. | Registered at the G.P.O. as a Newspaper. | MONDAY, JANUARY 20, 1919 | [16 PAGES.] | One Penny.

DEATH OF YOUNGEST SON OF KING AND QUEEN

Prince John on one of his earliest mounts.

Out for a spin on his bicycle.

Driving his own motor-car at Sandringham.

One of the most successful portraits of the Prince

Enjoying a visit to the London Zoological Gardens.

It is with the deepest regret that *The Daily Mirror* announces the death of Prince John, the King and Queen's youngest son. The Prince, who was thirteen years of age, had been in delicate health for some time, and had been living in retirement at Sandringham, where, on Saturday, he passed away.

20ᵗʰ January 1919

DEATH OF PRINCE JOHN, YOUNGEST SON OF THE KING AND QUEEN

Passed Away in Sleep at Sandringham After an Epileptic Attack

ROYAL PARENTS CALLED TO BEDSIDE

Life-Long Affliction that Gave Their Majesties Continual Anxiety – A Merry Boy

Deep sympathy will be felt by everyone with the King and Queen, whose youngest son, Prince Joñ, died on Saturday night at Sandringham, in his fourteenth year.

The following official communique was issued last night – Sandringham, Saturday Evening, Jan. 18th.

H.R.H. the Prince Joñ, who has since his infancy suffered from epileptic fits, which have lately become more frequent and severe, passed away in his sleep following an attack at 5.30 this afternoon at Sandringham.

Signed ALAN REEVE MANBY M.D.

The nurse in charge said that when the Prince passed away his face bore an angelic smile.

The funeral will be private, and it is expected will be at Sandringham Church to-morrow.

BIDDEN TO BEDSIDE

Grief of Royal Parents – Son's Lifelong Affliction

"The King and Queen have suffered a sad loss through the death of H.R.H. the Prince Joñ, fifth son of their Majesties, who died suddenly this (Saturday) afternoon at Sandringham."

So runs the announcement in the Court Circular, which adds that "the King and Queen, Queen Alexandra, the Queen of Norway, with the Crown Prince of Norway, Princess Mary, Princess Victoria, Prince Henry and Prince George attended divine service at Sandringham Church yesterday morning.

"In the afternoon the King decorated Private Thomas Ricketts, 1st Battalion Royal Newfoundland Regiment, with the Victoria Cross."

A Sandringham correspondent says that when the Prince passed away the nurse immediately summoned the King and Queen to the bedside.

Their Majesties and the members of the Royal Family are greatly shocked at Prince Joñ's death.

It will be readily understood now from the official bulletin how great has been the anxiety occasioned to the King and Queen by the almost lifelong affliction of their Majesties' youngest son.

A HAPPY PRINCE

At first the complaint did not greatly affect the patient's general health, and he looked a sturdy, healthy and happy lad. But the condition became more serious as the Prince grew older, and the risk of seizure made it necessary that he should almost constantly have an attendant.

The young Prince was never seen with the members of the Royal Family on public occasions for this reason, and although he was held in the highest affection – an affection all the greater because of his sad affliction – he was usually kept in comparative privacy and quiet.

The sad news was received with very deep regret by all classes at Windsor, where the late Prince was exceedingly popular.

Although he was unable to participate in game and frolics with as much energy as others, he dearly loved a boy's life, and his boyish pranks in which he took so much delight manifested the high spirits in which he lived.

FOND OF SOLDIERS

The Queen's Guest and Tale of Golden Curls that Came Off

The boy Prince spent the greater part of his time in the open air and almost invariably wore a sailor suit.

He was exceedingly fond of soldiers, and on one occasion, when there was a military display at the Castle, he climbed up on to a gate in order to get a good view.

At another time, when the guard was changing the Quadrangle, he walked up and down, in an endeavour to keep step with the troops and had a toy rifle at his shoulder.

On one occasion a young matron was having tea with the Queen. She was very anxious to renew acquaintance with Prince Joñ, and so the Queen sent for him.

A TEA-TIME EXPLOIT

He was very pleasant and polite when he came, and his salutations over, he amused himself as he pleased, while the Queen and her guest took no further notice of him.

Meanwhile the Prince climbed upon an ottoman behind the guest and was apparently admiring a diamond ornament in the back of her hat.

When the guest rose to leave a disconcerting sight met her gaze. On her chair were several golden curls, Prince Joñ having employed his time in unfastening the hairpins which held them.

Some years ago, when out driving in London with the Queen and Princess Mary, he asked for something which his mother refused.

The little Prince was not in the humour to be denied. "If you don't let me," he said, "I shall stand up and shout 'Votes for Women'." A royal compromise followed.

On another occasion he asked the workmen who were painting the front of Buckingham Palace if they had any little boys and girls at home. These he invited to the Palace on a given day to a party. The King and Queen knew nothing of the invitations, but when the children turned up the little Prince was filled with delight. Needless to say, there was a "party" – and a happy, unconventional gathering it was.

⬅ The brother of Prince Joñ, the Prince of Wales, later to become Edward VIII, as a boy with his mother and father, George V and Queen Mary.

BACKSTORY

Prince Joñ, the uncle of the present Queen, was something of a royal secret – kept out of public view for fear his "weakness" would reflect poorly on the royal line. His story was long hidden until a TV drama *The Lost Prince*, directed by Stephen Poliakoff, was broadcast in 2008.

THE DAILY MIRROR, Monday, February 3, 1919.

GLASGOW POLICE RAID—SOLDIERS ON ROOFS

The Daily Mirror

CERTIFIED CIRCULATION LARGER THAN THAT OF ANY OTHER DAILY PICTURE PAPER

No. 4,765. | Registered at the G.P.O. as a Newspaper. | MONDAY, FEBRUARY 3 1919. | [16 PAGES.] | One Penny.

GLASGOW'S ARMY OF OCCUPATION ACTS AS A DAMPER

An incident during one of the baton charges.

A damaged tramway-car. About twelve of these vehicles were attacked by the angry mob and the windows smashed.

Soldiers, with stacked rifles, at Central Station.

Guarding a railway bridge. Sentries are posted at all the principal points.

Military with fixed bayonets escorting a transport wagon. The men are in full service kit, and the majority wear their steel helmets.

Signalling from a hotel roof.

Glasgow has recovered most of its calm. Though always a storm centre industrially, the citizens agree that never before has there been such turmoil. The military are now in full possession of the more important points of the city, such as the post-office, railway stations and electric power stations.—(Daily Mirror photographs.)

3rd February 1919

POLICE RAID IN GLASGOW: MORE STRIKERS ARRESTED

Correspondence at the Labour Council Offices Examined and Names Taken

SOLDIERS IN CITY SAID TO NUMBER 10,000

Ten thousand troops, according to an unofficial estimate, are quartered in Glasgow, and soldiers yesterday occupied the roofs of important buildings. Further reinforcements arrived last night. All was quiet.

Three more strikers have been arrested, including a Socialist orator on his way to address a Sunday meeting. Police raided the Labour Council offices, examined correspondence and took names.

A movement has started to form a Loyalist Workers' League, in order to get rid of extremist dictators.

London this week is threatened with an engineers' strike of 200,000 men and also with railway trouble.

STRIKE ORATOR ARRESTED ON WAY TO HALL

English Socialist To Be Charged To-day

Large crowds gathered yesterday in George Square and in Glasgow-green in anticipation of meetings being held, but no meetings took place, and gradually the crowds dispersed.

Three more arrests have been made in connection with the riots, amongst these being George Ebury, a well-known English Socialist.

The three men will be brought up at the police court today on a charge of inciting to riot.

Ebury was to have addressed a big meeting in St Mungos Hall yesterday afternoon, and he was arrested while on his way to the hall.

The number of soldiers in Glasgow at present is unofficially stated to be something like 10,000. Some excitement was caused by the arrival of a fresh detachment last night.

The Chief Constable of Glasgow states that protective measures will be taken to ensure the safety of those who resume work today.

LOYALIST MOVEMENT

Anti-Extremist League Forming – Meeting: Condemns Violence

A movement has been started to form a Patriotic Workers' League on Clydeside, the object being to take the control of trade unions out of the hands of extremists and appoint shop stewards to work in harmony with the official union leaders.

A big demonstration will be held to-morrow at Whiteinch, Glasgow, to discuss the matter.

A crowded meeting convened by local workers was held in Govan district yesterday afternoon.

Councillor Wardley, a Labour man, presided. There were many interruptions and interjections, but the following resolution was carried: "That we trades unionists condemn wholeheartedly the democratic and unconstitutional methods to force us to take part in the strike. We pledge ourselves to stand by the representatives of the

trades unions in this country and to use our influence to maintain law and order."

Strikers' Defiance – The following is an extract from the Strike Bulletin. "The Government delude themselves if they imagine that the display of military force will break the strike! The strike will go on as before, only with increased resolution."

RAILWAYS GUARDED

Large crowds yesterday, especially in the vicinity of the rioting, watched the soldiers doing sentry-go with fixed bayonets and steel helmets. The military authorities had taken precautions against any repetition of rioting. Barbed wire and wireless apparatus had been placed inside the City Chambers.

BACKSTORY

In the aftermath of the First World War, returning soldiers had been promised a land fit for heroes. The reality was somewhat different. With unemployment rising, wages threatened and an era of economic and political turmoil in progress, there was the genuine prospect of revolution in Britain.

One of the bitterest disputes came in Glasgow where striking workers brought the city to a standstill. An initially peaceful march erupted into direct confrontation with police, and a reading of the riot act amid what came to be known as the Battle of George Square. The government sent the army in – pitting armed Britons against striking countrymen just months after the First World War had ended.

The tensions and disputes persisted almost throughout the inter-war period. In 1926, reflecting the widespread fear and feverish atmosphere of the time, many listeners to a spoof BBC radio bulletin reporting a revolution believed it was genuine. Just five months later the General Strike made that outcome a possibility (above left) as the strike bit hard – and rudimentary newspapers were produced by non-striking staff.

Away from the clashes on the streets, the suffering caused by the Great Depression took a heavy toll: in 1934 the *Mirror* reported that a young mother had starved herself in order to feed her children (above right).

PREMIER'S TRADE TERMS TO M. KRASSIN TO-DAY

The Daily Mirror

CERTIFIED CIRCULATION LARGER THAN THAT OF ANY OTHER DAILY PICTURE PAPER

No. 5,181. | Registered at the G.P.O. as a Newspaper. | MONDAY, JUNE 7, 1920 | [16 PAGES.] | One Penny.

TOPLIS SHOT DEAD

Toplis, wanted for the Andover murder, was shot dead by the police at Plumpton, five miles from Penrith, Cumberland, last evening. "I am Toplis," he said to a constable when challenged. He got away, but later on was found again, fired on the police, who returned the fire, killing him.

WRECKED IN DOCK 'AVALANCHE'

Capsized craft lying along the wall at the Alfred Dock, on the River Mersey. Altogether sixteen boats were sunk in the avalanche of water.

SIR C. MATHEWS DEAD.

Sir Charles Mathews, Bart., Director of Public Prosecutions since 1908, has died in his sixty-ninth year. He had been lying ill in a nursing home for several days, and his death was announced in London late last night.

Sunken barge and men at work on another craft which has turned turtle.

The opening to the Alfred Dock where the gates were. A diver is at work below.

As the result of the Countess, a Glasgow collier of 600 tons, striking the gate of the Albert Dock, Birkenhead, an avalanche of water was let loose, and the scene was described by a witness as "just like the Niagara Falls." The Countess headed a procession of smaller craft at sixty miles an hour into the River Mersey, fifteen feet below. At first it was feared that many had been drowned, but Lloyds reports no loss of life. Over fifty men were rescued by tug-boats and other craft.

ROAD TRAGEDY SEQUEL.

Charles Douglas Barnard, a young airman, of Watford, has been charged with the manslaughter of Alfred Sharp, who was recently killed by a motor-car just after midnight. A coat button found on his car, it is alleged, furnished a clue.

TOPLIS SHOT DEAD AFTER MOTOR CHASE BY POLICE

Toplis was shot dead at Plumpton, five miles from Penrith (Cumberland) between eight and eight-thirty last night. The points in the drama are as follows –

At 4.30 p.m. a man in khaki, when challenged by Sergeant Fulton, admitted he was Toplis, and threatened the officer with a revolver, and made off. The police officer warned headquarters, and a police motorcar was sent out. They found Toplis walking along the road, this time dressed in a brown suit and wearing a trilby hat.

He was carrying a parcel under his arm. When the police approached he covered them with a revolver, fired, and made off. The police left the car and pursued the man, who fired at them. The police returned his fire, and Toplis was shot in the breast. The son of the chief constable, who rode a motor cycle in pursuit of the man, was earlier threatened by Toplis' revolver.

The inquest will be held on Wednesday.

A MAN WITH PARCEL UNDER HIS ARM

Sergeant's First Meeting with Armed Stranger

"I AM TOPLIS"
(from our own correspondent)

Penrith, Sunday

When Sergeant Fulton was cycling near Plumpton at half-past four this afternoon he saw a man dressed in khaki, who said "I am Toplis." And he drew out a revolver and pointed it at the officer, ordering him to retreat.

The constable dashed off on his bicycle, and soon got into touch with Penrith Police Station. Thereupon a motor-car containing Inspector Ritchie and other officers started out in search of the man.

It was about 8 p.m. that the police officers saw a man dressed in a brown suit and wearing a trilby hat walking along the road. It was Toplis. And he had changed from khaki into the brown suit.

Under his right arm was a parcel, and the motor-car passed by him. Then the car, under the instruction of the inspector, repassed Toplis. As the car drew opposite him Toplis changed the parcel from under his right arm to under his left arm.

He put his hand in his pocket and drew out a revolver, with which he covered the car.

Then he fired a shot, but the car, on instruction, had forged ahead at full speed. Toplis made off, and the police went in pursuit; he reached the cover of a cottage and was finally shot dead – the bullet entering his breast.

The driver of the car told me: "I heard three shots, and when I came back I found Toplis dying."

I am informed that the man came down to Carlisle by train.

HUE AND CRY FOR TOPLIS

Lonely Heath Murder That Led to Exciting Chase

The crime which started the hue and cry for Percy Toplis was committed at a lonely spot on Thruxton Down, near Andover, about midnight on Saturday, April 24.

The victim was Sidney George Spicer, a married man, of twenty-seven, living at Salisbury, and employed as a chauffeur.

His body, with a bullet wound in the head, was found in a hedge on the heath on Sunday morning. It had apparently been dragged a considerable distance across a field before being laid there.

On the Monday Spicer's car was found abandoned in a suburb of Swansea.

Later, Private Harry Fallows. M.T., R.A.S.C., said in court that he rode in the car to Swansea with Percy Toplis, who, he said, picked him up at Bulford Camp, "I went with him, but did not know what he had done until I read it in the papers," Fallows added.

After his disappearance from Swansea, Toplis, against whom the coroner's jury returned a verdict of Wilful Murder, led the police all over the country a lively chase.

POLICE ON NEW SCENT

He has been seen, according to reports, in many places. It was believed that from Swansea he took a train to London. A report was current later that he had boarded the Cunard liner Carmania as a fireman.

Last week a new scent was started. A police-constable and a farmer at Tomintoul, Banffshire, were shot and severely wounded by a man they found in a gamekeeper's hut on the moor, and who afterwards rode away on a bicycle.

The description of the man resembled in many respects that of Percy Toplis. The fugitive was last reported fifteen miles north of Aberdeen, where he got a lift in a minister's cart.

All the police in the country were on the track of the man, and it seemed impossible that he could escape. There was evidence that he was working southward.

BACKSTORY

Percy Toplis (above) was the so-called "Monocled mutineer". Toplis had a long criminal record before joining the army. He was wounded in fighting at Gallipoli and later deserted a number of times, covering his tracks by re-enlisting under a false name and disguise – including that of a monocle-wearing officer.

Sent to the notorious Bull Ring training camp at Etaples in 1917, he was one of the leaders of a revolt against the brutal treatment soldiers were subjected to in the camp.

Slipping back into England, after the war he operated in the black market and shot and killed an alleged petrol smuggler Sidney Spicer. Marked out as the most wanted man in Britain, Toplis went on the run until he was killed in Penrith. He was buried in an unmarked grave in a secret cemetery, with the authorities keen to suppress the legend of his mutiny. The plan worked until Toplis's life was dramatized for TV in 1986.

NEW DISCLOSURES AT IRENE MUNRO INQUEST

The Daily Mirror

CERTIFIED CIRCULATION LARGER THAN THAT OF ANY OTHER DAILY PICTURE PAPER

No. 5,272   Registered at the G.P.O. as a Newspaper.   TUESDAY, SEPTEMBER 21, 1920   [16 PAGES.]   One Penny.

MRS. BAMBERGER'S TRIAL OPENS AT THE OLD BAILEY

A photograph of the accused woman taken while she was released on bail during the time of her convalescence after the operation for appendicitis which she underwent.—(Daily Mirror.)

Mrs. Bamberger arriving at the Old Bailey, with her solicitor, Mr. H. Olley, yesterday morning, to stand the trial so long deferred by her serious illness.

Mr. Cecil Hayes, who is defending Mrs. Bamberger at the Old Bailey.

Waiting to see Mrs. Bamberger leave the court at luncheon time. She remained within.

Mr. Robert Wemyss Symonds, one of the principal witnesses.

The trial of Mrs. Thelma Dorothea Bamberger, on charges of perjury in connection with her divorce proceedings, opened yesterday at the Old Bailey before Mr. Justice Rigby Swift. Mrs. Bamberger, who appeared to have made a good recovery from her illness, pleaded "Not guilty" in a firm, clear voice. The court was crowded to the limit of its accommodation, fashionably-dressed women forming a considerable proportion of those present. The court officials alone received over 600 written applications for seats.

21st September 1920

MRS. BAMBERGER'S SOBBING DENIAL

Lover's Remarkable Story in Perjury Trial

DIVORCE DRAMA

Tale of Infatuation That Turned to Hate

"Not guilty!" These two words, spoken in a low voice, were Mrs. Thelma Dorothy Bamberger's answer at the Old Bailey yesterday to an indictment charging her with committing perjury in one of the most remarkable divorce cases of recent years.

Five years ago Mrs. Bamberger, a petite and handsome young woman, divorced her second husband, Mr. Henry Theodore Bamberger, a stockbroker.

On the intervention of the King's Proctor, who alleged that Mrs. Bamberger herself had committed misconduct, the decree nisi was subsequently annulled, and she was arrested on the charge of perjury.

The sensational events which followed – the estreating of the accused woman's bail on the ground that witnesses had been interfered with, and her operation for appendicitis which led to her trial being twice postponed – lent additional public interest to yesterday's proceedings.

PALE AND WEEPING

Mrs. Bamberger, looking very pale and wearing a fawn-grey tailor-made costume, with a plum-coloured velvet hat, sobbed bitterly while the jury was being sworn. She was given a seat in the dock, in which a wardress also sat.

MY IDEAL MAN

Letters to Lover after Final Parting – Short-Lived Marriage at 18

"Where a petitioner, for the purpose of getting a divorce, commits perjury," said Sir Richard Muir [prosecuting], in his opening speech, "it strikes at the root of the administration of justice in this country if such evidence were to be treated lightly and passed over."

Counsel described the marriage, when eighteen, of Mrs. Bamberger, who was the daughter of an evangelistic preacher, to Mr. F. W. Jenkins, who divorced her four years later, the co-respondent, being Henry Theodore Bamberger, whom, she subsequently married, and lived with until he joined the Army in October 1914.

At the end of that year Mrs. Bamberger met a man named Robert Wemyss Symonds and from January 1915, until May, 1919, it was alleged, they lived together practically constantly as man and wife.

They had quarrels – according to Symonds the woman had an exceedingly violent temper – but they were very fond of one another, so Symonds, who did not at first know that she was already married, told her she must get a divorce from her husband and, as a result, she filed her petition on August 19, 1915, and a decree nisi was pronounced on December 7, 1917.

When the King's Proctor intervened, Mrs. Bamberger admitted misconduct with Symonds, but pleaded that her husband had coerced her into associating with men for money, which he shared. One man mentioned was Ernest Stein.

Mrs. Bamberger appeared to think that Symonds had given information regarding Stein, whereupon she withdrew her previous admissions.

"CRAZY WITH LOVE"

Apparently, said counsel, she had conceived a great hatred for Symonds, the man whom she formerly loved. In the Divorce Court she accused him of having thrown corrosive fluid in her face for the purpose of spoiling her looks.

About July, 1919, counsel proceeded, after a quarrel Symonds left her, and she wrote to him: 'To be told that a man has ceased to care for you when you have lived with him for four years, when everybody knows about it, would be a great blow, to put it mildly, but for him to chuck you out as if you were so much dirt is something one cannot get over.'

"This," said Sir Richard, "is the letter of a woman who said she never committed misconduct with Symonds."

Symonds and the accused made things up at a later date but in January, 1919, he heard of an incident, in which Mrs. Bamberger was charged with having robbed a man in a flat for which she was acquitted, telling Symonds she had been mistaken for her twin sister.

In May or April of 1919 Symonds left her finally, and she wrote to him a number of letters. In one she said, "I am simply crazy with love for you, my ideal man."

On another occasion Mrs. Bamberger wrote – "Come to arms that really love you better than life. No one could ever love you as your own Baby Pops."

BACKSTORY

The trial of Thelma Bamberger was a sensation that held readers spellbound during the course of remarkable proceedings. Bamberger (above, convalescing after an operation for appendicitis) was found guilty of perjury in claiming she was a virgin despite being married twice and involved in a number of alleged affairs and liaisons.

In the language of the time, reports would not be so explicit as to suggest she was sexually active – phrases such as "misconduct" implied as such. But the nature of the case, in which there was salacious testimony inferring with delicate subtlety that she had worked as a high-class prostitute, provided the nation's newspapers with scandal that they lapped up.

The public couldn't get enough. Huge crowds gathered outside the Old Bailey. When it was over, on the day when Bamberger was sentenced to nine months' imprisonment, her defence counsel said she was being "punished for the sins of society for the past fifty years".

ULTIMATUM TO STRIKERS BY TUBE COMBINE

The Daily Mirror

NET SALE MUCH THE LARGEST OF ANY DAILY PICTURE NEWSPAPER

No. 6,427.   Registered at the G.P.O as a Newspaper.   THURSDAY, JUNE 12, 1924   One Penny.

YOUTHS CHARGED WITH MURDER "FOR SPORT"

The two accused, Nathan Leopold, jun. (second from left), and Richard Loeb, between Loeb's uncle (left) and Leopold's father, in court.

Richard Loeb (extreme right) leading the search for the little victim's belt.

Robert Franks, the victim, a schoolboy.

The home of Nathan Leopold, sen., the millionaire.

Nathan Leopold, jun., one of the accused students.

Mr. Jacob Franks, the multi-millionaire and father of the murdered boy, with his son Jacob.

These pictures, illustrating the sensational murder near Chicago in which the sons of two millionaires are alleged to have confessed to committing the crime "in a spirit of adventure," have just reached London. After his father had received a demand for his ransom the body of Robert Franks, the fourteen-year-old son of a third millionaire, was found in a swamp, and later Nathan Leopold, jun., and Richard Loeb, two University students, were arrested. It is alleged that in their search for a victim to be murdered "for the experience" they drove round a school and through binoculars watched boys playing games. They selected Franks when he was umpiring a baseball match.

June–September 1924

KIDNAPPED SON OF MILLIONAIRE

Murder 'Confession' by Two University Graduates

SPRAYED WITH ACID

Cinema Blamed for increase of Juvenile Crime in U.S.

Two sons of Chicago millionaires are stated to have confessed to the kidnapping and murder of Robert Franks, son of another millionaire.

Both youths, who are University graduates, have, the police say, admitted abducting Franks as he left school in a motor-car.

While they were travelling along a main street he was hit on the head with a chisel, gagged and choked, and acid was then used to disfigure his face to make identity difficult. This and the growth of juvenile crime in the U.S. generally are largely attributed to the influence of the cinema on young minds.

GAGGED IN CAR

Police Allege Use of Acid To Disfigure Abducted Boy's Face
(from our own correspondent)

New York, Sunday

A sensation has been caused here by the alleged discovery yesterday by the Chicago police that Robert Franks, the fourteen-year-old son of the millionaire Jacob Franks, was kidnapped and murdered on May 21, on his way home from school, by Nathan Leopold, junior, and Richard Loeb, also sons of Chicago millionaires.

According to the police, they confessed to the crime after an all-night examination. Both youths are nineteen years old, and are post-graduate students of the University of Chicago. Leopold is reputed to be the youngest graduate at that institution, and Loeb the youngest at the University of Michigan.

They admitted, the prosecution alleges, that they seized the boy, placed him in a hired motorcar and killed him five minutes afterwards, while the car was driving through a main street.

First hitting him on the head with a chisel, they ensured his death by choking him with a gag. They put acid on his face in an effort to disfigure it so that identity would be difficult.

Demand For Ransom

Leopold wrote a letter to Jacob Franks, demanding £2,000 ransom, and it was Loeb who telephoned to Franks' home from a drug store and gave directions for the delivery of the ransom.

The ransom and "adventure" of the crime were the motives for the deed, although both youths received a liberal allowance from their parents.

Cinema pictures are considered responsible to a great extent for the increase of juvenile crime all over the United States.

Kidnapping is a capital offence under Illinois laws as well as murder, so that should the youths be proved guilty they are liable to be sentenced to death under two counts.

11th September 1924

LIFE SENTENCES ON BOY MURDERERS

Laughed When Taken to Gaol and Ordered Steaks

BETTING ON SENTENCE

Chicago, Wednesday

Amazing scenes were witnessed in Chicago to-day when Nathan Leopold and Richard Loeb, the wealthy American students who "murdered for sport," were sentenced to imprisonment for life.

Both are millionaires' sons aged nineteen, and had pleaded guilty to killing Robert Franks, a fourteen-year-old schoolboy.

Youth was the deciding factor in the decision of Judge Caverly, a London-born man. He said that no minor had ever been sentenced to death in Illinois on a plea of guilty.

In addition to the life sentence the boys were also formally sentenced to ninety-nine years' imprisonment on the charge of kidnapping Franks. – Reuter

"The crime singular in its atrocity, is, in a sense, inexplicable, but none the less inhuman and repulsive," said Judge Caverly in passing sentence.

"There are no mitigating circumstances."

Leopold and Loeb made no effort to hide their feelings when taken back to gaol. They laughed and chatted, and ordered: "Thick steaks smothered with onions and all side dishes."

Leopold in his cell offered to bet even money that he would be executed. Chicago betting was three to one that the boys would not be executed.

Owing to the threats received by the Judge, he was escorted to court by detectives and two rifle squads, says the Exchange.

BACKSTORY

The Leopold–Loeb murder trial was a shocking case revolving around the apparent desire of two rich young men to commit the "perfect" murder – simply for their own entertainment.

The famous attorney Clarence Darrow was able to spare the pair from execution but, 12 years later, Loeb was murdered in prison. Leopold was released on parole in 1958 and died in 1971.

Given that cinema was claimed to have played such a central part in the rise of juvenile crime and the murder of Franks, it was with some irony that director Alfred Hitchcock (above) would later make a successful film based on the Leopold–Loeb murder, entitled *Rope*.

GREAT NEW SERIAL BEGINS TO-DAY ON PAGE 17

Daily Mirror

28 PAGES

THE DAILY PICTURE — NEWSPAPER WITH THE LARGEST NET SALE

No. 7,536   Registered at the G.P.O. as a Newspaper   MONDAY, JANUARY 9, 1928   One Penny

ANXIOUS LONDON FACES THREAT OF NEW FLOODS

The rising tide yesterday afternoon forcing its way through the sandbag barrier at Grosvenor-road.

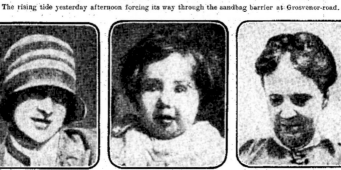

Miss Lilian Harding.   Irene Watson, of Putney.   Rosina Harding.   Mrs. Quick, a cripple.   Miss Florence Harding.

A night of fear for Londoners by the river was followed yesterday by a day of tense anxiety lest there should be a repetition of the disastrous flood which took a toll of fourteen lives on Saturday. At Grosvenor-road, where four of the five persons whose portraits appear above were drowned, strong barriers of earth and sandbags were erected to take the place of the broken embankment. Similar precautions were taken at other danger points, and handcarts laden with clay were kept in readiness to be rushed to any spot that showed signs of weakening. Official warning is given that the Thames tides will increase until to-morrow and will then gradually lessen.

OVER 5,000 HOMELESS IN LONDON FLOOD DISASTER

Workers Strengthen Damaged River Wall As Danger Hour Arrived This Morning

50,000 CROWD HAMPERS WORK OF POLICE

Amazing Scenes in Stricken Districts – Relief Funds Opened – Graphic Stories of Wave of Death

While men worked feverishly to strengthen parts of the Thames Embankment damaged by the floods, the high tide danger hour at three o'clock this morning passed without further serious flooding.

One of the most ominous points was in Grosvenor-road, Victoria, where six of the fourteen victims on Saturday lost their lives. Here the water lapped the sandbag and clay ramparts erected when the wall was broken, but they withstood the strain.

The Port of London Authority has issued a warning that the Thames tides will increase in height until to-morrow. Each one will be a little more dangerous than that before it, and the authorities appeal to the public to keep away from the danger area.

Yesterday great crowds on the Embankment seriously hampered the work of relief and rampart building.

The homeless now number over 5,000. The Lord Mayor appeals for funds on behalf of the sufferers. The Mayor of Westminster's Fund reached over £2,000 last night.

3 A.M. VIGIL AT RIVER DANGER POINTS

Clay Piled Up Against Ramparts in Grosvenor Road

In the early hours this morning workmen were busy strengthening the damaged points in the Thames Embankment as the high tide danger hour approached.

There was every sign, however, that the early morning tide during the "danger" period would be passed without further flooding.

CLAY AGAINST RAMPARTS

At 1.30 this morning men were still hard at work piling up clay against the ramparts in Grosvenor-road.

The water was just beginning to lap the lower part of the sandbags. All the streets in the flood-swept area were quiet, and few people, besides the workers, were about.

At 2.30 workmen were being served with tea from Salvation Army stalls. At Putney Bridge, the Thames at 2.30 a.m. looked like a sheet of glass; that was about an hour before high tide there.

The upper windows were well lit in Hurlingham Court-mansions, where the basements were swamped and two people drowned on Saturday morning.

Batteries of alarm clocks could be heard tinkling about this time from rows of houses near the river bank, and people began to gather.

The Embankment for several miles was one huge promenade for the greater part of the day. "Like crowds going to a football match" was one angry official's description. It is calculated that 50,000 people visited the "danger zone" during the day.

CAUGHT "LIKE RATS IN A TRAP"

Father Who Heard Calls for Help as Children Drowned

VAIN RESCUE DIVES

The flood came with devastating swiftness early on Saturday.

At various points along the Victoria Embankment the water cascaded into the streets.

Meanwhile, between Lambeth and Vauxhall Bridges and beyond a great tragedy was taking place.

Here policemen and boatmen saw the river's rapid rising and grew uneasy.

Then, with the first rush of the waters when the retaining wall crashed, they dashed to warn the sleeping occupants of houses.

Householders saw a raging torrent at their doors. Some took refuge in upper rooms.

Death In Twenty Seconds

Others, less fortunate, were caught like rats in a trap in basement rooms, and were drowned.

One of the most terrible tragedies was the drowning of four sisters, aged eighteen to three, at 8 Grosvenor-road.

Here the Embankment wall gave way for fifty yards, and in the great rush of water that followed the sisters, who were sleeping in the basement, lost their lives within twenty seconds.

"I saw them at 11.30 and said to them 'Goodnight and God bless you'," said the distracted father later.

The four girls were hopelessly trapped, as there were iron bars in front of the window.

"I heard one of the girls crying: 'Daddy, daddy, open the door!' I dived down time after time, trying to reach the door, but the weight of water against me was too great.

"I did not stop till long after the last cry. It was terrible."

Flood Items

Ceiling Rescue – A man trapped in a basement in Westminster escaped through a hole cut in the ceiling by rescuers.
Crash of Waters – Water rushed down two Battersea streets and met with a noise like an explosion.
Darkness Amid Floods – Electricity gave out in the Isle of Dogs and darkness added to the terror of the floods.
Fish in Police Station – A small fish was caught in Battersea Police Station yard.

IMPORTANT NEW FILM FEATURE ON MONDAY: See p. 2

Daily Mirror

THE DAILY PICTURE NEWSPAPER WITH THE LARGEST NET SALE

No. 7,595 | Registered at the G.P.O. as a Newspaper | SATURDAY, MARCH 17, 1928 | One Penny

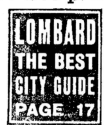

NAVAL SENSATION—THREE OFFICERS SUSPENDED

A striking *Daily Mirror* picture of Royal Oak, Rear-Admiral B. St. G. Collard's flagship, taken from Queen Elizabeth. It was in Royal Oak that the trouble occurred.

Rear-Admiral B. St. G. Collard. He commanded the First Battle Squadron, Mediterranean Fleet.

Captain K. G. B. Dewar. He was Flag Captain and Chief Staff Officer to Royal Oak.

Commander H. M. Daniel, D.S.O., was second in command of Royal Oak.

Admiral Sir Roger Keyes, by whose order the court of inquiry was held at Malta.

Captain F. O. B. S. Osborne, under whose command Royal Oak put to sea from Malta.

Sensational reports of incidents involving Rear-Admiral B. St. G. Collard and two of his officers, Captain K. G. B. Dewar and Commander H. M. Daniel, were followed yesterday by the statement from the Admiralty that as a result of a Court of Inquiry held at Malta, where the incidents took place, the three officers concerned were suspended from duty. Captain Dewar and Commander Daniel have arrived in London; Rear-Admiral Collard remains at Malta. There has been nothing in the nature of a revolt,

17th March 1928

NAVAL SUSPENSIONS: DEMAND FOR FULL ENQUIRY

Admiral Captain and Commander in Royal Oak Battleship Incident

MYSTERY OF "PERSONAL DIFFERENCES"

Three naval officers, one a Rear-Admiral, have been suspended as the result of trouble in the Royal Oak, the flagship of the First Battle Squadron Mediterranean Fleet.

The Admiralty announced yesterday that the suspensions were the result of a court of Inquiry held by order of the Commander-in-Chief. The suspended officers are:

Rear-Admiral B. St. Q. Collard, Captain Kenneth G. B. Dewar and Commander H. M. Daniel.

Naval M.P.s took the view last night that a sworn inquiry should be held. Meanwhile, the Admiralty is awaiting a full report on the incidents.

The origin of the trouble is attributed in naval circles to personal disagreements between the officers concerned. There has been no revolt.

PEACE EFFORTS BY THE C-IN-C. FAIL!

What further action will follow the suspension from duty of three officers of Royal Oak?

The position last night was that no decision could be taken until the report of Sir Roger Keyes had reached the Admiralty and been considered by them.

Naval M.P.s take the view that the whole affair should be investigated by a tribunal which is able to take evidence on oath and a demand for an inquiry of this description will probably be made in the House of Commons next week.

Evidence on oath is not taken at a naval inquiry, and in the Lobby yesterday this form of investigation was regarded as unsatisfactory, writes The Daily Mirror Lobby correspondent.

Surprise was expressed that, although the incidents are reported to have occurred as far back as last Sunday, the Admiralty were not in possession of complete information five days afterwards.

Disciplinary Matters

The only Admiralty statement issue so far is as follows –

A Court of Inquiry was held at Malta by order of the Commander-in-Chief, Mediterranean Station (Admiral Sir Roger Keyes), to investigate certain disciplinary matters in which Rear-Admiral Bernard St. G. Collard, C.B., D.S.O., Captain Kenneth G. B. Dewar, C.B., R.N. and Commander H. M. Daniel, I.S.O., R.N., were involved.

As a result of the inquiry the three officers concerned were suspended from duty by the Commander-in-Chief, whose report has not yet been received at the Admiralty.

Since the First Lord made his statement in the House to-day he has ascertained that Rear-Admiral Collard's flag has not been transferred to another ship so he had inferred from an earlier telegram, but has been struck and that he is still at Malta.

Captain K. G. B. Dewar and Commander H. M. Daniel, of the Royal Oak, have arrived in London, and called at the Admiralty yesterday morning.

It is learned authoritatively that the Admiralty does not regard the incident as in the nature of a revolt or mutiny. The matter in naval circles is thought to be a personal one between the Admiral and his officers.

ADMIRAL'S SUGGESTION

How Sir Roger Keyes Tried to Settle the Trouble

Malta, Friday

According to an unofficial version of the Royal Oak incident, the affair started with a regular formulated complaint and culminated in personal disagreements between the three officers concerned. Service questions, it is said, were definitely involved.

The Commander-in-Chief, Admiral Sir Roger Keyes, made efforts to pour oil on the troubled waters, suggesting as the only possible solution that Rear-Admiral Collard should transfer his flag to the Resolution, but this course did not appeal to the Rear-Admiral.

Therefore the Commander-in-Chief granted his request to be allowed to haul down his flag and Captain Dewar and Commander Daniel were allowed to leave for England. –Reuter

The combined Mediterranean and Atlantic Fleets, numbering nearly 100 ships, arrived at Gibraltar yesterday afternoon.

Mr. Bridgeman (First Lord of the Admiralty), answering a private notice question by Mr. Aramon in the Commons yesterday, said:

"I regret that I am unable to give any details of what happened in the Royal Oak. All we have got at present is a wireless report, a great deal of which, owing to interrupted transmission, is not very easy to decipher."

BACKSTORY

So what was all the fuss about that the Admiralty seemed at such great pains to keep quiet? It turned out that this mysterious disagreement on the high seas hinged on a long-running feud between officers, the bewildering complexities of Royal Navy etiquette and what was, for the time, rather un-shipshape language from a senior commander.

The story begins with the above-named officers assembled for a dance on the quarterdeck of the *Royal Oak*. Also in attendance was a Royal Marines Bandmaster called (almost incredibly) Percy Barnacle (above).

Rear Admiral Collard criticized Commander Daniel for supposedly not providing female guests with dance partners, and took umbrage with Captain Dewar for not remonstrating with Daniel.

Compounding the row was that Collard thought Barnacle's band were rubbish. He ordered them to stop playing and reputedly said "I'm not going to have a bugger like that on this ship."

This sparked letters of complaint from Dewar and Daniel which were judged to be "subversive" and ultimately ended their naval careers.

REMARKABLE STORIES OF "CAPTAIN BARKER"

Daily Mirror

THE DAILY PICTURE PAPER WITH THE LARGEST NET SALE

No. 7,896 — Registered at the G.P.O. as a Newspaper. — THURSDAY, MARCH 7, 1929 — One Penny

WOMAN WHO MASQUERADED AS ARMY CAPTAIN

An exclusive photograph of " Captain Leslie Bligh Barker

Another exclusive picture. Among the British and foreign medals are the D.S.O.

West End building where " Captain Barker " conducted a cafe.

" Captain Barker " at Hampton.
" He " weighs 16st.

Numerous fresh stories were told yesterday of the amazing exploits in various parts of London of " Captain Leslie Bligh Barker," who, having posed for years as a man, confessed at Brixton Prison to being a woman. Although some people with whom " he " came in contact were at times suspicious, their doubts were dissipated by " his " manly pose as an ex-Army officer and latterly as a reception clerk in a West End hotel. " He " was arrested in connection with bankruptcy proceedings.

7th March 1929

REMARKABLE STORIES OF THE LIFE OF "CAPTAIN" BARKER

Woman Who Posed for Years as a Man Refuses to Reveal Her Identity

RODE TO HOUNDS AND PLAYED IN CRICKET TEAM

Adventurous Career That Included Training Alsatians and Running a Restaurant

More of the astonishing history of "Captain" Victor Barker, the woman who for years posed as a man, was disclosed yesterday.

She is now in Holloway Prison for contempt of court following bankruptcy proceedings, and still refuses to reveal her identity.

The woman who was known to hundreds of people as Captain Barker's wife, the *Daily Mirror* learns, is a member of a distinguished titled Irish family.

The "captain" has hunted and played cricket, run a furniture shop and a restaurant, trained Alsatian dogs and been reception clerk at an hotel.

FOUR YEARS SPENT AS A MAN

'Captain's' Many Changes of Home and Occupation

VALET'S SUSPICIONS

"Captain" Barker's career as a man has been traced back to May, 1925, when she appeared at Andover, saying she had come from Brighton.

At Andover she opened an antique furniture shop, but it was not successful, and she went to live in a bungalow at Weyhill.

The next move was to Dudley, where for eighteen months she managed a kennel establishment.

For a few months "Captain" Barker lived at Hampton-on-Thames, saying he was employed at the War Office.

Next came the opening of the Mascot Cafe, Litchfield Street, Charing Cross-road, "Captain" Barker then living in an expensive flat in Hertford-street, Mayfair.

The restaurant had to be abandoned early last year, and the "Captain" was next heard of in September last, when she became reception clerk at the Regent Palace Hotel.

Until her arrest on Friday last she had lived for some time in a maisonette in Markham Square, Chelsea.

Threw Like A Woman

"Captain" Barker was accompanied at Andover by a "wife", a boy, three, four or five years old, and a governess.

After opening an antique furniture shop she secured a large circle of acquaintances.

She hunted with the Tidworth Hounds, and played several times for the Andover Town Cricket Club.

A member of the club told a Daily Mirror reporter yesterday he remembered that when the team was playing at Emham he commented to his colleagues on the fact that "Barker" threw the ball like a woman. Her sex was not suspected, however.

The proprietor of a well-known hotel in Andover said: "Captain Barker was a regular customer here, but from the first 'he' was regarded with some suspicion. After a little time many people were prepared to lay odds that he was a woman, his voice went funny at times, and his figure was distinctly feminine."

When it became clear that the furniture shop was not a success she went to live in a bungalow at Weyhill and kept pigs.

Major Batten, who now lives at Andover, was then acting as her groom and chauffeur.

TRAINER OF DOGS

Brilliant Speech to Ex-Officers – and a Brickworks Employee

At Dudley, where "Captain" Barker next went, she was manager of the Dundas Dog Kennels, Oakham, where Alsatians were trained on a large scale.

She showed great skill in the training of the animals.

She took keen interest in the social life of the town, attending many functions. In 1926, in full uniform and decorated with medals, she attended a dinner of the ex-officers and made a brilliant speech.

The "captain" always appeared to be down on her luck, although she seemed to be bright.

Mr. J. W. Thomas, who was manager of the house in Hertford-street, Mayfair, in which "Captain" Barker had a flat, said to a Daily Mirror reporter yesterday –

"For some months I acted as 'Captain' Barker's valet. At first I had my suspicions that he was not a man, but as he used to allow me to go into his room without knocking my suspicions seemed without ground, and I dismissed them from my mind.

"He frequently wore the uniform and badges of a cavalry colonel and rows of military decorations. Often, however, he was slovenly dressed.

"I was suspicious when he told me that he had refused from the King the Order of the British Empire but had accepted instead a pair of cuff links.

"He attempted to form two branches of the Mons Club and spoke to ex-Servicemen in the language of a genial hard-bitten cavalry colonel.

"In his manner of telling good stories and taking refreshment he acted in real Army style."

BACKSTORY

'Captain Victor Barker' was a cross-dressing woman who posed as the fictitious officer and duped scores of people for years – including, it was reported, her wife. She boxed and is also said to have been at political demonstrations against left-wing groups that often ended in violence, in which she supposedly enthusiastically engaged.

Barker's real name was either Lillian Smith or Valerie Arkell-Smith. She was able to pass herself off as a man until debts brought bankruptcy proceedings, and eventually charges of perjury for claiming in the High Court to be a man during a previous unrelated appearance.

The case exposed the entrenched views about sexuality at the time, and reflected general misunderstandings about gender and identity. Note the confusion in the report about whether to call Smith 'he' or 'she'.

TUNING-UP FOR OUR OUTBOARD TROPHY RACE

WE COVER HOLIDAY ACCIDENTS

Daily Mirror

THE DAILY PICTURE — PAPER WITH THE LARGEST NET SALE

No. 8,054 — Registered at the G.P.O. as a Newspaper. — MONDAY, SEPTEMBER 9, 1929 — One Penny

NEW £1,000 PICTURE PUZZLE

BRITAIN'S SCHNEIDER TRIUMPH AT 328 M.P.H.

Crowds on Southsea Beach watch a British 'plane. Inset, Waghorn between D'Arcy Greig (wearing coat) and Atcherley.

Flying-Officer Waghorn banks round the Cowes pylon

On the Orient liner Orford after the presentation of the Schneider Trophy to the winner. In the group are Mr. R. MacDonald, Lord Thomson, Sir Philip Sassoon, General Balbo and members of the rival teams.

World's speed records were snattered by Britain's representatives in the Schneider Trophy race contested over the Solent in ideal weather and in the presence of thousands of thrilled spectators who crowded on land and in ships and boats of every description. Flying-Officer Waghorn won at 328.63 m.p.h., with Warrant-Officer Dal Molin, Italy, second and Flight-Lieutenant D'Arcy Greig third. The winner's time greatly exceeded the best previously recorded in the history of the race, and Flying-Officer Atcherley, unluckily disqualified for failing to round a pylon by mistake, completed the fastest lap at 332 m.p.h. Two Italian machines were forced down. See also page 13.

9ᵗʰ September 1929

BRITAIN'S BID FOR STILL GREATER AIRSPEED TOMORROW

Schneider Team Captain to Challenge World Record in 'Plane That Won Trophy

VICTORY AT 328 MILES AN HOUR

Following her wonderful victory in the Schneider Trophy race on Saturday, Britain will, to-morrow attempt to set up a still higher world's speed record.

The attempt will be made by Squadron-Leader Orlebar, the captain of the Schneider Trophy team, and he will use the plane in which Flying-Officer Waghorn won the race at 328 miles an hour. A second 'plane will be tested by Flight-Lieutenant Stainforth and may also make an attempt on the record.

The record at present stands at 332 miles an hour, the speed reached by Flying-Officer Atcherley, who had the misfortune to go off the course and be disqualified. The best Italian average speed was 284 miles an hour, and two of their 'planes came down, one pilot being injured.

Waghorn's average speed was 47 miles an hour more than that with which Flight-Lieutenant Webster won the trophy at Venice two years ago.

TWO PILOTS LIKELY TO ATTACK RECORD

Second Machine To Be Tested at Calshot To-day

ITALIANS GOING HOME

It was officially announced, at Calshot last night that Squadron-Leader Orlebar will attempt to set up a new world's speed record to-morrow.

He will use the Supermarine Rolls Royce S 6, in which Flying-Officer Waghorn won the Schneider Trophy.

The Italian team were busy at Calshot all yesterday packing their machines into huge packing cases. They expect to leave Calshot to-night.

Lieutenant Monti, who was injured in the race, is progressing favourably.

THREE AMAZING LAPS

How Waghorn Set Up Records and Broke Them – The Silver Bullet

Two hours of thrills and breathless excitement – that was the effect of Saturday's great Schneider Trophy race on the multitude gathered on the shores below.

Great Britain's victory exceeded even the most sanguine expectations. Pilots and machines proved magnificent, and but for the error in direction which led to the disqualification of Flying-Officer Atcherley, Britain would have gained the first two places. The official placings were:

1–Waghorn (Great Britain) 328.63 m.p.h.
2–Dal Molin (Italy) 284.20 m.p.h.
3–D'Arcy Greig (Great Britain) 282.11 m.p.h.

The great drama of the race occurred in the first twenty minutes. When Flying-Officer Waghorn took [to] the air the world's record speed – the fastest at which a man had ever travelled – stood at 319 miles an hour.

Within twenty minutes that record had been broken three times on average lap speeds.

The crowd roared itself hoarse as Waghorn's speed mounted, setting up record after record as follows –

First lap 324 m.p.h.
Second lap 329 m.p.h.
Third lap 331 m.p h.

But better was to come, for in his sixth lap Flying-Officer Atcherley reached 332 miles an hour, and Britain had broken the world's record for the fourth time that day.

The impression two million people formed of Waghorn was a silver bullet shooting the air, a roar and a flash, and he was gone.

One great thrill was when the first Italian plane – the Macchi 52 – shot into the air with Warrant Officer Dal Molin in the cockpit. Like a flash he passed over the starting line and disappeared into the blue.

With the two machines together the spectators had their first great thrill – Dal Molin was on the straight for the finish of his first lap when Waghorn came behind him. It was a moment which left everybody gasping.

Waghorn raced ahead, and a burst of cheering came from the thronged pier. Dal Molin was on his tail, and the roar of their engines contrasted strangely with the quietude of the yachts and ships basking on the sunlit waters.

Fortune was not with the Italians. Dal Molin alone completed the course, but his average was only 284 miles an hour.

➥ The victorious Gloster Napier-powered Supermarine S6 being launched at Cowes for the 1929 Schneider Trophy, with the *Mauretania* in the background.

BACKSTORY

The 'Roaring Twenties' was a period of great excitement, and the daring attempts to break speed records captivated huge crowds. Few contests were as thrilling as the Schneider Trophy for seaplanes.

Running from 1911 to 1931, the races provided a remarkable spectacle, reaching a peak in the late 1920s and drawing a massive crowd to the Solent in 1929, when the record was smashed several times. A new mark of 355.8mph was eventually set, before Britain won the trophy outright in 1931.

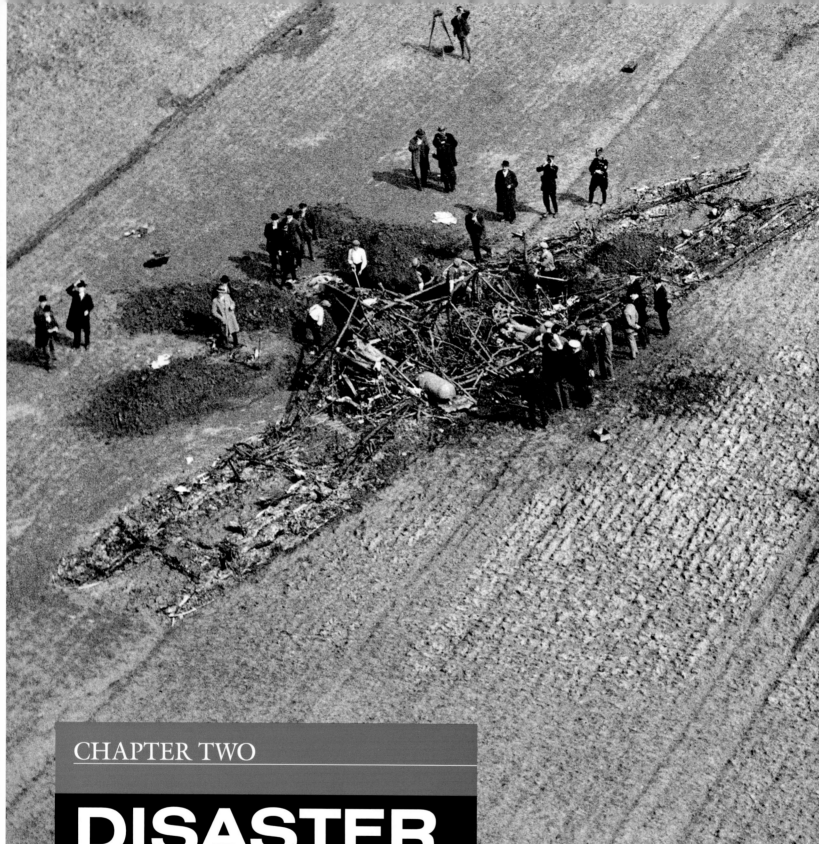

CHAPTER TWO

DISASTER
IN ONE
MINUTE

The dramatic scene of the City of Liverpool air disaster (see page 66).

MORE GUINEAS FOR MOTORISTS ON SUNDAY

150 FREE HAMPERS WINNERS' NAMES

Daily Mirror

THE DAILY PICTURE PAPER WITH THE LARGEST NET SALE

No. 8,213   Registered at the G.P.O. as a Newspaper.   SATURDAY, MARCH 15, 1930   One Penny

WIRELESS PROGRAMMES ON PAGE 17

CALCUTTA CUP SURPRISE

WEIRD STATUE

J. G. Askew, who was announced to be unfit last night.

J. C. Hubbard, the Harlequins player, who will take Askew's place.

P. W. Brook, selected yesterday to fill the vacancy left in the pack.

B. H. Black, badly hurt in inter-collegiate final, Oxford, is now fit.

The news that Askew would not play for England in the match against Scotland—the Rugby season climax—at Twickenham to-day was a big surprise. It will be Hubbard's first international.

CHANNEL TUNNEL IN SIGHT AT LAST—SCHEME APPROVED

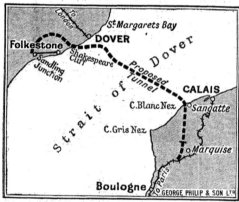

How the proposed tunnel would join England and France.

The late Mr. William Low, of Wrexham, who was the originator of the Channel Tunnel scheme and prepared the first plans in 1866.

The top of an almost completely filled-in shaft at the foot of the Shakespeare Cliff, Dover. It is all that remains of work done in connection with Channel Tunnel plans in 1885. The Committee of Inquiry set up by the Government expresses complete approval of the scheme in a report issued yesterday.

A strange statue recently set up on a high brick pedestal in a new quarter of Breslau in Germany. It represents the Holy Virgin carrying her Child and astride a donkey, as during the flight into Egypt. The smaller picture shows the human figures.

15th March 1930

CHANNEL TUNNEL SCHEME ADVOCATED BY COMMITTEE

"None of the New Forms of Communication is a Satisfactory Alternative"

£30,600,000 COST OF THREE UNDER-SEA TUBES

'Element of Doubt' Until Part of Work Has Been Done – Opening in 1938 a Possibility

Complete approval of the plans for a Channel Tunnel connecting Britain with France is given in the report issued yesterday of the Committee of Inquiry set up by the Government.

After examining other methods proposed, the committee found that none of them could be regarded as a satisfactory alternative to the tunnel. Although recognising the difficulties, the committee does not believe they are insurmountable. There will, however, be 'an element of doubt' until a pilot tunnel has been made.

The cost of the complete work is put at £30,600,000. There would, it is stated, be no difficulties in the way of operation or upkeep.

Lord Ebbisham is the only member of the committee to raise objections and he states that he does so on economic grounds.

TUNNEL WITHOUT GOVERNMENT AID

Committee Urges That Work Be Done Privately

£500,000 A YEAR COST

Only one member of the Channel Tunnel Committee, Lord Ebbisham (a former Lord Mayor of London), is against the scheme.

The report of the others is strongly in favour of railway connection between France and England.

"None of the new forms of cross-Channel communication suggested to us can be regarded as a satisfactory alternative to a Channel tunnel," they state, continuing –

"It appears probable that the geological and engineering difficulties likely to be encountered could be successfully overcome, but there must remain an element of doubt until the proposed pilot tunnel, estimated to cost £5,600,000, has been successfully driven across the Channel."

Pilot Tunnel

"If the pilot tunnel is successfully constructed the practicability of constructing traffic tunnels may be regarded as established. The cost of the main tunnels is estimated at about £25,000,000.

"If a Channel tunnel is constructed we consider that on economic grounds the work should be carried out by private enterprise and not be accorded any special financial assistance by the Government.

"We believe that a Channel tunnel could be built, maintained and operated by private enterprise at a cost which would permit of the traffic through it being conveyed at rates not higher than those at present in force on the short cross-Channel route.

"We believe that although some interests would probably be adversely affected, the construction of a Channel tunnel, by creating new traffic and thus increasing trade, would be of economic advantage to this country."

From an independent survey of existing statistics the committee came to the conclusion that the tunnel, if opened in 1938, would secure 2,357,000 passengers in that year.

The cost of maintenance and operation of the tunnel is put in certain circumstances at £500,000 a year.

The committee (excepting Lord Ebbisham) do not believe that the effect on agriculture, as a result of the possibility of increased competition from abroad, would be serious.

WHAT RAILWAYS THINK

Southern Belief That Tunnel Would Bring 15 Per Cent More Passengers

The Southern Railway Company assume, continues the report, that a Channel tunnel could be opened in 1936, and that the whole of the passengers carried by the short sea routes would be diverted to the tunnel.

It would also, they believed, attract additional passenger traffic equivalent in volume to fifteen per cent of the number of passengers carried on these routes.

On this basis the Southern Railway estimate that if a Channel tunnel was opened in 1936 it might be expected to secure 1,524,943 passengers.

BACKSTORY

The Channel Tunnel had long been a dream – or a nightmare, depending on an individual Briton's point of view – for over a century before the 1930 scheme was launched. Yet while advances in technology and the economics of the scheme made it a realistic prospect, entrenched opposition meant it would be more than 60 years before the vision became a reality.

Despite the best efforts of the committee and encouraging support from the Southern Railway, serious doubts were held by many within government and business as to its viability. The plan was narrowly defeated in a vote on support in the Houses of Commons in June 1930.

WHAT DO 'CHANNEL-TUNNELPHOBES' THINK NOW?

◀ Opposition to the tunnel had been expressed in cartoon form in 1914. Note the reference to a perceived threat from the French Army – despite Britain and France signing the *Entente Cordiale* in 1904, lingering suspicions about the "old enemy" did not fade.

AMAZING "RIPPER" TRIAL IN GERMANY

WIRELESS
PROGRAMMES
IN FULL
ON PAGE 18

Daily Mirror

THE DAILY PICTURE PAPER WITH THE LARGEST NET SALE

No. 8,547 — Registered at the G.P.O. as a Newspaper. — TUESDAY, APRIL 14, 1931 — One Penny

£100
FREE
CROSSWORD
PUZZLE

BOTTLED TEA FOR MR. GEORGE LANSBURY

HAPPY TIME AT PLAYING FIELDS PARTY

THE TWO BELLES OF NEW YORK

Mrs. Lewisohn (Edna May), the original Belle of New York, with Miss Kathleen Burgis, who takes the part in the present revival of the musical comedy at Daly's Theatre, prior to last night's performance.—("Daily Mirror" photograph.)

Mr. George Lansbury at a holiday party at the playing fields on the Foundling Hospital site. Cheers were given for Lord Rothermere, who has promised £50,000 of the £475,000 required to retain the site. See pages 14 and 15.

THREAT TO ALFONSO'S POWER.—Senor Zamora, the Spanish Republican leader, who last night issued what is in effect an ultimatum to King Alfonso (right) warning him that a Republic will be established if he does not surrender his powers.

14th April **1931**

"RIPPER'S" OWN STORY OF HIS CRIMES

GRIM RECITAL OF IMPULSE TO KILL

"I Was Embittered Against Humanity"

GIRL VICTIMS

Scissors Carried in His Pocket
"To Stab Someone"

Accused of five murders and seven attempted murders, Peter Kuerten, aged 48, when placed on trial at Dusseldorf yesterday, told the story of his life of crime.

With an amazing callousness, Kuerten related to the Court details of the terrible crimes he says he has committed.

The son of a drunken father, he said he was often in prison, and because of severe punishment became embittered against humanity.

Prominent criminologists and jurists from many countries are attending the trial.

5 MURDERS IN CHARGE

Kuerten's Amazing Disclosures in Terrible Story of His Life

Dusseldorf, Monday

During the reading of the indictments – sixteen crimes in all, including five murders and seven attempted murders – Kuerten remained "wooden." Then he told the terrible story of his life.

He was born forty-eight years ago of working class parents in Mulheim. As a youth he was frequently in prison for theft.

Kuerten related the circumstances of the first murder on the list, that of Christina Klein, the nine-year-old daughter of a restaurant proprietor at Mulheim, on May 2, 1913, with a callousness which caused shudders in court.

He intended to steal something from one of the Kleins's bedrooms. In the second room he entered he saw little Christina lying peacefully in bed. He left a corpse.

He would not have killed the child, he said, but for the fact that vivid memories of his prison sufferings drove him to it.

The president asked Kuerten if he would describe the murders without going into too many revolting details. The accused agreed.

Kuerten then described assaults on men, women and children, speaking with a halting but calm voice. Describing his attempt to murder a married woman of fifty named Appelonia Kruhn [sic], the second crime on the charge list, Kuerten admitted having a pair of scissors in his pocket with which to stab someone.

Five days later he left his dwelling at night in brutal mood. He saw Rosa Ohliger crying in a street of Slingen. He stabbed her to death.

On the second day he visited the body, intending to burn it by means of petrol, but he did not use the petrol until the following day. He wanted, as in the case of other victims, to gaze at the body.

He confirmed the details of Maria Hahn's murder and of her burial on the Papendall farm.

When the Court adjourned Kuerten appeared totally unaffected by his ordeal. – Reuter

TWO MURDERS IN NIGHT

One Girl Told to Wait While the Ripper Killed Her Companion

The Court was agape, adds the British United Press, as Kuerten told how he murdered two girls in one evening. They were Louise Lenzen, aged fourteen, and Gertrude Hamacher, aged six. He met them on a lonely road.

"I made their acquaintance, and then told Gertrude to wait while I went ahead with the Hamacher girl. I cut her throat. As Louise came past I pounced upon her and strangled her."

While relating his life story Kuerten made remarkable references to the effect of his prison sentences on his mind.

"I became embittered against humanity," he said, "because of the severe punishment inflicted upon me while in prison."

"RIPPER" A WRECK

Still Uncertain if the Man of Many Murders Will Be Executed

BERLIN, Thursday.

Peter Kuerten, the Dusseldorf "Ripper," on whom a ninefold sentence of death was passed for various murders, is now a complete physical and mental wreck owing to the uncertainty of his fate.

There is still a doubt whether he will go to the guillotine, and it is this terrible suspense that has unnerved the "Ripper."

BACKSTORY

Peter Kuerten (or Kürten) was one of the most infamous of all serial killers. A depraved, sadistic murderer who gained sexual gratification from his ghastly crimes, he was dubbed the "Vampire of Düsseldorf" for the rumour that he drank the blood of his victims.

Kuerten cited his experiences in prison as the spark that set him on the path to his life of monstrous crime. He had a brutal childhood, raised in a family of 13 children living in a one-room apartment ruled by an alcoholic and abusive father. Kuerten probably first killed at the age of nine in 1892, drowning two school friends in an incident that was described as an accident at the time.

By the time he was caught in 1931 he had killed at least nine times along with a string of attempted murders and violent attacks. He was convicted and executed by guillotine on 2nd July 1931.

BEGIN OUR GREAT NEW SERIAL ON PAGE 15

Daily Mirror

THE DAILY PICTURE   PAPER WITH THE LARGEST NET SALE

No. 8,594   Registered at the G.P.O. as a Newspaper.   MONDAY, JUNE 8, 1931   One Penny

£3,000 CROSSWORD TO-DAY

Wireless Programmes in Full on Page 16

SEVEREST BRITISH 'QUAKE EVER RECORDED

FELT FROM NORTH OF SCOTLAND TO SOUTH COAST

WOMAN INJURED—STREET DAMAGED

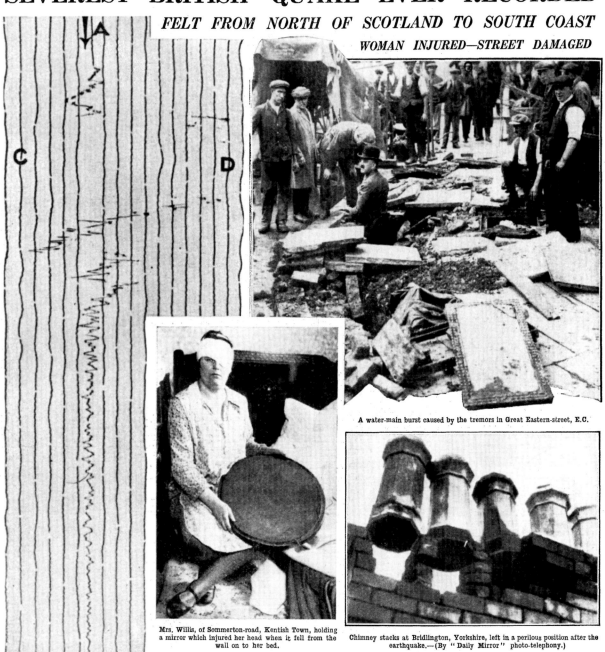

A water-main burst caused by the tremors in Great Eastern-street, E.C.

Mrs. Willis, of Sommerton-road, Kentish Town, holding a mirror which injured her head when it fell from the wall on to her bed.

Chimney stacks at Bridlington, Yorkshire, left in a perilous position after the earthquake.—(By "Daily Mirror" photo-telephony.)

The most severe and widespread earthquake ever recorded in Britain was felt from the extreme north of Scotland to the south coast early yesterday. There were two tremors, which lasted about twenty seconds, causing considerable alarm to thousands of people. The left picture shows Kew Observatory's record of the earthquake. So violent were the oscillations that the marking point, travelling from A to B, which registered the earth movement, failed to record the tremors adequately, leaving a gap between C and D.

8th June 1931

WORST SHOCKS EVER FELT IN GREAT BRITAIN

QUAKE AREA OF 150,000 SQ. MILES

Country Shaken from End to End in Night 20-second
shocks Observatory Seismograph Runs Off the Paper
The most severe and widespread earthquake ever recorded in Britain
occurred shortly before 1.30 a.m. yesterday.

Tremors lasting about twenty seconds were felt from John
o'Groats to towns on the South Coast, with the exception of a
few areas.

At Kew Observatory the lines of the seismograph ran completely
off the paper in several places.

It is estimated that the shock was felt over an area of 150,000
square miles.

TWO TREMORS

Area Affected from North of Scotland to the South Coast

"The shocks were the greatest ever recorded in England on our
instruments, which were installed at the beginning of the century,"
said Mr P. A. Sheppard, seismologist at Kew Observatory.

PEOPLE RUSH FROM THEIR BEDS

Bells Rung by Force of Quake – A Swaying Engine – "Explosion" Alarm in a Police Station at Scarborough

Jumping Beds – People awakened by the shock at Woodbridge
(Suffolk) were terrified by their beds rising half an inch.

Pit Disaster Fears – Ambulance workers rushed to collieries in the
Doncaster district fearing that there had been a disaster.

Ireland Immune – The *Daily Mirror* Dublin correspondent stated
that there were no reports of tremors in Ireland.

Babies Hurled into Air – Mothers at Driffield report that several
children were thrown out of their beds but all escaped serious injury.

Seeing Double – A man who reported to a Hull policeman that he
had seen a church steeple sway was told to "go home and sleep it off."

"Quake as Bellringer" – The shock made the bells of Clare Church,
Sudbury, Suffolk, ring for about a minute. Bells were also rung
at Peterborough.

Leaning Steeple – The upper part of the 100ft. steeple of a Wesleyan
church in Filey was seen to be slightly out of the perpendicular after
the tremor.

Shock for Birds – The shock was felt by people sleeping in boats
on the Norfolk Broads, and all the wildfowl immediately set up a
chorus of warning calls.

Sleepers Rush Into Street – At Grimsby many folk ran into the street
in their night attire, fearing their houses would fall, and in some
districts panic almost prevailed.

Hit by Falling Bricks – Chimneys fell through roofs in Bridlington.
Miss Elizabeth Chadwick was bruised by falling bricks while in bed
when a coping stone fell on to the roof, crashed through the slates,
and fell on to the pavement.

Moving Floor – Mr. C. Morris, Knightland-road, Upper Clapton,
jumped out of bed and then felt the floor moving from under
him. He told the *Daily Mirror* that he was quite scared and went
downstairs and took some medicine.

Zoo, Not Affected – Neither at the Zoological Gardens in Regent's
Park nor at the new zoo at Whipsnade were the animals affected.

The Ghost Train – A railwayman on duty at Berwick Station
thought a train was passing and dashed out to see, as no train
was due.

Swaying Railway Engine – At King's Lynn an engine driver found
his engine swaying so violently that he was afraid it would overturn,
and he had to stop.

The Worst Scare – The shock at Lowestoft was described as the
worst scare since the bombardment and air raids during the war.

Busy Telephones – Additional staffs had to be put on many
telephone exchanges yesterday to answer the flood of inquiries about
the earth tremors.

Policemen's Search – Officers in Scarborough police station, which
was rocked, searched for a mine which they thought had exploded
on the shore.

Burglars! – At Sneinton Hill, Nottingham, a woman ran into the
street and complained to the police that burglars were wrecking
her house.

Not Felt at Sea – Five ocean liners arrived at Plymouth between
4 a.m. and 10 a.m. yesterday and in no case did they report
encountering any oceanic disturbance.

Dr. Crippen Beheaded – Statues of Primo Camera and Dr. Crippen
at Madame Tussaud's were decapitated and a model of Helen Wills
lost an arm. Most damage was caused in the Chamber of Horrors.

BACKSTORY

This was the biggest ever recorded quake in this country.

The magnitude 6.1 shock had its epicentre at Dogger Bank in
the North Sea, about 65 miles from Great Yarmouth. Damage was
reported across the country but mercifully there were few injuries and
only one reported death – a woman in Hull dying from a heart attack.

In the aftermath, scientists warned the quake could "alter the
climate". The mistaken fear was that the quake had occurred in the
mid-Atlantic and could disrupt the course of the Gulf Stream.

HELEN OF TROY APPEAL ALLOWED

Daily Mirror

Theatre & Cinema Guide: P. 22

THE DAILY PICTURE   NEWSPAPER WITH THE LARGEST NET SALE

No. 8,878 | Registered at the G.P.O. as a Newspaper. | SATURDAY, MAY 7, 1932 | One Penny

£2,500 MUST-BE-WON CROSS-WORD TO-DAY

Wireless on Page 20

ASSASSINATION OF THE FRENCH PRESIDENT

RUSSIAN SHOOTS M. DOUMER—EXCLUSIVE PICTURE

An exclusive "Daily Mirror" photograph of the seventy-five-year-old French President, M. Doumer, being placed in his car after he had been fatally wounded by two of four shots fired at him by a Russian described as a Dr. Paul Gorguloff when entering an exhibition at a Paris hotel yesterday. The President was rushed to hospital, where the bullets were removed following two blood transfusions, but he became gradually weaker and died early this morning. Born of humble parents, M. Doumer (also left) was a leading figure in French politics for twenty-six years. See page 24.

7th May 1932

FRENCH PRESIDENT ASSASSINATED

CROWD TRIES TO LYNCH GUNMAN

Paul Doumer, the seventy-five-year-old President of France, died in hospital in Paris this morning from wounds inflicted by a Russian doctor who fired four shots while M. Doumer was visiting an exhibition yesterday. Mme. Doumer was at her husband's bedside during his last hours.

A detective and an author were also shot by the assassin, who was arrested after the police had saved him from lynching by the infuriated crowd.

The President, a much-loved figure in France, who lost four sons in the war, was, by the irony of fate, shot when attending a charity for ex-soldiers.

The King sent a message to Mme. Doumer expressing "profound horror at the dastardly attack." Telephone inquiries were made from Buckingham Palace until shortly before the President's death.

"DEATH TO THE ASSASSIN"
Assailant Says He Kidnapped Lindbergh Baby

INFURIATED CROWD

M. Paul Doumer, the seventy-five-year-old President of the French Republic, died in hospital this morning from bullet wounds received yesterday afternoon while he was paying a visit to a book exhibition.

Shortly after 1 a.m. President Doumer took a turn for the worse.

"The effects on the brain produced by the wound at the base of the skull are becoming more marked," a bulletin stated. "Weakness is increasing."

Oxygen was administered, and his family was summoned to the bedside. The Premier, M. Tardieu, was also called. Then at 2.45 this morning it was stated to be a question of minutes with the President. A quarter of an hour earlier he had fallen into a state of coma.

STRUGGLE WITH GIANT

Injured Men Hurl Themselves at Assassin and Disarm Him

The attack took place while M. Doumer was attending a sale of books for ex-soldiers at the Maison Rothschild.

A giant Russian doctor, Paul Gorguloff, described as an ex-president of the Russian Fascists, stepped forward and fired four shots at M. Doumer, one at M. Claude Farrere, the well-known author, who was accompanying him, and one at M. Paul Guichard, a high police official.

The President collapsed, seriously wounded. Although injured, M. Farrere and M. Guichard hurled themselves at the Russian.

Others went to their assistance and he was disarmed. Only the intervention of the police saved the Russian from the infuriated spectators, who shouted: "Death to the assassin."

President Doumer was carried to his own car and driven, with the other two wounded to the Beaujon Hospital.

Brain Just Missed
Even before the car entered the courtyard a crowd had gathered,
looking on in sorrowful silence, so quickly did the news of the attack spread.

Professor Gossett, the famous surgeon, who examined the President, found that he had two bullet wounds.

One at the base of the skull had traversed the nose and a cheek without touching the brain; the other was between the arm and the shoulder.

Two blood transfusions – one from a nurse – were necessary before the surgeon attempted to remove the bullets.

When the President woke and found himself in hospital he expressed surprise. "You have had a motor accident," he was told.

EYE-WITNESS'S STORY

The following description of the attack was given by an eye-witness, Mme. Paulette, the manageress of a Paris theatre –

"Seven of us at the exhibition were puzzled by the attitude of a big man wearing heavy black glasses, who seemed very nervous.

"We saw him ask M. Claude Farrere to autograph three of his books for him.

"M. Paul Doumer had smilingly crossed the room and approached M. Farrere's stand.

"At that moment a shot rang out, and then, after a pause, several others in quick succession.

"I saw M. Doumer wave an arm and then collapse, his hands clutching at the wounds, M. Claude Farrere was also wounded in the hand, and his wrist was covered with blood.

"M. Paul Guichard and others hurled themselves on the would-be assassin to disarm him while people shouted, 'Look out'."

M. Pietri, the Minister of National Defence, was standing close by, but the Russian fired too quickly for the Minister to stop him.

He seized his wrist, however, and that was how M. Guichard, Director of Municipal Police, was able to seize him.

M. Pietri stated that he tried to disarm the assailant, but it was impossible.

"It took five of us to master the giant, who was over 6ft. 3in," he said. At the police station Gorguloff, after refusing for some time to answer questions, at last admitted that he had come specially from Monaco to attempt to assassinate the President.

Charles Lindbergh, the famous American aviator, whose child Gorguloff bizarrely claimed to have kidnapped.

BACKSTORY

The murder of Doumer was one of a spate of assassinations and attacks amid the political turmoil of the time. Revolution in Russia, the rise of fascist dictators, and battles between left and right set the scene for crazed fanatics like Gorguloff to make their infamous mark on history.

Daily Mirror

THE DAILY PICTURE • NEWSPAPER WITH THE LARGEST NET SALE

No. 9,117   Registered at the G.P.O. as a Newspaper.   SATURDAY, FEBRUARY 11, 1933   One Penny

MACARTNEY ON THE TEST PAGE THREE

WIRELESS PAGE 20   AMUSEMENTS PAGE 20

MUTINY SHIP BOMBED: 18 DEAD

Set on Fire by Air Attack

CREW SURRENDER AND TAKE TO BOATS

After a stern sea chase lasting nearly a week, the runaway Dutch battleship De Zeven Provincien, with its crew of mutineers, was bombed into surrender from the air off Sumatra yesterday.

Eighteen men on board, including three Europeans, were killed in the bombing and fourteen more injured, among them one of the ship's officers, Baron de Vos van Steenwyk, who was being held prisoner.

The battleship was set on fire by a bomb and the mutineers took to the lifeboats. They were picked up by the pursuing vessels and placed under arrest.

Such was the dramatic climax to one of the most amazing episodes in naval history.

10-MINUTE DRAMA

Ultimatum — Bombs — and Then the White Flag

BATAVIA, Friday.

It was at dawn to-day, says Reuter, that the runaway warship was sighted by the pursuing squadron. This consisted of the Dutch cruiser Java and two destroyers, which were accompanied by eight Dornier flying-boats and a number of other craft.

De Zeven Provincien was steaming slowly along the south-east coast of Sumatra in the direction of Sourabaya, the Dutch naval base in Java.

The squadron commander summoned the mutineers by wireless to "strike their flag" unconditionally, otherwise force would be used.

He called on them to stop the ship and show a white cloth on the awning deck. He gave them ten minutes to comply.

The mutineers replied curtly: "Do not hinder us."

Then the attack began.

Island Exile

Without further delay a flying-boat was ordered over De Zeven Provincien, and at the expiry of the ultimatum a warning bomb was dropped alongside.

As no sign of surrender was forthcoming, a second bomb was dropped. This hit the deck, killed eighteen of the rebels instantly and set fire to the ship.

A minute later the rebels ran up the white flag, and they were immediately ordered to leave the ship in the lifeboats.

They were received on board the various pursuing vessels, and are to be imprisoned on the island of Ourust, near Batavia.

The Dutch tug Kraus, owned by a private firm, picked up four of the mutineers who had jumped overboard, and transferred them to the cruiser Java.

Messages received here show that sixteen officers, nine Europeans and three native petty officers, forty-four European warrant officers and 184 European ratings were aboard De Zeven Provincien.

Plan of Piracy

That the purpose of the mutineers in making for Sourabaya was to release the arrested naval ratings there was avowed in a wireless message they sent out, according to a statement made in the People's Council (the Dutch East Indies Legislature) by the Dutch naval commander to-day.

They further, he alleged, revealed a plan to loot trading ships encountered in case food ran short.

Meanwhile, trouble is reported to have broken out among members of the crew of De Zeven Provincien who were left behind when the vessel was seized by the mutineers at Oleleh, Sumatra, on Saturday. Reuter.

The Dutch warship De Zeven Provincien. Left: Captain Eikenboom, commander of the vessel, who was on land when the mutineers sailed away. Right: First-Officer Meijer, who was held prisoner by the mutineers.

TWO MEN BLOWN THROUGH WINDOW

Two men employed by South Metropolitan Gas Company, while working in the front room of this house in Robson-road, West Norwood, were blown through the window by an explosion. One was taken to hospital.

NEW AMBASSADOR ? — Mr. Norman Davis, who, it is expected, will be appointed U.S. Ambassador to London. Mr. Mellon will retire when Mr. Roosevelt's Administration takes over in March.

11th February **1933**

MUTINY SHIP BOMBED: 18 DEAD

Set on Fire by Air Attack

CREW SURRENDER AND TAKE TO BOATS

After a stern sea chase lasting nearly a week, the runaway Dutch battleship De Zeven Provincien, with its crew of mutineers, was bombed into surrender from the air off Sumatra yesterday.

Eighteen men on board, including three Europeans, were killed in the bombing and fourteen more injured, among them one of the ship's officers, Baron de Vos van Steenwyk, who was being held prisoner.

The battleship was set on fire by a bomb and the mutineers took to the lifeboats. They were picked up by the pursuing vessels and placed under arrest. Such was the dramatic climax to one of the most amazing episodes in naval history.

10-MINUTE DRAMA

Ultimatum – Bombs – and Then the White Flag
Batavia, Friday

It was at dawn to-day, says Reuter, that the runaway warship was sighted by the pursuing squadron. This consisted of the Dutch cruiser Java and two destroyers, which were accompanied by eight Dornier flying-boats and a number of other craft.

De Zeven Provincien was steaming slowly along the south-east coast of Sumatra in the direction of Sourabaya, the Dutch naval base in Java.

The squadron commander summoned the mutineers by wireless to "strike their flag" unconditionally, otherwise force would be used.

He called on them to stop the ship and show a white cloth on the awning deck. He gave them ten minutes to comply.

The mutineers replied curtly: "Do not hinder us."

Then the attack began.

Island Exile

Without further delay a flying-boat was ordered over De Zeven Provincien and at the expiry of the ultimatum a warning bomb was dropped alongside.

As no sign of surrender was forthcoming, a second bomb was dropped. This hit the deck, killed eighteen of the rebels instantly and set fire to the ship.

A minute later the rebels ran up the white flag, and they were immediately ordered to leave the ship in the lifeboats.

They were received on board the various pursuing vessels, and are to be imprisoned on the island of Ourust, near Batavia.

The Dutch tug Kraus, owned by a private firm, picked up four of the mutineers who had jumped overboard, and transferred them to the cruiser Java.

Messages received here show that sixteen officers, nine Europeans and three native petty officers, forty-four European warrant officers and 184 European ratings were aboard De Zeven Provincien.

Plan of Piracy

That the purpose of the mutineers in making for Sourabaya was to release the arrested naval ratings there was avowed in a wireless message they sent out, according to a statement made in the People's Council (the Dutch East Indies Legislature) by the Dutch naval commander to-day.

They further, he alleged, revealed a plan to loot trading ships encountered in case food ran short.

Meanwhile, trouble is reported to have broken out among members of the crew of De Zeven Provincien who were left behind when the vessel was seized by the mutineers at Oleleh, Sumatra, on Saturday. – Reuter

BACKSTORY

Against a backdrop of budget cuts amid the Great Depression, the armed forces were not immune. The mutiny of 1933 on the *De Zeven Provinciën*, was sparked among its mainly non-Dutch crew, inspired by revolutionary zeal.

With the captain ashore at that time, the agitators took control of the ship before being met with swift retribution by Dutch commanders. The incident led to uproar at home and major changes to the navy: all men suspected to be a socialist were dismissed from the ranks.

The *De Zeven Provinciën* mutiny was not an isolated incident. In the British Royal Navy there had been disputes, notably in the Invergordon Mutiny of 1931 during the Great Depression. Sailors from ships moored at the base sang 'The Red Flag' and went on strike over severe cuts in pay.

The Admiralty panicked and the government made concessions, but the leaders of the strike were later jailed, and hundreds of others dismissed. The wider economic impact led to Britain being forced off the Gold Standard.

↞ Two companies of men from HMS *Rodney* march through Invergordon after docking at the naval base in July 1931. Two months later many of the same men were in open mutiny.

Daily Mirror

THE DAILY PICTURE ● NEWSPAPER WITH THE LARGEST NET SALE

No. 9,125   Registered at the G.P.O. as a Newspaper.   TUESDAY, FEBRUARY 21, 1933   One Penny

THE DUCHESS BUYS AT THE B.I.F.
—Page 5

WIRELESS PAGE 20   AMUSEMENTS PAGE 21

'WED' TO MOTHER AND DAUGHTER!

K.C.'s Amazing Story of Secret Wives

"LIVED TOGETHER IN SAME HOUSE"

That a man had gone through a ceremony of marriage with a mother and her daughter while both of them were still alive, without either of them knowing that he had "married" the other, was asserted in the Probate Court yesterday.

The case concerned the will of Mr. John Byers Maxwell, a former London editor of a provincial newspaper, who died in 1931 in a mental hospital at Whittingham, Lancashire.

Mrs. Amy Madeleine Maxwell, otherwise Macintosh, of Cambridge-road, Hove, claimed that she was sole executrix under a will of July 7, 1926.

The defendant was Mrs. Maxwell's brother, Mr. Frank Arthur Wilmer, of Upper Tollington Park, Stroud Green, London. He claimed, as his mother's executor, that the will of July 7 was not duly executed, alternatively that it was revoked, and counter-claimed for the establishment of a will of November 3, 1926, or a will of September 1, 1926.

Mrs. Maxwell's reply was that the execution of these wills was obtained by undue influence of Mrs. Mary Newton Wilmer, her mother, who died in 1930, aged seventy-four.

An extraordinary story was unfolded by Mr. J. D. Cassels, K.C., for Mrs. Maxwell.

He said that Maxwell, who made five wills, lived with two women in the same house—lived with them in the broadest sense of the word—and they were mother and daughter.

He married them both, or went through a ceremony of marriage with them, first the daughter and then the mother, in the lifetime of both of them.

Married Before

The question of the legality of the daughter's marriage might arise, because she had been married fifteen years before, and her husband had deserted her.

Mr. Maxwell was sixty-five when he died. Mrs. Mary Wilmer, the mother, was sixty-nine when she went through a ceremony of marriage with Maxwell.

In October, 1921, Maxwell and plaintiff went through a form of marriage at St. Pancras Church, London, she describing herself as a widow and he as a bachelor.

It was Maxwell's desire that this marriage should be kept secret from the mother.

They all continued to live together in the same house. The mother and Maxwell went away on holiday together. The daughter went to live at Sheen Park. While there she received intimation that her mother and Maxwell had been married at a register office in the Isle of Thanet. It was a great shock to her.

"WIFE FOR YEARS"

Mr. Cassels described a violent scene when plaintiff, having heard that a will had been made in her favour, went to Park-road, Richmond, and asked that her side of the case should be considered.

The mother was incensed, and the daughter was incensed, too, and announced that she was Maxwell's wife and had been for years. That was the first the mother knew of the marriage.

Maxwell admitted the marriage to the daughter, and went out of the room. He was followed upstairs. The mother assaulted Maxwell and the daughter rescued him. He went downstairs, and the mother was described as "belabouring him unmercifully with a heavy book." Plaintiff took Maxwell to her home in Sheen Park. He sat there for two days looking very dazed.

Maxwell later went to a nursing home. He returned to live with the daughter at Sheen Park for a week. He then disappeared, and the daughter never saw him again, nor did she hear of him until 1931, when she was told he was dead.

Maxwell, in his final will dated November 3, 1926, left everything to the mother.

In December, 1927, continued Mr. Cassels, the mother secured Maxwell's admission as a pauper and a person of unsound mind into a mental hospital near Blackpool, describing him as "single," and herself as "friend."

The hearing was adjourned until to-day.

Mr. John Maxwell. He died at Whittingham, Lancs., in 1931.

MOLLISON IN BRAZIL.—Mr. J. A. Mollison on his arrival at Rio de Janeiro following his great solo flight across the South Atlantic. Major N. Braga (wearing leather coat), who welcomed him, flew the South Atlantic with Senor R. de Barros in 1927.

JOYCE WETHERED BEGINS WORK

"I Have Given Up Competitive Golf for Good"

Miss Joyce Wethered, the famous woman golfer, who (as exclusively reported in the *Daily Mirror*) has joined the staff of Messrs Fortnum and Mason, Piccadilly, as adviser on sports matters, began her new duties yesterday.

She was soon hard at work on a large green carpet facing a golf net and surrounded by rows of clubs.

Asked what her attitude was to the suggestion that she might lose her amateur status by accepting this post, Miss Wethered said: "I want it to be understood clearly that I am not demonstrating or teaching in any way. I am here only to advise.

"In any case, I have definitely decided—and nothing will alter my decision—that now I have gone into business I have given up competitive golf for good.

"Any question of amateur status only arises if I do enter competitive golf, so the point can never arise."

An official of the firm stated: "Miss Wethered has already designed a special bag for women who carry their clubs, and she will co-operate with the manufacturers in suggesting improvements in clubs and equipment."

U.S. and Status

Commenting on Miss Wethered's appointment, the New York *World Telegram*, quoted by Reuter, declares: "The amateur status of England's greatest all-time woman golfer is seriously threatened.

"That is an important fact to America, because Miss Wethered has always been looked upon as a reserve British power whenever the American invasion looked particularly threatening.

"Under the ruling, John Dawson, Chicago golfer, who is connected with a sports goods house, is ineligible to compete in the amateur championships, although he is not a professional and does not play for pay.

"Bobby Jones withdrew as an amateur when he entered the movies, and Mary K. Browne, of Cleveland, was barred from amateur golf play for several years because of her excursion in the professional tennis ranks with Mlle. Suzanne Lenglen.

"The United States Golf Association always has been strict in applying the amateur definition, and the U.S. rules would definitely bar Miss Wethered from further tournament competition."

Miss Joyce Wethered (hatless) beginning her new duties as sports adviser in London yesterday.

21st February 1933

'WED' TO MOTHER AND DAUGHTER!

K.C.'s Amazing Story of Secret Wives

"LIVED TOGETHER IN SAME HOUSE"

That a man had gone through a ceremony of marriage with a mother and her daughter while both of them were still alive, without either of them knowing that he had "married" the other, was asserted in the Probate Court yesterday.

The case concerned the will of Mr. John Byers Maxwell, a former London editor of a provincial newspaper, who died in 1931 in a mental hospital at Whittingham, Lancashire.

Mrs. Amy Madeleine Maxwell, otherwise Macintosh, of Cambridge-road, Hove, claimed that she was sole executrix under a will of July 7, 1926.

The defendant was Mrs. Maxwell's brother, Mr. Frank Arthur Wilmer, of Upper Tollington Park, Stroud Green, London. He claimed, as his mother's executor, that the will of July 7 was not duly executed, alternatively that it was revoked, and counter-claimed for the establishment of a will of November 3, 1926, or a will of September 1, 1926.

Mrs. Maxwell's reply was that the execution of these wills was obtained by undue influence of Mrs. Mary Newton Wilmer, her mother, who died in 1930, aged seventy-four.

An extraordinary story was unfolded by Mr. J. D. Cassels, K.C., for Mrs. Maxwell.

He said that Maxwell, who made five wills, lived with two women in the same house – lived with them in the broadest sense of the word – and they were mother and daughter.

He married them both, or went through a ceremony of marriage with them, first the daughter and then the mother, in the lifetime of both of them.

Married Before

The question of the legality of the daughter's marriage might arise, because she had been married fifteen years before, and her husband had deserted her. Mr. Maxwell was sixty-five when he died. Mrs. Mary Wilmer, the mother, was sixty-nine when she went through a ceremony of marriage with Maxwell.

In October 1921, Maxwell and plaintiff went through a form of marriage at St. Pancras Church, London, she describing herself as a widow and he as a bachelor.

It was Maxwell's desire that this marriage should be kept secret from the mother. They all continued to live together in the same house. The mother and Maxwell went away on holiday together. The daughter went to live at Sheen Park. While there she received intimation that her mother and Maxwell had been married at a register office in the Isle of Thanet. It was a great shock to her.

"WIFE FOR YEARS"

Mr. Cassels described a violent scene when plaintiff, having heard that a will had been made in her favour, went to Park-road, Richmond, and asked that her side of the case should be considered.

The mother was incensed, and the daughter was incensed, too, and announced that she was Maxwell's wife and had been for years. That was the first the mother knew of the marriage.

Maxwell admitted the marriage to the daughter, and went out of the room. He was followed upstairs. The mother assaulted Maxwell and the daughter rescued him. He went downstairs, and the mother was described as "belabouring him unmercifully with a heavy book."

Plaintiff took Maxwell to her home in Sheen Park. He sat there for two days looking very dazed.

Maxwell later went to a nursing home. He returned to live with the daughter at Sheen Park for a week. He then disappeared, and the daughter never saw him again, nor did she hear of him until 1931, when she was told he was dead.

Maxwell, in his final will dated November 3, 1926, left everything to the mother. In December 1927, continued Mr. Cassels, the mother secured Maxwell's admission as a pauper and a person of unsound mind into a mental hospital near Blackpool, describing him as "single," and herself as "friend."

The hearing was adjourned until to-day.

23rd February 1933

SECRET OF TWO "WIVES"

Court Story of "Perfectly Proper" Household

Remarkable entries in the diary of a woman who, at sixty-seven, was married to a man who was stated also to have married her daughter, were read in the Maxwell will suit in the Probate Court yesterday.

She alleges that a will dated November 3, 1926, which her brother, Mr. Frank Arthur Wilmer, of Upper Tollington Park, Stroud Green. N., seeks to establish, was obtained by undue influence and fraud on the part of her mother, Mrs. Maud Mary Wilmer, now dead.

Plaintiff's counsel had stated that Maxwell went through ceremonies of marriage with the mother and her daughter while both of them were alive, without either knowing that he had "married" the other.

Mrs. Maxwell was yesterday called for cross-examination by Mr. Cotes Preedy, K.C., regarding entries in her mother's diary for 1926.

An entry on May 30 – the date of Mrs. Wilmer's "marriage" to Maxwell –read: "My darling: at last, Maud Mary Maxwell. Bought Jack (Maxwell) ring. Went at night to Canterbury Cathedral. 'Holy, Holy. Holy, early in the morning: our song shall rise to Thee.' Very impressive."

On the following day was the entry: "Jack returned to Amy as suggested by me, owing to his distressed condition, the day after our ceremony."

Mr. Cotes Preedy asked about an entry of June 21: "Amy showed me her engagement ring from George." Mrs. Maxwell said she never had an engagement ring from the man referred to.

Do you suggest that your dead mother made that up? – Yes. I do.

Were you going about with this man as if you were engaged? – No, I was not. I was married.

Mr. Cotes Preedy read from the diary: "Lost my daughter ten years ago," and asked: "What happened in l916?"

Mrs. Maxwell said she did not know. She denied that she had "got into trouble or something" at that time.

BACKSTORY

This was a complicated yet faintly titillating case of a respectable newspaper editor seemingly marrying both a mother and her daughter. In the event, Mr Maxwell passed away, leaving it to his wife – both of them – to unravel the messy legacy.

Daily Mirror

THE DAILY PICTURE ● NEWSPAPER WITH THE LARGEST NET SALE

No. 9,156 — Registered at the G.P.O. as a Newspaper. — WEDNESDAY, MARCH 29, 1933 — One Penny

OFFICER'S TRIAL RESULT—P. 2

WIRELESS PAGES 20-21 AMUSEMENTS PAGE 18

15 DEAD IN BRITISH AIR LINER
WONDERFUL PICTURES BROUGHT BY AIR

Burning wreckage of the giant Imperial Airways air liner City of Liverpool, which crashed in flames near Dixmude, Flanders, killing eleven British people and four foreigners. Everyone on board the machine, which was flying from Cologne to Croydon, lost their lives. The victims include three women and a girl. Two passengers tried to escape by leaping from the 'plane as it nose-dived in flames from 600ft. See page 24.

29th March 1933

MID-AIR EXPLOSION WRECKS GIANT 'PLANE

Couple Leap Into Space from Blazing Liner

15 PEOPLE DIE IN CRASH

Wing Drops from the Machine

"ALL'S WELL," THE LAST MESSAGE

EYE WITNESS'S VIVID STORY

The greatest disaster in the history of British civil aviation cost fifteen lives yesterday when the Imperial Airways liner, City of Liverpool, on the Cologne-Croydon service, crashed in flames near Dixmude, close to the Belgian coast.

Everyone on board, including three women and a girl, perished in the crash, which is believed to have been caused by fuel-tanks exploding.

The 'plane hurtled to earth from 500 feet.

A wing fell off.

Two passengers were seen leaping into mid-air.

The machine struck the ground at 125 m.p.h.

Shortly before the crash the wireless operator gave the machine's position and added "All's well." Below is a graphic account of the disaster by an eye-witness.

DISASTER IN ONE MINUTE

'Air Liner Hurtles to Earth a Ball of Fire'
(from Reuter's special correspondent)

Ypres, Wednesday Morning

Within a mile of the British trenches held in the war at Wounen I saw at midnight the still smouldering remains of the giant Imperial Airways liner, City of Liverpool, which yesterday fell in flames an hour after leaving Brussels.

An elderly Belgian infantry colonel named Massart, whose property adjoins the scene of the accident, told me:

"When I saw the 'plane it appeared to be only just overhead.

"There was a white flash of flame, which enveloped the body of the aeroplane.

"Then the entire machine became a ball of flaming fire.

"A woman either jumped or was propelled from the aeroplane by the force of an explosion.

"She seemed to have a parachute attached to her, but she dropped to earth and her shattered body was found later.

"Meanwhile, the pilot, who must have been suffering agonies from the flames, was evidently bent on landing his 'plane without thought for his own safety.

"At a height of about 500ft. the machine turned twice, then dived in flames.

"A wing fell off and the machine crashed into a field 200 yards from my house."

Only a Minute
"Tremendous flames of burning oil and petrol leapt high in the air and left no hope of anyone escaping from the wreckage."

Another eye-witness said that a man had jumped from the 'plane just before the woman. His mangled body, with his watch stopped at 2.20 p.m., was 500 yards away.

Only a few minutes before the disaster the Wireless operator sent out the machine's position, and added: "All's well."

The liner seems to have gone out of control about half a mile away from the scene of the crash.

It was then at a height estimated by one witness at 6,000ft.

There was but a minute between the first flash of flame and the disaster.

During the afternoon Dixmude fire brigade extinguished most of the flames, but when I visited the scene about midnight some of the wreckage was still smouldering and was being extinguished by two gendarmes on duty.

It is believed that the charred remains of thirteen people, including the pilot, mechanic and wireless operator, are still in the debris.

Pieces of the aeroplane are scattered over several hundreds of yards, but the main framework is still distinguishable.

The machine seems to have struck the ground at a slight angle and the engines are completely buried in the soft earth.

The airliner was broken into three parts, which are lying about twelve yards apart. They consist of the wings and the front of the fuselage, the tail and rear part of the fuselage, and then the rudder.

Another message says that the disaster is believed to have been caused by the fuel-tanks exploding.

Portions of the 'plane, luggage and three bags of mail were picked up by police.

The mailbags were practically undamaged and were handed to the judicial authorities at Furnes for forwarding to London.

Was It An Omen?
Major Teesdale, secretary of the Junior Aero-Club in London, last night stated that a collection of drawings of aircraft was yesterday taken down and cleaned, and the only one damaged was a picture of the City of Liverpool, the glass of which was badly smashed.

BACKSTORY

The advent of air travel was an exciting development between the wars and its image of glamour and wealth was a captivating story choice for newsmen. Inevitably, when disaster struck, it made for headline news.

Airships were also frequently in the news, whether in reports of their manufacture and launch or their demise. The fate of the US airship *Akron* made for horrifying yet compelling reading (above)

Daily Mirror

THE DAILY PICTURE NEWSPAPER WITH THE LARGEST NET SALE

NEW £700 GOLF TOURNAMENT

WIRELESS PAGE 16   AMUSEMENTS PAGE 12

No. 9,206   Registered at the G.P.O. as a Newspaper.   SATURDAY, MAY 27, 1933   One Penny

MR. & MRS. JOHN AMERY ARRESTED

Mr. John Amery and his wife, formerly Miss Una Wing, at the Surete Generale, the French C.I.D., in Paris yesterday Mr. Amery was detained, but Mrs. Amery was released.

Police Visit to Paris Hotel

ACTRESS BRIDE RELEASED

FROM OUR OWN CORRESPONDENT

PARIS, Friday.

Mr. John Amery, the son of Mr. L. S. Amery, the former Dominions Secretary, and his wife, who before her marriage was Miss Una Wing, an actress, were arrested in Paris to-day.

I understand that Mr. and Mrs. Amery were staying at an hotel in Montmartre, where two detectives called to inspect the list of new arrivals.

They had in their possession a list of all persons wanted under extradition orders by foreign countries, and they were visiting all the hotels according to routine in search of persons on that list.

When they saw the names Mr. and Mrs. John Amery they asked to see the couple.

Mr. and Mrs. Amery were informed by them of the extradition proceedings instituted by the Greek Government, and were placed under arrest.

No Concealment

Later Mrs. Amery was released, but Mr. Amery is being detained at the headquarters of the Sureté Generale, the French C.I.D., awaiting the result of the application of the Greek authorities for their extradition to Greece on a charge relating to a cheque.

While the Greek authorities are applying for Mr. and Mrs. John Amery's extradition, Mr. Amery in turn is trying to arrange for bail, and negotiations are being carried on with Mr. Amery's father.

"I am certain that Mr. Amery did not expect to be arrested," the hotel proprietor stated, "for he has been coming and going in a normal fashion and making no effort to conceal his whereabouts.

"He and his wife did not have their meals in the hotel. They paid regularly, and I believe they have never left Paris since they came here, at any rate not for any length of time."

Wedding Ban

Mr. John Amery's announcement last summer that he was to marry Miss Una Wing, a twenty-two-year-old actress, resulted in action being taken by his family to prevent the ceremony on the ground that he was under age.

When the couple presented themselves at Chelsea Register Office to be married, they

(Continued on back page)

MISS HALSEY'S ALL WHITE WEDDING

White was the dominant note at the wedding yesterday of Miss Joan Halsey, elder daughter of Admiral Sir Lionel Halsey, Comptroller and Treasurer to the Prince of Wales, and Lady Halsey, of Old Warden, Beds, to Mr. George Lockhart Wood, only son of the late Captain T. L. Wood, and Mrs. Wood, of The Hoo, Great Gaddesden, Herts.

Masses of white flowers were used in the decoration of Old Warden Church, and the bride wore a dress of white satin with a long train of similar material, edged with old Brussels lace.

She wore a wreath of orange blossom, and the bridal bouquet was a sheaf of lilies. Pearls set off the whiteness of her dress.

The bridesmaids—Misses Ruth Halsey, Alice Wood, Pamela McCorquodale, Patricia Wells, Anne Campbell and Betty Wood—wore gowns of white satin with long tight sleeves.

The Prince of Wales was represented at the ceremony, and the presents included gifts from him and Prince George.

Dr. Furse, Bishop of St. Albans, officiated, assisted by Canon F. Halsey, uncle of the bride.

The bridal party left the church amid the cheers of villagers

The bridal procession down a lane from the church after the wedding. Above, the bride and bridegroom.

27ᵗʰ May 1933

MR. & MRS. JOHN AMERY ARRESTED

Police Visit to Paris Hotel

ACTRESS BRIDE RELEASED
FROM OUR OWN CORRESPONDENT

Paris, Friday

Mr. Joñ Amery, the son of Mr. L. S. Amery, the former Dominions Secretary, and his wife, who before her marriage was Miss Una Wing, an actress, were arrested in Paris to-day.

I understand that Mr. and Mrs. Amery were staying at an hotel in Montmartre, where two detectives called to inspect the list of new arrivals.

They had in their possession a list of all persons wanted under extradition orders by foreign countries, and they were visiting all the hotels according to routine in search of persons on that list.

When they saw the names Mr. and Mrs. Joñ Amery they asked to see the couple.

Mr. and Mrs. Amery were informed by them of the extradition proceedings instituted by the Greek Government, and were placed under arrest.

No Concealment

Later Mrs. Amery was released, but Mr. Amery is being detained at the headquarters of the Surete Generale, the French C.I.D., awaiting the result of the application of the Greek authorities for their extradition to Greece on a charge relating to a cheque.

While the Greek authorities are applying for Mr. and Mrs. Joñ Amery's extradition, Mr. Amery in turn is trying to arrange for bail, and negotiations are being carried on with Mr. Amery's father.

"I am certain that Mr. Amery did not expect to be arrested," the hotel proprietor stated, "for he has been coming and going in a normal fashion and making no effort to conceal his whereabouts.

"He and his wife did not have their meals in the hotel. They paid regularly, and I believe they have never left Paris since they came here, at any rate not for any length of time."

Wedding Ban

Mr. Joñ Amery's announcement last summer that he was to marry Miss Una Wing, a twenty-two-year-old actress, resulted in action being taken by his family to prevent the ceremony on the ground that he was under age.

When the couple presented themselves at Chelsea Register Office to be married, they were told that the ceremony could not take place.

An hour before the time arranged for the marriage two telegrams – one from Lord Greenwood and the other from Lady Greenwood, Mr. Amery's uncle and aunt – were received at the office, giving instructions not to proceed with the marriage as their nephew was under age.

In September Mr. Amery made a spectacular night dash to France in a motor-boat, and it was understood that Miss Wing had crossed to Dunkirk in a steamer.

They were unable, however, to find any country in which they could be married. They returned to this country and Mr. Amery had a heart-to-heart talk with his father.

It was not until March 30 last that the young lovers' quest ended in success. They were then married in Athens.

⬆ Joñ Amery was hanged despite his father's last-minute attempts to earn a reprieve, based on a claim his son was insane.

BACKSTORY

The colourful love life of Joñ Amery was just one episode in a much darker tale.

Born to a wealthy and politically influential family, Amery was the classic rebellious rich boy who struggled to live a worthwhile adult life. His elopement to marry Una Wing, most likely a former prostitute, caused a scandal, but it was his later actions that gained him deserved infamy.

Becoming a fascist, he joined up with Franco's Nationalists during the Spanish Civil War and by 1942 was in France trying – and failing – to recruit a British POW 'Legion of St George' to fight against the Allies. He made radio broadcasts similar to those of Lord Haw-Haw before being caught while on the run to Switzerland in April 1945.

Amery was brought back to Britain to be charged and was found guilty of treason after an eight-minute trial. He was executed by hanging at the age of 33. He is said to have walked to the gallows with great composure and bravery, but became, as the *Independent* would later describe him, "the traitor Britain forgot".

Daily Mirror

Broadcasting - Page 24

THE DAILY PICTURE • NEWSPAPER WITH THE LARGEST NET SALE

DRESS-SUIT ORDER FOR NEW POLICE —PAGE 2

No. 9,365 — Registered at the G.P.O. as a Newspaper. — WEDNESDAY, NOVEMBER 29, 1933 — One Penny

TRIAL BY FURY—U.S. LYNCH LAW

Frenzied Mob Storm Another Gaol

SOLDIERS' BOMBS DEFIED

Lynch law is spreading in the United States. Here are two contrasting pictures:—

IN MARYLAND
Something like civil war broke out yesterday when a mob attacked the State Armoury in an attempt to release four lynchers arrested by order of the Governor.

IN CALIFORNIA
The Governor publicly pardoned people involved in the storming of a prison and lynching two kidnappers, which was "a fine lesson to others."

The situation in Maryland grew so serious that the State Militia had to be mobilised. They hurled tear gas bombs at the mob, which replied with bricks. Shots followed, but it is not known whether they were fired by the crowd or the troops.

Martial law has been proclaimed.

SECRET SEARCH

Police Guarded by Troops Armed with Machine Guns

BALTIMORE, Tuesday.

A fierce clash between an infuriated mob and soldiers at Salisbury (Maryland) in which tear gas bombs and bricks were hurled and shots fired, came as a climax to the arrest of four lynchers by order of Governor Ritchie.

The men are alleged to have killed a negro who had attacked an aged white woman.

When the State Attorney refused to arrest the men a secret house-to-house search was ordered by Governor Ritchie.

Police, under the protection of troops armed with machine-guns, tear gas bombs and riot guns, hauled the wanted men from their beds last night. They were taken to the State armoury at Salisbury.

Yelling Crowd

The report of their arrest spread like wildfire, and crowds of townspeople soon gathered around the armoury.

Antagonism against the Governor's action flared up, and later a yelling crowd surged against the building.

The State Militia was called out, and a pitched battle took place.

Troops hurled tear-gas bombs into the advancing mob, but still they came on and drove the soldiers into the armoury.

A general fire alarm was sounded, and brought a fire brigade full speed to the assistance of the troops.

CAR OVERTURNED

A fusillade of bricks was launched against the armoury and shots followed.

The firemen appeared to be sympathetic towards the crowd, because they poured water into the tear gas, apparently in an effort to deaden the effect of the fumes.

After the riot had died down the troops departed in motor-cars, apparently heading towards Baltimore. It is not known if the arrested men were with them.

The crowd did not molest the troops, but they seized and overturned a motor-car which was said to belong to the State Attorney.

The negro, for whose lynching the men were arrested, was done to death by a mob at Princess Anne.

Defying a barrage of tear gas bombs and the truncheons of twenty police, more than a thousand people burst into the county gaol and carried off the negro.

The victim was stripped and dragged through the town by a rope round his neck and hanged to a tree next to a Judge's house.

Later the body was cut down and burned in the public square.—Reuter.

According to Exchange, the Maryland authorities have proclaimed martial law.

Telegraphing and telephoning were banned during the arrests.

SHOTGUN GUARD

Four Gangsters Cleared of Kidnapping Charge

A jury at St. Paul, Minnesota, yesterday acquitted four gangsters, led by Roger Tuohy, who were accused of kidnapping Mr. William Hamm, junr., a young and wealthy brewer, states Reuter.

The gang were also indicted by the grand jury in Chicago for the alleged kidnapping last July of Jacob Factor, the financier accused of share-pushing frauds.

Crowds jammed the corridors of the courthouse to learn the verdict. Guards around the court were reinforced and sheriffs stood on each stairway with shot-guns ready.

Factor Case

After their acquittal the four men were served with "fugitive warrants" accusing them of participation in the kidnapping of Jacob Factor.

They will be taken to Chicago for trial in the Factor case, regardless of their acquittal yesterday.

Mr. William Hamm, junr., was kidnapped in June, but was released a few days later after a ransom had been paid. It was stated at the time that this ransom was much less than the £20,000 originally demanded.

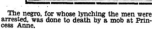

Leaders of the mob battering in the doors of the county gaol at San Jose, California, prior to the lynching of Thurmond and Holmes, two alleged kidnappers.

Governor Ritchie, of Maryland, who has had four lynchers arrested.

Governor Rolph publicly pardoned people involved in the San Jose lynching.

The sentence of lynch law carried out at San Jose. Thousands of onlookers cheered the spectacle. (Pictures by radio.)

29th November 1933

TRIAL BY FURY – U.S. LYNCH LAW

Frenzied Mob Storm Another Gaol

SOLDIER'S BOMBS DEFIED

Lynch law is spreading in the United States. Here are two contrasting pictures –

IN MARYLAND

Something like civil war broke out yesterday when a mob attacked the State Armoury in an attempt to release four lynchers arrested by order of the Governor.

IN CALIFORNIA

The Governor publicly pardoned people involved in the storming of a prison and lynching two kidnappers, which was "a fine lesson to others."

The situation in Maryland grew so serious that the State Militia had to be mobilised. They hurled tear gas bombs at the mob, which replied with bricks.

Shots followed, but it is not known whether they were fired by the crowd or the troops. Martial law has been proclaimed.

SECRET SEARCH

Baltimore, Tuesday

A fierce clash between an infuriated mob and soldiers at Salisbury (Maryland) in which tear gas bombs and bricks were hurled and shots fired, came as a climax to the arrest of four lynchers by order of Governor Ritchie.

The men are alleged to have killed a negro who had attacked an aged white woman.

When the State Attorney refused to arrest the men a secret house-to-house search was ordered by Governor Ritchie.

Police, under the protection of troops armed with machine-guns, tear gas bombs and riot guns, hauled the wanted men from their beds last night. They were taken to the State armoury at Salisbury.

Yelling Crowd

The report of their arrest spread like wildfire, and crowds of townspeople soon gathered around the armoury.

Antagonism against the Governor's action flared up, and later a yelling crowd surged against the building.

The State Militia was called out, and a pitched battle took place.

Troops hurled tear-gas bombs into the advancing mob, but still they came on and drove the soldiers into the armoury.

A general fire alarm was sounded, and brought a fire brigade full speed to the assistance of the troops.

CAR OVERTURNED

A fusillade of bricks was launched against the armoury and shots followed.

The firemen appeared to be sympathetic towards the crowd, because they poured water into the tear gas, apparently in an effort to deaden the effect of the fumes.

After the riot had died down the troops departed in motor-cars, apparently heading towards Baltimore. It is not known if the arrested men were with them.

The crowd did not molest the troops, but they seized and overturned a motor-car which was said to belong to the State Attorney.

The negro, for whose lynching the men were arrested, was done to death by a mob at Princess Anne.

Defying a barrage of tear gas bombs and the truncheons of twenty police, more than a thousand people burst into the county gaol and carried off the negro.

The victim was stripped and dragged through the town by a rope round his neck and hanged to a tree next to a Judge's house. Later the body was cut down and burned in the public square. – Reuter

According to Exchange, the Maryland authorities have proclaimed martial law. Telegraphing and telephoning were banned during the arrests.

SHOTGUN GUARD

Four Gangsters Cleared of Kidnapping Charge

A jury at St. Paul, Minnesota, yesterday acquitted four gangsters, led by Roger Tuohy, who were accused of kidnapping Mr. William Hamm, junr., a young and wealthy brewer, states Reuter.

The gang were also indicted by the grand jury in Chicago for the alleged kidnapping last July of Jacob Factor, the financier accused of share-pushing frauds.

Crowds jammed the corridors of the courthouse to learn the verdict. Guards around the court were reinforced and sheriffs stood on each stairway with shotguns ready.

Factor Case

After their acquittal the four men were served with "fugitive warrants" accusing them of participation in the kidnapping of Jacob Factor.

They will be taken to Chicago for trial in the Factor case, regardless of their acquittal yesterday.

Mr. William Hamm, junr., was kidnapped in June, but was released a few days later after a ransom had been paid. It was stated at the time that this ransom was much less than the $20,000 originally demanded.

BACKSTORY

Public lynchings – usually of black victims – in the United States were all-too-frequent even nearly 60 years after the end of the American Civil War. That these savage attacks took place away from the Deep South was perhaps more of a surprise.

The Baltimore victim was George Armwood, a man said to be of limited intelligence who was accused of raping and robbing an elderly white woman. He was taken to a jail in Princess Anne. A mob stormed the jail, beat, and then mutilated Armwood, before hanging him from a tree and setting fire to the corpse. A month later, there were riots to attempt to free the men accused of the lynching.

The contrasting public slaying in California came when a frenzied mob stormed Santa Clara County Jail. They were after two suspected kidnappers, Thomas Thurmond and John Holmes, who had been arrested for the abduction and murder of Brooke Hart, the son of a wealthy department store owner. Both Thurmond and Holmes were hanged in a local park.

Broadcasting - Page 20

Daily Mirror

THE DAILY PICTURE — NEWSPAPER WITH THE LARGEST NET SALE

FIVE YEARS FOR DESERT LOVE FEUD MURDERER
— Page 3

No. 9,726 — Registered at the G.P.O. as a Newspaper. — **WEDNESDAY, JANUARY 30, 1935** — One Penny

KIDNAPPED BOY SENSATION

Court Sequel 31 Years After He Vanished

FOUND IN AMERICA

SPECIAL "DAILY MIRROR" NEWS

SENSATIONAL details of a kidnapping drama—details which will touch both sides of the Atlantic and bridge a gap of thirty-one years—will be revealed in Sheffield police court to-morrow.

It was on Tuesday, October 18, 1904, that the first act of the drama was played, for on that day Johnny Whitnear, aged five, of Woodbourn-road, Sheffield, vanished.

Johnny's mother is now Mrs. Woodward, and lives in Cobble-street, Sheffield. She has received a subpœna to attend the police court.

She understands that her appearance is in connection with Johnny's disappearance as a boy. Other people, it is stated, have also been called to attend the court.

Johnny Whitnear—thirty-six years old now—is believed to be in Sheffield, but his address is not revealed. He has been served with a court notice.

On the day the child vanished, a man aged about thirty-five had asked the permission of his mother to take him fishing at Keveton, seven miles away.

He did not come back. For weeks the anxious parents searched in vain. Months passed into years. They had nearly given up hope of ever seeing him again. Then they got news.

At the beginning of March, 1909, the Sheffield police were informed by a man, who did not wish his identity disclosed, that the alleged kidnapper was living under an assumed name in Newark, New Jersey, with a boy who was almost certainly Johnny Whitnear.

But the American police insisted that a member of the family must identify the child before he could be given up.

All Their Money Gone

The boy's father, an artisan in a Sheffield steel works, was not well enough to make the journey to America, so the eldest son, William, aged twenty-one, was chosen to go in his stead.

All the resources of the family went to pay for that journey, but it brought their boy back.

(Continued on page 3)

Johnny Whitnear in his mother's arms when he was restored to her in 1909.

AIR LINER'S LOST GOLD FOUND

Digging by Night to Recover £22,000

3 FEET DOWN

BURIED three feet beneath the frozen ground in a field near Oisement, two and a half miles from the main Paris-Treport road, the missing consignment of £22,000 worth of gold, lost from a Hillman aeroplane flying from Le Bourget to London on Saturday, was found last night (states Reuter).

A woman walking across a field in the Department of the Somme noticed the debris of a wooden case. There was no sign of any gold, but the woman immediately informed the police.

Gendarmes at once organised a digging party with the help of a few local inhabitants.

The ground was frozen hard and darkness had already set in. Torches and flares cast a yellow flickering light on the diggers working silently in the deserted countryside.

In spite of the cold great beads of sweat stood out on their foreheads as they dug into the iron ground.

Eleven bars of gold have already been retrieved and it is believed that all will be recovered.

According to French law, adds the Exchange, the woman who noticed the broken boxes will receive ten per cent. of the total value of the gold recovered.

FOUR MILES UP

PARIS, Tuesday.

The French airwoman, Madeleine Charnoux, with another woman flyer on board, Miss Edith Clark, to-day reached an altitude of 20,100ft.—nearly four miles—the highest altitude ever attained by a woman piloting a small aeroplane. The previous record was 15,000ft.—Exchange.

OXFORD COLLEGE FIRE

Firemen from Oxford and Abingdon fighting the flames yesterday when fire destroyed the west wing of Ripon Hall, the famous Oxford theological college at Boar's Hill. They were severely handicapped by shortage of water. The library reading room was involved in the blaze but thousands of valuable books were saved as well as furniture. See page 2.

Oxford Boat Race Crews May Desert the Isis

"RIVER IS NOT FIT FOR TRAINING"

IF Oxford wins the Boat Race this year, the Varsity Eight will never again be seen in home waters until the Isis is improved. "We have been going to Henley," the Oxford President, Mr. Michael Mosley, told the *Daily Mirror* last night, "because the river there is fit for training, and at Oxford it is not.

"We used to sneer at Cambridge's little ditch, but the Cam is far superior to the river at Oxford.

"The journey to Henley every day does not take so much longer than it used to take us to negotiate one of the locks.

"We have had no illness this year, while in previous years there has been nothing but illness in the crew.

"The crew has improved tremendously."

Mr. Mosley suggests the dredging of the river at Oxford, the building of a tow-path all the way to Abingdon and the removal of Iffley lock.

An appeal for some of these improvements to be made is likely if Oxford win.

Mr. M. H. Mosley

BOHEMIA "LET LOOSE" AT TRIAL

FONTAINEBLEAU, Tuesday.

SCENES reminiscent of a Bloomsbury highbrow party were seen in court here to-day when Jean Charles Millet, grandson of the famous French landscape painter, was charged with selling forgeries of the master's works.

Along with him was charged M Paul Cazot, a professional picture copier.

The public benches, crowded with eccentrically-dressed Bohemians, were a sea of gesticulating hands and raised eyebrows.

"Amazing sense of perspective "—"What a skyline "—"An obvious forgery "—"A mediocre copy "—were among the expressions heard on all sides.

The verdict was postponed for a week.—Reuter.

30th January 1935

KIDNAPPED BOY SENSATION

Court Sequel 31 Years After He Vanished

FOUND IN AMERICA

SPECIAL "DAILY MIRROR" NEWS

SENSATIONAL details of a kidnapping drama – details which will touch both sides of the Atlantic and bridge a gap of thirty-one years – will be revealed in Sheffield police court to-morrow.

It was on Tuesday, October 18, 1904, that the first act of the drama was played, for on that day Johnny Whitnear, aged five, of Woodbourn-road, Sheffield, vanished.

Johnny's mother is now Mrs. Woodward, and lives in Cobble-street, Sheffield. She has received a subpoena to attend the police court.

She understands that her appearance is in connection with Johnny's disappearance as a boy. Other people, it is stated, have also been called to attend the court.

Johnny Whitnear – thirty-six years old now – is believed to be in Sheffield, but his address is not revealed. He has been served with a court notice.

On the day the child vanished, a man aged about thirty-five had asked the permission of his mother to take him fishing at Keveton, seven miles away.

He did not come back. For weeks the anxious parents searched in vain. Months passed into years. They had nearly given up hope of ever seeing him again. Then they got news.

At the beginning of March, 1909, the Sheffield police were informed by a man, who did not wish his identity disclosed, that the alleged kidnapper was living under an assumed name in Newark, New Jersey, with a boy who was almost certainly Johnny Whitnear.

But the American police insisted that a member of the family must identify the child before he could be given up.

All Their Money Gone

The boy's father, an artisan in a Sheffield steel works, was not well enough to make the journey to America, so the eldest son, William, aged twenty-one, was chosen to go in his stead.

All the resources of the family went to pay for that journey, but it brought their boy back. William sailed on Saturday, March 6, 1909 on the Mauretania.

He reached Newark, New Jersey, on March 12, and with an escort of detectives he paid a visit to the alleged kidnapper who, it was said, confessed.

Johnny there and then left with his brother. The pair sailed for Liverpool on the Mauretania, landing on March 23.

On Wednesday, March 24, 1909, the "Daily Mirror" gave a full front-page photograph of the kidnapped boy's return. It was headed, "Affecting meeting between Johnny Whitnear and his mother at Liverpool."

The whole family were reunited at their home. Woodbourn-road was strung with flags.

Fully a thousand people watched the homecoming and shouted themselves hoarse; John had to be shown at the window before they would disperse.

William's double journey was of over 6,000 miles. It was one of the strangest and swiftest then on record. He had less than ten pounds weight of luggage and he accomplished the journey in less than three weeks.

BACKSTORY

The incredible case of John Whitnear and his abduction was a mystery that was only in part resolved 31 years later.

A 69-year-old man called Henry Ross, recently returned to the UK in 1935, was charged with taking John away from his parents to live in the United States. Once his case reached Leeds Assizes, a different story emerged.

It was initially claimed that Ross asked the boy's mother in 1904 if he could take John on a fishing excursion. She consented and that was the last time she saw her boy for five years.

Ross went on to claim that he was in fact the father of the child, and that his mother had asked him to take her son away, a statement Mrs Woodward fiercely denied. The case collapsed when the Judge (Mr Justice Atkinson) recognised it was a case of one word against another, decades after the events concerned. He directed the jury to return a verdict of not guilty.

"Do you think," he said, "that any Court is going to inflict any punishment? It is preposterous."

This wasn't the only case of extraordinary reunions and outcomes spanning decades. On 4th January 1936, the Mirror reported that two brothers "lost" in the war met again in hospital 18 years later:

"Eighteen years ago two brothers went 'over the top' together into the Battle of Cambrai. Each had since believed the other killed. Yesterday they met in adjoining beds of a London hospital.

"Edward and Charles Walters are the brothers. Edward lay in a London County Council hospital, recovering from an operation when a patient was brought in to occupy a bed.

"'The new patient has the same name as yours,' the nurse said, and Edward looked, hesitated, stared and spoke. A fervent handclasp reunited the brothers."

THE DAILY MIRROR, Friday, May 31, 1935

Daily Mirror

THE DAILY PICTURE NEWSPAPER WITH THE LARGEST NET SALE

Broadcasting - Page 22

No. 9,829 — Registered at the G.P.O as a Newspaper. — FRIDAY, MAY 31, 1935 — One Penny

FRENCH PREMIER COLLAPSES
—Page 3

Amusements : Pages 26 and 27

BRITAIN LOOKS TO 1960
World Air-Mail Service Daily

HER HUSBAND'S JOKE.—Mrs. Roosevelt, wife of the American President, laughs as she listens beside Mr. Josephus Daniels, to the presidential speech to Congress on the Soldiers' Bonus Bill.

'PRESS-THE-BUTTON' CARS ON OUR ROADS

BRITAIN is looking to the future. The next twenty-five years will be as rich in progress and achievement as have been the years of King George's reign. Men are everywhere visualising the brave new world that lies before them.

With the Channel crossed by car and an expert's prophecy of an autogiro to run on roads, the prospect of a sea-and-air motoring era has this week been opened up. Yesterday, the Postmaster-General, speaking at Swansea, said that in 1960 we should have telephones in every home, air mails daily from most parts of the world, and events presented to us by television.

During the next three years the Post Office will be spending £34,000,000 mainly on telephone development. That figure is one small item in the bill of progress.

What else does 1960 hold in store for us? Signalling systems on roads, cars driven by touching switches, films in schools, Hollywood extinct. Those were some of the forecasts given to the *Daily Mirror* last night.

HOLLYWOOD DOOMED?

"WHAT is your dream of 1960?" the *Daily Mirror* last night asked leading figures in industries and art. And these were their answers:—

MOTORING
Still Restrictions

SIR HERBERT AUSTIN:—England will be intersected with great arterial roads, reserved for high-speed traffic.

No doubt these roads will be governed in the same way as railway lines are to-day—probably with a similar system of signalling and level crossings.

Our present roads will in many cases become more or less obsolete or only used by farmers and slow traffic.

Except for the steering cars in those days will, I think, be controlled simply by pressing various buttons, as is done in elevators at the present time.

No doubt the increase of speed will bring with it many dangers, and I think that in 1960 there will still be some form of restriction in congested or dangerous areas—even the arterial roads.

One must realise that even now the average speed of a fast car equals the average speed of many railway trains.

FILMS
Talkies as an Art

MR. HERBERT WILCOX:—We shall have coloured and stereoscopic films.

There will be a central dissemination of films from some organisation similar to the B.B.C. and films will be televised on different wave-lengths into the home.

I think that would be a good thing for the film industry, as it would popularise actors as wireless has done.

I think Hollywood in 1960 will be derelict. It has served a useful purpose, but in the years to come talking pictures will grow as an art.

Hollywood is 3,000 miles away from the nearest intellectual centre, which is New York.

Films will be universally adopted as a medium for education in schools. This would make teaching so much more effective, particularly in the case of geography

SHIPPING
Comfort Before Speed

MR. FRANK CHARLTON (Director of Cunard-White Star Line and financial expert):—People will travel abroad in comfort. The tendency now is to build with a view to the comfort of passengers as well as speed.

I do not think that 1960 will see any bigger vessel than the Queen Mary, and it is almost
(Continued on back page)

FELL 800 ft. TO DEATH
Parachutist Killed Before Crowd

WATCHED by hundreds of people, Ivor Price, twenty-seven, a parachute jumper attached to Sir Alan Cobham's air display, fell 800ft. to his death while making a parachute jump at Woodford (Cheshire) Aerodrome last night.

Price's jump was the last event of the evening, in which he and Miss Naomi Heron-Maxwell did a double leap from two 'planes.

Price jumped off a few seconds before Miss Heron-Maxwell. His parachute did not open and he could be seen turning over and over as he hurtled to the ground. Women in the crowd fainted.

Miss Heron-Maxwell landed safely.

Princess Otto von Bismarck, whose husband is Counsellor of the German Embassy in London, with their baby son, Count Karl Alexander, after his christening yesterday at the German Church, Montpelier-place.

Execution 'Divine Law'
CORONER'S REBUKE TO MRS. VAN DER ELST

Mrs. Van der Elst's demonstration was a protest against the divinely instituted moral law. She would be wiser if she devoted her energy to saving souls.

SO said the Salford coroner, Mr. R. Stuart Rodger, yesterday, during the inquest on John Harris Bridge, the twenty-five-year-old Salford murderer.

He was referring to the scenes which occurred outside Strangeways Prison, Manchester, yesterday as the execution was taking place

Last night Mr. Stuart Rodger told the *Daily Mirror* that he believed that the moral laws which were given to Moses, as opposed to the ceremonial laws, were intended for all persons and all times.

But he did not develop his argument. He said he had been very ill for eight weeks.

SET AFIRE BY LORRY

Playing a hose on a railway coach which caught fire on Dover Admiralty Pier yesterday from a blazing Army lorry. The wreck of the lorry is seen lying across the rails. It was loaded with 6in. blank shells and blazed up after being in collision with a locomotive.

Girl Golf Star in a Scene

THIRTY caddies nearly ruined the final of the British women's golf championship at Newcastle, Co. Down yesterday.

The caddies were annoyed because Miss Pam Barton, the eighteen-year-old London girl who, after a gallant fight, was beaten in the final by Miss Wanda Morgan by three and two —changed her caddie just before going out.

George Murphy had been carrying Miss Barton's clubs all the week, but yesterday she was dissatisfied with him and dispensed with his services Another lad carried the clubs.

Other caddies thereupon followed the match in the first round, applauding loudly every winning stroke by Miss Morgan.

On completion of the first round Miss Barton spoke to officials of the Ladies' Golf Union.

Murphy was then paid the fee of six shillings to which he would have been entitled had he carried Miss Barton's clubs.

Before the second round began the caddies were addressed by Mrs. J. B. Walker, the Irish international golfer, who asked them to be "good sports." There was no further demonstration.

Miss Barton told a reporter that she was not worried by the "barracking."

31st May 1935

BRITAIN LOOKS TO 1960

'PRESS-THE-BUTTON CARS' ON OUR ROADS

BRITAIN IS looking to the future. The next twenty-five years will be as rich in progress and achievement as have been the years of King George's reign. Men are everywhere visualising the brave new world that lies before them.

Yesterday, the Postmaster-General, speaking at Swansea, said that in 1960 we should have telephones in every home, air mails daily from most parts of the world, and events presented to us by television.

What else does 1960 hold in store for us? Signalling systems on roads, cars driven by touching switches, films in schools, Hollywood extinct. Those were some of the forecasts given to the *Daily Mirror* last night.

HOLLYWOOD DOOMED

MOTORING
Still Restrictions
SIR HERBERT AUSTIN – England will be intersected with great arterial roads, reserved for high-speed traffic.

No doubt these roads will be governed in the same way as railway lines are to-day – probably with a similar system of signalling and level crossings.

Our present roads will in many cases become more or less obsolete or only used by farmers and slow traffic.

Except for the steering, cars in those days will, I think, be controlled simply by pressing various buttons, as is done in elevators at the present time.

FILMS
Talkies as an Art
MR. HERBERT WILCOX – We shall have coloured and stereoscopic films.

There will be a central dissemination of films from some organisation similar to the B.B.C., and films will be televised on different wavelengths into the home.

I think that would be a good thing for the film industry, as it would popularise actors as wireless has done.

I think Hollywood in 1960 will be derelict. It has served a useful

purpose, but in the years to come talking pictures will grow as an art.

Hollywood is 3,000 miles away from the nearest intellectual centre, which is New York.

Films will be universally adopted as a medium for education in schools. This would make teaching so much more effective, particularly in the case of choreography.

SHIPPING
Comfort Before Speed
MR. FRANK CHARLTON (Director of Cunard-White Star Line and financial expert) – People will travel abroad in comfort.

The tendency now is to build with a view to the comfort of passengers as well as speed. I do not think that 1969 will see any bigger vessel than the Queen Mary, and it is almost an impossibility to improve on the speed of such a magnificent vessel as she is.

AVIATION
Stratosphere Flying
MR. JIM MOLLISON – 'Planes will fly from London to New York in three hours. It is possible at the present time to fly the journey by 'plane in nine hours. Stratosphere flying will reduce that time by at least a third.

These things may happen even by 1940. The aeroplane will, I think, have supplanted other modes of travel for long journeys by 1960.

The motor-car owners of to-day will be the aeroplane owner of to-morrow.

PHILOSOPHY
The Machine Age
MR. C. E. M. JOAD – Human life will be more dependent upon machinery.

If the present rage for the mechanisation of our work and entertainment goes on people will in turn develop into "robots" unable to appreciate art which I think is half dead already.

But by 1960 the population will probably have decreased by about 5,000,000, and a reaction may set in. People may turn for relief to the simpler modes of living.

THEATRE
No Change
MR CEDRIC HARDWICKE – People will still long for flesh-and-blood presentations on the stage.

Television entertainment will be easily obtained, but there is a "herd" instinct that drives people to seek entertainment in a crowded place.

I cannot visualise theatres being turned into palatial palaces such as the modern cinemas. Such buildings would lack the atmosphere necessary for the enjoyment of a good play.

Besides many people are never happier than when they are struggling for a ticket at the theatre or sitting on a camp stool outside the entrance.

➥ Unlike Miss Winifred Brown, sitting in an Avro Avian aeroplane at the Manx air races in 1932, not all "motor-car owners of to-day will be the aeroplane owner of to-morrow".

BACKSTORY

Not all the *Mirror*'s prophecies were to come true, but some observations by the paper's specialist correspondents looked to be impressively accurate.

Broadcasting - Page 20

Daily Mirror

THE DAILY PICTURE NEWSPAPER WITH THE LARGEST NET SALE

No. 10,062   Registered at the G.P.O. as a Newspaper.   SATURDAY, FEBRUARY 29, 1936   One Penny

Amusements: Page 22

HITLER'S "LET'S BE FRIENDS" PLEA TO WORLD

An Exclusive Interview with "Daily Mirror"

"I APPEAL TO REASON"

Passionately... fervently... in the plain words of a Man of the People, Adolf Hitler, Leader and Master of Germany, in an exclusive interview with the "Daily Mirror" yesterday, pleaded with the world:—

"LET'S BE FRIENDS"

"I appeal to reason in international affairs," he said. "I want to show that the idea of eternal enmity is wrong. We are not hereditary enemies."

The "Daily Mirror" challenged his views with those in his book, "My Struggle." "My justification," said the Leader, "I shall write in the great book of history."

Man of Destiny Speaks

By BERTRAND DE JOUVENEL

IN the room where the destiny of Germany is planned her Man of Destiny sat to receive me.

Simply dressed, sitting at his desk, he unburdened to me his heart . . . his hopes . . his fears.

He eyed me keenly for a moment.

Then . . . slowly, this man who sees into the mind, said:

"Yes, I know what you are thinking.

"You say to yourself, 'Hitler makes peaceful declarations to us, but is it in good faith? Is he sincere?'

"Instead of giving yourselves up to psychological guesses, would you not do better to reason, to make use of logic?

"This logic, in which the French profess implicit belief—does it not lead you to think that it would be obviously to the advantage of France and Germany to maintain friendly relations?

"Would it not be ruinous for them to meet in conflict on new fields of battle?

"Is it not logical that I should wish for what is the most advantageous for my country?

"AND THE BEST THING FOR MY COUNTRY IS PEACE.

"People imagine me as someone quite different from what I am.

"They know quite well that I started at the bottom, and have become the master of Germany, which is rather an astonishing achievement, and there must be some extraordinary reasons for it.

"Mysticisms, Chance, or—?"

"Some say that it is due to violence that I became chief of the German nation. As you know, there was only a handful of us to begin with. We would have had our work cut out to capture by violence a nation of 68 million.

"Others say that my success is due to the mysticisms that I have created. Still others declare that it is due to chance.

"I must tell you what has brought me to where I am—"

Hitler's face took on a change. His eyes took on their fighting light; his fists clenched.

"Political problems appeared complicated. The German people did not understand them.

"They preferred, in such conditions, to leave to professional politicians the task of freeing them from these complications.

"I simplified these problems. I reduced them to simple terms.

"The Germans understood—and they followed me!

"And so the class-war—that notorious war of the classes—was shown to be an absurdity.

"I demonstrated its absurdity and the people understand me!

"I made an appeal to their reason.

"NOW I AM MAKING AN APPEAL TO REASON IN INTERNATIONAL AFFAIRS.

"I WANT TO SHOW MY PEOPLE THAT THE IDEA OF EVERLASTING ENMITY IS ABSURD; AND THAT WE ARE IN NO WAY HEREDITARY ENEMIES. THE GERMAN PEOPLE UNDERSTAND THAT, TOO.

"The German people have followed me in a reconciliation that has been infinitely more difficult—the reconciliation of Germany and Poland.

"By some the agreement between Germany and

(Continued on back page)

Rest of the News

Countess Haugwitz-Reventlow, formerly Miss Barbara Hutton, the Woolworth heiress, who gave birth to a son on Monday, was last night stated to be gravely ill after an operation. See back page.

29th February **1936**

HITLER'S "LET'S BE FRIENDS" PLEA TO WORLD

An Exclusive Interview with "Daily Mirror"

"I APPEAL TO REASON"

Passionately . . . fervently . . . in the plain words of a Man of the People, Adolf Hitler, Leader and Master of Germany, in an exclusive interview with the "Daily Mirror" yesterday, pleaded with "LET'S BE FRIENDS."

"I appeal to reason in international affairs," he said. "I want to show that the idea of eternal enmity is wrong. We are not hereditary enemies."

The "Daily Mirror" challenged his views with those in his book, "My Struggle". "My justification," said the Leader, "I shall write in the great book of history."

Man Of Destiny Speaks

By Bertrand de Jouvenel

IN the room where the destiny of Germany is planned her Man of Destiny sat to receive me. Simply dressed, sitting at his desk, he unburdened to me his heart . . . his hopes . . . his fears.

He eyed me keenly for a minute.

Then . . . slowly, this man who sees into the mind said:

"Yes, I know what you are thinking.

"You say to yourself: 'Hitler makes peaceful declarations to us but is it in good faith? Is he sincere?'

"Instead of giving yourselves up to psychological guesses would you not do better to reason, to make use of logic?

"This logic, in which the French profess implicit belief – does it not lead you to think that it would be obviously to the advantage of France and Germany to maintain friendly relations?

"Would it not be ruinous for them to meet in conflict on new fields of battle?

"Is it not logical that I should wish for what is most advantageous for my country?

"AND THE BEST THING FOR MY COUNTRY IS PEACE.

"People imagine me as something quite different from what I am.

"They know quite well that I started at the bottom and have become the master of Germany which is rather an astonishing achievement.

"Some say that is due to violence that I became chief of the German nation. As you know there was only a handful of us to begin with. We would have had our work cut out to capture by violence a nation of 73 million.

"Others say that my success is due to the mysticisms that I have created. Still others declare that it is due to chance.

"I must tell you what has brought me to where I am."

Hitler's face took on a change. His eyes took on their fighting light. His fists clenched.

"Political problems appeared complicated. The German people did not understand them.

"I simplified these problems . . . The Germans understood – and they followed me!

"And so the class war – that notorious war of the classes – was shown to be an absurdity.

"I demonstrated its absurdity and the people understood me!

I made an appeal to their reason. Now I am making an appeal to reason in international affairs . . ."

I raised a hand and the Leader ceased. "But," I said "if we read with satisfaction your peaceful declarations, nevertheless, we are still anxious because other signs are not so encouraging.

"I want to call your notice to Mein Kampf [in which Hitler called for the annihilation of France]. This book is looked upon through Germany as a political bible. It circulates without author's corrections to what you said in it.". . .

The Leader eyed me calmly.

"I was in prison when I wrote that book." He said. "It was a moment of great tension between France and Germany. I was on the side of my country. . . Today there is no further reason for conflict."

. . .

"We must not lose sight of the fact that Soviet Russia is a political factor, having at its disposal a faith in revolutions and armaments on a vast scale.

"As a German it is my duty to take such a situation into consideration. Bolshevism has no chance of being successful in Germany but there are other nations that are not so well protected against the Bolshevik virus."

THE DICTATOR

BACKSTORY

This astonishing interview with history's most infamous figure is an extraordinary insight into the period – and the barefaced lies Adolf Hitler was telling. In the build-up to war, and with many willing to appease the Nazis, the French philosopher Bertrand de Jouvenel challenged the dictator on his aims and queried his claims that he desired peace against the beliefs laid out in his book *Mein Kampf*.

It was a remarkable time and 13 years after Hitler's picture had first appeared in the newspaper (above).

Broadcasting - Page 22

Daily Mirror

THE DAILY PICTURE   NEWSPAPER WITH THE LARGEST NET SALE

BEST GUIDE FOR FLAT RACING —Page 31

No. 10,079   Registered at the G.P.O. as a Newspaper.   FRIDAY, MARCH 20, 1936   One Penny

Amusements: Pages 26 and 27

BRITON LOST AMONG KILLER TRIBE

"No Explorer Has Returned Alive"—Radio Silent

BY A SPECIAL CORRESPONDENT

SOMEWHERE in the wilds of Ecuador, South America, Captain Eric Erskine Loch, D.S.O., a British officer, searching for a phantom tribe of Indians, is cut off from the civilised world.

He is in a country where live the Auka Indians, a race of gigantic naked men who kill men on sight with their long barbed spears. Women they carry away alive to their unknown jungle fastnesses.

Captain Loch had kept in touch with New York by radio, but for six weeks his wireless transmitter has been silent.

Jungle and Desert

No explorer has ever returned alive from the wild country of jungle, scrub and desert which this lost explorer has penetrated. Bodies have been found stuck with fifty Auka spears.

Death for death's sake is believed to be the tribe's religion. They never rob the bodies of their victims.

I spoke last night with Captain Loch's twenty-three-year-old nephew, Mr. Alasdair Loch. He has just come back to England from the death country of the phantom people.

Malaria compelled him to leave the expedition. He made his way foodless through swamps for fourteen days back to the nearest point of civilisation.

"Captain Loch, the leader, was the only Briton left in the expedition when I struggled back," said Mr. Alasdair Loch.

"The others are Georges Brum, of Havre; Peter Prime, of Oconomowoc, Wisconsin; and John Ohman, the Swedish-American wireless operator.

Ambush from Trees

"They have about a dozen Indian servants.

"The naked Aukas hunt in bodies of a hundred or more. They ambush their victims from trees.

"The Aukas are rightly known as the Phantom People. Only one has ever lived for a time among more civilised tribes.

"If the party is attacked it has only repeating rifles and very little ammunition.

"The Phantom People are the terror of the unknown land, which they share with boa constrictors, lions and fever-carrying mosquitoes.

"The expedition found and shot a hairy tapir—a great beast like a cross between a bear and a rhinoceros.

"It mapped hundreds of square miles of the country. It located the lake under which is reputed to be the vast gold hoard of the Incas.

"Captain Loch's last words to me were that he intended to return to blow up the lake after making contact with the Phantom People."

Captain Eric Erskine Loch, D.S.O

Heiress to See Dying Mother

FROM OUR OWN CORRESPONDENT

NEW YORK, Thursday

A DRAMATIC death-bed reunion is expected between Mrs. Maryon Cooper Hewitt and her heiress daughter, whom, it is alleged, she caused to undergo an operation rendering her incapable of motherhood.

News to-night reached Jersey City Hospital, where the mother is desperately ill, that Miss Ann Hewitt was planning a dash to her bedside from California. Mrs. Cooper Hewitt's condition is regarded as hopeless.

A warrant of arrest on the charge of maiming her daughter was issued against Mrs. Hewitt six weeks ago

MUSEUM MAN HUNT

POLICE surrounded the British Museum last night, following a report that a man had been seen on the roof.

Early this morning the *Daily Mirror* learned that police searched the whole interior but found no trace of any intruder

Peace—A World Conference

A WORLD conference to discuss Hitler's Peace Plan is expected in three months' time as a result of talks in London yesterday between the Locarno Powers.

Disarmament will also be discussed.

—See page 3.

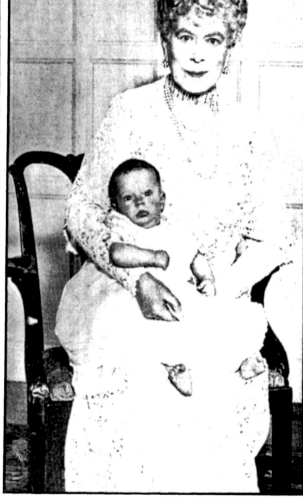

Queen Mary at Sandringham holding on her lap her grandson, Prince Edward, the baby son of the Duke and Duchess of Kent. This picture and another on page 16 were taken before the death of King George.—"*The Times*" World Copyright.

Curly Tail Keeps Him Straight

KING'S Folly is a greyhound with a twist in his tail.

The faster he goes the more curls his tail.

Such an uncompromising curl it is that by the time King's Folly is at full stretch his curly tail won't let him turn

That is what Mrs. Clara Gardiner Mitchell, of Winchell, Gloucestershire, found when she bought King's Folly from Mr. J. McKeown, of Newcastle.

She told the Newcastle County Court about it yesterday when she claimed £40 from Mr. McKeown—and won

78

20ᵗʰ March 1936

BRITON LOST AMONG KILLER TRIBE

"No Explorer Has Returned Alive" – Radio Silent

BY A SPECIAL CORRESPONDENT

SOME WHERE in the wilds of Ecuador, South America, Captain Eric Erskine Loch, D.S.O., a British officer, searching for a phantom tribe of Indians, is cut off from the civilised world.

He is in a country where live the Auka Indians, a race of gigantic naked men who kill men on sight with their long barbed spears. Women they carry away alive to their unknown jungle fortresses.

Captain Loch had kept in touch with New York by radio, but for six weeks his wireless transmitter has been silent.

Jungle and Desert

No explorer has ever returned alive from the wild country of jungle, scrub and desert which this lost explorer has penetrated.

Bodies have been found stuck with fifty Auka spears.

Death for death's sake is believed to be the tribe's religion. They never rob the bodies of their victims.

I spoke last night with Captain Loch's twenty-three-year-old nephew, Mr. Alasdair Loch. He has just come back to England from the death country of the phantom people.

Malaria compelled him to leave the expedition. He made his way foodless through swamps for fourteen days back to the nearest point of civilisation.

"Captain Loch, the leader, was the only Briton left in the expedition when I struggled back," said Mr. Alasdair Loch.

"The others are Georges Brum, of Havre; Peter Prime, of Oconomowoc, Wisconsin; and John Ohman, the Swedish-American wireless operator."

Ambush from Trees

"They have about a dozen Indian servants.

"The naked Aukas hunt in bodies of a hundred or more. They ambush their victims from trees.

"The Aukas are rightly known as the Phantom People. Only one has ever lived for a time among more civilised tribes.

"If the party is attacked it has only repeating rifles and very little ammunition.

"The Phantom People are the terror of the unknown land, which they share with boa constrictors, lions and fever-carrying mosquitoes.

"The expedition found and shot a hairy tapir – a great beast like a cross between a bear and a rhinoceros.

"It mapped hundreds of square miles of the country. It located the lake under which is reputed to be the vast gold hoard of the Incas.

"Captain Loch's last words to me were that he intended to return to blow up the lake after making contact with the Phantom People."

BACKSTORY

The expedition to Ecuador undertaken by Captain Eric Erskine Loch was the stuff of derring-do seemingly belonging to another age – but also an illustration of how the developed world still viewed "savages" in uncharted places.

Loch's expedition was supposedly made in search of fabled Inca gold – and made for sensational, if not entirely accurate, claims from the expedition members.

The *Mirror*'s report the next day was headlined "Explorers escape from jungle of death", and revealed how Loch had turned up safely.

"WE are back, and safe." These five words, sent out by a small portable wireless transmitter from a wild, unmapped region of Ecuador, South America, revealed yesterday that Captain Eric Erskine Loch, the explorer, and his three companions, have survived the terrors of the jungle.

Never before has a white man returned alive from the dense jungle and oozy swamp country of the Auka Indians – a tribe of spearmen whose religion is to kill men on sight and carry women off as captives.

Captain Loch's secretary, Miss Eula McClary, speaking over the transatlantic telephone from the New York headquarters, told me of the party's future plans.

"It was wonderful, after the terrible silence, to get the radio message that they were safe," she said. "But I expect they failed to encounter the Aukas.

"The message stated that they would be back in New York in May. Captain Loch's companions all went down with jungle fever, and their experiences were terrible – they had to cut their own trail to escape man-traps.

"They dared not take their radio into the interior in case the noise of the generator gave the alarm.

"That accounts for the silence, which lasted for seven weeks, for they had to cut their way back to the base again – the growth is so quick that a path soon disappears.

"He wanted to return to a lake he located, where the Incas' huge gold treasure is supposed to be hidden, but that will have to be some other time, as the rainy season is now on, and the ground is impassable.

"The district of the lake is 'taboo' to the Indian servants during the rains – just as the Auka country is always 'taboo' to them, for that wild tribe has driven all the other Indians away in terror.

"No, Eric is not married – but I should say he is a most desirable bachelor. As far as I know he is not likely to get engaged – he has had a very distinguished career in the British Army, campaigning in India and Africa, and winning the D.S.O., and the Army has made a bachelor-soldier of him."

Broadcasting - Pages 22 & 23

Daily Mirror

THE DAILY PICTURE NEWSPAPER WITH THE LARGEST NET SALE

No. 10,156   Registered at the G.P.O as a newspaper.   FRIDAY, JUNE 19, 1936   One Penny

WEEK'S WEATHER CHART —Page 10

Amusements : Pages 24 and 25

QUADS TO BE ON SHOW—6D. A LOOK

Only Way to Balance Budget

PUBLIC FUND FAILS

FROM OUR SPECIAL CORRESPONDENT

ST. NEOTS, Thursday.

Britain's famous quads—Ann, Paul, Ernest and Michael Miles—are going to start earning their own living when they are eight months old—in three weeks.

THEY are to be put on public exhibition in the new sun nursery that is being built on to the country house, The Gables, the new home of their parents.

By paying 6d. visitors will be able to walk up a staircase on to a balcony surrounding the nursery and look through windows into the room where the quads will lie in their cots.

This course has been decided upon as the only possible way of raising the money.

So far, the bulk of the cost has been borne by Dr. Harrisson, who brought them into the world and who has been the means of keeping them alive—" one chance in ten thousand that came off through the doctor's constant care," say the experts.

It was hoped that the public would contribute by supporting a fund that was opened, but that has been a failure.

Already Cost £2,000

The only way left of meeting the steadily rising bills for their upkeep, Dr. Harrisson thinks, is to copy the idea of the Canadian Quins and put the Quads on exhibition.

Their parents have no option but to agree. Mr. Miles is still working as a lorry driver.

He earns no more than £3 a week, and as the cost of upkeep of the new house will be heavy, apart from maintaining his wife and two-year-old son, he will be unable to contribute much towards the rearing of the Quads.

Already over £2,000 has been spent upon them. For the first few weeks of their lives they were costing £15 a day, as four nurses were engaged.

Since then, Dr. Harrisson has managed to raise £750 to buy The Gables, but he has himself had to guarantee the £450 needed to build the new sun nursery.

Even now, one nurse, Miss Murrant, will have

(Continued on back page)

A Day with Shirley

WHAT is Shirley Temple really like? This question is answered by Reginald Whitley, the "Daily Mirror" film expert, who has just returned from Hollywood.

Turn to page 12 and read what he says about a day he spent with the charming, unprecocious little girl who, at seven years of age, is the sweetheart of the world.

GIRL PAT IS "SIGHTED" AGAIN

Mystery Deepens

MYSTERY OF THE GIRL PAT, TRUANT GRIMSBY TRAWLER, DEEPENED LAST NIGHT.

Two days after being reported wrecked with three white men dead on board in the Bahamas, she was "sighted" off Georgetown, British Guiana, nearly 2,000 miles away.

And her skipper, George Osborne, was reported to have been taken from Inagua, Bahamas, to Haiti in the sloop, Malake, and to be now in Jamaica.

The vessel off Georgetown, says Reuter, answered closely to the description of the Girl Pat. She anchored two miles off the town.

A seaplane flew out The white crew on board seemed to signal for help.

A police launch then left port, but the vessel made off after claiming that her name was the Kiaora.

On Wednesday Mr. J. H. Jarrett, K.C., Colonial Secretary of the Bahamas Islands, sent the chief magistrate of the Mayaguan Island to Atwood Cay, sixty miles away.

Yesterday, over the long distance telephone at Nassau, the capital of the Bahamas, Mr. Jarrett said:—

"Not having heard from Mr. Forbes, the Justice of the Peace at Mayaguana, I have now sent an aeroplane from Nassau to Atwood Cay.

"If the wreck is that of the Girl Pat I shall know within the next few hours."

RIFLE AND GAS "WAR" ROUND U.S. FACTORY

FROM OUR OWN CORRESPONDENT

NEW YORK, Thursday.

FOURTEEN people are stated to have been shot or gassed in a fierce battle at Kent, Ohio, between pickets and strike breakers.

Eye-witnesses compared the fighting to wartime scenes in France. There was a constant crackle of rifle fire and bursting of gas bombs.

The trouble started when lorries containing forty strike breakers drove through hostile pickets into a factory yard behind a barrage of tear gas.

The women of the district are in a state of hysteria.

"DEAD SOLDIERS" IN CARNIVAL

A tableau depicting two dead soldiers entangled in barbed wire and wearing gas masks appeared in a carnival procession at Carlisle last night.

It was entered by the Carlisle Peace Council, and caused considerable adverse comment.

Milady in a Fix

Victorian crinoline and modern car set a problem for little bridesmaid bound for the wedding at Christ Church, Didsbury, Manchester, yesterday of Captain S. Whipp and Miss Noreen Carlyle.

The King George—Sister Ship for the Queen Mary

THE Queen Mary, Britain's wonder liner, is to have a sister ship—and M.P.s think she will be named King George. Mr Neville Chamberlain announced in the Commons yesterday that he had received an application from the Cunard-White Star Company for authority to use the sum available under the North Atlantic Shipping Act for the construction of a sister ship

The Chancellor said the company had obtained preliminary tenders from various yards and he understood that, after considering them, they would negotiate in the first instance with Messrs. John Brown and Co

The Government, however, still reserved the right to further consultation before any contract is signed.

It is believed that John Brown's are practically certain to secure the contract (writes our Political Correspondent), since the stocks on which the Queen Mary was built are available, and the present ship is said to be highly satisfactory.

The order will mean work for nearly 200,000 men, in many cases for three years, and Clydeside is delighted. It is suggested that a start will be made in August.

Meanwhile the Queen Mary is making excellent progress on her second trip across the Atlantic. By noon yesterday she had covered 566 miles since leaving Cherbourg breakwater, at 5.30 a.m. on Wednesday.

LIFE AMBITION TO KILL A GIRL

WHEN the twenty-eight-year-old son of a wealthy real estate operator confessed, according to the San Francisco police, that he strangled a girl of twenty-four and then assaulted her, he said:

"I have done everything possible to hurt women since I was fourteen. I have ruined as many as I could. An incident which occurred when I was fourteen turned me against them.

"This killing is no surprise to me. I knew that eventually I would achieve my supreme vengeance—that I would kill a woman."

The police say the man's story is that he met the girl a fortnight ago and made violent love to her, which she repulsed. Two nights ago he went to her apartment

Again he made love to her and she rejected his advances. He then caught her by the throat and tied a silk stocking round her neck. Most of her clothes were stripped off

Walter left the apartment and walked the streets "for twenty-four hours" before going to the police, says the British United Press.

He told the police: "I don't want a lawyer. I want to plead guilty and get it over as soon as possible." He is living apart from his wife, who, when informed of his confession, exclaimed: "Oh, what can I do to help him?"

19th June 1936

QUADS TO BE ON SHOW 6D. A LOOK

Only Way to Balance Budget

PUBLIC FUND FAILS
FROM OUR SPECIAL CORRESPONDENT

St. Neots, Thursday

Britain's famous quads – Ann, Paul, Ernest and Michael Miles – are going to start earning their own living when they are eight months old in three weeks.

They are to be put on public exhibition in the new sun nursery that is being built on to the country house, The Gables, the new home of their parents.

By paying 6d. visitors will be able to walk up a staircase on to a balcony surrounding the nursery and look through windows into the room where the quads will lie in their cots.

This course has been decided upon as the only possible way of raising the money. So far, the bulk of the cost has been borne by Dr. Harrisson, who brought them into the world and who has been the means of keeping them alive – "one chance in ten thousand that came off through the doctor's constant care," say the experts.

It was hoped that the public would contribute by supporting a fund that was opened, but that has been a failure.

Already Cost £2,000

The only way left of meeting the steadily rising bills for their upkeep, Dr. Harrisson thinks, is to copy the idea of the Canadian Quins and put the Quads on exhibition.

Their parents have no option but to agree. Mr. Miles is still working as a lorry driver.

He earns no more than £3 a week, and as the cost of upkeep of the new house will be heavy, apart from maintaining his wife and two-year-old-son, he will be unable to contribute much towards the rearing of the Quads.

Already over £2,000 has been spent upon them. For the first few weeks of their lives they were costing £15 a day, as four nurses were engaged,

Since then, Dr. Harrisson has managed to raise £750 to buy The Gables, but he has himself had to guarantee the £450 needed to build the new sun nursery.

Even now, one nurse, Miss Murrant, will have to stay on indefinitely to help Mrs. Miles rear her babies. The other remaining nurse is expected to leave in a fortnight, as Mrs. Miles's mother, Mrs. Mason, is to live with the family and help with the work.

"Heavy as the expense is now, it will be heavier shortly," Miss Harrisson, the doctor's daughter, told me.

"They are growing so rapidly that new clothes are always needed and they will soon start eating soft foods.

"Besides, toys will be needed when they begin crawling. You can't share one teddy bear between four.

"All this expense is a great worry to us, as the public have not helped as we expected.

"So to put them on show is the only way we have left. We feel sure that hundreds of people will be willing to pay to see them . . . They really are wonderful babies."

It will be a month before the sun nursery is completed and the quads exhibition opened. There will be no risks taken with the children's health. Whenever they show signs of being unwell – even with a cold – visitors will not be allowed.

But, as Miss Harrisson pointed out, "once people have seen Ernest kicking his cot about in glee, it will need a police patrol to keep them away."

BACKSTORY

The Miles children were the first quadruplets to have survived for more than a few days, and naturally they charmed the nation during the 1930s. Their new nursery was unveiled by politician George Lansbury, they adorned the front page of the *Mirror* to ring in Christmas Eve (above), and were given star billing when they made their stage debut aged three in a local play.

But as time wore on, and their parents wanted to raise a normal family rather than live in the public gaze, the Miles quads inevitably faded from view – although the four children were pictured again in 1947 (left), when they turned out for a Scouts and Girl Guides jamboree, and would occasionally surface in newsreels.

THE DAILY MIRROR, Friday, July 17, 1936.

Broadcasting - Page 28

DailyMirror

THE DAILY PICTURE • NEWSPAPER WITH THE LARGEST NET SALE

No. 10,180 | Registered at the G.P.O. as a newspaper. | FRIDAY, JULY 17, 1936 | One Penny

ATTEMPT ON THE KING'S LIFE

HERE IS THE MAN WITH LOADED PISTOL

And The 'Special' Who Saved The King

George Andrew McMahon under arrest in Constitution Hill yesterday after an attempt on the life of the King. Helping to hold him is Special-Constable Dick (wearing peaked cap), of Hackney, whose prompt action saved the King's life. He was on duty for the day only. His eye caught the glint of metal in the sunshine, and he saw a man on the outskirts of the crowd holding a revolver. He threw himself between the revolver and the King, and, pouncing on the man, knocked the revolver into the roadway. He then arrested McMahon. Full story on pages 2 and 3; the King's speech page 4; world opinion page 5; other pictures on pages 12, 14, 16, 17 and 19.

17th July 1936

ATTEMPT TO KILL THE KING WITH REVOLVER

Policeman, on Day's Duty, Hurls Himself Before Gun

THE KING, UNMOVED

AFTER FACING DEATH AT THE HANDS OF A MAN ARMED WITH A REVOLVER YESTERDAY MIDDAY, KING EDWARD VIII WAS HARD AT WORK AT ST. JAMES'S PALACE, LAST NIGHT, ON STATE BUSINESS.

IN THE AFTERNOON HE HAD PLAYED A ROUND OF GOLF AT COOMBE HILL GOLF COURSE, AND HE HAD PLAYED CONFIDENTLY, SHOWING NO TRACE OF THE TERRIBLE ORDEAL HE HAD BEEN THROUGH.

For three hours before as, with the Duke of York, he rode to Buckingham Palace after presenting the Colours to the Guards in Hyde Park, a man had pointed straight at him a nickelplated pistol loaded in four of its five chambers.

Without flinching the King rode on. At Buckingham Palace Queen Mary who, driving ahead, had seen nothing of the incident, was one of the first to congratulate her son on his safe return.

Later a man was charged at Bow-street with being in possession of a firearm and attempting to endanger life. He was George Andrew McMahon, aged about thirty-four, a journalist, of Westbourne-terrace, Paddington. He is a Scotsman who had lived in London for many years.

The King was saved by a middle-aged Hackney Special Constable, who was only on duty for the day.

Special Constable Dick, of Woodford Green, Essex, was watching the procession when he saw a glint of metal in the sun.

He turned to a man on the outskirts of the crowd and saw he was holding a revolver close to his body.

With complete disregard of his own safety the special constable pounced on the man. His body came between the revolver and the King.

With a sweep of his arm he knocked the weapon out from the crowd to hit the hoofs of the King's horse.

"Don't Hurt Me"

A spectator said that Special Constable Dick when he saw a revolver gleaming in the sunshine, leaped forward and struck fearlessly at the weapon.

It went spinning in the air over the heads of the crowd.

When Special Constable Dick grasped the man by the neck he cried, "Don't hurt me."

There was a struggle, and other policemen rushed forward.

Commandant L. V. Dawe told the Daily Mirror last night of his pride in having "the man who saved the King" – Special Constable Dick of the "J" Division – under his command.

"I am naturally delighted that one of my men was able to be of such service." Commandant Dawe said, "particularly because it shows that Specials are able to do more than merely keep a crowd back and watch a procession go by.

"Special Constable Dick showed that he could 'jump to it' in an emergency. And it is also most gratifying to notice that Dick used an effective regulation police hold in his share of the arrest.

"It shows that theoretical training can be of enormous value when a man puts it immediately into practice in so great an emergency."

The King's Courage

The crowd turned on the man. He was seized and roughly handled by men and women. Only the arrival of the police saved him from being beaten to death.

They forced a way into the struggling mass, and holding the man high over the crowd's heads, passed him from hand to hand to the rear of the ranks.

Then he was taken to Bow-street Police Station.

Greatest incident of the attempt was the courage of the Soldier King. As he rode by his eye caught the flash of the revolver. He looked sideways.

HE SAW THE GUN POINTING AT HIM; HIS EYES NEVER LEFT IT; BUT HIS FACE UNCHANGED AND UNMOVED, HE RODE CALMLY ON AS THOUGH ON PARADE.

A second man, John William Remes, aged thirty-two, of Hollingbury-place, Ditcham-road, Brighton, was detained by the police after striking the man who had the revolver.

Mr. Remes, a porter at the Hotel Metropole, Brighton, is staying at Streatham on holiday. He was released after being kept at the police station for several hours, and later told the Daily Mirror . . .

"My wife said: 'Look, an insult to the King.' I struck the man on the spur of the moment – feeling the indignation any patriotic Englishman would.

"A little later we were taken – the man and myself – to Cannon-row Police Station . . ."

Mrs. Remes, who was badly shaken by the incident, said: "My husband only did what any other man would have done."

A woman who saw the attempt to murder Queen Victoria in 1882, and was present again at yesterday's incidents –seventy-eight-year-old Mrs. Mary Ann Clarges, of Marylebone-road, N.W.1 – told the "Daily Mirror" her story.

"To-day my daughter took me to see the King. The King came riding towards us and we started to cheer. Then I heard someone scream and a woman cried: 'Oh, look! Stop him, stop him!'

"I turned and saw a revolver waved in the air only a few paces away. I screamed, and then a hand appeared as though from nowhere and thrust up the one holding the revolver.

"I saw the police pull the man away, and then I fainted . . ."

BACKSTORY

The dramatic attempt on the life of King Edward VIII – just a few months before his abdication – centred on the curious character of George Andrew McMahon (real name Jerome Bannigan).

McMahon was found guilty at the Old Bailey in September 1936, of intent to alarm His Majesty, and sentenced to 12 months' hard labour. McMahon had claimed he had been paid £150 by a "foreign power" to assassinate the king, going so far as to suggest he had informed MI5 and deliberately failed to shoot.

Later accused of being a pro-Nazi, McMahon maintained his innocence and subsequent enquiries and claims suggested he was associated with various suspect individuals and groups – so his story might not have been as fanciful as assumed.

Daily Mirror

THE DAILY PICTURE   **NEWSPAPER WITH THE LARGEST NET SALE**

No. 10,273   Registered at the G.P.O. as a newspaper.   TUESDAY, NOVEMBER 3, 1936   One Penny

FAMOUS K.C. DIES AS DINERS LAUGH AT HIS JOKES

BY A SPECIAL CORRESPONDENT

With 400 of the most distinguished patrons of sport, the arts and the theatre still laughing at one of his jokes, Sir Henry Curtis-Bennett, K.C., and fifty-seven-year-old 18st. "Falstaff of the Bar," collapsed and died at a London banquet last night.

HE was the second chairman of London Sessions to have dropped dead in less than a month. Sir Percival Clarke, the previous chairman, died on October 5 in his room in a London hotel.

Twenty-three years ago Sir Henry's father dropped dead at a meeting at the Mansion House within a month of his appointment as Chief Metropolitan Magistrate.

By another amazing coincidence Sir Henry's intimate friend, Mr. Frederick Freke Palmer, well-known solicitor, collapsed and died at a banquet in London in January, 1932, just as he finished a speech full of humorous anecdotes, when he fell back into his chair.

Last night Sir Henry was replying to the toast of the "Guests" at the dinner of the National Greyhound Racing Society at the Dorchester.

A few moments before he rose to deliver his speech he turned to a friend and said: "I feel as nervous as a kitten to-night." "Oh, nonsense," was the answer, "the number of times you have spoken in public."

Sir Henry stood up. With tragic and unconscious prophecy, he began by saying that it might be the last speech he would make. On his appointment to the Bench he would have to learn to listen to other people.

For fifteen minutes he kept his audience rocking with merriment as he told story after witty story. Finally, he came to the tale of a journey which he had recently made from Scotland to England.

He said that the train seemed to be stopping far more frequently than usual, and at last, when it came to a Border town where it should not have halted, he put his head out of the window and asked a man in uniform why it had stopped.

The man replied, "Well, sir, we are getting a new engine, for this one does not seem to be able to get enough steam pressure. Somehow the train seems to be overladen to-night."

Crash of Glass

As the guests were laughing at Sir Henry's story, obviously directed against himself, there was a crash of glasses.

Sir Henry was seen to stagger, put his hand to his side, and slowly topple over on to the floor, his bulk knocking chairs and cutlery out of the way and spilling the wine from the glasses which smashed to splinters as he slowly sank on to the carpet.

In a second his brother, Sir Noel Curtis-Bennett, was by his side, calling frantically for a doctor. Quickly two rushed to his side. One of them was Sir Henry Jackson. Screens were put around the top table.

A deep silence fell over the room, while the doctors brought water to Sir Henry's lips, and fanned him with napkins.

Then an announcement was made that the dinner would be abandoned.

Guests filed slowly out.

Before Sir Henry Curtis-Bennett could be carried from the banqueting hall to an ambulance he had died.

Sir Henry had been a K.C. since 1919.

Murder trials in which he was briefed included those of Ronald True, Armstrong, Mrs. Thompson, Field and Gray, the Crumbles murderers, Patrick Mahon and Vaquier.

He acted as counsel for Miss Irene Savidge in the famous Savidge inquiry.

He was knighted in 1922, and had been at the Bar for thirty-four years.

This exclusive picture of Sir Henry Curtis-Bennett was taken at the dinner last night a moment before he fell to the floor and died.

As will be seen, Sir Henry was smiling broadly at a joke (told in adjoining column) about his weight. Guests round him, and even the waiters, were still laughing uproariously at the story when the great Judge and lawyer fell.

£1,000,000 GEMS IN TO-DAY'S PAGEANT OF PARLIAMENT

BY A SPECIAL CORRESPONDENT

A million pounds worth of diamonds will be worn by peeresses at the opening of the new session of Parliament by the King to-day.

TIARAS in which one stone alone may be worth £1,000, priceless ermine and crimson velvet robes will make the House of Lords the scene of the most impressive pageant known in the modern world.

So great has been the rush to see the King make his first appearance in Parliament as Sovereign that more than 500 peeresses have been unable to obtain seats.

In the heavy gold carriage of state, drawn by eight horses, accompanied by a Sovereign's escort of Life Guards, the King will start from Buckingham Palace punctually at 11.20.

At 11.25 the procession will be in the Mall; 11.35, Horse Guards Parade; 11.40, Whitehall, and 11.45, House of Lords.

It will be the first Royal procession to Westminster for many years in which no woman has ridden.

The drive will be notable, too, as the first appearance of Lord Colebrooke in the recently revived office of Master of the Robes.

A woman secretary stood on guard by a telephone in Westminster last night while, with nerves on edge, Miss Florence Horsbrugh, M.P. for Dundee, was re-reading the speech she will make when she moves the address in reply to the King's Speech.

When a "Daily Mirror" representative asked if Miss Horsbrugh would come to the telephone to be congratulated on being the first woman to have the honour, the secretary was firm. "She has had so many congratulations, she needs protecting from them," declared the secretary.

"She's still nervous. She'll be nervous right up to the moment for making her speech."

Traffic Arrangements—see page 23

DROPPED SPANNER SHOCK AT OPERA

BY A SPECIAL CORRESPONDENT

HERR Von Ribbentrop, the German Ambassador, and Frau Ribbentrop made their first public appearance in London society at the performance of "Der Rosenkavalier" by the Dresden State Opera Company at Covent Garden last night.

Nearly all the German colony in London were present.

The first excitement occurred when an electrician dropped a spanner in the middle of the first act.

The house was hushed for the singing of a newcomer to Covent Garden Marta Fuchs, when a terrific crash was heard back-stage. The singer jumped, then went on as though nothing had happened.

3rd November 1936

FAMOUS K.C. DIES AS DINERS LAUGH AT HIS JOKES

BY A SPECIAL CORRESPONDENT

With 400 of the most distinguished patrons of sport, the arts and the theatre still laughing at one of his jokes, Sir Henry Curtis-Bennett, K.C., and fifty-seven-year-old 18st. "Falstaff of the Bar", collapsed and died at a London banquet last night.

HE was the second chairman of London Sessions to have dropped dead in less than a month. Sir Percival Clarke, the previous chairman, died October 5 in his room in a London hotel.

Twenty-three years ago Sir Henry's father dropped dead at a meeting at the Mansion House within a month of his appointment as Chief Metropolitan Magistrate.

By another amazing coincidence Sir Henry's intimate friend, Mr. Frederick Freke Palmer, well-known solicitor, collapsed and died at a banquet in London in January, 1932, just as he finished a speech full of humorous anecdotes, when he fell back into his chair.

Last night Sir Henry was replying to the toast of the Guests at the dinner of the National Greyhound Racing Society at the Dorchester.

A few moments before he rose to deliver his speech he turned to a friend and said: "I feel as nervous as a kitten to-night." "Oh, nonsense," was the answer, "the number of times you have spoken in public."

Sir Henry stood up. With tragic and unconscious prophecy, he began by saying that it might be the last speech he would make. On his appointment to the Bench he would have to learn to listen to other people.

For fifteen minutes he kept his audience rocking with merriment as he told story after witty story. Finally, he came to the tale of a journey which he had recently made from Scotland to England.

He said that the train seemed to be stopping far more frequently than usual, and at last, when it came to a Border town where it should not have halted, he put his head out of the window and asked a man in uniform why it had stopped.

The man replied, "Well, sir, we are getting a new engine, for this one does not seem to be able to get enough steam pressure. Somehow the train seems to be overladen to-night."

Crash of Glass

As the guests were laughing at Sir Henry's story, obviously directed against himself, there was a crash of glasses.

Sir Henry was seen to stagger, put his hand to his side, and slowly topple over on to the floor, his bulk knocking chairs and cutlery out of the way and spilling the wine from the glasses which smashed to splinters as he slowly sank on to the carpet.

In a second his brother, Sir Noel Curtis-Bennett, was by his side, calling frantically for a doctor. Quickly two rushed to his side. One of them was Sir Henry Jackson. Screens were put around the top table.

A deep silence fell over the room, while the doctors brought water to Sir Henry's lips and fanned him with napkins.

Then an announcement was made that the dinner would be abandoned.

Guests filed slowly out.

Before Sir Henry Curtis-Bennett could be carried from the banqueting hall to an ambulance he had died.

Sir Henry had been a K.C. since 1919. Murder trials in which he was briefed included those of Ronald True, Armstrong, Mrs. Thompson, Field and Gray, the Crumbles murderers, Patrick Mahon and Vaquier.

He acted as counsel for Miss Irene Savidge in the famous Savidge inquiry.

He was knighted in 1922, and had been at the bar for thirty-four years.

BACKSTORY

During the 1930s the *Mirror*, among other newspapers, appeared to have something of a fascination for unfortunate people "dropping down dead" and the phrase frequently appeared in headlines and copy.

Sir Henry Curtis-Bennett was an avuncular figure involved in a number of high-profile cases, notably the Savidge Inquiry, when he acted on behalf of Miss Irene Savidge. She was a young North London woman who had been seen in intimate contact in Hyde Park with the influential economist and politician Sir Leo Money.

Money and Savidge were charged with indecent behaviour, but the case was thrown out in magistrates' court. The police suspected Money had used his establishment connections to gain his acquittal, but the police themselves were accused of improper questioning of Miss Savidge (pictured below, during the enquiry), including the absence of a female officer and intimate questions about her sex life.

THURSDAY, APRIL 22, 1937

Daily Mirror

No. 10416   Registered at the G.P.O. as a Newspaper. **ONE PENNY**

LATE LON ED

CLARK GABLE SAYS "I'M NO PAPA—GOT 2 WIVES TO PROVE IT"

FROM OUR OWN CORRESPONDENT

NEW YORK, Wednesday.

CLARK Gable grinned at the reporters as he pushed his way through a clamouring horde of women fans outside Los Angeles court-house for the Norton trial to-day. "I'm no papa," he wise-cracked, "and I'll show you two wives to prove it."

In court his attorney announced that Gable's first wife, Josephine Dillon, and his second, Ria Langham, from whom he separated "on a friendly footing" in 1935, have offered to give evidence for him against forty-seven-year-old Violet Wells Norton, the Englishwoman who accused him of being father of her love-child in an Essex romance.

Women are rallying to their hero. This morning he got up to find a record mail. Rabbits' feet, sacred statues, lucky coins and psychic handkerchiefs poured in from admirers all over America as tokens of sympathy and good luck in the trial.

With them came letters begging Clark to wear the lucky symbols in court.

One girl sent him the first verse of Kipling's "If," which includes the lines: " If you can trust yourself when all men doubt you . . . or being lied about don't deal in lies . . ."

At the court house Clark sought refuge behind locked doors in a private room. His peace ended when Frau Deorfleur, a friend of the old days, got leave to enter with a band of Pressmen.

"He Was with Me"

"I'll do anything to help Clark," she cried. "He's always been the swellest guy I know."

She told reporters he couldn't have lived with Mrs. Norton in Essex, as is alleged, because at that time he happened to be with her.

Many men joined the throngs of women in court hoping to hear Mae West give evidence of a letter written by Mrs. Norton which said: " You will be surprised to know Gable is the father of my daughter Gwendoline, who looks exactly like him. Now, Miss West, would you be a fairy godmother to my girl and put Clark to shame ?"

At the start of to-day's hearing the defence failed in a move for a directed verdict acquitting Mrs. Norton and Jack L. Smith, a private detective, who are accused of attempting to obtain money from Gable by fraud.

STRIKE WILL HOLD UP LINERS

SURPRISE strike order threatened to stop the Queen Mary sailing from New York yesterday—but a two-hour truce enabled her to leave to schedule.

Mr. Joseph Ryan, president of the International Longshoremen's Association, later informed Reuter that the strike was to be resumed because members of the independent union at Montreal returned to unload the Andania and the Alaunia.

A hundred and fifty dockers at once ceased work on the Cunard cargo steamer Maidan at Boston.

A strike has also been called against all vessels of Furness, Withy and Co. and associated lines in North American ports.

FASCISTS IN STREET CLASH

Fighting broke out in St. George's Highstreet, Shadwell, last night, when about 600 Blackshirts, marching to the Limehouse headquarters, passed an anti-Fascist meeting. Police soon cleared the fighters and one arrest was made.

Miss Adele Royle, actress-mannequin, who is suing Lord Kingsborough for alleged breach of promise.

"YOU SILLY BLIGHTER" AND "YE GODS!" BROADCAST MYSTERY

BY A SPECIAL CORRESPONDENT

VARIETY had just ended in the B.B.C.'s London Regional programme yesterday afternoon at 4.45.

Then that 'tween-items silence . . . but crashing through it came a protesting voice. It said clearly, if rather more-in-pain-than-in-anger:—

" You silly blighter."

. . . the 'tween items silence descended on the air again, but then the listener heard:

" Ye Gods ! "

. . . silence once more, then the same voice, not so much in pain as in anger this time, said :

" Give me the— "

—but what listeners will never know.

The voice, to their regret, faded out and a clear, correct polite announcer urbanely read a reading from the works of Edmund Spenser.

* * *

Answer by the B.B.C. to a question by the *Daily Mirror:* "There does seem to have been a slight hitch during the change-over. Oh ! no, we cannot confirm, nor would we deny, that unintended remarks were broadcast."

FAITHFUL MARY SAYS—

"FATHER DIVINE AIN'T NO GOD! JUST A MAN"

" He ain't God ! He's just a damned man —no more God than anybody else."

THIS was how " Faithful Mary," middle-aged mulatto wife of Father Divine, debunked the black, self-styled Messiah, to New Yorkers yesterday, says British United Press.

Father Divine is being sought by the police following the stabbing of Harry Green, white process server, who tried to thrust a writ into his hand at a sacred banquet in the Harlem temple.

The charge against him is " felonious assault."

Faithful Mary revealed that after the stabbing Father Divine asked her to hand over to him the deeds of a hotel and its 165 acres of ground at High Falls, New York State. She refused.

Next to Father Divine, Faithful Mary has been the most powerful figure in the sect which hails him as God.

Scores of different properties are in her name, including " Heavens," " Promised Lands," farms, dress shops, and "Glory Be to Father Divine " restaurants.

VISCOUNT DENIES PROMISE TO WED

VISCOUNT Kingsborough, thirty-nine-year-old heir of the Earl of Kingston, is being sued by a West End actress-mannequin, Miss Adele Royle, for damages for alleged breach of promise to marry her.

The action is in the list for hearing before a special jury in the King's Bench Division. The defence is a denial that any promise to marry was ever made.

Titian-Haired Beauty

Miss Royle, who is thirty-four, is tall and good-looking, with long Titian hair which she wears coiled in plaits. She lives at The White House, Albany-street, Regent's Park, London, N.W.

Lord Kingsborough is the Earl of Kingston's only son. He has three sisters.

He was educated at Eton and at the Royal Military College becoming a lieutenant in the Royal Scots Greys and serving in the war.

In 1927 he retired from the Army owing to ill-health.

He is a keen yachtsman, and in 1930 won the endurance race organised by the Marine Motoring Association at Poole.

The Earl of Kingston, who lives at Kilronan Castle, Keadue, and Oakport, Boyle, Co. Roscommon, is the ninth earl and is a Deputy-Lieutenant for Co. Roscommon.

He served in South Africa in 1900 and 1902 and also served in the Great War, when he was wounded.

Viscount Kingsborough.

22nd April 1937

CLARK GABLE SAYS "I'M NO PAPA – GOT 2 WIVES TO PROVE IT"

FROM OUR OWN CORRESPONDENT

New York, Wednesday

CLARK Gable grinned at the reporters as he pushed his way through a clamouring horde of women fans outside Los Angeles court-house for the Norton trial to-day. "I'm no papa," he wise-cracked, "and I'll show you two wives to prove it."

In court his attorney announced that Gable's first wife, Josephine Dillon, and his second, Ria Langham, from whom he separated on a friendly footing in 1935, have offered to give evidence for him against forty-seven-year-old Violet Wells Norton, the Englishwoman who accused him of being father of her love-child in an Essex romance.

Women are rallying to their hero. This morning he got up to find a record mail. Rabbits' feet, sacred statues, lucky coins and psychic handkerchiefs poured in from admirers all over America as tokens of sympathy and good luck in the trial.

With them came letters begging Clark to wear the lucky symbols in court.

One girl sent him the first verse of Kipling's "If", which includes the lines: "If you can trust yourself when all men doubt you . . . or being lied about don't deal in lies . . ."

At the court house Clark sought refuge behind locked doors in a private room. His peace ended when Frau Deorfleur, a friend of the old days, got leave to enter with a band of Pressmen.

"He Was with Me"

"I'll do anything to help Clark," she cried.

"He's always been the swellest guy I know." She told reporters he couldn't have lived with Mrs. Norton in Essex, as is alleged, because at that time he happened to be with her.

Many men joined the throngs of women in court hoping to hear Mae West give evidence of a letter written by Mrs. Norton which said: "You will be surprised to know Gable is the father of my daughter Gwendoline, who looks exactly like him. Now, Miss West, would you be a fairy godmother to my girl and put Clark to shame?"

At the start of to-day's hearing the defence failed in a move for a directed verdict acquitting Mrs. Norton and Jack L. Smith, a private detective, who are accused of attempting to obtain money from Gable by fraud.

BACKSTORY

At the height of Hollywood's pre-war golden age, Clark Gable was one of the biggest stars, and – naturally – the subject of overwhelming attention and fascination. Crowds clamoured to see the outcome of the sensational court proceedings against Violet Wells Norton and Jack Smith, in which it was claimed Gable had fathered an English child called Gwendoline in 1922 and had been known, according to Wells Norton, as plain old Frank Billings.

Violet's performance in the Los Angeles witness box was a tour de force, veering from breathless sobbing to angry accusations. A letter to Gable was read out in court in which Norton had penned, "I give you my heart and mind. You've had my body." The jury found in Gable's favour, with the judge saying "There is no evidence to support [Violet Norton's] claim that Gable was ever in England, or ever knew her." She was found guilty of misuse of the mail but not of extortion and sentenced to a year in prison, before being deported.

◗ Clark Gable in less stressful times, teeing off at Newquay Golf Course in June 1952.

TUESDAY, NOVEMBER 23, 1937

Daily Mirror

No. 10600   Registered at the G.P.O. as a Newspaper.   ONE PENNY

TYPHOID MENACE SPREAD TO THREE NEW DISTRICTS LAST NIGHT

LABOUR STAFF "APPALLED" BY B.B.C. JOKE

THE B.B.C. has "appalled" the Ministry of Labour Staff Association. A comedian's wisecrack in last Saturday's Music Hall broadcast was the cause of it.

Mr. R. D. Crook, secretary, has written to tell the Corporation that the joke was of a type that gives offence to thousands, and he hopes that kind of thing will not be repeated.

Comedians "sought to obtain a laugh," he goes on, by referring to someone who fainted.

"What was expected to raise a laugh was the rejoinder—when the other comedian asked what made the person faint—that the person fainting had just been given a civil answer by a Labour Exchange clerk."

"A joke does not need to be based on fact if it is in good taste, but when it is in such thorough bad taste as this form of humour it is relevant to inquire as to the basis for such a false allegation."

Conduct of staffs at the exchanges, he adds, has been praised by successive Ministers of Labour and M.P.s of all political schools of thought.

A B.B.C. official said last night: "The letter will have the consideration of the B.B.C. when received."

£10,000 GIFT TO EMPLOYEES

A gift of £10,000, to be divided among their lower paid employees as their Christmas box, is announced by Messrs. Dorman, Long and Company, Ltd., Middlesbrough, "in recognition of the extremely good work they have done

★
Man Lost Off Liner Begged Her To Wed
★

"He asked me to marry him. I refused. He was always threatening to commit suicide, then he was lost overboard."

In these disjointed phrases, Mrs. Hedwig Self, German-born wife of a film artist, spoke at St. Pancras Station, London, yesterday, of her ordeal in the liner Llangibby Castle, from which Mr. Gervase Lambton, twenty-five-year-old cousin of the Earl of Durham, was lost overboard in the Red Sea while on his way to Kenya.

Mrs. Self, seen on arrival, was greeted at the station by her husband, Mr. Frederick George Self, London film "stunt" artist.

Before disappearing, Mr. Lambton left a note: "I have kept my promise sooner than you imagined. By the time you receive this I shall be in the sea."

CROYDON'S TYPHOID SCOURGE IS SPREADING. LAST NIGHT CASES WERE REPORTED FROM THE NEIGHBOURING AREAS OF WALLINGTON, PURLEY AND COULSDON.

TWELVE cases were reported to Coulsdon and Purley Council—residential district adjoining Croydon—and two of the victims have died.

Warning that more cases might increase in Croydon within the next few days has been given in a statement by the town clerk. But it was added that the incubation period would end then and the epidemic should wane.

Thirteen notifications of cases in Croydon within twenty-four hours brought the total to 149.

A sixth death was reported, but this was from para-typhoid, and the patient's symptoms appeared before the epidemic.

Last night came an announcement from Minister of Health Sir Kingsley Wood that the inquiry into the causes of the epidemic and steps taken to deal with it would take place "at an early date."

Mr. H. L. Murphy, K.C., will conduct it and assessors will be Sir Humphry Rolleston and Mr. H. J. F. Gourley.

Hospital Ready

First case in Wallington (Surrey)—a seven-and-a-half-year-old child, of Forester's-drive, and pupil at a private school in South Croydon—was sent to Wandle Valley Isolation Hospital yesterday.

Dr. P. J. O'Connell, medical officer of Wallington Borough Council, confirmed the case at last night's Council meeting, said he had made plans for the hospital to receive any fresh cases at once.

All the cases from the areas round Croydon resulted from contact made in Croydon with the polluted water.

As hundreds of people in the outside areas work in the borough, the neighbouring authorities are uneasy.

Islington has a suspected case. A boy of six is under observation in a London County Council isolation hospital.

Kensington reported another suspected case last night—a twelve-year-old girl named Newman, of Beecher-street. She is in the Western Fever Hospital.

Her father and mother have died of typhoid. Two other members of the family and a woman living in the same house are victims—the only cases reported in Kensington.

POLICE WATCH LOVERS COLLECT GIRL'S "BOTTOM DRAWER"

TWO police-sergeants walked up and down outside Mr. Alfred Scammell's house in Fairholme-crescent, Hayes (Middlesex), last night while his seventeen-year-old daughter, Edith, and her fiancé, collected belongings, which included part of the girl's "bottom drawer."

Under the eyes of the police the young lovers stacked the parcels in a car they had hired. Then Mr. Scammell made them write a list of the articles and sign for them.

Earlier in the day Mr. Scammell had been ordered by Uxbridge magistrates to return the young lovers their property.

Edith told the Court that after she had left home for lodgings, she and her fiancé, twenty-year-old Sidney Smith went back for their possessions.

"My father asked me where I had been, and said I had no right to leave home," said Edith. "I refused to answer him, and he ordered my young man out of the house."

The Chairman: Your father has every right to know why you left home.

"I am quite old enough to know my own mind" . . . seventeen-year-old Edith Scammell, in Uxbridge, with her fiancé, Sidney Smith, yesterday.

IN HIS OWN AMBULANCE

The ambulance he usually drives took Fireman Hanson, of Central Station, Hounslow, to Hounslow Hospital yesterday, critically injured by a fall down the station coal-shaft.

LOST GIRL THEORY

The mother of fifteen-year-old Violet Cook, factory girl, of Shillington-street, Battersea, S.W., who has been missing from home since last Friday, believes that her daughter has eloped.

"All her prettiest frocks are missing from her wardrobe." Mrs. Cook told the Daily Mirror yesterday.

SOVIET ARCHBISHOP FACES FIRING SQUAD

FROM OUR OWN CORRESPONDENT
WARSAW, Monday.

TWENTY-TWO high priests of the Russian Orthodox Church have been sentenced to death for treason by the military court of Oriel, a big city in Central Russia, 300 miles from Moscow.

Ten of the priests were executed and the remainder are awaiting death in their cells, found guilty of plotting against Stalin and the State.

Among the sentenced were the aged Archbishop of Central Russia, two bishops and six canons.

A last-hour attempt is being made to save the Archbishop and the surviving priests from the firing squad.

All day Archbishop Dionisys, of the Orthodox Church in Poland, has been telephoning to the head of the Rumanian Orthodox Church in Bukarest to secure "joint diplomatic efforts of Poland and Rumania" on behalf of the condemned Archbishop.

It was reported in Warsaw to-night that King Carol himself may be induced to join in the appeal to Stalin.

According to Exchange the Soviet paper, Izvestia, reports that three Archbishops are among the clergy exposed as "agents of Fascist States" plotting terroristic acts.

23rd November 1937

TYPHOID MENACE SPREAD TO THREE NEW DISTRICTS LAST NIGHT

CROYDON'S TYPHOID SCOURGE IS SPREADING. LAST NIGHT CASES WERE REPORTED FROM THE NEIGHBOURING AREAS OF WALLINGTON, PURLEY AND COULSDON.

TWELVE cases were reported to Coulsdon and Purley Council – a residential district adjoining Croydon – and two of the victims have died.

Warning that more cases might increase in Croydon within the next few days has been given in a statement by the town clerk. But it was added that the incubation period would end then and the epidemic should wane.

Thirteen notifications of cases in Croydon within twenty-four hours brought the total to 149.

A sixth death was reported, but this was from para-typhoid, and the patient's symptoms appeared before the epidemic.

Last night came an announcement from Minister of Health Sir Kingsley Wood that the inquiry into the causes of the epidemic and steps taken to deal with it would take place "at an early date."

Mr. H. L. Murphy, K.C., will conduct it and assessors will be Sir Humphry Rolleston and Mr. H. J. F. Gourley.

Hospital Ready
First case in Wallington (Surrey) – a seven-and-a-half-year-old child, of Forester's-drive, and pupil at a private school in South Croydon – was sent to Wandle Valley Isolation Hospital yesterday.

Dr. P. J. O'Connell, medical officer of Wallington Borough Council, confirmed the case at last night's Council meeting, and said he had made plans for the hospital to receive any fresh cases at once.

All the cases from the areas round Croydon resulted from contact made in Croydon with the polluted water.

As hundreds of people in the outside areas work in the borough, the neighbouring authorities are uneasy.

Islington has a suspected case. A boy of six is under observation in a London County Council isolation hospital.

Kensington reported another suspected case last night – a twelve-year-old girl named Newman, of Becher-street. She is in the Western Fever Hospital.

Her father and mother have died of typhoid.

Two other members of the family and a woman living in the same house are victims – the only cases reported in Kensington.

24th November 1937

"Business and pleasure as usual" is the order in Croydon, although fourteen new notifications yesterday brought the total of typhoid cases to 163.

Death toll stands at six.
"The public may confidently continue to shop and take their amusements in Croydon," says a statement by the Town Clerk, Mr. E. Taberner, which has been posted outside shops and cinemas all over the district.

"The new cases now reported may have been infected three weeks ago," it is explained.

"Elementary precautions," however, are advised by the Town Clerk. He urges the utmost personal cleanliness, "especially when preparing or handling food before eating."

Meanwhile, Ministry of Health officials are working with the Corporation in an effort to track down every possible source of infection.

They are not satisfied that the well at Addington, supplying water to parts of South Croydon, is entirely to blame. Streams are being examined, watercress beds tested, and a thorough overhaul being made of every source of water supply.

Report of the bacteriological examination of Croydon water issued yesterday states that, as in earlier samples, the water is wholesome.

Yesterday's fourteen new cases – the highest day's total since last Thursday – were all in Croydon, and none are reported in the surrounding districts.

Dr. Somerville Hastings, chairman of Hospitals and Medical Services Committee of the London County Council, said yesterday that the incidence of typhoid in London has not been exceptional in the last few weeks.

There were always a few cases of the disease in London, but it had not assumed epidemic proportions . . .

A nurse with typhoid has been taken to Worcester Isolation Hospital. She went from Croydon on October 27 to nurse a private patient.

Kensington's total of cases remains at five but a daughter of Mr. and Mrs. Newman who died of typhoid last week, is suspected.

A case of typhoid – that of an adult – has been notified at a village near Folkestone. The Medical Officer of Health, Dr. D. MacDougall, said that the case had no connection with the Croydon outbreak.

Not Scared!
Watercress was used as a garnishing last night for one of the dishes at the City Livery Club's banquet at the Guildhall. Despite the broadcast reference to watercress in connection with the typhoid outbreak, it was left on very few plates.

BACKSTORY

The Croydon typhoid outbreak was a stark reminder that for all the advances in science and public health, killer diseases of the unsanitary past still posed a real threat in Britain well into the 20th century. The outbreak was eventually traced to a well in which construction work was taking place. One of the workers there was carrying the disease and there had been a lack of chlorination.

While typhoid cases were relatively common and the Croydon outbreak was not an epidemic, the seniority of the officials on the investigative enquiry illustrated the seriousness with which it was treated.

It was also not the last typhoid scare. As late as 1964, Aberdeen was hit by an outbreak – thankfully without fatalities – traced to an infected batch of tinned corned beef in a supermarket (above).

THURSDAY, NOVEMBER 3, 1938

Daily Mirror

FOR BRITAIN AND THE EMPIRE

No. 10893
Registered at the
G.P.O. as a
Newspaper.
ONE PENNY

LATE LONDON

SHELLED SHIP SINKS OFF NORFOLK COAST: FIVE CHILDREN AND MOTHERS ON BOARD

The Cantabria.

WHILE a crowd watched from the Norfolk shore, a Spanish cargo ship, with three women and five young children among the 45 people aboard, was yesterday shelled and wrecked by the guns of a Spanish Insurgent cruiser, ten miles off the English coast.

For three hours the guns of the cruiser flashed fire. Then the doomed cargo ship, riddled with gunshot, drifted away and foundered eight miles north of Cromer.

The captain's wife and two children were rescued by lifeboat, but the fate of the other children—one a baby of three months—is not yet known.

The Cromer lifeboatmen, who had watched the drama of the high seas as the windows of the coast houses rattled to the roar of the guns, launched their boat and hurried, unasked, to the rescue.

As they sailed, the boom of the guns faded and the explosions that had lit the afternoon mists died away.

Then, when night fell, Coxswain Bloggs—risen from a sickbed to lead the rescue —steered his boat to the derelict.

They found her to be the Cantabria. She was holed above and below water. She listed heavily to starboard.

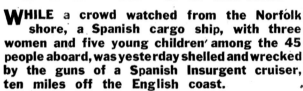

Sixty-two-year-old Coxswain Bloggs. . . . Hardly recovered from appendicitis, he took the Cromer lifeboat out to the rescue.

'In the Thames Next'

"The Spanish war comes nearer home," said Mr. Noel Baker in the Commons last night.

"A Spanish merchant ship on time charter to a British company has been attacked off Cromer by an insurgent trawler, said to be armed from Germany."

A member: "They'll be in the Thames next."

Mr. Baker voiced the suspicions of M.P.s of all parties who wondered why a Spanish ship was operating so far from home, who armed her, in what foreign port she sheltered.

But even as the raider opened fire, Mr. Chamberlain was telling the House: "My mind is clear that the Spanish question is no longer a menace to Europe."

As the shells tore great holes in her hull and swept away her deck-houses, the radio operator's wife carried her children to a cabin and lay on top of them to protect them. The cook's wife and baby daughter, aged three, were on board. They have not yet been found.

True to the traditions of the sea, the captain had refused to leave his sinking ship. And his wife chose to face death with him and their two children, rather than seek the safety of one of the ship's boats.

One member of the crew stayed with the stricken family.

"The woman and her children showed magnificent courage," Coxswain Bloggs said.

"One was a boy of six, the other his sister, aged eight. Their parents are middle-aged.

"For hours they had faced death by gunshot and fire, yet when we took them aboard I heard not a whimper from the children, saw not a sign of a tear in that brave woman's eyes.

"So exhausted were the youngsters that they curled up in the bottom of our boat and dropped off to sleep.

"The sinking ship must have been holed badly below water. Her list was so heavy that when we came alongside, her starboard rails were level with the lifeboat.

"It was too dark to see what damage she had suffered, but I reckon that she could not have lasted much more than an hour after we left her.

"**WE LIFTED THE LITTLE ONES OFF FIRST, THEN TOOK THEIR MOTHER ABOARD, THEN THE SAILOR. ONLY AFTER THAT WOULD THE SPANISH CAPTAIN ABANDON SHIP.**

"All this time the Spanish warship lay only two boatlengths away, but she made no attempt to hamper us.

"The rest of the crew had already left the ship when we arrived and the captain told me that some had been picked up by a British steamer."

Picked Up by Warship

"The others had taken off in one of the ship's boats and were picked up by the warship which had been bombarding them.

"When the captain came into our boat he made it clear that the last thing he wanted to do was to go near the cruiser. It seemed

(Continued on back page)

FISHING FLEET SURROUNDED THE RAIDER

A BRITISH fishing fleet operating on the scene of the Franco warship's raid tried to stop the attack on the Cantabria.

That dramatic incident in the North Sea shelling was revealed last night when rescued men were landed at Yarmouth.

"The attacking cruiser was an armed merchantman or passenger vessel," one sailor said, "and she steamed towards us in full view of the fishing fleet. When it was seen that she intended to attack us the drifters closed in with sirens shrieking.

Raider Armed in Germany

"The attacker drew off as the fishing fleet neared him, but some time later returned to the attack and opened fire.

"The first shell carried away part of the bridge. Then she opened up with her guns in earnest. Our hull was holed in four places, and we were lucky to escape with our lives."

Mr. C. L. Burbridge, director of Mid-Atlantic Shipping Company, Ltd., the London firm which has been acting as agents for cargo vessels taken over by the Spanish Government, said he had been told that the Nadir, the raiding ship, had been to Germany for arms, and was on her way back to Spain.

FAMILIES FLEE FROM FIRE

After an hour's fight to stop the spread of a factory fire in Gainsborough-road, Walthamstow, E., late last night, police told people in neighbouring streets to prepare to leave their homes.

Some families ran out in their nightclothes as flames shot up 40ft.

The fire, which at one time threatened a store of explosives, was extinguished at 1 a.m.

3rd November 1938

SHELLED SHIP SINKS OFF NORFOLK COAST

WHILE a crowd watched from the Norfolk shore a Spanish cargo ship, with three women and five young children among the 45 people aboard, was yesterday shelled and wrecked by the guns of a Spanish Insurgent cruiser, ten miles off the English coast.

For three hours the guns of the cruiser flashed fire. Then the doomed cargo ship, riddled with gunshot, drifted away and foundered eight miles north of Cromer.

The captain's wife and two children were rescued by lifeboat, but the fate of the other children – one a baby of three months – is not yet known.

The Cromer lifeboatmen, who had watched the drama of the high seas as the windows of the coast houses rattled to the roar of the guns, launched their boat and hurried, unasked, to the rescue.

As they sailed, the boom of the guns faded and the explosions that had lit the afternoon mists died away.

Then, when night fell, Coxswain Bloggs – risen from a sickbed to lead the rescue – steered his boat to the derelict.

She was holed above and below water. She listed heavily to starboard. As the shells tore great holes in her hull and swept away her deck-houses, the radio operator's wife carried her children to a cabin and lay on top of them to protect them. The cook's wife and baby daughter, aged three, were on board. They have not yet been traced.

True to the traditions of the sea the captain had refused to leave his sinking ship. And his wife chose to face death with him and their two children, rather than seek the safety of one of the ship's boats.

One member of the crew stayed with the stricken family.

"The woman and her children showed magnificent courage," Coxswain Bloggs said.

"One was a boy of six, the other his sister, aged eight. Their parents are middle-aged.

"For hours they had faced death by gunshot and fire, yet when we took them aboard I heard not a whimper from the children, saw not a sign of a tear in that brave woman's eyes.

"So exhausted were the youngsters that they curled up in the bottom of our boat and dropped off to sleep.

"The sinking ship must have been holed badly below water. Her list was so heavy that when we came alongside, her starboard rails were level with the lifeboat.

"It was too dark to see what damage she had suffered, but I reckon that she could not have lasted much more than an hour after we left her . . .

"All this time the Spanish warship lay only two boat lengths away, but she made no attempt to hamper us.

"The rest of the crew had already left the ship when we arrived and the captain told me that some had been picked up by a British steamer . . .

"When the captain came into our boat he made it clear that the last thing he wanted to do was to go near the cruiser. It seemed to be standing by waiting to see the last plunge of its victim.

"As we pulled back for Cromer – eight miles to the south-west – the last we saw of her was her masthead lights still burning.". . .

The captain is Manuel Arguelles. He said that the Cantabria came from Santander, and was chartered by the Mid-Atlantic Shipping Company, of London. She was bound from Immingham to London with a cargo of ballast.

"As we passed into the North Sea we noticed that we were being followed by what appeared to be an armed trawler.

"We kept on our course, but, without warning, the trawler suddenly opened a terrific bombardment. They were firing broadside on and my crew, with members of my family, making a total of forty-five, rushed to take cover on the other side of the ship.

"Shells were falling all round us. At least twenty shells fell near us or on the ship. Many of them hit the hull, and soon water was pouring in.

"We had wireless on board, and from the moment the armed trawler, which bore the name Nadir, began firing our operator kept sending SOS, SOS . . .

Captain Arguelles said that the warship, as far as he could see, carried about six guns, which were firing the whole time.

On board his ship, while the shells whined over him, the captain had been ordered by the raider to strike his flag.

"I will die first," he shouted back, and shook his fist at the warship. After three hours' shelling the cruiser spoke again, "Abandon your ship now or we sink you," came the cry.

Then Captain Arguelles knew that the Cantabria was doomed. He called together his crew, ordered them to leave.

As the crew took to the boats the captain, his wife Trinidad, their son Ramon, aged six, their daughter Veyona, aged eight, and a steward walked aft. Then the Cromer lifeboat was seen approaching.

The captain's little girl, who would not leave her father's side, said in Spanish when she came ashore: "Thank you brave English sailors for rescuing us. Thank you very much for saving my daddy and my mammy.". .

◀ The SS *Pattersonian*. This ship and her crew played a brave and key role in the rescue of the *Cantabria*'s crew.

BACKSTORY

The Spanish Civil War came close to British shores in 1938, in the shape of the extraordinary attack on the Republican-controlled *Cantabria*. The vessel had been impounded earlier in the year with the Nationalist leader, General Franco, contesting but then losing the case to gain the ship. He vowed to either capture or sink her – and his threat was carried out off the coast of Cromer.

THE FORGOTTEN WAR

The Second World War produced hundreds of unforgettable narratives, thousands of well-known events and countless individual tales. There were also the stories that were briefly front-page news, but were soon overshadowed by even more momentous, history-shaping days, and subsequently neglected.

Here are a just a small selection of the Second World War reports that have, for a variety of reasons, not been quite as well remembered as others.

In the early months of the conflict the British Expeditionary Force was back on the continent – and some people found their jokes too saucy.

As the *Mirror*'s Bernard Gray reported, "A popular broadcaster sang a song called 'Dirty Songs,' [and] put it over so well that the troops nearly brought the place down with their cheers. Some people complained."

Laughs would soon be in short supply, however. Many of those troops admonished for their sense of humour would be laying down their lives or facing mortal danger at Dunkirk (below).

It wasn't all bravery and a feeling of "we're all in this together", however. Across bomb-shattered cities, there was the scourge of looting. The problem was so serious that the *Mirror* called for offenders to be hanged. The report also cited a war reserve policeman who had been caught stealing from the home of a dead Blitz victim who he was supposed to have been protecting from looters.

There was similar outrage over abuses of the rationing system. The *Mirror*'s star writer and columnist Cassandra investigated the scandal of how there came to be plenty of high-quality, meat-based delicacies available – as long as an individual had the money to pay for it.

This astonishing, evocative image illustrates the bravery, determination and sheer stoicism of ordinary British people in standing up to the terror of war. In an unnamed Kent village (place names were often censored), an ARP warden, Mrs Mary Couchman, sprang into action to protect her children, including her young son Brian, as bombs fell close by. A *Mirror* photographer was on hand to capture the scene. "You are a brave woman," he said to Mrs Couchman. "Oh, it was nothing. Somebody had to look after the children," she replied.

◀ On the day of a great triumph for Allied forces in North Africa, in January 1941 back home the government was shutting down the left-wing newspaper the *Daily Worker*. While police officers were ordering staff to literally stop the presses, the authorities were suppressing the newspaper and a sister magazine, claiming they "systematically publish matter calculated to foment opposition to successful prosecution of the war."

▶ October 1942 saw the remarkable story of two British soldiers reported missing after Dunkirk. They escaped from a Nazi prison camp in France and walked 1,600 miles in freezing weather through Belgium, Holland, Germany and Poland to reach safety in Russia.

One of them, Sgt Louis Massey, was pictured in Moscow with a Russian soldier.

▶ The war provided remarkable stories of personal sacrifice in the face of dreadful suffering. Lady Rachel Workman MacRobert of Aberdeenshire had lost three pilot sons. The eldest, Sir Alastair, had been killed before the war in a flying accident. Sir Roderick was killed in action in the Middle East, just a month before Sir Iain was reported missing. In tribute to them, Lady MacRobert donated £25,000 to launch a Stirling bomber to be named *MacRobert's Reply*.

"I have no more sons to carry on the fight," said Lady MacRobert, "but I want to make a mother's reply, attacking in the way my boys would have attacked – sharply, straight to the mark . . . I give you £25,000 to buy a bomber to carry on their work."

To this day, the RAF still flies an aircraft that carries the name *MacRobert's Reply*.

◀ Over 70 years on, the report of eight-year-old Tommy Wakenshaw receiving the Victoria Cross on his dead father's behalf is still immensely moving.

Private Adam Wakenshaw, of the Durham Light Infantry, died winning his VC in Egypt. Despite losing an arm and being in terrible pain, Private Wakenshaw continued to fire an anti-tank gun alongside Private Eric Moñ, who was soon killed. Wakenshaw was injured again yet somehow managed to fight on until he was killed by a direct hit. When the combat died down, he was later found stretched beside the ammunition box, still at his post.

The story moved the nation. The *Mirror* reported that Tommy and his mother Dorothy, brother Joñ and sister Lilian lived in a hard-up area of Newcastle, and they received donations to move into a new furnished home.

The Wakenshaw family story came on the day after the Betñal Green Tube Disaster, in which 173 people died. They were caught up in a crush during an air raid as people tried to get into the station, which was being used as a deep shelter. Censorship prevented this tragedy being reported until two years later.

Daily Mirror ...

HUNS EXPECT US TO INVADE NEXT WEEK

To wed man she has never seen

WHILE THE NAZI AIR BASES IN OCCUPIED TERRITORY WERE BEING BOMBED AT THE RATE OF ONE EVERY THREE HOURS, GERMAN RADIO DECLARED LAST NIGHT "EVERYTHING IS READY FOR THE ALLIED INVASION ZERO HOUR NEXT WEEK."

AIR BLITZ MAY HAVE CUT ITALY IN HALF

Couple—93, 86—quarrel over bacon

DUTCH BOMB HOLLAND AND FRENCH FRANCE ON 6TH DAY OF BIG ATTACK

Chocolate saves soldier

Wartime paint for essential work

Goebbels admits crisis after crisis, attacks 'raid cowards'

TERMS: ROME FISHING?

CADBURY means QUALITY

▶ A strange tale of divorce proceedings caused by bacon. Mrs Frances Lush, aged 86, of Leigh-on-Sea, Essex, wanted to split from her husband, James Lush, aged 83, after a row about the poor quality bacon he had brought home.

The *Mirror* reported that Mr Lush was deaf.

▶ Miss Amelia King was a 26-year-old Londoner who had volunteered for the Women's Land Army but was barred because she was, as the *Mirror* put it, "coloured".

The Women's Land Army denied to the *Mirror* they had imposed a colour bar, and blamed farmers who refused to "take coloured girls".

The issue was raised in the House of Commons. Miss King's father was in the Merchant Navy and her brother was serving in the Royal Navy. Amelia's own determination to serve was eventually rewarded when she was offered work on a farm, but she successfully insisted it was officially organised by the Land Army.

Daily Mirror ...

5TH IN SIGHT OF DYING CITY OF NAPLES

Slav troops fight Huns in Trieste

BIG NEW SOVIET GAINS AT THREE KEY POINTS: ONLY TEN MILES FROM SMOLENSK

Giraud feted in Corsica

ELECTIONS HITCH

Doctors' attack on medical officers

BECAUSE SHE'S COLOURED

WLA accuses farmers of imposing bar

FRY'S Makers of Good Chocolate

◀ The extraordinary story of merchant sailor Poon Lim was one of the most astonishing feats of human survival, yet in the midst of a raging global conflict received only scant attention in the newspaper:

"Chinese seaman Poon Lim who, after his ship had been torpedoed, spent 133 days on a raft – a record – arrived yesterday at a Scottish port, but at first refused to talk about his experiences till he had told them to the King.

"He is going to Buckingham Palace shortly to receive the British Empire Medal, and he felt it would be discourteous to tell his story beforehand. Ministry of War Transport officials who welcomed Poon Lim were nonplussed.

"After they had persuaded him that they were representatives of the King he talked a little. But it was only after he had gone to Glasgow and had been greeted by Lord Provost Welsh."

Lim had survived a U-boat attack on the SS *Benlomond* by eating fish and seabirds, and drinking rainwater, before being rescued by fishermen off the coast of Brazil.

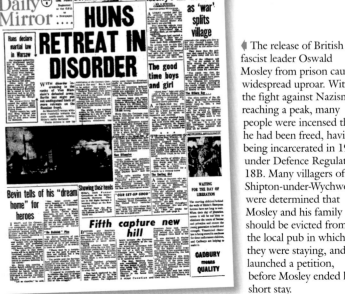

OCTOBER 20, 1943

Page 5

PRINCESS
ugh?
estion

MADAME SWEEP

'Married' a dying widow 'to make last days happy'

Poon Lim's sealed lips
By FIORA

I. SCHMIDT W THE ULT

Referee jibbed at his job!

Champagne and oysters in divorce suit story

FOOD FACTS

HOUSEHOLD MILK DRIED EGGS ONIONS

POINTS CHANGES

Daily Mirror ....

Berlin: Further back yet

Mosley's inn 'bombed' as 'war' splits village

Huns declare martial law in Warsaw

HUNS RETREAT IN DISORDER

WITH disorder growing in the crossing of the ranks of the Warstain's defeated army, Berlin last night declared martial law and underlined limits of more retreats on the Russian front.

The good time boys and girl

Bevin tells of his "dream home" for heroes

Showing their heels

Fifth capture new hill

ONIONS for WINTER

WAITING FOR THE DAY OF LIBERATION

CADBURY means QUALITY

◀ The release of British fascist leader Oswald Mosley from prison caused widespread uproar. With the fight against Nazism reaching a peak, many people were incensed that he had been freed, having being incarcerated in 1940 under Defence Regulation 18B. Many villagers of Shipton-under-Wychwood were determined that Mosley and his family should be evicted from the local pub in which they were staying, and launched a petition, before Mosley ended his short stay.

On 5th June 1944 the American Fifth Army took one of the major European capitals. It was a milestone in the war – a vivid symbol that the fascist and Nazi domination of Europe was coming to an end. But just hours later the Allies launched the massive land, air and sea invasion of Normandy – D-Day – and the battle for Italy was knocked off the headlines.

A French bomber attacks the Piteccio Viaduct in central Italy, cutting the Nazi supply lines in 1944.

As Britain readied itself for the post-war era and the general election that was to transform the country, one much-despised villain was about to face his comeuppance.

William Joyce, aka the infamous Lord Haw-Haw, who had been loathed for his traitorous radio broadcasts from Germany, was cornered and captured as he attempted to cross the German–Danish border. Joyce (below first left, next to Oswald Mosley) had been a leading British fascist before the war.

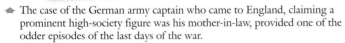

The case of the German army captain who came to England, claiming a prominent high-society figure was his mother-in-law, provided one of the odder episodes of the last days of the war.

"Captain Klaus" claimed he was married to Jacqueline de Broglie, daughter of the socialite and fashion icon Daisy Fellowes, who was good friends with the Duke (formerly King Edward VIII) and Duchess of Windsor.

With the war at last over, it was revealed that Hitler had intended to use the power of the sun as a new terror weapon. German scientists were said to have been planning to install huge reflectors on platforms 5,000 miles above the Earth, and to then focus the sun's beam onto a specific target, thus vaporizing it in intense heat.

One small problem: space travel was to elude mankind for a generation yet.

CHAPTER THREE

IT WILL BE A LONG MARRIAGE

Elizabeth Taylor, a glamorous young superstar ideal for a new, forward-looking post-war age. She is pictured here arriving at London Airport and was accompanied by her second husband Michael Wilding (see page 108).

e to
ett
ut'

, the Prime
erday—and

minutes to
ree wickets.

nap'
e

ATOM SCIENTISTS MAY TURN BRITAIN INTO A LAND OF SUNSHINE

"Daily Mirror" Reporter

PRODUCTION of the atomic bomb may bring Britain warm and sunny weather, lead to the discovery of new continents under the Polar ice, revolutionise human life at home and at work.

BUT—all that won't come for a long time, Sir John Anderson warned last night. There is a huge amount of scientific work to be done, and so far no work worth mentioning has been carried out on the invention for peace purposes.

Sir John suggested that the cost of using the discovery in peace might be prohibitive—£500,000,000 was spent in four years' research.

But it was pointed out last night that this was the cost to the United States for nine days of war against Japan.

When, however, science has harnessed the new discovery to the needs of peace here are some of the things that may happen:

Weather.—Our climate could be made warm and sunny.

Clouds over the experimental station in America where the first atom-bomb exploded just vanished in the heat of the explosion.

The dull, grey clouds over England could be dispersed by a similar controlled emission of heat.

Land.—New warm continents may be opened up in the Arctic and the Antarctic.

Using the enormous heat given out by exploding atoms, countries possessing ice-covered territories may be able to melt the thick ice which makes these areas uninhabitable.

Rich mineral deposits in the Arctic could then be worked, large areas there and in Siberia made habitable.

Homes.—Electricity will still heat and light our homes. But dynamos making the electricity would be run at a fraction of present cost by atomic power units, or turbines fed with steam from atomically-heated boilers.

Labour.—There would be less toil for hundreds of thousands of miners, transport workers, dockers.

Transport.—Quicker and cheaper.

Coal and Petrol.—As obsolete as charcoal.

Petrol Engines.—Will be superseded by small high-powered atomic engines.

Industry.—Readjusted to use the new labour-saving energy to the best advantage.

Ships.—Gigantic liners could be built to run on atomic energy.

Aeroplanes. — Designers will work out plans for huge plywood or plastic planes, capable of carrying thousands of passengers. Weight of engines and fuel will be negligible. These aeroplanes will weigh less than modern all-metal planes. Jet propulsion will be boosted by the new discovery

Motor Cars. — The future motor car designer will not now have to take into account the weight of the engine. More comfortable and roomier cars can be built.

Navy barracks "like prisons"

THE British sailor in barracks in the Far East feels like a convict or a pauper, according to the Pacific Fleet's official organ, *Pacific Post.*

"Take away the atmosphere of prisons and workhouses, and build barracks bright, so the sailors can take pride in making them their home," says the paper.

"And for heaven's sake let us have modern laundries, galleys, decent rest rooms, decent writing rooms, bigger libraries

Bomb brought villa folk close to death

"Daily Mirror" Reporter

LITTLE did the people living in the small suburban villas surrounding the National Physical Laboratory at Teddington realise the extent of the scientific research taking place behind the high brick walls.

Least of all did they know that, at one stage in the experiments which led to the final creation of the atomic bomb, they might all have been blown sky high.

Like a College

Something like a collection of small factories surrounding a country mansion; something like a college; something like a public garden with an abundant display of flowers and green lawns—that was one of the places concerned in the first experiments.

Sir Charles Darwin, director of the laboratory, the man who played a leading role in the discovery, has a small, modest room in one building.

Both these children were "in court" yesterday—two-year-old Patricia Barney (left) and her sister Joyce, aged nine. At North London Police Court 22-year-old Elsie Wright was sent for trial charged with unlawfully taking Patricia away.

It was stated that the woman had a daughter named Pat, who was living with her husband, from whom she was separated. The prosecution allege that after bigamously marrying another man she told him she would fetch her own Pat—but instead she brought Pat Barney.

McAVOY'S K.O. WIN

Jock McAvoy knocked out Johnnie Clements, Scottish middle-weight contender in the sixth round at Portsmouth.

Vince Hawkins beat Corporal Tommy Jones (Derby) on points.

ER

r

fiancee were
e roof of a
g the prizes.

?

bit of luck it
er of Gordon
ys at New-
tes Bouverie.
ng for him to
Leger filly,
alencay, Fair-
Tresa all
particularly
o showed fine
at the last

me Valencay
f there is a
thorn's race
the one to
lections —

2.0, Naishapur
Ponte Tresa
armugant f.
LE: 'Ponte

Minister's home is still 'No. 36'

"Daily Mirror" Reporter

SIX steps down from a leafy country road, at the end of a marigold-bordered footpath, stands No. 36, Tan-y-coed—a house no different from 209 houses that make up the garden suburb of Burry Port, Carmarthenshire.

But it's a show place just the same.

For behind its dinky curtains and cream cement washed walls lives Jim Griffiths, Llanelly's Member of Parliament and Britain's new Minister of National Insurance.

At least, it's the place they point out as the house Jim Griffiths lives in. But ask his tall, pleasant wife and she'll murmur:

"Well, you can hardly say Jim 'lives' here. 'Stays,' or 'pops in' would be better. And goodness knows how often I'm going to see him from now on."

Jim—no one dreams of calling him Mr. Griffiths—hasn't the least idea either but he means to go there from London as often as he can, though it means six hours in a train and more often than not a mile walk from the station after midnight.

There's a constant procession of callers—miners, steel workers, Servicemen's families—when Jim's at No. 36.

When they come tall, 50-year-old Mrs. Winifred Griffiths shuts the little study door on them and slips into her speckless kitchen to wonder if the rations will squeeze out another cup of tea.

"We don't get much time to ourselves, but we've got used to that now," she told me.

"Been in Parliament since 1936," says husband Jim, throwing her an affectionate glance. "We certainly should be used to it by now, m'dear.

"For the last year how many week-ends have we had together? Twenty? Yes, about that. Just twenty. Not many, is it?"

They've lived in No. 36 for nine years now and they don't intend moving.

"We shan't leave," says Jim's wife. "We pay rent like everybody else. We all own a small share in our houses. There are 210 altogether belonging to the Welsh Housing Trust Garden Suburb. Dear me, we should be lost if we had to move, wouldn't we, Jim?"

"Move? No fear," says Jim. "We've got our roots here, right among the people.

"Lots To Do"

"And what with Rugby at Stradey Park on Saturday afternoons—been missing it lately—and walking with Win up the mountain or down on the strip of beach or to the pictures in the village, we find lots to do."

Mrs. Griffiths runs her simply furnished eight-roomed house single handed, cooks, sews and darns for herself and Sheila, 17, and Arthur, 13½, both at Llanelly County School, and nurses her eighty-year-old mother, lying ill in the front bedroom.

Another son, Harold, he's nineteen-and-a-half, is training with the RAF in Canada.

When he sets off to catch the London train Jim's wife packs a few sandwiches and some of her currant cakes for him to eat on the train.

"Win's packet of sandwiches always reminds me of my pit days," says the new fifty - four - year - old Minister with the £5,000 salary. "Sixteen years I had at Ammanford Anthracite carrying a box and jack.

"Sixteen years—and I was very lucky to get through without a scratch. One of my brothers, we were ten children

altogether, was killed in a pit explosion."

Mrs. Griffiths remembers, too. "I was a miner's wife for two years before Jim went to the Labour College in London," she says.

"He came back and had another year underground—and since then he's been a traveller."

Ask her what she thinks of her husband's steady climb up the ladder and she'll smile with quiet pride—"Well, he seems to know what he's about, and people seem to think a good deal of him. But he's just Jim to me and to everybody else around here."

—and the cake ea

Tea-time at No. 36, Tan-y-coed. Cream sandwich and, of course, the fair... the oven. Jim Griffiths (on left) emphasises a point. His audience lis...

MYSTERY SOLDIER FELT GUILTY

MYSTERY soldier found shot dead at Keele Hall Camp, North Staffordshire, had a guilty conscience, witnesses said at yesterday's inquest.

Although a Russian—he was called "Russo"—the mystery man teamed up with Cypriots and told them he had committed a murder in Russia and was afraid to go back.

Inquest was adjourned to a date not yet fixed.

8th August 1945

ATOMIC SCIENTISTS MAY TURN BRITAIN INTO LAND OF SUNSHINE

PRODUCTION of the atomic bomb may bring Britain warm and sunny weather, lead to the discovery of new continents under the Polar ice, and revolutionise human life at home and at work.

BUT – all that won't come "for a long time", Sir John Anderson warned last night. There is a huge amount of scientific work to be done, and so far no work worth mentioning has been carried out on the invention for peace purposes.

Sir John suggested that the cost of using the discovery in peace might be prohibitive – £500,000,000 was spent in four years' research.

But it was pointed out last night that this was the cost to the United States for nine days of war against Japan.

When, however, science has harnessed the new discovery to the needs of peace here are some of the things that may happen . . .

Weather – Our climate could be made warm and sunny. Clouds over the experimental station in America where the first atom-bomb exploded just vanished in the heat of the explosion.

The dull, grey clouds over England could be dispersed by a similar controlled emission of heat.

Land – New warm continents may be opened up in the Arctic and the Antarctic.

Using the enormous heat given out by exploding atoms, countries possessing ice-covered territories may be able to melt the thick ice, which makes these areas linkable.

Rich mineral deposits in the Arctic could then be worked. Large areas there and in Siberia habitable.

Electricity will still heat and light our homes. But dynamos making the electricity would run at a fraction of present cost by atomic power units or turbines fed with steam from atomically-heated boilers.

Labour – There would be less toil for hundreds of thousands of miners, transport workers, dockers.

Transport – Quicker and cheaper.

Coal and Petrol – As obsolete as charcoal.

Petrol Engines – Will be superseded by small high-powered atomic engines.

Industry – Re-adjusted to use the new labour-saving energy to the best advantage.

Ships – Gigantic liners could be built to run on atomic energy.

Aeroplanes – Designers will work out plans for huge plywood or plastic planes, capable of carrying thousands of passengers.

Weight of engines and fuel will be negligible. These aeroplanes will weigh less than modern all-metal planes. Jet propulsion will be boosted by the new discovery.

Motor Cars – The future motor car designer will not now have to take into account the weight of the engine. More comfortable and roomier cars can be built.

BACKSTORY

The nuclear age heralded an era of great promise, but also one of fear. While petrol wasn't quite made as redundant as charcoal, and the skies over Britain remained resolutely grey, nuclear power did make significant inroads in electricity production.

With the detonation of atomic bombs that same August over Hiroshima and Nagasaki, however, the terrifying prospect of nuclear Armageddon became a terrifying reality.

Daily Mirror

SAT., APRIL 19

WEATHER

Mainly cloudy; bright intervals. OUTLOOK: Mainly fair.

2 mothers at bed of girl bitten by snake

AFTER police had searched for her, the mother of Ann Price, six-year-old Bridgend (Glamorgan) girl who was bitten by an adder, was located at Exeter and was last night at her child's bedside in a Bridgend hospital.

Ann, who was severely bitten in the leg, was still ill, though her condition showed a slight improvement.

With the arrival of her mother, Ann had two "mothers" at the hospital, for Mrs. Emily Nelson, of New-road, Pencoed, near Bridgend, who has been looking after Ann and her sisters, Avril, eight, and Julia, five, was there, too.

The children were taken out of their mother's care by Court order and were entrusted to Mrs. Nelson three years ago.

As she left the ward Ann's mother, who said she had remarried since she lost her husband in the Army during the war, said her name was now Mrs. Winifred Dilworth, of Exeter.

"Ann is my child and I am going to stay at the hospital with her until she gets better," she declared.

Ann got the bite while walking home from school.

Doctors have used anti-snake serum, for which an S O S was broadcast on Thursday.

DIAMOND GIFT

Princess Elizabeth was presented with a six-carat diamond worth £1,500 when she visited the diamond town of Kimberley yesterday. Princess Margaret received one valued at £1,000.

4 FOUND ALIVE IN BLAST CITY

FIREMEN in asbestos suits got into the Monsanto chemical factory in shattered Texas City for the first time last night, forty-eight hours after the explosion, and found four girls still alive.

Washington has demanded an immediate Congress inquiry into the disaster because of "high international tension."

Death-roll so far is 400, with 3,000 hurt. Damage is £7,000,000 . . . and oil is still blazing.

The King has sent a message to President Truman, expressing the deep sorrow of the Queen and himself at the catastrophe.

"May I express through you the horror which this tragic disaster has evoked in my people and their wholehearted sympathy towards all those affected," says the message.

Labour control on miners, farm workers, to go

BY the end of the year the last war-time labour controls will have gone.

Yesterday, the Prime Minister met executive members of the National Union of Mineworkers and agreed to lift the Control of Engagements Order from the mining industry.

It is left to the N.U.M. and the National Coal Board to discuss the most convenient time. Lifting of the control means that miners will be free to leave the industry when they wish.

The miners are to have representation of Government committees responsible for developing machinery for the mines, following talks with Mr. Attlee.

It is understood that by the end of the year workers in agriculture, too, will be freed from restriction.

THE NAVY PAYS AN ACCOUNT

The fortress of Heligoland, in the North Sea—major nuisance to the British Navy in two great wars—was blown up by the Navy yesterday. The picture shows the effects as 6,700 tons of T.N.T. wrecked the island's military installations, underground forts and submarine pens—everything the R.A.F.'s bombs couldn't reach during the war.

Class may tell in Esher Cup at Sandown

By BOUVERIE

BAD luck contributed to Saravan's defeat in the Free Handicap, and in choosing another "class" horse in Nebuchadnezzar for Sandown's Esher Cup I am hoping for better fortune for to-day's topweight.

Fine Prospect, with Gosling claiming the allowance, Lucky Bag, Red Flag and Anatolia are all favourably mentioned, and Super is expected to win soon. Fine Prospect seems the one for a place.

Richest two-year-old prize of the season to date, the Stud Produce Stakes, attracts several

youngsters with reputations of being more than "useful." Among them are Long Ago, Straight Play and Masala, and in choosing Long Ago I do so in the belief that she will pay to follow even if failing here.

Scotland's Grand National at Bogside may be fought out between Musical Lad, Rowland Roy and Silver Fame. My preference is for the last-named.

Coloured School Boy, ridden this time by J. Moloney, and Lovely Cottage, will also be in the field to make it a first-class race.

WINNERS AND S.P. AT THREE MEETINGS

MARSHMALLOW—THIRD TIME UNLUCKY

By NEWSBOY

MARSHMALLOW, who had won his two previous races this season, was expected to make it a three-timer by taking the Tudor Stakes at Sandown Park yesterday. He failed—by a neck.

Refresher obtained first run on Marshmallow, but the latter ran on again near the post, and was only narrowly beaten.

Relique, third in this race, is a good type, and will show great improvement.

Edward Tudor won the valuable Twickenham Stakes much easier than the official verdict of a neck indicates. Gordon Richards was last on this good horse turning into the straight, but he brought him on the outside and was only cantering when Patter put in a quick challenge.

Richards had to get Edward Tudor going again very quickly to stave off defeat.

Quatrain, the French challenger, never looked likely to win throughout the last halfmile.

Edward Tudor unseated

Gordon Richards in the paddock and he received a knock on the head, but was able to ride the winner of the following race.

Stockade, like Edward Tudor, was badly in need of a race, but this did not stop the son of Big Game completing a double for Mrs. Macdonald-Buchanan. F. Darling and G. Richards.

The Athlone Handicap provided Gordon Richards with his third winner of the day when old Sugar Palm got up in the last few strides to beat Magrew and William Tell.

BIG RACE PRICES

USELESS EUSTACE

"I know I'm incompetent, sir, that's why I work twice as 'ard when you don't know 'ow to do it."

Printed and Published by the DAILY MIRROR NEWSPAPERS Ltd at Geraldine House, Rolls Bldgs Fetter-lane. London E.C.4 —Saturday. April 19, 1947 Tel Holborn 4321

104

17th–19th April 1947

IF YOU HEAR THE BANG DROP THEM A LINE

TOMORROW the biggest bang since the atom bomb blasted Bikini is due to take place – and the Air Ministry would like anybody in Britain who hears it to tell them.

The island fortifications of Heligoland, the former German North Sea naval base, are being blown up at 1 p.m.

A sound wave through the high atmosphere is expected to reach Britain about half an hour after the explosion.

Reports should be made on a postcard to the Director (M.0. 15), Meteorological Office, Air Ministry, Kingsway, London, W.C.2, and, should state the place and time and the nature of the sound heard.

Lieutenant-Commander Francis Mildred, 43, of Stamford Hill, London, stands by the button aboard H.M. cable-laying ship *Lasso*, anchored nine miles from Heligoland.

If mist does not cause a postponement of the plans, he will press it at the fourth pip of the B.B.C.'s one o'clock time signal today – and 6,000 tons of explosives will blow up the fortified island's 130 acres in the biggest bang since the Bikini atom test.

People on the German coast thirty miles away have been warned not to come into the open.

THE NAVY PAYS AN ACCOUNT

The fortress of Heligoland, in the North Sea – major nuisance to the British Navy in two great wars – was blown up by the Navy yesterday. The picture shows the effects as 6,700 tons of T.N.T. wrecked the island's military installations, underground forts and submarine pens – everything the RAF's bombs couldn't reach during the war.

▶ Unexploded bombs plagued the post-war world and continue to show up even today.

BACKSTORY

The strategic island of Heligoland, a tiny archipelago 29 miles off the German coast, was a thorn in the side of the Allies during the Second World War. Once a territory of Britain, it provided the Nazis with a base bristling with defences that remained all but impervious through the conflict.

Two years later, the Royal Navy finally got its revenge, smashing the main island to pieces, and in the process causing the destruction of many homes – much to the islanders' lasting resentment. Even today, there are still unexploded bombs, a legacy of the heavy air raids.

Daily Mirror

MON MAY 8 1950

ONE PENNY

No. 14,459

Registered at G.P.O. as a Newspaper.

FORWARD WITH THE PEOPLE

It will be a long and happy marriage, says Elizabeth Taylor

—'WE BOTH ADORE OVERSIZE SWEATERS AND HAMBURGERS'

AFTER her £20,000 Hollywood wedding fit for a princess, English-born film star, Elizabeth Taylor, 18, told a thousand champagne-sipping guests why her marriage to her third fiance, Conrad Nick Hilton, 23, heir to a £44,000,000 hotel fortune, would be "long and happy."

"We both adore oversize sweaters and hamburgers with onions," she said.

Then the couple slipped away on a private plane to a secret hide-out where they are honeymooning before beginning a three-month European trip (cables Stan Mays).

Radiant and poised before 3,000 onlookers, Elizabeth walked down the aisle of the Beverly Hills church one step behind her art-dealer father, instead of on his arm.

That gave the guests on both sides a good view of the £1,200 wedding dress of twenty yards of white satin. It was a last-minute idea by a Press agent, hailed by the studio as "brilliant."

After Nick had slipped a £3,500 platinum ring studded with diamonds on his bride's finger he kissed her for five seconds. Then Elizabeth flung her arms round Nick and hugged him.

Scores of screen celebrities in the audience tittered, but the front pew, filled with Metro-Goldwyn-Mayer directors, shush-shushed for silence as the battery of studio cameramen ground away. FOR THE STUDIO WAS PAYING FOR EVERY PENNY OF IT.

As the couple marched down the aisle, Elizabeth paused to kiss her father and mother.

In the crowd outside the church was an English girl "fan," Miss Rose Goldigg, of Leeds, who said she waited five hours for the wedding procession.

Three dining rooms of a country club were taken over for the reception. Each room featured as a centre-piece a symbolic statue carved from ice, depicting two kissing doves and a replica of the wedding church.

Elizabeth and Nick after the wedding.

'BIG 3' WILL DRAW PLAN TO HALT RUSSIA

By BILL GREIG

FIVE big problems will face the Foreign Ministers of Britain, France and the United States when they meet in London this week in an effort to hammer out a "united front" economic and foreign policy:

1 Getting the initiative back from Russia, both in Europe and the Far East.

Mr. Dean Acheson, U.S. Secretary of State, believes the Western Powers have been reduced to countering Russia's moves rather than forestalling them.

2 The problem of Berlin. Russia is stiffening up the pressure on Berlin from Eastern Germany. An answer to this must be found.

3 The problem of re-creating Germany as a nation capable of taking her full place in the economic life of Europe.

The Occupation Statute must be revised soon and the Ministers must decide how far they can go.

4 The Far East. How can the Western Powers help to buttress the countries now threatened by Communism?

5 The deadlock over China now threatening to wreck the United Nations.

Mr Acheson who is already in Paris sees M. Schuman, the French Foreign Secretary, today.

Tomorrow he will meet Mr. Bevin in London alone and on Thursday all three will sit down together with their experts.

The agenda for the talks is long and complicated containing almost as many items as an auctioneer's catalogue.

Missing trawler— 'Faint message'

THE mystery of the missing trawler Milford Viscount deepened yesterday when a faint wireless message was picked up at Tarbat Ness lighthouse near Inverness.

The message, received at 4.30 a.m., said: "This might be last call. Batteries going flat. Position 72 degrees 40 mins north 17 west."

The lighthouse could not reply as it has no transmitting radio.

The message was heard by William Smith, a brother of Alex Smith, skipper of the missing trawler.

William is convinced that it was his brother's voice he heard.

He went to the lighthouse on Saturday to try to confirm that messages being picked up by the keepers were from the Viscount.

The position given in yesterday's message is north of Iceland and east of Greenland.

A U.S. Air Force B17 bomber took off from Iceland to search the area, and the sloop Cygnet, heading for Iceland, was radioed to keep a look-out for the missing trawler.

Derby 1-2-3: All French, says trainer

From TOM PHILLIPS

PARIS, Sunday

AN Englishman stood outside stable No. 59 on the beautiful Long-champs racecourse here today and made the proud boast 'French horses will fill the first three places in the Derby on May 27.'

Proud? Yes, for Richard Carver has trained numerous winners for French owners and has frequently carried off big prizes with French horses in England.

He added to his prophecy: "And I think mine will be first."

He had just seen L'Amiral fourth favourite for the Derby, win the Prix Hocquart by half a length from Lacaduv with Pardal, one of M Boussac's Derby candidates a further four lengths away third.

Carver trains L'Amiral for Mme Volterra; he also trained My Love, winner of this race before he went on to win the 1948 Derby.

After L'Amiral's convincing victory, I spoke to Mme Volterra widow of the famous Paris sportsman and theatre magnate, as she posed for pictures beside her horse.

Then she sat under a chestnut tree looking very beautiful with her white hat fitting closely over blonde hair and her black and white check suit with fox furs A Frenchman congratulated her on L'Amiral's success: he said: "Now for the Derby."

Mme Volterra's flush deepened. She smiled and replied: "Oh, la, la. I think so. I hope so. I'm certain."

I am not so sure. The fluctuations in French form between now and the Derby almost invariably complicate the issue by the time the numbers go up in the frame at the great Epsom classic.

There are several other French horses to be taken into consideration, but there can be no denying that this fine French colt bred by Admiral Drake, a very successful sire, won

Continued on Back Page

WIDOW OF FAMOUS PAINTER IS ATTACKED IN 20-ROOM HOUSE —HUNT FOR BLOODSTAINED MAN

POLICE were yesterday seeking a man with blood-stained clothes after a mysterious attack on a woman painter, widow of a famous Royal Academician.

The widow, Mrs. Maude Stanhope Forbes, 70, was found with serious head injuries in the drawing-room of her twenty-roomed home Higher Faughan Newlyn Cornwall.

She had been attacked by a man who had concealed himself in the drawing-room. He dragged off her wrist watch and a platinum ring from her finger.

Mrs. Forbes's screams were heard by her housekeeper's husband. As he ran downstairs the assailant rushed from the house.

Mrs. Forbes, who has herself exhibited at the Royal Academy, is the widow of Stanhope Forbes, R.A., founder of the Newlyn school of artists.

Her husband was famous for his paintings of Cornish street scenes and country lanes

His "The Health of the Bride" was spoken of with admiration by Sir Alfred Munnings, ex-president of the Royal Academy, last year, when he opened a memorial exhibition of Mr Forbes's work at Newlyn.

Higher Faughan, where the attack occurred is the place where Forbes did his best work. It overlooks Newlyn and Mount's Bay and is circled by trees

Yesterday a police guard stopped callers

8th May 1950

IT WILL BE A LONG AND HAPPY MARRIAGE, SAYS ELIZABETH TAYLOR

WE BOTH ADORE OVERSIZE SWEATERS AND HAMBURGERS

After her £29,000 wedding fit for a princess, English-born film star, Elizabeth Taylor, 18, told a thousand champagne-sipping guests why her marriage to her third fiancé, Conrad Nick Hilton, 23, heir to a £44,000,000 hotel fortune, would be "long and happy."

"We both adore oversize sweaters and hamburgers with onions," she said.

Then the couple slipped away on a private plane to a secret hide-out where they are honeymooning before beginning a three-month European trip (cables Stan Mays).

Radiant and poised before 3,000 onlookers, Elizabeth walked down the aisle of the Beverly Hills church one step behind her art-dealer father, instead of on his arm.

That gave the guests on both sides a good view of the £1,200 wedding dress of twenty yards of white satin. It was a last-minute idea by a Press agent, hailed by the studio as "brilliant."

After Nick had slipped a £3,500 platinum ring studded with diamonds on his bride's finger he kissed her for five seconds. Then Elizabeth flung her arms round Nick and hugged him.

Scores of screen celebrities in the audience tittered, but the front pew, filled with Metro-Goldwyn-Mayer directors, shush-shushed for silence as the battery of studio cameramen ground away.

FOR THE STUDIO WAS PAYING FOR EVERY PENNY OF IT.

As the couple marched down the aisle, Elizabeth paused to kiss her father and mother. In the crowd outside the church was an English girl "fan," Miss Rose Golding, of Leeds, who said she waited five hours for the wedding procession.

Three dining rooms of a country club were taken over for the reception. Each room featured as a centre-piece a symbolic statue carved from ice, depicting two kissing doves and a replica of the wedding church.

BACKSTORY

Sadly Elizabeth Taylor's first marriage was not a particularly long one. She and Hilton lasted just a year together, before she took the plunge with matinée idol Michael Wilding. The couple had two sons before splitting in 1957.

Tragedy struck when Liz's third husband, Mike Todd, died in a plane crash in 1958, and then Taylor and her new beau Eddie Fisher caused a sensation by marrying. Singer Fisher had been married to Taylor's friend Debbie Reynolds and was Todd's best friend.

Amid a welter of rumours about affairs and flings with a number of famous men, Taylor and Fisher lasted five years, before the British-born actress embarked on what was to be the most tumultuous of all Hollywood romances with Richard Burton. The pair married twice, finally divorcing for good in 1976.

Liz wasn't finished yet, however, and married Republican senator John Warner, only to divorce in 1982. She finally called time on married life in 1996 after five years of wedded bliss with construction worker, Larry Fortensky.

Daily Mirror

FRI
AUG. 31
1951

1½d

No. 14,868

FORWARD WITH THE PEOPLE

Registered at G.P.O. as a Newspaper.

MADNESS VILLAGE IS PRAYING: LIFT THE CURSE OF OUR FATHERS' SIN

From AUDREY WHITING

Pont St. Esprit, Thursday.

THE vineyards need spraying. The dairy cows need milking.

But as the warm wind blows a fine layer of white dust over the red-topped cafe tables, this tiny South of France village is praying.

Inside the tiny grey-stone Roman Catholic Church of St. Pierre, Frenchmen and their families are clasping earthworn hands and whispering, "Do not make us pay for the sins of our fathers . . ." Groaning and crying, strapped in their beds are 187 villagers suffering from a "strange disease of the mind."

'We Know We Are Accursed'

Three local doctors, two French Ministry of Health specialists and three poison experts from Marseilles police laboratory have tried to console the village by saying: "A strange germ has entered your bread. You are suffering from an unknown poison."

But this village in the Gard region of France, where Van Gogh painted some of his most famous pictures, could only cry: "We know we are cursed."

In his book-lined office in the town hall, the mayor, M. Albert Hebrard, pored, frightened over a history book told me: "We are paying for unkind deeds. We are cursed."

At Page 366, he was staring down at a story about a plague which struck the village in 1610. "At that time eighty men and women died from madness—they, too, were poisoned by flour," he said.

Since Sunday morning doctors have tried to calm the village.

Today there was a melancholy tolling of church bells. A black velvet awning cover the porch as the village paid homage to an old couple who died from the "bread plague."

There will be two more funerals tomorrow.

Thirty-six people are "out of their minds" in the local asylum. And 187 people in their own homes are "suffering from hallucinations."

After three days' research scientists are still not sure of the cause of the strange malady.

Professor Olivier, police researcher, told me: "All we can say is that a parasite called ergot was mixed with the flour.

This morning eight-year-old Marie Martine Perreu suddenly screamed as she was playing hop-scotch: "A big elephant is chasing me. Take him away."

All the villagers will say is: "She is paying for the sins of her ancestors."

Today all windows were shuttered. When I arrived in the village I felt well—I am leaving with a bad cold.

Georges Ellis who runs the main bar in the village, said: "You are cursed, too. If you lived here you would have gone mad. As you are on a visit, you have been given grace."

And, the terrifying thing was, that he believed what he said.

Stranded trippers rush for air seats home

LAST hope of getting home of hundreds of British holidaymakers stranded in Eire, because of a threatened strike by Irish seamen, was dashed yesterday when the Irish air line, Aer Lingus, announced: "We can only take forty extra passengers."

All day long desperate tourists, many running short of money after their holiday, besieged the air line's Dublin offices. Officials explained, "Our services are at their peak already —we can only put on two extra aircraft."

Other Britons who dashed to Belfast to try to get a passage on the unaffected Belfast-Liver-pool service found last night's ship already fully booked.

The British and Irish Steam Packet Company suspended all their services between Dublin-Liverpool and Cork-Fishguard yesterday, when the Irish Seamen's and Port Workers' Union threatened to call out their members over a pay dispute with the company.

Under an agreement between that union and the British Seamen's Union, all crews on ships registered in Eire are members of the Irish union and vice versa.

Only cross-channel passenger ships from Eire not affected by the threat are those operated by British Railways (all British registered ships), and even those services face disruption if the unsettled unofficial ten - days - old strike of British seamen on the Heysham (Lancs)-Belfast run spreads.

Hundreds of people due to start their holiday in Eire yesterday cancelled their bookings.

MAN ACCUSED OF 2 MURDERS WAS TWICE IN MENTAL HOMES

COURT TOLD

JOHN THOMAS STRAFFEN, 21, accused at Bath, Somerset, yesterday, of murdering Cicely Batstone, 8, was twice certified as being mentally defective, it was stated.

Detective-Inspector T. J. Coles, head of Bath C.I.D., said Straffen was still n licence.

Straffen is also accused of murdering Brenda Goddard, aged six.

Earlier, Mr. P. Donal Barry, prosecuting, had said that on the evening of the day when Cicely left her home in Camden-road, Bath, to go to a cinema, a detectives wife, Mrs. Violet Mabel Cowley, was walking down Broomfield-road with her dog.

She reached a point where there were farm buildings on one side of the road and large gates leading to a field on the other side.

Mrs. Cowley saw a man and a little girl walking from the gates into the field towards a large tree, said Mr. Barry.

'Stopped to Watch'

She knew that this field was not used by the public and so she was interested and stopped to watch these two people. She saw them walk up the path and disappear round the back of a hedge.

The child's dress was very like the dress Cicely wore when she left home.

"Mrs. Cowley particularly noticed the man so well, that at a later date at an identification parade she was able to pick out the man she saw

◎ Continued on Back Page

6039136— her lucky number

Yesterday was the loveliest day in little Joyce Dickinson's life—"nicer even than when I was a bridesmaid." For Joyce, 11, of Putney, London, was the 6,039,136th visitor to the South Bank Exhibition. She was the one to top the figures for the 1851 Exhibition. She was given a stick of rock 5ft. 0½in. long—1in. taller than herself (above). From a Festival kiosk she chose a three-rope pearl necklace.

Sir Gerald Barry, Festival Director, asked Joyce to lunch, and her father let her have a sip of champagne.

Alderman wins 'kiss' appeal

EIGHT magistrates and a K.C. decided yesterday that it was "quite unsafe" to accept a woman's story of a stolen kiss, and Alderman Fred W. Davis's appeal against conviction and a £3 fine for assault was allowed.

"All the evidence tends to indicate that her story is not true," said Mr. G. A. Thesiger, the K.C., who presided at the West Kent Appeal Committee's hearing.

Davis, 64, a J.P. and railway inspector, of Livingstone - road, Gillingham (Kent), was found guilty of the offence on July 25.

He sat immediately below the witness-box when Mrs. Susan Whittingstall, 56, wife of a crossing-keeper, retold her story yesterday.

Describing the scene after the alleged kiss, she said: "I drew back away from him, but he said: 'Come on.' I said: 'No, Mr. Davis, I am not that sort of woman.' He said: 'Am I forgiven?' I was only testing you.' I asked him what right he had to test me. I told him that I should tell my husband."

"The only reason I took the case to court was to stop my husband taking the law into his own hands," she said later.

Davis said Mrs. Whittingstall had complained to him previously about the behaviour of other persons.

Mr. Curtis-Bennett: Had you the smallest desire to kiss her ? — None whatever —or any other woman.

Describing what happened on the day of the alleged kissing, he said: "I turned round, not knowing she had followed me into the office, and brushed her on the shoulder. I said 'Sorry.'"

Addressing the committee Mr. Curtis-Bennett said certain women of Mrs. Whittingstall's age, frustrated in some way, enjoyed making allegations.

They wished to make out that they were so glamorous and attractive that men could not resist them. It was pathetic rather than wicked.

The committee reached its decision in five minutes.

Alderman Davis said later: "I am very happy this has been cleared up."

---

5 saved as car sinks in ditch

FLOUNDERING waist deep through slime, three men struggled yesterday to rescue six people, two of them children, trapped in a car that lost a wheel, overturned into a ditch and sank in seven feet of water.

The driver of the car, Robert Davis, of Duncan-drive, Greasby, Cheshire, was drowned.

Two of the passengers, Mrs. Marjorie Davis, his wife, and Mrs. Josephine Sherman, of Roslyn-road, Hoylwall, Cheshire, were last night in hospital seriously hurt.

'Disappeared'

The others, Mr. and Mrs. Davis' two children, Beryl, 15, and Bryan, 7, and Mr. John Sherman, were not badly injured.

The accident was at East Brent, Somerset — on a main highway to South West resorts.

Mr. Davis and his passengers were returning from holiday.

The three men who went to their aid were Farmer George Hill, of South View Farm, East Brent, his farm-worker, Harold Kick, and an unknown car driver.

'Nobody Helped'

"The car had completely disappeared when we reached the spot." said Mr. Hill.

"We wrenched the driver's door open and pulled the driver and the boy clear.

"I kept shouting for the crowd of about thirty people who had collected to come and help us. But none of them would move an inch. They just stood watching us. I was furious."

To get the other four passengers out, Mr. Hill said the three of them lifted the car and smashed a back window.

31st August **1951**

MADNESS VILLAGE IS PRAYING: LIFT THE CURSE OF OUR FATHERS' SIN

From Audrey Whiting
Pont St. Esprit, Thursday

THE vineyards need spraying. The dairy cows need milking. But as the warm wind blows a fine layer of white dust over the red-topped cafe tables, this tiny South of France village is praying.

Inside the tiny grey-stone Roman Catholic Church of St. Pierre, Frenchmen and their families are clasping earth-worn hands and whispering, "Do not make us pay for the sins of our fathers . . ." Groaning and crying, strapped in their beds are 187 villagers suffering from a "strange disease of the mind."

'We Know We Are Accursed'

Three local doctors, two French Ministry of Health specialists and three poison experts from Marseilles police laboratory have tried to console the village by saying:

"A strange germ has entered your bread. You are suffering from an unknown poison."

But this village in the Gard region of France, where Van Gogh painted some of his most famous pictures, could only cry: "We know we are cursed."

In his book-lined office in the town hall, the mayor, M. Albert Hebrard, pored, frightened over a history book told me: "We are paying for unkind deeds. We are cursed."

At Page 366, he was staring down at a story about a plague which struck the village in 1610. "At that time eighty men and women died from madness they, too, were poisoned by flour," he said.

Since Sunday morning doctors have tried to calm the village.

Today there was a melancholy tolling of church bells. A black velvet awning covered the porch as the village paid homage to an old couple who died from the "bread plague".

There will be two more funerals tomorrow.

Thirty-six people are out of their minds in the local asylum. And 187 people in their own homes are "suffering from hallucinations."

After three days' research scientists are still not sure of the cause of the strange malady.

Professor Olivier, police researcher, told me: "All we can say is that a parasite called ergot was mixed with the flour."

This morning eight-year-old Marie Marline Perreu suddenly screamed as she was playing hop-scotch: "A big elephant is chasing me. Take him away."

All the villagers will say is: "She is paying for the sins of her ancestors."

Today all windows were shuttered. When I arrived in the village I felt well – I am leaving with a bad cold.

Georges Ellis who runs the main bar in the village, said: "You are cursed, too.

BACKSTORY

The strange mass-madness that struck the pretty village of Pont-Saint-Esprit, was most likely a bizarre, but not unheard of, example of ergot poisoning.

Four people died and over 250 were affected by the condition, caused by a fungus that contaminates cereal grains. It can cause shocking side effects on people who consume the infected flour – from the agonizing burning sensation of "St Anthony's Fire" to the collective madness seen at Pont-Saint-Esprit.

The kind of hallucinations and mass psychosis the villagers experienced have been recorded a number of times before, particularly in medieval Europe. Ergot has even been cited as a possible factor in the Salem witch trials of the 1690s.

The Pont-Saint-Esprit poisoning came in the same year as a series of terrible avalanches that struck not far away in the Alps. As the *Mirror* reported on 22nd January, "Terrific avalanches of snow and ice roaring down the mountainside during the night turned the Swiss village of Vals into a shambles yesterday. Houses were crushed and swept away.

"Estimates put the death toll from avalanches in the Swiss, Austrian and Italian Alps during the week-end at 104. Officials fear, however, that the final figure will be much higher than this."

This grim prediction came horribly true. In what became known as the "Winter of Terror", over 250 people were killed in a series of devastating avalanches.

If you lived here you would have gone mad. As you are on a visit, you have been given grace."

And, the terrifying thing was, that he believed what he said.

➤ A tranquil Alpine scene – but the winter of 1951 was one of disaster and tragedy.

Daily Mirror

WED
FEB. 27
1952

1½d

No. 15,020

Registered at G.P.O as a Newspaper.

FORWARD
WITH THE
PEOPLE

CHURCHILL SAYS NO NEW U.S. PACT—'BUT ATTLEE MADE SECRET AGREEMENT'

Shock for Labour M.P.s

MR. CHURCHILL, in the Foreign Affairs debate last night, gave a solemn assurance to the House of Commons that he made no secret pact with America concerning Korea or China during his visit to Washington.

He said: " There is no truth in the suggestion that any secret or private arrangement was made, or any change of policy agreed upon, formally or informally, actual or implied, by me or the Foreign Secretary during our joint visit to the United States."

THEN HE SURPRISED THE HOUSE BY DECLARING THAT THE LABOUR GOVERNMENT HAD THEMSELVES GIVEN A SECRET PLEDGE ON KOREA TO AMERICA IN MAY LAST YEAR.

He said the Labour Government, in answer to an inquiry from America, then decided that in the event of heavy air attacks on U.N. forces in Korea from bases in China " they would associate themselves with action not confined to Korea."

The disclosure was a surprise to most Labour back-benchers. They thought that when Labour went out of office the whole question of Korea and Red China was still open to discussion.

Mr. Churchill made his statement in a six-hour stormy debate on the Labour Party motion seeking to censure him for failing to make it clear while in Washington that he adhered to the Labour Government's policy on Korea and China which had been endorsed by the present Government.

Twenty-minute Storm

With the Liberals voting with the Government this motion was defeated by 318 votes to 285, a majority of 33.

There was an extraordinary twenty-minute storm when Mr. Churchill made his statement on the Attlee Government's pledge to America. Mr. Aneurin Bevan immediately demanded production of the document from which Mr. Churchill was quoting.

Mr. Bevan said the Prime Minister's statement was " shameful." Mr. Attlee and Mr. Morrison joined in the demand, and there were excited scenes before Mr. Churchill could continue his speech.

Mr. Churchill said he was not quoting. He was entitled, he said, in defence of the Government and in view of the shameful attack on them, to place the House in possession of the facts.

Mr. Morrison said the members of the Labour Government had nothing to be ashamed of. Discussions with America had been confined to " what would you do if you are attacked from airfields over the border ? "

'Cannot Stand By'

He added: " In principle we cannot stand by in that case and do nothing about it." There were loud Conservative cheers.

Mr. Churchill next went on to say that in September last the Labour Government agreed to an American proposal that in the event of a breakdown in the Korea armistice talks and the resumption of large-scale fighting " certain action should be taken of a more limited character."

He added: " In my view that justifies the words I used to the U.S. Congress— 'prompt, resolute and effective.'"

Report of debate starts in Page 5.

THE BRIGADIER CUFFED ME, SAYS MORRISON

MR Herbert Morrison, in the Commons last night, said that he had received a cuff on the head from the Government Whip, Brigadier H R. Mackeson.

After the Whip had announced the Government's victory in the Foreign Affairs division, he was seen to flick his arm in Mr. Morrison's direction.

Labour M.P.s jumped to their feet. Mr. Michael Stewart (Lab., Fulham E.) said the act was trivial but it represented an attitude of vulgarity and ignorance of the politeness required of a Government Whip.

Brigadier Mackeson said that if he had been in any way discourteous he offered Mr. Morrison his unqualified apology.

This was accepted by Mr. Morrison.

Man who never went out for 25 years had hair 5ft. 8in. long

"DAILY MIRROR" REPORTER

A MAN aged about forty, with a matted beard reaching almost to his feet, hair 5ft. 8in. long, and 3in. finger nails, was yesterday taken from an aged spinster's house at Bristol where he had lived unknown to the neighbours for twenty-five years.

During those twenty-five years it is thought that he never once left the crumbling twelve-roomed home of the four Tucker spinster sisters, of whom only Miss Louisa Tucker, 84, is now living.

A police inspector said last night that the man was named Harry Tucker, and that it was believed Miss Louisa Tucker was his aunt.

" Ever since he left school it seems that he has been in the Tucker sisters' house," the inspector added.

A policeman found the man when he was called to the house at midnight after neighbours had reported that Miss Tucker was throwing bottles, money and bedclothes out of the windows. The man was crouching naked in a corner among rickety furniture.

With Miss Tucker he was taken to a home to be cared for. And within an hour of arriving his matted beard and hair were cut off.

He was fairly well nourished, but obviously frightened by his first contact with the outside world for twenty-five years," said a welfare officer.

Thought He Had Died

Last night the strange story of the Tucker house was being pieced together. People who have lived all their lives near the house in Somerset-street, Kingsdown, recalled that a curly-headed schoolboy had once stayed with the Tucker sisters.

"That was more than twenty-five years ago," said Mrs. Hall who lives two doors away. "We all thought he had gone away or died."

But a welfare officer confirmed that the hairy man and the curly-headed schoolboy were the same person.

Louisa Tucker's last remaining sister died three years ago, and sympathetic neighbours often called at the house because they thought she was lonely. But, said the neighbours, she never allowed them in.

HOUSE WITH A SECRET
The Tucker sisters' home

WHITHER LABOUR?

THIRD article in this important series on the future of the Labour Party is by Mr. ANEURIN BEVAN and is on Page Two.

Tomorrow's contribution will be by Mr. SAM WATSON, miners' leader and member of the Labour Party National Executive.

The girl you'll see in shop windows

THE men who choose TV announcers turned down twenty-three-year-old Audrey White (above) because they thought her breathtaking beauty would make such an impression on viewers that they would just look at her without listening.

Now Audrey's beauty is going to make another kind of impression.

She is going to have plaster spread over her and from the shape she leaves in the mould will be cast hundreds of shop window models.

Audrey said last night: " I intend to make a good impression."

27th February 1952

MAN WHO NEVER WENT OUT FOR 25 YEARS HAD HAIR 5 FT. 8 IN. LONG

A MAN aged about forty, with a matted beard reaching almost to his feet, hair 5ft. 8in. long, and 3in. finger nails, was yesterday taken from an aged spinster's house at Bristol where he had lived unknown to the neighbours for twenty-five years.

During those twenty-five years it is thought that he never once left the crumbling twelve-roomed home of the four Tucker spinster sisters, of whom only Miss Louisa Tucker, 84, is now living.

A police inspector said last night that the man was named Harry Tucker, and that it was believed Miss Louisa Tucker was his aunt.

"Ever since he left school it seems that he has been in the Tucker sisters' house," the inspector added.

A policeman found the man when he was called to the house at midnight after neighbours had reported that Miss Tucker was throwing bottles, money and bedclothes out of the windows. The man was crouching naked in a corner among rickety furniture.

With Miss Tucker he was taken to a home to be cared for. And within an hour of arriving his matted beard and hair were cut off.

"He was fairly well nourished, but obviously frightened by his first contact with the outside world for twenty-five years," said a welfare officer.

Thought He Had Died

Last night the strange story of the Tucker house was being pieced together.

People who have lived all their lives near the house in Somerset-street, Kingsdown, recalled that a curly-headed schoolboy had once stayed with the Tucker sisters.

"That was more than twenty-five years ago," said Mrs. Hall, who lives two doors away. "We all thought he had gone away or died."

But a welfare officer confirmed that the hairy man and the curly-headed schoolboy were the same person.

Louisa Tucker's last remaining sister died three years ago, and sympathetic neighbours often called at the house because they thought she was lonely. But said the neighbours, she never allowed them in.

THE SMALL DOG THAT CAN'T UNDERSTAND THE SHUT DOOR

FOR one caller, the mysterious house in Somerset-street always had a welcome. Every day for three years the door had opened to his call and every day Spot, the little mongrel dog, had been given a snack.

Yesterday he stood outside and barked. There was no answer. He scratched at the door. But it stayed shut. Dejectedly, Spot, whose owner lives three doors down the street, trotted away, unable to understand what seemed to be a rebuff.

And while Spot was trotting up and down Somerset-street, Bristol, Miss Louisa Tucker, 84, who could have explained everything to him, lay seriously ill in Bristol Hospital.

Her nephew, Harry Tucker, who spent twenty-five years in the house in Somerset-street without once being seen by the neighbours, was taken to an institution two days ago after police called.

Yesterday, welfare officers spent hours hunting through the twelve-roomed house, trying to learn the background to one of the strangest, most fantastic cases any of them can remember.

The search revealed several pieces of worm-eaten but once beautiful Chippendale and Sheraton furniture. Over £100 in notes was also found.

But why was Harry Tucker found wrapped in a mouldering blanket in the corner of a candlelit room?

The welfare officers are still trying to piece that story together.

Daily Mirror

MON
AUG. 18
1952

1½d

FORWARD
WITH THE
PEOPLE

No. 15,167
Registered at G.P.O. as a Newspaper.

Where the flood fury hit

Lynmouth

A few days ago this was the road from Barnstaple which wound down through the hills into quiet Lynmouth. It was the road the deluge took. Bursting its way from the rocky slopes above, the torrent hurled before it huge boulders, great spears of pine trees, ton upon ton of cloying red mud. The debris was bottlenecked by the first few houses and Lynmouth became a giant concrete mixer, the rocks and trees twisting and tumbling in the cataract, smashing against the buildings all round. . . .
Picture by "Daily Mirror" photographer Ted Heanly. More dramatic pictures and stories in other pages.

DEATHS MAY NUMBER OVER FIFTY

FAMILY OF 4 MISSING

A MAN and wife and their two children are named as missing in a flood-victim list issued early today by Barnstaple police.

The list which is incomplete—it does not include a number of people still unaccounted for—gives twenty-four as missing presumed dead, and seven missing. Named in it are:

MISSING PRESUMED DEAD: Miss Elsie Cherry, 50, Gladsmuir-road, Highgate, N.19; Benjamin Coutt, 54, and Mrs. Emma Coult, Langley Park, Co. Durham;
Gabriel Litson, William Watts, Mrs. Maud Watts, Mrs. Mulle, Edwin Smith, Mrs. Barwick, Charles H. Litson, Miss Hannah Jarvis and Miss Cannon, all

of Lynmouth; Miss Mary Anne Floyde, Frederick Floyde, Mrs. Doris Bowen, Ronald Bowen, David Bowen, Kenneth Bowen, Mrs. Emma Ridd, Rodney Dimmock, all of Barbrook; and two unknown girl cyclists named Gwen and Joyce;
Miss Jessie Whitbread, of London-road, Bedford, and Miss Stella Bates, of Putnoe-lane, Bedford.

MISSING: William Richards, Mrs. Gwendoline Richards, and their two children; Miss Anne Branston, Miss Emmy Branston, and Mrs. Olive Frisby, all of Lynmouth.

This list is in addition to the three Boy Scouts, the Parracombe postman, William Leamorthy, and an unidentified family of three, known to be dead.

From Geoffrey Chambers — Lynton, Monday, 2 a.m.

THE list of people drowned in the North Devon flood disaster may number more than fifty—when the tragic tally is completed, according to police estimates here today.

Early today it was possible to list a total of forty-two people dead or unaccounted for. Some were not named. In addition, police believe that a number of other people—such as holiday-makers who were in the area, but did not sign hotel registers—may be missing.

It may be a week before the position is sorted out. Devon's Chief Constable, Lieutenant-Colonel R. R. M. Bacon, told me: "Many holidaymakers may have left the area without notifying anyone. We hope anyone with information will contact us."

Damage in Lynmouth—the village split and shattered by the raging River Lyn—is estimated at £250,000. Over the whole of the flood-ravaged area it may reach

Continued on
Back Page

18th August 1952

DEATHS MAY NUMBER OVER FIFTY

Some Power Saved Me, Says Man Who Lost Family

From Geoffrey Chambers Lynton, Monday, 2 a.m.

THE list of people drowned in the North Devon flood disaster may number more than fifty – when the tragic tally is completed, according to police estimates here today.

Early today it was possible to list a total of forty-two people dead or unaccounted for. Some were not named. In addition, police believe that a number of other people – such as holidaymakers who were in the area, but did not sign hotel registers – may be missing.

It may be a week before the position is sorted out. Devon's Chief Constable, Lieutenant-Colonel R. M. Bacon, told me: "Many holidaymakers may have left the area without notifying anyone. We hope anyone with information will contact us."

Damage in Lynmouth – the village split and shattered by the racing River Lyn – is estimated at £250,000.

Over the whole of the flood-ravaged area it may reach £31,500,000. It was a daylong deluge of rain on Friday that caused the disaster. Nine inches of rain – more than three months' normal fall – fell during the day at Longstone Barrow, four miles from Lynton.

And last night ominous dark clouds were again piling up over this holiday countryside. More rain was forecast.

In Lynton's raftered Town Hall, weary councillors were told yesterday that it would be six months before the "ghost town" of Lynmouth could be restored to life . . .

All day bulldozers have been working in the remnants of Lynmouth, heaving rocks and tons of earth into the false river caused when the Lyn changed its course.

Royal Engineers, blasting a new bed for the River Lyn, detonated charges to break up some of the huge boulders which the torrent had pushed away from the river bank.

Another squad of sappers threw a girder footbridge across the Lyn, joining Lynmouth and Lynton.

War-Time Warden

Gangs of local volunteers, under the control of wartime head warden of Lynton, Mr. W. H. Tall, and Army and RAF working parties, salvaged furniture, bedding and clothing from the wrecked homes.

Firemen disinfected the broken sewerage drains and electricians worked all day to restore the current. Amidst the rock-strewn devastation of the town, Devon's Chief Constable controlled a police search of wrecked houses, shops and hotels by walkie-talkie radio.

Bodies are still believed to be buried in the rubble of the Bath Hotel . . .

Last night, military police cordoned roads leading into Lynmouth and stopped all unauthorised persons entering, because of the fear of looting from the devastated area . . .

As dawn broke yesterday morning, the August sunshine seemed to mock the plight of the homeless people standing about grey faced in bewildered groups.

Many had slept rough in Lynton's Jubilee Hall, rapidly improvised as a rest centre. There were not enough mattresses to go round. Householders queued for drinking water from Army and RAF tankers.

Tired and weeping queues of homeless trooped into the Post Office here to draw on savings to take them away from the devastation.

In the Town Hall, patient information bureau staff checked alphabetical lists of names as crying relatives came to ask for news.

Walking aimlessly through the town, Councillor Tom Floyde, a 63-year-old postman, who lost his wife, son, a daughter, son-in-law and two grandchildren when his cottage at Barbrook collapsed, stopped me ashen faced and trembling.

"I am a God-fearing man," he said weeping.

"But I just cannot understand it. With my family I was dragged down to the river bed, but some almighty Power drew me back and saved me."

Mr. Floyde showed me ugly bruises on his arms and legs where he was buffeted against boulders.

Even grief such as his did not prevent him from attending church. He sat at the back and prayed during a children's service.

"All I have left of my household is my dog Tim," he said.

He passed his hand across his eyes and added: "I've been to the Post Office for a new uniform to start work. But they told me to rest."

Twenty-four-year-old Eric Randell was on leave at his parents' home. He was talking to his crippled twenty-six-year-old brother Cyril and his nephew, little Arthur Rose, on holiday from Cheddar.

"Suddenly the waters of the East Lyn demolished the house. I went down the street to try to find Cyril. We managed to get the furniture upstairs as the water rose higher.

"Finally, my father carried my mother on his back and little Arthur in his arms, and waded up to his neck to safety . . ."

BACKSTORY

The Lynmouth flood disaster claimed 34 lives and left the county of Devon and beyond in grief. The terrible devastation (left) attested to the power of nature – but conspiracy theories were soon being raised.

Some believed that the nine inches of rain that fell in just a matter of hours was not the result of some freak weather, but due to cloud seeding experiments being conducted by the military on nearby Exmoor. The claims have since been rubbished by various experts.

Just six months later, Britain and the Low Countries were hit by an even greater flood disaster. The North Sea Flood of 31st January/1st February 1953 brought devastation as a storm surge of almost 19 feet led to vast tracts of East Anglia and the Thames Estuary being swamped with floodwater. Whole villages were laid waste, thousands had to be evacuated and the damage was costed at over £1bn in today's money. But the death toll was the grimmest statistic. 307 died in England, 19 in Scotland – and over 1,800 in Holland.

Daily Mirror

WED MAY 6 1953

1½d

FORWARD WITH THE PEOPLE

No. 15,388 ✦ ✦ ✦

'MAD MAJOR' FLIES UNDER 15 LONDON BRIDGES

"Daily Mirror" Reporter

TENS of thousands of Londoners saw a tiny plane swoop down to the Thames at lunch-time yesterday and shoot under bridge after bridge in a dare-devil up-river flight.

According to eye-witness reports, it skimmed through the arches of at least fifteen bridges ranging from Blackfriars, in the City, to beyond Kew.

AT TIMES THE LITTLE PLANE, WHICH THE POLICE SAID WAS AN AUSTER, SEEMED TO BE ONLY A FOOT OR SO ABOVE THE WATER.

But it was handled so skilfully that it completed its course without mishap.

Later Major Christopher Draper, 61, a World War I fighter pilot known as "the Mad Major," told me: "I was the pilot.

"I flew under fifteen bridges out of the total of eighteen over the Thames—starting at Waterloo Bridge. I missed Hungerford Bridge, Kew Bridge and one of the railway bridges because the air currents made it too dangerous for the lightweight Auster aircraft. She only has one engine, you know."

Friend in Plane

A friend who accompanied him on the flight said he was there to take a cine-film record of it for Major Draper's personal record.

Major Draper added that a chief inspector of police had asked him to come and see him at Waterloo police station tomorrow.

Police reported to Scotland Yard that the aircraft flew under the centre arches of Blackfriars and Waterloo Bridges, went over Hungerford Bridge, and then climbed to circle before going on to Westminster and Lambeth Bridges.

At Westminster two eighteen-year-old clerks, Jill Monday and Pamela Rogers, dived for cover with scores of other people on the bridge, as they watched the plane speeding towards them

'Terrible Noise'

"It made a terrible noise," Jill told me. "Nobody knew what was happening."

A group of bricklayers working on the entrance to Hungerford Bridge confirmed that the plane did not fly under that bridge.

"The pilot must have thought that it would be just a little too daring," said one man, who claimed to have had RAF experience.

Mr. G. Humphrey, of Degema-road, Chislehurst (Kent), who was working on a tower in Parliament-square, saw the plane come from the direction of St. Paul's Cathedral.

"It came as far as Parliament-square, circled and then flew towards Waterloo Bridge," he said.

"IT TURNED AGAIN AND DROPPED ALMOST TO THE RIVER LEVEL AND FLEW UNDER THE CENTRE ARCH OF WATERLOO BRIDGE, IT FLEW ALONG THE RIVER FOR ABOUT A MILE."

He thought the plane was an Auster Aiglet, a type widely used by flying clubs and schools. It has a 130 h.p. engine and a wing-span of 36ft.

Mr. S. Hawtree, of Hallsham-road, Romford (Essex), said: "The plane dived from the direction of Waterloo Bridge. It climbed and circled round County Hall and then came in low again to go under Westminster Bridge.

"Still flying low it went under two more bridges. Had it left it a minute later, there would have been a vessel coming up under the bridges."

Back in 1931 Major Draper flew under Tower Bridge and the low arch of Westminster Bridge. He was bound over by a Mansion House magistrate for his exploit—which earned him the name of "The Mad Major."

Christie: 33rd witness today

THE thirty-third and last witness to be called by the prosecution in the murder charges against John Reginald Halliday Christie is due to give evidence at the Clerkenwell, London, magistrates' court today, when the hearing is resumed.

He is Dr. L. Nickolls, chief of Scotland Yard's Forensic Science Laboratory.

Christie, a fifty-five-year-old haulage clerk, is accused of the murder of his wife and three women at No. 10, Rillington-place, Notting Hill.

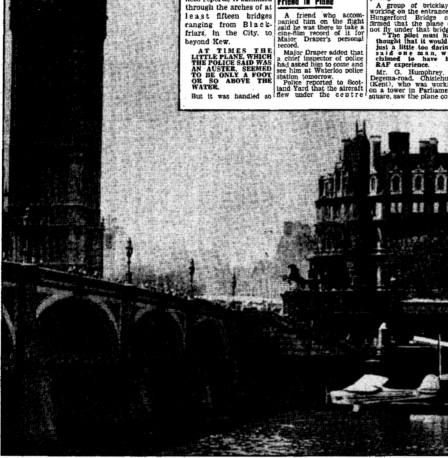

The Auster is seen above just before it flew through an arch of Westminster Bridge, during its flight up the Thames at lunch-time yesterday. Another dramatic picture—See Page Nine.

6th May 1953

'MAD MAJOR' FLIES UNDER 15 LONDON BRIDGES

TENS of thousands of Londoners saw a tiny plane swoop down to the Thames at lunchtime yesterday and shoot under bridge after bridge in a dare-devil up-river flight.

According to eye-witness reports, it skimmed through the arches of at least fifteen bridges ranging from Blackfriars, in the City, to beyond Kew.

At times the little plane, which police said was an Auster, seemed to be only a foot or so above the water.

But it was handled so skilfully that it completed its course without mishap.

Later Major Christopher Draper, 61, a World War I fighter pilot known as "the Mad Major," told me: "I was the pilot.

"I flew under fifteen bridges out of the total of eighteen over the Thames – starting at Waterloo Bridge. I missed Hungerford Bridge, Kew Bridge and one of the railway bridges because the air currents made it too dangerous for the lightweight Auster aircraft. She only has one engine, you know."

Friend in Plane

A friend who accompanied him on the flight said he was there to take a cine-film record of it for Major Draper's personal record.

Major Draper added that a chief inspector of police had asked him to come and see him at Waterloo police station tomorrow.

Police reported to Scotland Yard that the aircraft flew under the centre arches of Blackfriars and Waterloo Bridges, went over Hungerford Bridge, and then climbed to circle before going on to Westminster and Lambeth Bridges.

At Westminster two eighteen-year-old clerks, Jill Mondey and Pamela Rogers, dived for cover with scores of other people on the bridge, as they watched the plane speeding towards them

'Terrible Noise'

"It made a terrible noise," Jill told me. "Nobody knew what was happening."

A group of bricklayers working on the entrance to Hungerford Bridge confirmed that the plane did not fly under that bridge.

"The pilot must have thought that it would be just a little too daring," said one man, who claimed to have had RAF experience.

Mr. G. Humphrey, of Degerna-road, Chislehurst (Kent), who was working on a tower in Parliament square, saw the plane come from the direction of St Paul's Cathedral.

"It came as far as Parliament-square, circled and then flew towards Waterloo Bridge," he said.

"IT TURNED AGAIN AND DROPPED ALMOST TO THE RIVER LEVEL AND FLEW UNDER THE CENTRE ARCH OF WATERLOO BRIDGE.

IT FLEW ALONG THE RIVER FOR ABOUT A MILE."

He thought the plane was an Auster Aiglet, a type widely used by flying clubs and schools. It has a 130 h.p. engine and a wing-span of 36ft.

Mr. S. Hawtree, of Hailsham-road, Romford (Essex), said: "The plane dived from the direction of Waterloo Bridge. It climbed and circled round County Hall and then came in low again to go under Westminster Bridge.

"Still flying low it went under two more bridges. Had it left it

a minute later, there would have been a vessel coming up under the bridges."

Back in 1931 Major Draper flew under Tower Bridge and the low arch of Westminster Bridge. He was bound over by a Mansion House magistrate for his exploit – which earned him the name of "The Mad Major."

▲ "The Mad Major" pictured with his aircraft.

Daily Mirror

MON JAN. 17 1955

1½d FORWARD WITH THE PEOPLE
No. 15,915

BLACKOUT

LONDON GETS MIDNIGHT AT LUNCHTIME

SHIVERING Britain yesterday had its wildest weather mixture for years.

Snow. Gales. Rain. Fog. Floods. Britain had the whole lot. Plus a little hurricane.

But London had the strangest weather freak of all—a "black pudding" that brought midnight, and terror, at lunchtime.

The "black pudding"—that was the name a weather expert gave to it—was a slowly-moving cloud of smog.

It closed on the city soon after 1 p.m. There was no warning—just an eerie blackness that fell suddenly. With it came terror.

Frightened women sank to their knees in prayer.

DAILY MIRROR REPORTER

Others ran screaming for shelter.

Crowds in Piccadilly-circus groped their way through the darkness.

Cars crawled along. Though their headlights blazed, visibility was only two or three yards.

Then, as suddenly as it arrived, the terrifying black pudding rolled on. Within seven minutes Central London was clear. It was daylight again.

The "black pudding" was rolling southwards, bringing more fear.

'End of World'

It blacked out Croydon. There a bearded man walked up and down shouting: "This is the end of the world."

Another man said: "I really did think the end had come."

It blacked out Wimbledon. It blacked out Richmond. And Bromley, and East Grinstead, and Tunbridge Wells.

Thirty minutes later it was over Brighton and Hastings. Then the terror cloud disappeared out to sea.

"What WAS it?"

That was the question by hundreds of anxious phone callers who blocked the switchboards at the Air Ministry and the B.B.C. Many more phoned the Daily Mirror.

Trapped by Winds

The explanation from an Air Ministry weather expert:

"A cloud of smog was trapped between a northerly and a south-easterly wind and the temperature caused it to descend in a dense cloud roughly between a mile and two miles across."

London got the little hurricane, too. It swept through Highgate last night.

A 12ft. high wall was blown down. Trees were uprooted. Fences were flattened.

It was a hurricane from nowhere. And as suddenly as it arose it died.

'Get Your Bedsocks'

Elsewhere in Britain it was a weather story of chaotic road conditions.

What can Britain expect in the way of weather today?

The answer from the weather men is: "It may freeze all day."

London had a foretaste early on. The 1 a.m. temperature was 29 degrees—three degrees below freezing point.

That was a drop of nearly 20 degrees in twelve hours.

An Air Ministry forecaster said: "You'd better get your bedsocks out.

"It's likely to be even colder."

PAGE ONE

● Ray Morley, 28, whipped off his jacket and handed it to a bystander. Then Ray, clinging to a railing, saved a puppy drowning in a Hampstead Heath pond.

When the jacket was handed back £4 10s. was missing from a pocket.

BRIEF

1.30 p.m. IN PICCADILLY-CIRCUS YESTERDAY.

It's Marilyn versus Sheree

From LIONEL CRANE, New York, Sunday.

THE shape of things to come in Hollywood looks like being a girl called Sheree North.

Sheree walked in today as Marilyn Monroe walked out.

Marilyn was suspended by her studio for not turning up for work on a new film, "How To Be Very, Very Popular."

In it she was to play the part of a strip-tease dancer.

But Marilyn said she would rather be a serious actress and play in a gloomy Russian drama.

Now all filmland is waiting to see the result of the battle of beauties.

Sheree, who used to earn £13 weekly doing "wiggle" dances in night clubs, was brought to Hollywood two years ago as "the first real threat to Monroe."

At that time she said: "Marilyn's a fine actress. She has her own line. I wouldn't dream of imitating her." Sheree, a slimmer version of Marilyn, has hazel eyes, but she is not a blonde.

Most of her pictures show her with corn-coloured curls, but this is a wig. Her hair is black.

"This is my chance and I will use everything I've got to grab it," she told me.

THE DEFENCE SCANDAL
See Page Two

Marilyn.   Sheree.

17ᵗʰ January 1955

BLACKOUT

LONDON GETS MIDNIGHT
AT LUNCHTIME

SHIVERING Britain yesterday had its wildest weather mixture for years.

Snow. Gales. Rain. Fog. Floods. Britain had the whole lot. Plus a little hurricane.

But London had the strangest weather freak of all – a "black pudding" that brought midnight, and terror, at lunchtime.

The "black pudding" – that was the name a weather expert gave to it – was a slowly moving cloud of smog.

It closed on the city soon after 1 p.m. There was no warning – just an eerie blackness that fell suddenly. With it came terror.

Frightened women sank to their knees in prayer.

Others ran screaming for shelter.

Crowds in Piccadilly Circus groped their way through the darkness.

Cars crawled along. Though their headlights blazed, visibility was only two or three yards.

Then, as suddenly as it arrived, the terrifying "black pudding" rolled on.

Within seven minutes Central London was clear. It was daylight again.

The "black pudding" was rolling southwards, bringing more fear.

'End of World'

It blacked out Croydon. There a bearded man walked up and down shouting: "This is the end of the world."

Another man said: "I really did think the end had come."

It blacked out Wimbledon. It blacked out Richmond. And Bromley, and East Grinstead, and Tunbridge Wells.

Thirty minutes later it was over Brighton and Hastings. Then the terror cloud disappeared out to sea.

What WAS it?

That was the question by hundreds of anxious phone callers who blocked the switchboards at the Air Ministry and the B.B.C.

Many more phoned the *Daily Mirror*.

Trapped by Winds

The explanation from an Air Ministry weather expert:

"A cloud of smog was trapped between a northerly and a southeasterly wind and the temperature caused it to descend in a dense cloud roughly between a mile and two miles across."

London got the little hurricane too. It swept through Highgate last night.

A 12ft. high wall was blown down. Trees were uprooted. Fences were flattened.

It was a hurricane from nowhere. And as suddenly as it arose it died.

'Get Your Bedsocks'

Elsewhere in Britain it was a weather story of chaotic road conditions.

What can Britain expect in the way of weather today? The answer from the weather men is: "It may freeze all day."

London had a foretaste early on. The 1 a.m. temperature was 29 degrees – three degrees below freezing point.

That was a drop of nearly 20 degrees in twelve hours.

An Air Ministry forecaster said: "You'd better get your bedsocks out. It's likely to be even colder."

BACKSTORY

Britain in the 1950s was no stranger to smog. The toxic clouds of pollution caused by thousands of coal fires and factories (above) belching smoke into the atmosphere, combining with fog to create a deadly phenomenon, killed thousands of people vulnerable to such conditions.

The four-day smog of December 1952 was said to be so dense that people could not even see their feet (below). Up to 4,000 people – and quite likely more – died. The Clean Air Acts of 1956 and 1968 went some way to alleviating the problem.

Daily Mirror

MON JUNE 13 1955

1½d FORWARD WITH THE PEOPLE
No. 16,019

16th day of the rail strike

FOR THE LOVE OF MIKE
GET A MOVE ON !

THIS is the SIXTEENTH day of the railway strike.

Unless General Robertson and Driver Baty speed up their truce talks, the strike will soon have lasted for three weeks.

This is not good enough.

For the love of Mike, **GET A MOVE ON. HURRY. HURRY. HURRY.**

The British public have been very, very patient. But now they are very, very impatient.

The Trades Union Congress and the Daily Mirror advocated that peace talks should begin before the strike ended.

We were right.

But nobody advocated talks that go on and on and on while the country drifts to ruin.

We want express speed talks. But they are moving at the speed of a shunting engine on a dark night with the signals against it.

We want to switch the crisis from the main line to the conference room. But we don't want it to stay there as a permanent museum exhibit—like Puffing Billy.

Hurry, Sir Brian. Hurry, Mr. Baty.

DAILY MIRROR PAGE ONE COMMENT

Stop **CRAWLING** out of the crisis.
Look at what is happening:

❶ FOR thirty-eight days, Sir Brian Robertson, head of the Transport Commission, did not meet Mr. Jim Baty, leader of the union on strike, A.S.L.E.F.

On the thirty-ninth day they met.

They talked for five hours to clear up a point of honour that had nothing to do with the basic issues at stake.

They talked about how to conduct talks to get discussions going to make negotiations possible.

HERE WE GO ROUND THE MULBERRY BUSH!

Are Sir Brian and Mr. Baty still going round and round like a train on the London Inner Circle?

❷ THE peace talks started last Wednesday.
What is the position today?

There is still deadlock. Sir Brian offers more basic pay for Mr. Baty's drivers.

Mr. Baty stands out for more basic pay for his firemen and his cleaners as well.

The signal says STOP—and both sides obey the signal.

If it weren't for Sir Walter Monckton, the Minister of Labour, they might not be meeting again today. As far as man-to-man talks to end the strike were concerned, Sunday was a complete loss.

❸ WHY did they break off their talks on Saturday?

Apparently they needed twenty-four hours to reflect on what they had already been reflecting on for four days.

With the strike costing British Railways possibly £5,000,000 a week, twenty-four hours of reflection come pretty expensive.

We hope they pay dividends today when the peace talks resume. The "Mirror" repeats: **GET A MOVE ON. HURRY TO BREAK THE DEADLOCK. TALK FAST. TALK ALL DAY AND TALK ALL NIGHT, IF NECESSARY. BUT LET'S GET SOMEWHERE QUICKLY.**

Death toll rises to 85 in car-race horror

PRAYER FOR THE VICTIMS

A Frenchwoman dies after the Le Mans road-race disaster in which eighty-five people were killed. Over her a priest breathes a prayer. Another victim lies nearby. But the race went on. . . .

DAILY MIRROR REPORTER

THE death toll in the Le Mans road-race disaster rose to eighty-five last night.

Another 105 people are injured.

A Mercedes driven by Frenchman Pierre Levegh crashed off the track at 150 miles an hour, exploded and plunged into a spectators' enclosure on Saturday.

The race was not stopped. Sixty-odd cars droned on for the remaining twenty-one hours of the twenty-four-hour race.

The winner was twenty-six-year-old Mike Hawthorn, of Britain, in a Jaguar.

At Le Mans last night, soon after his victory, he said: "I am glad I won, but no one likes to see an accident, especially such a terrible accident as that."

Why the Horror race went on—Centre Pages.

DEATH TOLL RISES TO 85 IN CAR-RACE HORROR

THE death toll in the Le Mans road-race disaster rose to eighty-five last night. Another 105 people are injured.

A Mercedes driven by Frenchman Pierre Levegh crashed off the track at 150 miles an hour, exploded and plunged into a spectators' enclosure on Saturday.

The race was not stopped. Sixty-odd cars droned on for the remaining twenty-one hours of the twenty-four-hour race.

The winner was twenty-six-year-old Mike Hawthorn, of Britain, in a Jaguar.

At Le Mans last night, soon after his victory, he said: "I am glad I won, but no one likes to see an accident, especially such a terrible accident as that."

WHY THE HORROR CRASH RACE WENT ON

Daily Mirror Motoring Correspondent, Le Mans

WHY did the Le Mans 24-hour road race go on for another 21 hours after the biggest disaster in motor racing history?

How, people are asking everywhere, could sixty-odd cars have been allowed to go roaring on at speeds of up to 150 miles an hour AFTER THE CRASH THAT KILLED 85 PEOPLE AND INJURED 105 YESTERDAY?

Was it the drivers who wanted to go on racing?

Certainly Mike Hawthorn didn't. He and Ivor Bueb won in a British Jaguar.

'This is too much'

But before his victory during a stop at the pits after the accident, Mike said "I wish I did not have to race in this damn thing any more. This is too much for me."

Only subdued clapping greeted Mike when he sped over the finishing line in his Jaguar today – the crowd was still stunned by the memory of that moment last evening when a blazing car plunged like a torrent of death into a spectators' enclosure.

Some of the people seemed to be watching unwillingly, as if hypnotised.

One even asked his companion: "Why did this race have to go on?"

Elsewhere officials were explaining: "There might have been a panic if we had stopped the race."

'It's Essential'

Another – Monsieur Charles Faroux, the race president – looked into the future. "These twenty-four-hour Le Mans races will continue," he said.

"They are an essential element of the world's car industry."

Earlier M. Faroux had been pressed by local council leaders to cancel the race because of the disaster.

His answer to that was: "No. Thousands of people have come to Le Mans just to see the racing."

Only the Mercedes team asked for permission to drop out immediately after the crash – the car that hurtled off the road was driven by a team-mate.

After seven and a half hours the permission came, from Germany.

At that time a Mercedes driven by Britain's Stirling Moss was in the lead.

THE CRASH THAT KILLED EIGHTY-FIVE happened at 6.30 p.m.

A low, silver-coloured Mercedes-Benz, driven by veteran Frenchman Pierre Levegh, streaked up the track at 150 miles an hour.

It touched the back of an Austin Healey driven by Englishman Lance Macklin.

The Mercedes bounced from side to side, then plunged over a safety barrier into the crowd.

It blew up as it flew into the air among the screaming people like a blazing cat o'nine tails.

Many people were decapitated. Many others had head and chest injuries.

Pierre Levegh lay dead near the blazing wreckage of his car.

But the rest of the cars roared on – there were still 21 hours to go.

An SOS

In the enclosure there was a frantic appeal for doctors. Two from London, Dr. Geoffrey Dickson and Dr. Duncan McDermott, both of the Western Hospital, Hammersmith, worked in the operating theatre at Le Mans Hospital non-stop until the early hours.

Meanwhile experts tried to find out why the crash happened.

Some said the course is too narrow, the cars too fast and the safety precautions inadequate.

BACKSTORY

The death toll in the Le Mans disaster would be established as 84, with over 100 injured. It prompted reform in safety features, introducing a greater distance between the track and spectators, though the measures at the time were judged to be above standard. Nonetheless, Mercedes withdrew from all forms of motor racing for over 30 years.

Hawthorn was blamed by some for the accident in braking too sharply for a refuelling stop, though other experts reject this, citing a multitude of factors in the build-up to the accident. Hawthorn was killed in a road accident in Surrey in 1959.

The Austin Healy involved in the crash was sold at auction in 2011 for £843,000.

A graphic depiction of the scene at Le Mans, illustrating the sheer carnage of the disaster.

Daily Mirror

TUES MAY 15 1956

2ᵈ FORWARD WITH THE PEOPLE

No. 16,305

THE FROGMAN BLUNDER

THE SILENT MAN IN THE COMMONS LAST NIGHT

DOES MOUNTBATTEN KNOW THE ANSWER?

THERE was a silent figure in the Gallery of the House of Commons last night. He was:
FIFTY-FOUR-YEAR-OLD ADMIRAL THE EARL MOUNTBATTEN, THE FIRST SEA LORD.

Wearing a dark grey lounge suit, he sat in the front row of the Peers' Gallery listening to evasive replies from Sir Anthony Eden, the Prime Minister, in the debate on the Frogman Blunder.

Sitting next to him was the white-haired figure of Lord Cilcennin, aged fifty-two, First Lord of the Admiralty—Mountbatten's political chief.

They heard Sir Anthony say:

"I deplore this debate and I will say no more." . . . "I have not one word more to say than I announced on Wednesday." . . . "I am not prepared to discuss these matters in this House."

Without Authority of Ministers

Sir Anthony repeated that what was done in the affair of Commander Crabb was done without the authority of Ministers.

He emphasised: "That includes ALL Ministers and ALL aspects of this affair."

The first official statement that Commander Crabb was presumed dead was issued by the Admiralty. That was on April 29 —ten days after Crabb disappeared in Portsmouth harbour. The Service chief at the Admiralty is Lord Mountbatten.

IS HE THE ONLY MAN IN THE WORLD BESIDES THE PRIME MINISTER WHO KNOWS THE FULL FACTS OF THE MISSION AND THE FATE OF COMMANDER CRABB?

The Commons Debate is reported on the Back Page

15th May 1956

THE SILENT MAN IN THE COMMONS LAST NIGHT

The Frogman Blunder

THERE was a silent figure in the Gallery of the House of Commons last night. He was: FIFTY-FOUR-YEAR-OLD ADMIRAL THE EARL MOUNTBATTEN, THE FIRST SEA LORD.

Wearing a dark grey lounge suit, he sat in the front row of the Peers' Gallery listening to evasive replies from Sir Anthony Eden, the Prime Minister, in the debate on the Frogman Blunder.

Sitting next to him was the white-haired figure of Lord Cilcennin, aged fifty-two, First Lord of the Admiralty, Mountbatten's political chief.

They heard Sir Anthony say: "I deplore this debate and I will say no more.

"I have not one word more to say than I announced on Wednesday . . .

"I am not prepared to discuss these matters in this House."

Without Authority of Ministers

Sir Anthony repeated that what was done in the affair of Commander Crabb was done without the authority of Ministers. He emphasised: "That includes ALL Ministers and ALL aspects of this affair."

The first official statement that Commander Crabb was presumed dead was issued by the Admiralty. That was on April 29 – ten days after Crabb disappeared in Portsmouth harbour.

The Service chief at the Admiralty is Lord Mountbatten.

IS HE THE ONLY MAN IN THE WORLD BESIDES THE PRIME MINISTER WHO KNOWS THE FULL FACTS OF THE MISSION AND THE FATE OF COMMANDER CRABB . . .?

ANNOUNCING the death of Commander Crabb . . . the Admiralty said "He did not return from a test dive which took place in connection with trials of certain underwater apparatus in Stokes Bay, in the Portsmouth area, about a week ago."

WHAT EDEN SAID ...

WHEN he was questioned by M.P.s last Wednesday about the fate of Commander Crabb, the missing frogman, Sir Anthony Eden said: "What was done was done without authority or the knowledge of Her Majesty's Ministers. Appropriate disciplinary steps are being taken."

WHAT THE RUSSIANS SAID ...

THE Russian Note to Britain said that Rear-Admiral Burnett, Chief of Staff at Portsmouth, was told by the commanding officer of the Russian squadron that a frogman had been seen. The Note said Admiral Burnett categorically denied the possibility of a diver alongside the Soviet ships and stated that during that time no diving work whatsoever was carried out in the harbour.

10th June 1957

FROGMAN CRABB – IS IT HIS BODY?

THE body of a frogman was found yesterday floating in Chichester harbour, twelve miles from the spot in Portsmouth harbour where Commander Lionel "Buster" Crabb vanished fourteen months ago.

The body, which had obviously been in the water a considerable time, was dressed in the remains of a frogman's black rubber suit.

The head and hands were missing.

The police were called and they told the Admiralty of the discovery. A spokesman there said last night:

"We are standing by to help in identifying the body or the equipment."

Another Admiralty spokesman said: "It is not impossible for a body to disappear in the sea at Portsmouth and turn up twelve months or more later at Chichester."

There have been cases where bodies of people drowned in Portsmouth harbour have come to the surface a year later – some as far away as the Isle of Wight.

When ex-Navy frogman Commander Crabb mysteriously disappeared, the Russian cruiser Ordzhonikidze, which brought the Russian leaders Bulganin and Krushchev to Britain, was in Portsmouth harbour.

Commander Crabb, hero of many wartime frogman exploits, was on a secret mission when he disappeared.

Sir Anthony Eden, then Prime Minister, said in the House of Commons that Commander Crabb's activities in Portsmouth harbour were "unauthorised."

BACKSTORY

Lionel "Buster" Crabb was one of the great heroes of the Second World War – a daredevil diver who won the George Medal for stopping mines from blowing up British ships, and whose exploits were dramatized in the film *The Silent Enemy*.

After the war he continued to work for the Royal Navy on special missions. Mystery surrounded his disappearance in 1955. It was alleged he was spying on the Russian ship *Ordzhonikidze* which had docked in Portsmouth after bringing Soviet leaders Krushchev and Bulganin to the UK, and the secrecy of the Crabb case prompted the uproar in parliament.

When a body eventually turned up over a year later, his former wife and his girlfriend could not provide formal identification and the inquest resulted in an open verdict. But 50 years later Crabb's diving partner Sydney Knowles made the sensational claim that Crabb was threatening to defect to the USSR and was murdered by another diver working for British Intelligence while on the *Ordzhonikidze* mission.

Other theories and rumours abound, including Crabb being killed by the Russians using a secret underwater weapon; that a Russian frogman slit his throat while the Briton was trying to plant a mine; and that Crabb did in fact defect to the Soviet Union.

Only a drop in a petrol can, but...

IT'S OIL—AND IT'S OURS!

says NORMAN LONGMATE

THE little pumping engine swayed monotonously up and down in the fog. Around it a few cows shivered miserably as they grazed.

It looked like the pump for providing a water supply for a farm.

But a notice said: "No smoking within 200 feet."

And when a man huddled in an overcoat turned a tap, a greasy black liquid trickled out.

For this was Kuwait in England—the source of the only oil in the world we could still count on getting even if Nasser turned the whole Middle East against us and we hadn't a single dollar to buy American supplies.

Sleepy Village

There are no tall derricks . . . no hard-faced men driving heavy lorries loaded with explosives . . . no "gushers" flaming dramatically into the sky.

The heart of Britain's oilfield is called Eakring, Nottinghamshire — a tiny, sleepy village miles from the nearest railway station.

Instead of a booming "oil town" there are a few temporary wooden huts.

In place of soaring drilling rigs, 200 tiny "nodding donkey" engines—ignored except by the cows and an occasional maintenance man—are scattered about the Nottinghamshire fields.

Yet this is a battlefield. For oil in England is not waiting to bubble to the surface as soon as a borehole reaches it.

Every gallon has to be fought for.

WATER has to be forced below the layers of oil—which may be 3,000 feet down—to bring it part-way to the surface.

Pumps above ground have to struggle to drag it the rest of the way.

Elaborate machinery is needed to remove water from the oil.

Last year, in spite of the difficulties, the 650 men of the British Petroleum Company employed on home production of oil, won 15,000,000 gallons from the soil.

It sounds a lot. But it is less than one day's supply for the whole country.

For Britain last year used 23,000,000 TONS. The six oilfields near Eakring—plus one tiny one near Liverpool—supplied just 53,000 tons of that.

Production is rising . . . 65,000 tons last year . . . 80,000 tons expected this year. Perhaps more in the future.

But it will still be merely a drop in the petrol can.

The Difference

Summed up Scotsman William Watson, who had twenty-five years' experience of oil production in the Middle East before taking over as manager at Eakring:

"There is more oil in one well in Persia than in the whole of this field."

American production, too, is way ahead of Britain's, although the methods used, and the size of the wells, is the same.

But for every well in Nottinghamshire, Texas has 1,000.

Good Quality

Why do we bother about British oil?

One reason is that the oil produced is of good quality, comparable with that imported.

Another is that transport costs are much less. After a short trip by underground pipeline, oil from Eakring is carried direct by rail to the refineries in Scotland.

WHAT difference has the coming of oil meant to Eakring?

For the farmers who dreamed of making a fortune from rich "strikes" on their land, it has meant a big disappointment.

Oil deposits in England belong to the Crown, though the farmers receive compensation for any damage done—and may benefit from new roads and services put in by the oil men.

Local Recruits

For local workmen it has meant new opportunities. Though most of the staff are outside experts, a few workers are recruited locally.

Typical of these is forty-six-year-old Ernest Bartle, who used to be a farm labourer — it seemed a choice between that and working in the mines.

Today he works in the same fields — but as a pumpman supervising a collecting station, where the output of ten wells is pumped into the pipeline.

"I've still got the kind of outdoor job I like," he told me, " but pay and hours are better."

FOR the oil men, working in Britain is just another job.

Take Harry Warman, who is thirty-three. As soon as he qualified as a geologist he went to Persia for eight years to help search for oil.

It meant disappearing into the desert or the mountains with a mule caravan for weeks at a time. Coping with flies . . . and a heat of 126 degrees in the shade.

On Rations, Too

Next year he is off to the tropical jungle of New Guinea.

At the moment he is working in a comfortable laboratory in Eakring and driving to work every day in a large car.

"Oil is oil wherever you are," he says simply.

But there are differences, as the men of Eakring are finding out—for wherever I went in the "field" I heard one grievance.

Although there is little public transport, the men receive only a very small petrol ration.

So the blokes who produce 15,000,000 gallons of oil a year find it hard to get enough to take them to work.

IKE'S PLAN

Continued from Page One

six months ago Eden's Folly could never have occurred. There would have been no war with Egypt. No breach in the Atlantic Alliance.

The whole world knows **WHY** Eisenhower kept quiet.

He was frightened to intervene because of America's domestic election. He refused to formulate a policy for the Middle East until he was again firmly in the Presidential saddle.

There can be no more of this perilous nonsense if the Anglo-American partnership—essential to world peace—is to flourish. History will not wait, even for America. And America is the leader of the Western Alliance.

Let there be no major move in 1957 without prior consultation between the Western Powers.

President Eisenhower still deeply resents what he privately describes as the "deceit" of Prime Minister Eden. That is understandable.

But the partnership with Britain cannot be kept alive if he continues to snub the British people.

The wound must be healed by Britain.

The first urgent task for the Tory Party is to select a leader who can again walk into the White House—and be welcomed and trusted.

● The Task at Home

ANOTHER task confronts the Tories, with equal urgency.

On December 5 the Daily Mirror declared:

" How can WE help in the urgent business of making Britain great again ?

" Long-drawn-out games of political chess over Suez will solve nothing. They will not get Britain out of the mess.

" The debate is over. The time has come for a massive UNITED effort."

The Mirror asked the Tory Party to decide whether Sir Anthony Eden, after all that has happened, is capable of piloting the country through the pressing problems which face us at home.

Meanwhile, the announcement that he is stepping in to solve the fuel crisis has been received with grim amusement.

One month has passed since that question was asked.

How much longer must the nation wait for the answer ?

Dainty feet score at the Sales

VIEW POINT

I RECKON you have to be SMALL to get the best bargains.

My wife takes a tiny, size three-and-a-half shoe. Shops stock a few for display purposes but usually can't sell them all. So when the Sales come along the small shoes are offered at bargain prices. My missus steps in—and gets two pairs for the normal price of one.— Derek, London, E.2.

UNINSPIRED

WHAT gets into men once they're married and settled down?

When courting, my man was lively and gay. Now he's like a block of wood. He has no conversation. Nothing inspires him.— Housewife, Slough.

PENICILLIN

A COMMENTATOR in the "Voice of America" radio programme said streptomycin and penicillin were developed in a laboratory in Iowa. Now we all know that Sir Alexander Fleming discovered penicillin—but I'd like to know if the Government do anything to combat an inaccurate statement like this.—M. A. P., Alveston, Bristol.

USE FOR CARDS

WHAT to do with old Christmas cards? I write letters on them, and send them, with their envelopes to my relatives. It's not meanness, just another way of saving money.—(Mrs.) P. W., Mere, Wilts.

SACK O' SOIL

I HAVE sifted as much as twenty-two pounds of soil out of a hundred-weight sack of potatoes. It's not exactly easy money being a greengrocer as I am.—(Mrs.) F. Hodson, Sheffield, 7.

MATTER OF CHOICE

MY cat takes a great interest in the television programmes, and will sit on my lap for ages, staring at the screen. On the other hand my dog doesn't take the slightest bit of notice—until Big Ben chimes the hours, and then he howls his head off.—(Mrs.) K. N., Kingston-on-Thames.

DIG THIS!

CARTOONISTS often depict men shirking the work in the garden— but most of the men in my street seem as happy as sandboys when they are planting and weeding. Give them a spade and they'll dig all day. So lay off, cartoonists—you'll be giving them ideas.—(Mrs.) P. G., Peterlee, Co. Durham.

CHEER UP, GILBERT !

I WAS glad to hear Vera Lynn mention Gilbert Harding on TV recently. Since he has been in hospital there's been practically no mention of him. I suppose it's: "Out of sight, out of mind." Cheer up, Gilbert, I hope you'll be well soon.—H. F. H., Hounslow, Middlesex.

— GILBERT

7th January 1957

IT'S OIL – AND IT'S OURS!

Says Norman Longmate

THE little pumping engine swayed monotonously up and down in the fog. Around it a few cows shivered miserably as they grazed.

It looked like the pump for providing a water supply for a farm.

But a notice said: "No smoking within 200 feet."

And when a man huddled in an overcoat turned a tap, a greasy black liquid trickled out.

For this was Kuwait in England – the only source of oil in the world we could still count on getting even if Nasser turned the whole Middle East against us and we hadn't a single dollar to buy American supplies temporarily.

Sleepy Village

There are no tall derricks . . . no hard-faced men driving heavy lorries loaded with explosives . . . no "gushers" flaming dramatically into the sky.

The heart of Britain's oilfield is called Eakring, Nottinghamshire – a tiny sleepy village miles from the nearest railway station.

Instead of a booming "oil town" there are a few temporary wooden huts.

In place of soaring drilling rigs, 200 tiny "nodding donkey" engines – ignored except by the cows and an occasional maintenance man – are scattered about the Nottinghamshire fields.

Yet this is a battlefield. For oil in England is not waiting to bubble to the surface as soon as a borehole reaches it.

Every gallon has to be fought for.

Water has to be forced below the layers of oil – which may be 3,000 feet down – to bring it part-way to the surface.

Pumps above ground have to struggle to drag it the rest of the way.

Elaborate machinery is needed to remove water from the oil.

Last year in spite of the difficulties, the 650 men of the British Petroleum Company employed on home production of oil won 5,000,000 gallons from the soil.

It sounds a lot. But it is less than one day's supply for the whole country.

For Britain last year used 23,000,000 TONS. The six oilfields near Eakring – plus one tiny one near Liverpool – supplied just 53,000 tons of that.

Production is rising . . . 65,000 tons last year . . . 80,000 tons expected this year. Perhaps more in the future.

But it will still be merely a drop in the petrol can.

The Difference

Summed up Scotsman William Watson, who had twenty-five years' experience of oil production in the Middle East before taking over as manager at Eakring:

"There is more oil in one well in Persia than in the whole of this field."

American production, too, is way ahead of Britain's, although the methods used, and the size of the wells, is the same.

But for every well in Nottinghamshire, Texas has 1,000.

Good Quality

Why do we bother about British oil? One reason is that the oil produced is of good quality, comparable with that imported.

Another is that transport costs are much less. After a short trip by underground pipeline, oil from Eakring is carried direct by rail to the refineries in Scotland.

What difference has the coming of oil meant to Eakring?

For the farmers who dreamed of making a fortune from rich "strikes" on their land, it has meant a big disappointment.

Oil deposits in England belong to the Crown, though the farmers receive compensation for any damage done – and may benefit from new roads and services put in by the oil men.

For local workmen it has meant new opportunities. Though most of the staff are outside experts, a few workers are recruited locally.

Typical of these is forty-six-year-old Ernest Bartle, who used to be a farm labourer – it seemed a choice between that and working in the mines. Today he works in the same fields – but as a pumpman supervising a collecting station, where the output of ten wells is pumped into the pipeline.

"I've still got the kind of outdoor job I like," he told me, "but pay and hours are better."

FOR the oil men, working in Britain is just another job.

Take Harry Warman, who is thirty-three. As soon as he qualified as a geologist he went to Persia for eight years to help search for oil.

It meant disappearing into the desert or the mountains with a mule caravan for weeks at a time. Coping with flies . . . and a heat of 126 degrees in the shade.

On Rations, Too

Next year he is off to the tropical jungle of New Guinea. At the moment he is working in a comfortable laboratory in Eakring and driving to work every day in a large car.

"Oil is oil wherever you are," he says simply.

But there are differences, as the men of Eakring are finding out – for wherever I went in the "field" I heard one grievance.

Although there is little public transport, the men receive only a very small petrol ration.

So the blokes who produce 15,000,000 gallons of oil a year find it hard to get enough to take them to work.

◀ Mainland oil production in the UK wasn't limited to Nottinghamshire. This well was at Kimmeridge in Dorset.

Adrienne gets a wigging

RED-HEADED actress Adrienne Corri got a wigging from ITV last night—for wearing a BLONDE WIG on B.B.C. television.

Adrienne is pictured in the wig on the right as she signs autographs at the stage door of the B.B.C. studios at Shepherd's Bush.

She had just appeared (complete with wig) in the "What's My Line?" programme.

Miss Corri bought the £30 wig for her part in next week's ITV play called "Dangerous Word."

And ABC Television said she could not appear in the wig before the play unless she gave the show "a plug."

'Naughty Girl'

The B.B.C. said that as the wig was Adrienne's property, she could wear it any time she wanted. But she could NOT plug a rival channel.

Added a B.B.C. spokesman: "We're in the television business too." Commented an ABC spokesman: "ADRIENNE IS A NAUGHTY GIRL."

Adrienne said last night: "It was my wig—and I did ask the B.B.C. if I could wear it during 'What's My Line?' and play the play."

The only comment on the wig during "What's My Line?" came from chairman Eamonn Andrews. He gave a long, low wolf whistle.

MISS CORRI MINUS HER WIG

Adrienne Corri in her blonde wig, signs autographs outside the B.B.C. television studios.

QUEUES ON THE 100 mph MOTORWAY

SO many drivers wanted to use Britain's first motorway yesterday that there was a monster TRAFFIC JAM—a mile-and-a-half long.

The motorway, which cost £3,750,000, is the eight-and-a-quarter-mile-long Preston by-pass which was opened last week by the Prime Minister.

At one time, Automobile Association patrols estimated yesterday's flow of traffic on this Lancashire high-speed roadway to be at the rate of about 1,000 vehicles an hour in both directions.

Drivers who had been travelling at a mile a minute from Bamber Bridge had to wait up to half an hour to get back on to the old road at Broughton.

THERE WERE NO ACCIDENTS, BUT THERE WERE SOME BREAKDOWNS.

Radio - controlled breakdown vehicles went to the aid of about half a dozen cars and one car had to be towed away.

The A.A. official said that yesterday's speeds were "fast." At least six cars, he said, "reached 100 m.p.h."

That sit-down dog is back home again

THE little mongrel dog who sat by a main road for fourteen hours was back home with his owner yesterday.

Mr. Ernest Jolly, of Pheasant - road, Ipswich, Suffolk, claimed the dog, Pip, from the Ipswich headquarters of the Royal Society for the Prevention of Cruelty to Animals.

The R.S.P.C.A. took care of Pip on Friday after a phone call from a cyclist saying that the dog had been sitting by the road at Wherstead, near Ipswich, throughout the night.

Mr. Jolly, a milkman, said yesterday that Pip was taken for a car trip on Thursday and ran off when the car stopped.

"I waited about until it was too dark to see and then drove home," said Mr. Jolly. "When I went back next day there was no sign of him.

"Pip is very intelligent and I think he was waiting by the side of the road for my car to come along."

BOY 'SCIENTISTS' HURT IN BLAST

SCHOOLBOY "scientist" Tony Vine, 15, read about the "solid fuel unit" in the American Moon Rocket and decided it would be just the thing for his model jet aircraft.

So yesterday he and two of his schoolfriends started work on the unit. Last night one of them was in hospital and the others were being treated for shock after an explosion.

In hospital was Chris Turner, 15, with a badly cut leg. Roger Smith, also fifteen, was badly shocked

and Tony had a stomach injury.

The boys all live in Woodfield - avenue, Portsmouth.

Tony said last night: "We packed some potassium chlorate into a tube with some other chemicals to make a solid fuel unit.

"But one of us banged the tube and the whole lot went up."

Included in "the lot" was the little shed at the bottom of Tony's garden.

25th March 1958
COLOSSAL MOTORWAY

By Patrick Mennem

AN army of giant road-making machines lumbered past Transport Minister Harold Watkinson yesterday.

Within seconds they had pounded a strip of Bedfordshire into a different shape. Work on the London to Birmingham motorway had started.

The sixty-seven mile motorway is the single road scheme ever tackled in Britain.

SO BIG that the contractors will use a HELICOPTER to keep an eye on how the work is going.

SO BIG that 8,000,000 gallons of fuel will be needed for more than 1,000 pieces of machinery.

The motorway begun yesterday near Luton will stretch from the St. Albans by-pass in Hertfordshire to the Dunchurch by-pass near Rugby, Warwickshire.

Then the road will divide, one section going a few miles on to Birmingham, the other heading north, for Yorkshire.

Everything about the £20,000,000 scheme is colossal.

EACH of the twin carriage-ways will be 36ft. wide.

THERE will be more than 200 fly-overs and fly-unders.

THERE will be facilities every twelve miles for petrol stations, cafes and picnic parking places.

25th October 1958

TYPIST Elizabeth O'Dwyer yesterday became the first person to be prosecuted in Britain for a parking-meter offence – and she doesn't OWN a car and can't DRIVE.

Elizabeth, 19, got a summons because – at the request of one of her firm's representatives – she stopped on her way home to lunch and put a second shilling in the meter where his car was parked.

That, the magistrate was told at Marlborough street, London, was illegal.

If Elizabeth had not put a second shilling in the meter, the car-owner's two-hour parking time would soon have been up, said Mr Leonard Gost, prosecuting for Westminster City Council, which runs the meters.

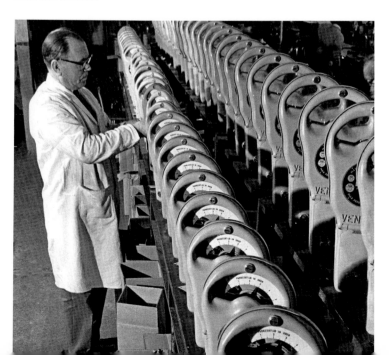

When the time was up, a penalty flag would have shown on the meter – and the car-owner would have had to pay a 10s. fine.

Mr Gost said it was forbidden to "feed" the meters with extra coins which stopped the penalty flag showing.

The magistrate, Mr Clyde Wilson, asked "If a person puts in 6d. for only one hour, can he not pay another 6d. for a second hour?"

Mr Gost: "No he can pay two sixpences at once and get two hours, but if he puts in only one sixpence he cannot go back later and pay another sixpence for the second hour."

Magistrate: "I cannot see the logic of that."

Mr Gost said the car had to be moved from the parking bay for at least an hour before the meter could be used again for the same car.

'Hardship'

Mr. W. H Chitty, a solicitor who pleaded guilty on behalf of Elizabeth, said the case seemed a great hardship for a girl who did not own the car and had not parked it.

Elizabeth, of Davidson road, Croydon, was given an absolute discharge and ordered to pay 2s. costs.

At her home last night, Elizabeth, who did not go to court, said: "I still don't really understand what I did wrong."

She added: "All I did was put a shilling in for one of our representatives. He was on the phone, and couldn't get out.

"When I put the shilling in, a meter attendant told me I was committing an offence and called two policemen."

8th December 1958
QUEUES ON THE 100 MPH MOTORWAY

SO many drivers wanted to use Britain's first motorway yesterday that there was a monster TRAFFIC JAM – a mile-and-a-half long.

The motorway, which cost £3,750,000, is the eight-and-a-quarter-mile-long Preston by-pass which was opened last week by the Prime Minister.

At one time, Automobile Association patrols estimated yesterday's flow of traffic on this Lancashire high-speed roadway to be at the rate of about 1,000 vehicles an hour in both directions.

Drivers who had been travelling at a mile a minute from Bamber Bridge had to wait up to half an hour to get back on to the old road at Broughton.

THERE WERE NO ACCIDENTS, BUT THERE WERE SOME BREAKDOWNS.

Radio-controlled breakdown vehicles went to the aid of about half a dozen cars and one car had to be towed away.

The A.A. official said that yesterday's speeds were "fast." At least six cars, he said, "reached 100 m.p.h."

BACKSTORY

Britain's embrace of the new motorway system got off to an exciting start with the opening of the Preston bypass and the construction of the M1 – but the introduction of a new traffic measure, in the shape of parking meters, brought an immediate unpopularity that has persisted ever since. The first meter in Britain was set up in London's Grosvenor Square, on 10th June 1958.

Daily Mirror

WED JAN 7 1959

2½ ★ ★ ★ FORWARD WITH THE PEOPLE No. 17,126

WINSTON KEEPS MUM

THEY GOT ME, PAL SAYS FLYNN

SWASHBUCKLING Hollywood film star Errol Flynn, 49, who was injured while with Castro's rebel army during the Cuban Revolution, talks to a fan by telephone from a Havana hotel. The fan wanted to know if Flynn—hero of many film battles—was seriously injured. He had slight wounds in an arm and leg. Slung casually over his right shoulder is a scarf—a gift from Castro.

Earlier, one of the star's secretaries in Hollywood said Flynn phoned him and said he got the injuries during an attack on a sugar mill.

Flynn had been with Castro's forces for about two weeks. "He has quite a story to tell," the secretary added.

The vigilant Castro—See picture on the Back Page.

By VICTOR KNIGHT

RUMOURS swept the political world last night that eighty-four-year-old Sir Winston Churchill had decided to retire from the House of Commons at the next General Election.

Speculation started when it was announced that Sir Winston was making a speech to about 100 leading Tories from his Woodford, Essex, constituency.

Newspaper reporters and cameramen packed the Kensington Palace Hotel, London, where the meeting was being held.

But if Sir Winston **HAS** decided to retire from Parliament he gave no clue whatever last night.

Though he spoke for fifteen minutes about domestic and world politics, not once did he mention his own personal position in the House.

But he **DID** mention the General Election.

They would have to organise themselves for it, he said, "sometime this year or next."

The Tory Party, he said, did not want a vote of thanks. They wanted a "vote of confidence."

When did the ex-Premier think the election would be?

"For my part," he said, "I am rather doubtful whether it is going to be so swift and sudden as is made out."

Smiles and Handshakes

After his speech, drinks were brought in and Sir Winston, wreathed in smiles, sat chatting and shaking hands with the local Tories.

A Party official explained that Sir Winston had asked for the meeting because he likes to meet the Woodford Tory Executive Council regularly and have a drink with them.

Last time this happened, said the official, was about a year ago.

● Sir Winston did not go to the meeting alone. Lady Churchill was with him. So was his daughter Mary—wife of War Secretary Christopher Soames.

7th January 1959

THEY GOT ME, PAL SAYS FLYNN

SWASHBUCKLING Hollywood film star Errol Flynn, 49, who was injured while with Castro's rebel army during the Cuban Revolution, talks to a fan by telephone from a Havana hotel.

The fan wanted to know if Flynn – hero of many film battles – was seriously injured. He had slight wounds in an arm and leg. Slung casually over his right shoulder is a scarf – a gift from Castro.

Earlier, one of the star's secretaries in Hollywood said Flynn phoned him and said he got the injuries during an attack on a sugar mill.

Flynn had been with Castro's forces for about two weeks. "He has quite a story to tell," the secretary added.

16th October 1959

'I INTEND TO DEVOTE MY LIFE TO WOMEN'

Errol Flynn Died Laughing

FABULOUS film star Errol Flynn, who died at Vancouver, Canada, after a heart attack yesterday . . . was laughing and joking minutes before he collapsed.

A few hours earlier fifty-year-old Flynn said: "I intend to devote the rest of my life to women."

HE WAS AN ACTOR TO THE END

From Lionel Crane Hollywood, Thursday

IN the last hour of his life Errol Flynn gave his finest performance.

Last night, while an audience of seven people in a doctor's house at Vancouver, Canada, rocked with laughter, Errol leaned nonchalantly against a wall in the living-room, pantomiming his entire fantastic career.

Racked with pain, but with a grin on his face, Errol made merciless fun of himself and the whole Hollywood merry-go-round.

"It was superb, magnificent," said his host, Dr. Grant Gould.

And no showman in the world could have beaten Errol's exit line. When he had finished his show he went towards another room

with seventeen-year-old Beverly Aadland, his protegee, who starred with him in his last film, "Cuban Rebel Girl."

'I Shall Return'

At the door Errol turned, raised a finger and said: "I shall return." But he did not.

A few minutes later Beverly rushed back into the living room and cried: "Errol's ill. Errol's ill."

In her hand she had a broken phial containing a drug. She told Dr. Gould she carried the drug with her because Errol had had two slight heart attacks.

She said she had broken the phial under his nose to try to revive him.

When the other guests went into the room Errol was lying on the floor. Beverly flung herself on top of the fifty-year-old actor. With her long blonde hair falling over her face, she tried to breathe life into him by putting her mouth to his.

When she was exhausted, George Caldough, a friend of Errol's, took over.

Firemen also tried, but it was no good. Errol died before they could get him into the ambulance.

Her Screams

Beverly ran screaming on to a balcony outside the flat and had to be restrained.

At the hospital she still would not believe Errol was dead. She threw herself on his bed, and later said to friends: "He is all right. He will be out tomorrow."

Friends led her away, saying that Errol WAS dead. With her she took a gold wrist watch bearing the initials "E.F."

His third wife, Pat Wymore, is returning to Hollywood later today. Pat's daughter's Amelia, is six.

Errol's two other daughters, both by Norah Eddington, are Rory, 13, and Deirdre, 14. He had a son by his first wife, actress Lily Damita.

Errol, who made and spent a fortune in alimony and court cases, said recently: "I earned seven million dollars for brandishing a sword, riding a horse and screaming 'Charge!'

"I did not deserve it, but I certainly didn't mind spending it. The public has always expected me to be a playboy and a decent chap never lets his public down."

Last Words

When he arrived in Vancouver he was asked if he intended to marry Miss Aadland. She said: "I don't believe in marriage," and Errol said: "That's the girl."

He also said that films were no longer important to him and added: "I intend to devote the rest of my life to women."

BACKSTORY

For fans more used to seeing their idol hogging the headlines for his movies and hell-raising lifestyle, it came as a surprise to see Errol Flynn (left) spending his later days with Fidel Castro's revolutionary army in Cuba.

The man who memorably played Robin Hood was sympathetic to Castro's cause, and while embedded with Castro's rebel troops worked as a correspondent, writing articles about their campaign. The film legend had his teenage girlfriend Beverly Aadland in tow, but his health was declining. Nine months later he died, aged just 50.

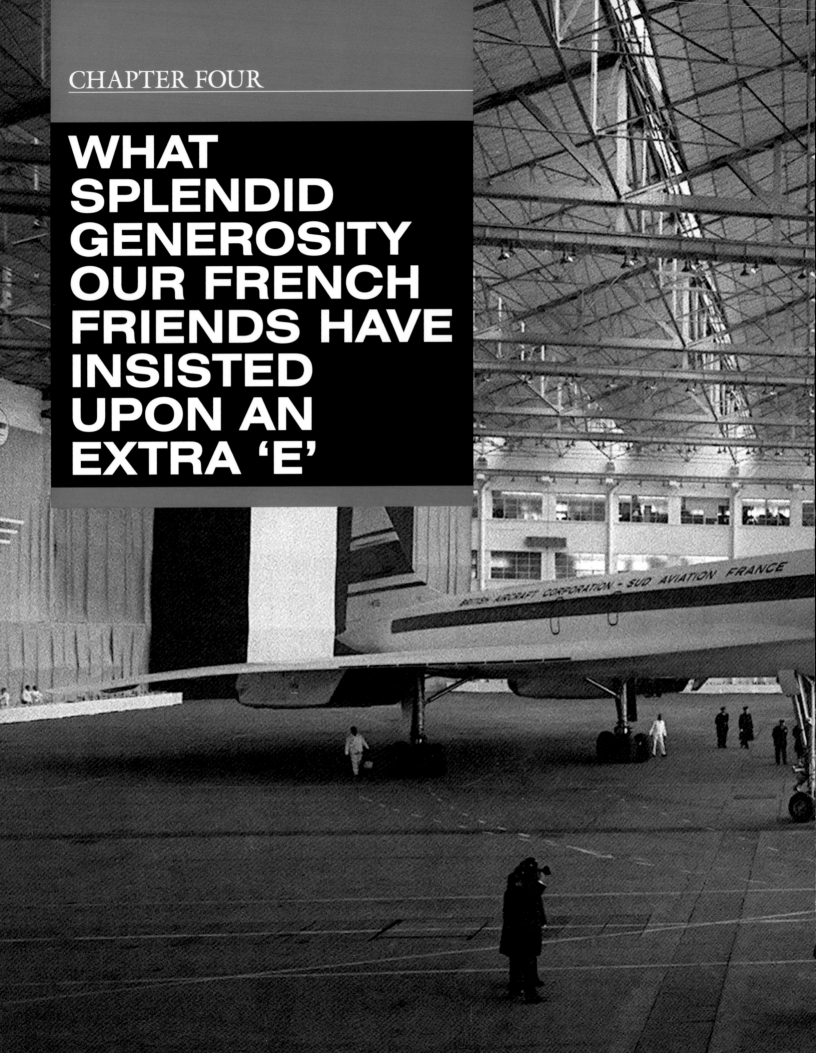

CHAPTER FOUR

WHAT SPLENDID GENEROSITY OUR FRENCH FRIENDS HAVE INSISTED UPON AN EXTRA 'E'

The BAC Aerospatiale Concorde 001 prototype is rolled out in Toulouse in 1968 (see page 142).

Daily Mirror

WED MAY 4 1960

2d • • • • No. 17,536

SHE IS TOLD: YOU MUST PAY £7,000

The Silent Duchess

THE Duchess of Argyll, 48, stayed silent in the High Court yesterday.

SHE did not go into the witness box.

SHE called no witnesses.

SHE was ordered to pay £7,000 damages to Mrs. Yvonne Mac-Pherson, 49, her former social secretary, for slander and libel.

'What Can I Say...?'

The Duchess, pictured here, was also ordered to pay Mrs. Mac-Pherson's costs—estimated at £2,000.

The Duke of Argyll, 56, gave evidence on Mrs. MacPherson's behalf.

So did Mrs. Alice Mary Wolkowicki, who was film and stage star Diana Napier and widow of singer (You Are My Heart's Delight) Richard Tauber.

Outside the court—

THE DUCHESS said: "What can I say that millions do not know already?

"My whole life has been made public in the last two days."

A Kiss from the Duke...

THE DUKE pecked Mrs. Mac-Pherson on the cheek—and made no comment.

MRS MacPHERSON — now social secretary to the Marchioness of Dufferin and Ava, said:

"I just can't believe that, after three years, this enormous cloud has suddenly vanished. I just can't take it in.

"I brought the action to clear my name — and that has been done."

★ Court story begins on Page Four.

4th May 1960

SHE IS TOLD: YOU MUST PAY £7,000

The Silent Duchess

THE Duchess of Argyll, 46, stayed silent in the High Court yesterday.

SHE did not go into the witness box.

SHE called no witnesses.

SHE was ordered to pay £7,000 damages to Mrs. Yvonne MacPherson, 49, her former social secretary, for slander and libel.

'What Can I Say ...?'

The Duchess was also ordered to pay Mrs. MacPherson's costs – estimated at £2,000.

The Duke of Argyll, 56, gave evidence on Mrs. MacPherson's behalf.

So did Mrs. Alice Mary Wolkowicki, who was film and stage star Diana Napier and widow of singer (You Are My Heart's Delight) Richard Tauber.

Outside the court –

THE DUCHESS said: "What can I say that millions do not know already?

"My whole life has been made public in the last two days."

A Kiss from the Duke ...

THE DUKE pecked Mrs. MacPherson on the cheek – and made no comment.

MRS MACPHERSON – now social secretary to the Marchioness of Dufferin and Ava, said:

"I just can't believe that, after three years, this enormous cloud has suddenly vanished. I just can't take it in.

"I brought the action to clear my name – and that has been done."

THE Duchess of Argyll, 46, said no word in her own defence yesterday before a High Court jury decided she should pay £7,000 damages to Mrs. Yvonne MacPherson, 49, for slander and libel.

The Duchess – whose husband, the Duke, has started divorce proceedings, sat with downcast eyes during the closing speech in the case.

Damages

The jury assessed the damages in this way:

£2,500 for the slanders – in which the court had been told, the Duchess said Mrs. MacPherson had abused her position as a confidential secretary by supplying information about the Duke and the Duchess to the Press for pay.

£4,500 for the libel – said to be contained in a 'file' telegram the Duchess sent to the Duke and which was signed with Mrs. MacPherson's Christian name, Yvonne.

The telegram said: "All is ready as we planned to tear strips off Margaret (the Duchess) financially – and otherwise."

Before the announcement that the Duchess would call no witnesses, the court had heard evidence on Mrs. MacPherson's behalf.

When the DUKE OF ARGYLL resumed his evidence in the case yesterday he was further cross-examined by Mr. Gerald Gardiner, QC for the Duchess.

Mr. Gardiner asked the Duke if he had broken into his wife's desk on April 20, 1959, and taken her private diaries and documents.

The Duke said the diaries were in an open drawer. The

documents were in a locked cabinet, and he had a key made to open it. He then removed the documents.

'Fine Point'

Mr Gardiner: "Did they include all the letters you had written to her and all the letters she had received since she was 18?"

The Duke: "They included a good many of the letters I had written to her."

Mr. Gardiner: "Not to put too fine a point on it, you pinched them?"

The Duke: "That is not a matter for this court."

Daily Mirror

3d. Tuesday, December 10, 1963   No. 18,654

Singer Frank's ordeal—son vanishes

KIDNAPPERS SILENT AFTER SINATRA GRAB

Lord Mancroft: Six Questions

SOME aspects of the embarrassing affair over the Norwich Union insurance group and Lord Mancroft may benefit from a public airing this crisp December morning.

The facts are simple, the policy haywire, the consequences deplorable.

Lord Mancroft, a man of distinction on the board of Sir Isaac Wolfson's Great Universal Stores, is no longer on the London advisory board of the Norwich company.

The reason? Arab interests informed the company he was associated with "other business interests" and that therefore Norwich insurance policies would no longer be accepted.

MIRROR PAGE ONE COMMENT

Bluntly, old man, Lord Mancroft is a Jew: his father was Arthur Samuel, an antique dealer. Of Norwich.

Even the incident of Sherlock Holmes's non-barking dog is not as curious as the situation since the Norwich company and Lord Mancroft parted. If it hadn't been for the vigilant Press, only the Arabs would have known what really happened—and why. Which would have handed them a jumbo-size chuckle.

From the Institute of Directors, usually so earsplitting, there comes an eerie silence though Lord Mancroft is a prominent member.

Does the Institute approve of commercial blackmail? Does it agree

Continued on Page Two

Frank Sinatra Junior pictured in Hollywood with his father and mother—whose marriage was dissolved.

From BARRIE HARDING, Reno, Nevada, Monday

SINGER Frank Sinatra kept to his hotel room in this gambling city tonight, hoping for a telephone call from the kidnappers of his 19-year-old son, Frank Jnr.

Sinatra flew here from his home in Palm Springs, California, soon after he heard the news that two gunmen had forced his son into a car at Lake Tahoe, a mountain resort near Reno.

G-men, who with hundreds of armed police are tonight hunting the kidnappers, are faced with a complete mystery.

So far, there has been no ransom demand—and no apparent motive for the kidnapping.

Earlier, two men were suspected — Joseph Sorce, 23, and Thomas Keating, 21. Both were on the run from a Californian prison and also wanted for alleged armed robbery and kidnapping.

But the men were later arrested — and cleared by the FBI of any connection

Police with their guns ready for action stop a car . . . and draw another blank. This was one of the many roadblocks set up around Lake Tahoe.

with the Sinatra kidnapping.

Young Sinatra was abducted from his Lake Tahoe hotel room while he was waiting to give a show at the exclusive Harrah's Club.

He was appearing at the club with the band originally formed by the late Tommy Dorsey — the man who put his father on the road to fame.

Jo Foss, a 24-year-old trumpet player, was in the room.

Gagged

Foss told police that there was a knock on the door and a man's voice said: "Room service."

Sinatra opened the door and two men, armed with revolvers, burst in.

Foss said that they forced him to the floor and gagged him. Then they tied Sinatra's hands together with tape and hustled him out, with a gun in his back.

Tonight, police were maintaining road blocks over a wide area. Others were searching the snow-covered passes in the surrounding mountains which rise to 7,200ft.

Cabins

Police believe that Sinatra might have been taken to one of thousands of motel rooms or hundreds of mountain cabins which have been closed down for the winter.

"It will take days to search the lot," a spokesman said tonight.

When Frank Sinatra, Snr, was first told of the kidnapping he said: "My God! I can't believe it."

His close friend, film star Dean Martin, said in Hollywood: "Frank loves that boy very much. He adores him. He tried to help him as much as possible."

Frank Sinatra's former wife, Nancy — the boy's mother — was being attended by a doctor at her Hollywood home tonight.

10th December 1963

KIDNAPPERS SILENT AFTER SINATRA GRAB

Singer Frank's ordeal – son vanishes

From Barrie Harding, Reno, Nevada, Monday

SINGER Frank Sinatra kept to his hotel room in this gambling city tonight, hoping for a telephone call from the kidnappers of his 19-year-old son, Frank Jnr.

Sinatra flew here from his home in Palm Springs, California, soon after he heard the news that two gunmen had forced his son into a car at Lake Tahoe, a mountain resort near Reno.

G-men, who with hundreds of armed police are tonight hunting the kidnappers, are faced with a complete mystery.

So far, there has been no ransom demand – and no apparent motive for the kidnapping.

Young Sinatra was abducted from his Lake Tahoe hotel room while he was waiting to give a show at the exclusive Harrah's Club.

He was appearing at the club with the band originally formed by the late Tommy Dorsey – the man who put his father on the road to fame.

Jo Foss, a 24-year-old trumpet player, was in the room.

Gagged

Foss told police that there was a knock on the door and a man's voice said: "Room service." Sinatra opened the door and two men, armed with revolvers, burst in.

Foss said that they forced him to the floor and gagged him. Then they tied Sinatra's hands together with tape and hustled him out, with a gun in his back.

Tonight, police were maintaining road blocks over a wide area. Others were searching the snow covered passes in the surrounding mountains which rise to 7,200ft.

Cabins

Police believe that Sinatra might have been taken to one of thousands of hotel rooms or hundreds of mountain cabins which have been closed down for the winter.

"It will take days to search the lot," a spokesman said tonight.

When Frank Sinatra, Snr, was first told of the kidnapping he said: "My God! I can't believe it."

His close friend, film star Dean Martin, said in Hollywood: "Frank loves that boy very much. He adores him. He tried to help him as much as possible."

12th December 1963

'IT WAS ROUGH' SAYS YOUNG SINATRA

SINGER Frank Sinatra today paid £85,700 to ransom his 19-year-old son from kidnappers – and now the hunt for the gang is hotting up again.

For Sinatra senior, announcing his son's return, said: "I've made no deal to protect the kidnappers. They are on their own now."

Sinatra junior, who was found walking on a Los Angeles boulevard by a patrolling "private eye," said he had "a rough two and a half days."

He thought the kidnappers were "a bunch of amateurs" from the way they operated, he told the private detective, Charles Jones, 50.

"They were more scared than I was," he added.

"One of them chickened out before they made the pick-up of the ransom money. He gave up on the whole deal."

Gunpoint

After phone negotiations, his father drove to a secret place on the Wilshire Boulevard in Los Angeles and left the £85,700 ransom money in dollar notes.

And, in the early hours of this morning, Sinatra junior was picked up on a Los Angeles street by Charles Jones.

He was smuggled past TV cameramen and reporters in the boot of Jones's car to the Hollywood home of his mother – Frank Sinatra's ex-wife, Nancy.

Knocked

Jones said today: "I knocked at the door, and Mrs. Sinatra was there.

"I said: 'Mrs. Sinatra, I have your boy in the boot of my car – and he is all right.'

"She gasped. She just stood there. Then Frank, the boy's father, came to the doorway and said: 'Let's get that boot open'."

Sinatra said: "This is my forty-sixth birthday, and it is about as good a birthday present as anyone could ask for."

BACKSTORY

The sensational kidnapping of the son of one of the most famous entertainers in the world came just a couple of weeks after the assassination of President Kennedy – and perhaps has therefore not lived so long in the memory.

It was a case swiftly solved once the ransom money – $240,000 – had been paid. The FBI had photographed the cash and traced the trail back to the house where Sinatra Jnr (above) had been held. With the kidnappers panicking, one of them, John Irwin, confessed to his brother who in turn called the FBI. Soon Irwin, Barry Keenan and Joe Amsler were arrested.

The defence tried to pin some responsibility on Sinatra Jnr, claiming he was complicit in the plot, but the jury disagreed and the hapless gang were convicted with heavy sentences. However, parole enabled Irwin and Amsler to serve three and a half years, and Keenan a year more. Singer Dean Torrence, of Jan & Dean fame, was a friend of Keenan and also caught up in the case.

Keenan went on to become a millionaire property developer. Joe Amsler briefly enjoyed a movie career as a stand-in actor.

Daily Mirror

4d.   Monday, July 26, 1965   No. 19,157

It looks like suicide, says the Yard

KILLER HUNT OFF—FREDDIE MILLS SHOCK

The man who **must** lead the Tories

FOR the first time in history, Tory MPs are selecting their leader by the democratic method of a secret ballot.

For the first time in history, the Tory Establishment, "the magic circle," the descendants of families that have ruled Britain for centuries, have no power to sway—or "interpret"—the decision.

Here at last is the chance for the back-bench Tories—finally set free from the Old Guard—to pick the best man for the job.

They will be voting not just for themselves. They will be voting for Britain—and Britain's future.

CHALLENGE

This is not a private fight. Nor is it a grown-up version of a contest to find the most popular boy in the form.

The Tories are choosing this week:

MIRROR PAGE ONE COMMENT

● The immediate leader of Her Majesty's Opposition.

● The man who will carry the challenge to Harold Wilson in the General Election.

● The man who could be the next Prime Minister: his task to further the speedy modernisation of Britain, to cope with Britain's serious, long-term problems.

CONTENDERS

Because this election is of such immense NATIONAL importance, the Mirror, which is not a Tory paper, feels it has a duty to speak its mind. Only two of the contenders for the leadership are capable of filling the great place in British life which now is vacant.

The two are, of course, REGINALD MAUDLING and EDWARD HEATH.

Unlike most of the men who have led the Tories, they do not come from illustrious landed or industrial families. They are not wealthy.

Every penny they possess has been earned. They would not know what to do with a grouse moor if somebody gave them one.

They have made their way through unfashionable schools and up Oxford and up the political ladder simply by their power of brain and force of character.

No ducal uncles, dowager aunts or well-placed cousins have been there to give them a shove at critical moments of their career.

Both belong to the right age group—under 50.

Continued on Page Two

THIS was the picture taken at the Freddie Mills Nite Spot one night in October, 1963.

Mills smiled as he posed for the photographer with an arm round laughing singer Michael Holliday.

When 35-year-old Holliday left the club that night, he went home, took an overdose of drugs . . . and died.

Now—less than two years later—his friend Freddie Mills is dead. Last night, detectives investigating the mystery believed that Mills, too, committed suicide.

But one mystery remained: What could have made Freddie Mills decide to die?

Mr. Andy Ho, the man who was Freddie Mills's partner for eighteen years, outside the Nite Spot in Charing Cross-road yesterday.

SCOTLAND Yard detectives investigating the death of one-time boxing champion Freddie Mills—found shot in a car near his West End night club—were almost certain last night that he killed himself.

At first, the investigation had been treated as a MURDER inquiry.

The belief that Mills committed suicide left the big question unanswered: Why would he do it?

Mills, 46—he was world light heavyweight champion from 1948 to 1950—was found dead early yesterday.

He lay on the back seat of his silver-grey Citroen car, in an alley behind the club—the Freddie Mills Nite Spot, in Charing Cross-road.

By **MIRROR REPORTERS**

Rifle

There was a 0.22 calibre bullet in his brain. A rifle lay on the seat, near him.

But WHY would Freddie Mills choose to die?

He had retired from boxing in 1950 after earning a reputed £100,000.

He had a wife and two daughters—Susan, 13, and Mandy, 9.

At the Freddie Mills Nite Spot, which he opened two years ago, he was known as a gay host.

But friends said last night that he had been worrying about the club.

Expenses were heavy. And the last Budget had hit most West End night spots.

A director of the Pigalle, the Stork Room and the Society, Mr. Bill Ofner, said:

"Freddie phoned me last week, and asked how business was.

"I told him it was disastrous. He said, 'Well, that's some consolation.'"

But Mills's partner, Chinese-born Mr. Andy Ho, denied that the Nite Spot was in trouble . . .

Mr. Ho, 50, said at home in Hartshorne - road, Bushey Heath, Herts: "Freddie had not approached me for help. His death was a complete shock to me."

What happens to the Freddie Mills Nite Spot now?

"There is no plan for the club at present." Mr. Ho said.

Mr. Ho's 26 - year - old daughter Nita, who works as a receptionist at the club on Saturdays, had a theory about Mills's death.

"For some time," she said, "Freddie hadn't appeared on television, or opened fetes—or any of the things he used to do.

"He wasn't happy about that. Maybe he wanted to make headlines once more, when he died."

Big-hearted Mills often helped his maiden aunt, Miss Kate Gray, who was in the Dorset County Coun-

Continued on Back Page

138

26th July 1965

KILLER HUNT OFF – FREDDIE MILLS SHOCK

It looks like suicide, says the Yard

SCOTLAND Yard detectives investigating the death of one-time boxing champion Freddie Mills – found shot in a car near his West End night club – were almost certain last night that he killed himself.

At first, the investigation had been treated as a MURDER inquiry.

The belief that Mills committed suicide left the big question unanswered: Why would he do it?

Mills, 46 – he was world light heavyweight champion from 1948 to 1950 – was found dead early yesterday.

He lay on the back seat of his silver-grey Citroen car, in an alley behind the club – the Freddie Mills Nite Spot, in Charing Cross-road.

Rifle

There was a 0.22 calibre bullet in his brain. A rifle lay on the seat, near him.

But WHY would Freddie Mills choose to die?

He had retired from boxing in 1950 after earning a reputed £100,000. He had a wife and two daughters – Susan, 13, and Mandy, 9.

At the Freddie Mills Nite Spot, which he opened two years ago, he was known as a gay host.

But friends said last night that he had been worrying about the club.

Expenses were heavy. And the last Budget had hit most West End night spots.

A director of the Pigalle, the Stork Room and the Society, Mr. Bill Ofner, said:

"Freddie phoned me last week, and asked how business was.

"I told him it was disastrous. He said. 'Well, that's some consolation'."

But Mills's partner, Chinese-born Mr. Andy Ho, denied that the Nite Spot was in trouble.

Mr. Ho, 50, said at home in Hartsbourne-road, Bushey Heath, Herts:

"Freddie had not approached me for help. His death was a complete shock to me."

What happens to the Freddie Mills Nite Spot now?

"There is no plan for the club at present." Mr. Ho said.

Mr. Ho's 26-year-old daughter Nita, who works as a receptionist at the club on Saturdays, had a theory about Mills's death.

"For some time," she said, "Freddie hadn't appeared on television, or opened fetes – or any of the things he used to do.

"He wasn't happy about that. Maybe he wanted to make headlines once more, when he died."

Big-hearted Mills often helped his maiden aunt, Miss Kate Gray, who was in the Dorset County Council's old people's home at Gillingham.

The matron, Mrs Winifred Mumford, said last night that he had planned a coach trip for the old folk.

"Then I had a letter from him," she said. "It was sad and pathetic. It talked about his business, how difficult things were, and then we heard nothing more."

Only a fortnight ago, Freddie visited a pub not two miles from his home at Denmark Hill – and asked for a job running a catering department.

Mr. David Cheetham, of Dulwich, a customer at the pub, said: "I gathered he wanted to try something new, but although the pub is a first-class money-maker, it was obviously a comedown for Freddie to ask for a job."

For the last eighteen years, Mills was in partnership with Andy Ho.

At first, they ran a Chinese restaurant. Two years ago, they changed it to a night club.

The club's opening day brought tragedy.

Actress Ellis Powell – the original radio "Mrs. Dale" – was to have opened the Nite Spot.

But that day, she killed herself with an overdose of drugs.

A few months later – in October, 1963 – Mills lost another friend. Singer Michael Holliday, 35, spent an evening at the club. He and Mills were photographed together laughing.

Then Holliday went home and killed himself with drugs.

Last Thursday, Mills and Mr. Ho were fined for liquor and gaming offences at the Nite Spot. Mills was upset by the case.

Late on Saturday night, Mills sent a message to the club.

Part-time doorman Bob Deacon, a blond, 21-year-old law student, said yesterday:

"A man told me Freddie wanted to talk to me.

"Freddie was sitting at the wheel of the car.

"He said he'd had a few drinks and was going to sleep it off.

"He asked me to wake him in half an hour.

"At 11.10 p.m. I went back. Freddie was awake.

"He asked how many customers were in the club. It was a quiet evening – I told him there were only eight.

"He said, 'Oh dear. I won't come in yet'."

BACKSTORY

An official enquiry concluded that former World Light Heavyweight champion Freddie Mills committed suicide in his car (below) – but that didn't stop the lurid rumours surrounding this colourful character. One theory is that Mills was murdered by business rivals, another that he was executed by gangland assassins. There is even a theory that Mills was a sadistic serial killer of prostitutes, and took his own life as police closed in on him.

Daily Mirror

4d. Saturday, January 28, 1967 US No. 19,625

3 MOON MEN KILLED

Top Spacemen die on Earth

The Moon explorers

DISASTER AT LAST —IN TRAINING ON CAPE KENNEDY LAUNCHING PAD

From JOHN SMITH, New York, Friday

THREE American "moon-men" were killed today as fire swept their Apollo 1 Spacecraft at the Cape Kennedy launching pad.

It was the disaster that everyone feared would happen. Until now, America has never lost an astronaut in a Space project. And, ironically, it happened on Earth.

The Spacemen were: Virgil "Gus" Grissom, 40, Edward White, 36, and Roger Chaffee, 31.

Grissom was one of America's first men in Space. White was the first U.S. Space walker. Chaffee was a "new boy" to the Space team.

REHEARSAL

The blaze apparently began in the electrical system and spread to the oxygen supply.

It broke out during the first big rehearsal for Apollo 1—which is due to be America's first manned Moon test flight on February 21.

The countdown for a mock launching was in progress . . .

Suddenly, smoke and flames filled the Spacecraft. The astronauts, in touch with ground control by radio, gave no warning of the fire.

THESE are the three pioneer Astronauts who died. They are from left: Virgil Grissom, Edward White and Roger Chaffee. Gus Grissom, 40, was the first man in history to go on two Space rocket flights —in 1961 and 1965.

On his last trip, he nearly drowned when his Spaceship Liberty Bell Seven sank after splashdown.

Grissom had two young sons. He said his one regret about being an astronaut was that he didn't have enough time with them.

Major Edward White, 36, was the first American to walk in Space.

He stepped out at the end of a gold-plated cord in June last year, 150 miles over the Pacific, from his Spaceship, Gemini IV. He stayed out for fourteen minutes.

Roger Chaffee, 31, was a "rookie" astronaut who had not made a Space flight.

Continued on Back Page

28th January 1967

3 MOON MEN KILLED

Top Spacemen Die on Earth

DISASTER AT LAST – IN TRAINING ON CAPE KENNEDY LAUNCHING PAD

From Joñ Smith, New York, Friday

THREE American "moon-men" were killed today as fire swept their Apollo I Spacecraft at the Cape Kennedy launching pad.

It was the disaster that everyone feared would happen. Until now, America has never lost an astronaut in a Space project. And, ironically, it happened on Earth.

The Spacemen were: Virgil "Gus" Grissom, 40, Edward White, 36, and Roger Chaffee, 31.

Grissom was one of America's first men in Space. White was the first U.S. Space walker. Chaffee was a "new boy" to the Space team.

REHEARSAL

The blaze apparently began in the electrical system and spread to the oxygen supply.

It broke out during the first big rehearsal for Apollo I – which is due to be America's first manned Moon test flight on February 21.

The countdown for a mock launching was in progress . . .

Suddenly, smoke and flames filled the spacecraft. The astronauts, in touch with ground control by radio, gave no warning of the fire.

They were trapped in the cockpit and died almost instantly.

Workmen, trying desperately to break open the hatches, were driven back by dense smoke. Later, the fire was put out.

The disaster, which came at the end of a day of tests, shocked officials of the National Aeronautical and Space Administration.

An official statement said: "The Spacecraft was located 218ft. above the launching pad. The crew entered it at 3 p.m.

"Minor difficulties had been encountered during the count. The accident occurred at 6.31 p.m.

"All data has been impounded pending an investigation."

Three hours later, the bodies of Grissom, White and Chaffee were still in the Spacecraft.

Smoke

The fire is believed to have sent smoke through the oxygen tubes of their space suits killing them before they had a chance to switch to emergency supplies.

Twenty-five of the launch pad crew were treated for smoke inhalation.

Science reporter Arthur Smith writes: Grissom, White and Chaffee were due to fly in their Apollo I on a fourteen-day mission in Earth orbit.

This was to be the first manned test of the Apollo moonship.

The disaster must mean a further delay of several months.

President Lyndon B. Joñson tonight sent a personal message of sympathy to the families of the three men.

He said: "Three valiant young men have given their lives in the nation's service."

Gus Grissom, 40, was the first man in history to go on two Space rocket flights – in 1961 and 1965.

On his last trip, he nearly drowned when his Spaceship Liberty Bell Seven sank after splashdown.

Grissom had two young sons. He said his one regret about being an astronaut was that he didn't have enough time with them.

Major Edward White, 36, was the first American to walk in Space.

He stepped out at the end of a gold-plated cord in June last year, 150 miles over the Pacific, from his Spaceship, Gemini IV. He stayed out for fourteen minutes.

Roger Chaffee, 31, was a "rookie" astronaut who had not made a Space flight.

BACKSTORY

The awful fate that befell Grissom, White, and Chaffee dealt the Apollo mission programme a severe blow. The Americans were undaunted, however, and the programme forged ahead.

There would be another two years of exhaustive missions and testing, before Apollo 11 successfully landed on the moon's surface, and Neil Armstrong took that momentous "one small step for man, one giant leap for mankind."

Daily Mirror

1d. Monday, July 21, 1969   No. 20,393

The time : 3.56 am, July 21, AD 1969

MAN WALKS ON THE MOON

The first step . . Astronaut Armstrong feels gingerly with his foot for the Moon surface

I'LL SEE LAWYER OVER JUDGE'S RAP, SAYS AIRPORT MAN

By GEORGE GLENTON

BUSINESSMAN Richard Pointer spoke last night of what he called an "astounding" remark made about him by a judge at the Old Bailey.

Mr. Pointer, chairman of Airpark Garages, Limited, was mentioned earlier by Judge Mervyn Griffith-Jones when he was sentencing twelve men for taking part in a fraud plot at London's Heathrow Airport car parks.

The judge told the twelve men—who were mostly employed at the car parks—that the amount of money stolen must have run into hundreds of thousands of pounds.

Part of the racket, the judge had been told, involved attendants altering dates and times on car-park tickets and pocketing fees paid by customers.

Worthy

The judge congratulated the detective team which took part in uncovering the fraud.

He said: "The discovery and the subsequent work by the police officers under Detective Chief Inspector Ronald Ashby is worthy of the highest commendation.

Among the sentenced men were car-park supervisor Thomas Henry Hayes, 45, who was jailed for seven years, and William Charles, 39, who got six years.

Sentencing Hayes, the judge told him: "In my view, you stand with William Charles as one of the two principals in this fraud, after and under Pointer."

Prosecuting counsel Mr. E. J. Cussen had said in his opening speech that Mr. Pointer had not been charged and was not in the dock.

William Charles, in evidence, alleged that Mr. Pointer had received some of the stolen money.

Mr. Pointer said last night: "I am astounded at the judge's remarks. Some 12 months ago I was interviewed by the police, and have given them every co-operation since.

"I have been available during the trial to give evidence, but was told that I would not be required to do so. . . . I have never had any knowledge of this racket that was going on.

Costs

"I am concerned now that the business I have built up in the past 12 years will be affected, and am consulting my legal advisers.

"The bulk of the money that has been stolen is money that should have been mine."

Hayes, of Raynton-close, Hayes, Middlesex, was ordered to pay £2,000 costs, and Charles, of Glebe-avenue, Ruislip, was ordered to pay £3,000.

The ten other men were jailed for terms ranging from four years to a year and also ordered to pay costs.

Women relatives screamed as the sentences were passed. Some were carried from the court.

Concorde —with an E for Excellent

THE great gleaming white dart they call the Concorde duly made its official debut yesterday.

It was an occasion for smiles all round, and dreamy talk of being able to pop over to Beirut for an evening out.

The French had special cause to smile, too. For they got their own way, as they so often do, on the one matter still unsettling with their British partners. The spelling of Concorde.

On this chill day in Toulouse, Mr. Anthony Wedgwood Benn, the Technology Minister, gave in to the French with great good grace.

Generosity

He said: "In English, Concorde ends with a plain 'D', exactly as it is pronounced. With splendid generosity our French friends have insisted upon an extra 'E'.

"No amount of argument or discussion, no series of committees or Ministerial meetings have ever produced an agreement on this point.

"It is intolerable that we should continue in this way. I have therefore decided to resolve it myself. From now on the British Concorde will also be spelt with an 'E.'"

Mr. Benn said the final "E" symbolised many things.

Bands

"It stands for excellence, for England, for Europe—towards which we are moving — and entry, and for Entente Cordiale." And cordiale was the word yesterday. A French band played the British national anthem and a Royal Air Force band played the French anthem.

But that was yesterday. Today, with the VIPs departed, the business goes on of preparing this first prototype for its maiden flight, due next February.

The Triofs Ahead—See Page 9.

MRS MOPP FINDS A TREASURE

CHARLADY Gladys Mott liked the look of the piece of mahogany among the rubbish she was clearing out of a cottage left to her by an aunt.

So instead of putting it on the bonfire, she gave the cracked mahogany panel to her employer, oil executive John Vagg.

Two years later, Mr. Vagg took it to art experts at Christie's in London . . . where it was auctioned for £60gns.

It turned out that the painting—of Ann, daughter of Emperor Paul I of Russia—was by the nineteenth-century Dutch artist Schelfhout.

The story of Mrs. Mott's find was revealed yesterday in Christie's "Review of the Year."

Last night, at her home in Horley-row, Horley, Surrey, Mrs. Mott said: "Mr. Vagg split the proceeds between himself, his wife and myself. I was amazed it fetched so much."

Princess in love pleads to marry

PRINCESS Maria Beatrice last night begged her father, ex-king Umberto of Italy, to let her marry her fiance, actor Maurizio Arena.

The ex-king and his 29-year-old daughter met at an hotel near Nice.

It was the princess's latest bid to persuade her parents to bring a happy ending to her romance and drop their attempt to have the marriage banned by a court in Rome.

Four weeks ago, the princess and Maurizio—son of a flower seller—gave up an attempt to marry at Reading, Berkshire, because they had to qualify by spending a fortnight in England.

Nosing proudly into a new era of flying, the first Concorde airliner is ready to leave its hangar in Toulouse. Picture by FREDDIE REED.

GIANT'S DEBUT

12ᵗʰ December 1967

CONCORDE WITH AN E – FOR EXCELLENT

THE great gleaming white dart they call the Concorde duly made its official debut yesterday.

It was an occasion for smiles all round, and dreamy talk: of being able to pop over to Beirut for an evening out.

The French had special cause to smile, too. For they got their own way, as they so often do, on the one matter still unsettled with their British partners.

The spelling of Concorde.

On this chill day in Toulouse, Mr. Anthony Wedgwood Benn, the Technology Minister, gave in to the French with great good grace.

He said: "In English, Concorde ends with a plain 'D', exactly as it is pronounced. With splendid generosity our French friends have insisted upon an extra 'E'.

"No amount of argument or discussion, no series of committees or Ministerial meetings have ever produced an agreement on this point.

"It is intolerable that we should continue in this way. I have therefore decided to resolve it myself. From now on the British Concorde will also be spelt with an 'E'."

Mr. Benn said the final 'E' symbolised many things.

"It stands for excellence, for England, for Europe – towards which we are moving – and entry and for Entente Cordiale."

And cordiale was the word yesterday.

A French band played the British national anthem and a Royal Air Force band played the French anthem.

But that was yesterday. Today, with the VIPs departed, the business goes on of preparing this first prototype for its maiden flight, due next February.

CONCORDE – THE TRIALS AHEAD

How the critics can be silenced

By Air Correspondent Peter Harris

THE first official public appearance of the Concorde yesterday was an occasion for ceremony, bunting and flags, toasts and brave speeches from Ministers from both countries.

But there is still reason to say plainly: On the British side, in marked contrast to the French, the enthusiasm is too little and could be too late.

Almost inevitably in Britain, twenty-four hours after the occasion, the critics were assessing chances of the project's cancellation. British Overseas Airways made a half-hearted and belated effort to show interest by producing their first Concorde captain-elect.

It is time to change the tune – before Concorde's prospects suffer the same undeserved fate as the VC 10, which is now never likely to gain the position in the world it deserves.

It is not BOAC's fault that they appear to the world hostile to British aviation products.

When Tory Aviation Minister Julian Amery appointed Sir Giles Guthrie as BOAC chairman, the instruction was: "Run the airline on a strictly commercial basis."

But there was a provision which said the Government might insist on an uneconomic move if it seemed in the overall interests of the country. If it resulted in a loss, BOAC could show it in their accounts.

Sir Giles is running a strictly commercial airline. Any balance-of-payments benefits Britain gains from the Concorde programme and the advanced technology know-how gained by industry will not show on Sir Giles's books.

Snipers

But a quiet Government guarantee would leave him free to push Concorde enthusiastically. Paradoxically, prospective American operators are already doing this.

A guarantee might even help to silence the critics, the half-informed snipers who would be better advised to ask "Can Britain AFFORD to cancel Concorde?"

Because the answer is NO. Britain lives by exporting technical products, and most industries have at some time benefited from the advanced research inspired by aviation needs.

Today, the main support of that technology in Britain is Concorde.

Concorde is probably the biggest single technical project we have in any field. And it is being designed and built by highly-qualified professionals.

Can we not try to give them the encouragement they deserve, instead of trying constantly to shout them down?

BACKSTORY

Peter Harris's warnings of opposition to the Concorde programme was a foretaste of things to come. Given the go-ahead in 1962, the project was dogged by complaints over cost and political wrangles. Nonetheless, commercial flights eventually started in 1976, and the aircraft became synonymous with supersonic travel, ferrying the rich and glamorous across the Atlantic.

On 24ᵗʰ October 2003, three of BA's remaining Concordes made an emotional final flight, landing together at Heathrow Airport (above) – their last journey over the capital watched by thousands.

Daily Mirror

5d. Friday, May 17, 1968 ✦ ✦ ✦ No. 20,028

THE GENTLE VOICE OF COMFORT

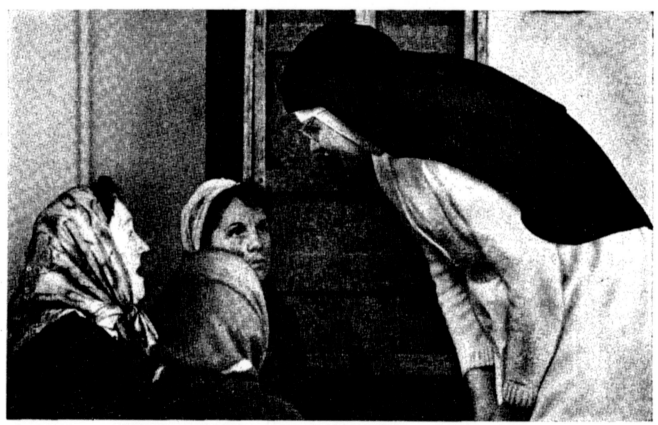

SOMEONE was needed to ease the shock of it all . . . to console those who were so close to the disaster.

When the Ronan Point flats fell apart yesterday, that someone was this nun.

Three women from the flats—fear etched plainly on their faces — found some comfort in the gentle words of the nun.

She wasn't as noticeable as the rescue workers.

But in her way, Just as valuable.

Picture by CHARLES LEY

SHATTERED SKYSCRAPER: MYSTERY OF 'A GAS LEAK'

By **KENELM JENOUR** and **NICK DAVIES**

DID a gas leak cause yesterday's Ronan Point flats disaster?

A policeman who was one of the first on the scene said last night that a gas leak had been reported at the flats. at Newham, in London's East End.

The North Thames Gas Board had been told of a leak on the eighteenth floor the night before the disaster, he said.

But a Gas Board spokesman said: "Leaks are treated as priority. If one was reported there would be no chance of it being overlooked."

Checked

He added: " We have checked very carefully and there is no evidence that any such report was made to us."

Four people died when an entire wing of the twenty-two-storey skyscraper collapsed. Thirteen were injured. Eighty families were left homeless.

Last night Home Secretary James Callaghan ordered a report by lunch-time today on the disaster.

Experts think the collapse was caused by a gas explosion in a kitchen as a woman was making tea.

The woman, 56-year-old cake decorator Miss Ivy Hodge, was in hospital last night.

She is suffering from burns.

Miss Hodge, whose home was Flat 90 on the 18th floor, said:

❝ I had just filled a kettle for my tea. Suddenly, I found myself on the floor of the kitchen.

I was able to get up and get out through the door, and some people helped me to get out of the building.

In the kitchen I don't remember turning the gas on, nor do I remember if I lighted a match. ❞

Carpets, beds, dressing tables and bits of curtain sagged from

◆ Continued on Back Page

17ᵗʰ May 1968

SHATTERED SKYSCRAPER: MYSTERY OF 'A GAS LEAK'

By Kenelm Jenour and Nick Davies

DID a gas leak cause yesterday's Ronan Point flats disaster?

A policeman who was one of the first on the scene said last night that a gas leak had been reported at the flats, at Newham, in London's East End.

The North Thames Gas Board had been told of a leak on the eighteenth floor the night before the disaster, he said.

But a Gas Board spokesman said: "Leaks are treated as priority. If one was reported there would be no chance of it being overlooked."

Checked

He added: "We have checked very carefully and there is no evidence that any such report was made to us."

Four people died when an entire wing of the twenty-two storey skyscraper collapsed.

Thirteen were injured. Eighty families were left homeless.

Last night Home Secretary James Callaghan ordered a report by lunch-time today on the disaster.

Experts think the collapse was caused by a gas explosion in a kitchen as a woman was making tea.

The woman, 56-year-old cake decorator Miss Ivy Hodge, was in hospital last night. She is suffering from burns.

Miss Hodge, whose home was Flat 90 on the 18th floor, said: "I had just filled a kettle for my tea. Suddenly, I found myself on the floor of the kitchen.

"I was able to get up and get out through the door, and some people helped me to get out of the building.

"In the kitchen I don't remember turning the gas on, nor do I remember if I lighted a match."

Carpets, beds, dressing tables and bits of curtain sagged from the jagged corner of the building.

Hours after the disaster, some of the refugees were allowed back in to rescue their most treasured belongings.

Others vowed never to set foot in the flats again.

Denis Smith, who escaped with his wife Janet and six-year-old son said: "Nothing in the world will induce me to go back into a block of flats again. It doesn't matter where it is or who built it."

Many more of the survivors said they would refuse to live in the block when it has been repaired. "Not in there, not ever," said one of them, Mrs. Jane Darlen. The building, completed only two months ago, was factory built and assembled on the site.

Mr. Geoffrey Davies, boss of Taylor Woodrow Anglian, the company which built the block, said:

"There was not the slightest evidence of structural failure. There must have been a very severe explosion."

He added: "These flats are built to the most stringent design regulations anywhere in the world.

"This type of building is no less structurally safe than any other kind of building."

Decide

Three separate full-scale inquiries into the disaster were announced last night.

The Government, the Newham Borough Council, and the building contractors are to hold independent investigations.

Mr. Callaghan will decide after today's lunch-time report what type of inquiry he wants.

The Queen, who toured Cheshire and Lancashire yesterday, asked for inquiries to be made on her behalf.

She expressed her concern over the accident – and her relief that the casualties were not greater.

Many people in the flats escaped with their lives by inches as walls fell away.

One man said: "Suddenly we found ourselves staring out over London."

Another man clung to a piece of concrete – and slid down with it as the rubble collapsed.

BACKSTORY

The public enquiry into the Ronan Point disaster found that a gas explosion had blown out a supporting wall, but that the building itself was structurally unsound.

Part of the nationwide move to clear slums and erect tower blocks, Ronan Point was a soaring tower built using prefabricated concrete panels. But there was significant criticism of the design and form of construction.

The tragedy led to changes in building regulations – and to a campaign against the high-rise housing model that would later see many blocks demolished. The rebuilt Ronan Point – itself the subject of lingering concerns over its safety – was torn down in 1986.

Daily Mirror

Friday, July 4, 1969

Telephone: (STD code 01)—353 0246

TWO NATIONS IN CUP ROW OPEN FIRE

Police ask guests at a royal party in the West End: Tone it down

DOZENS of people complained to the police early today about noise from a London party attended by Princess Margaret.

As the 400 guests of Prince Rupert of Loewenstein-Wertheim lived it up to the sound of two beat groups and a band, some of the people living nearby telephoned the Daily Mirror to complain.

Later, police said: "We have taken action. A car has been sent to the party to ask them to tone it down."

Prince Rupert said at his home in Holland Villas-road, Kensington: "We hope we're not inconveniencing any of our neighbours."

Banker

"The noise certainly doesn't seem too loud to me. We've got two beat groups, a band and 400 guests, including Princess Margaret."

Earlier, Miss Judith Spreckley, 23, of Addison-road, Kensington, said: "If I was living next door to the party, my china would be broken by now.

"When I rang the police they said they could not do anything about it. They would not interfere because Princess Margaret was there."

Prince Rupert, a member of a Bavarian family, is a City banker and businessman. He is a direct descendant of George III.

TWO TOP MEN QUIT FROM QE2 FIRM

Two key executives of Upper Clyde Shipbuilders, the firm which built the Queen Elizabeth 2, have resigned, it was revealed last night.

They are personnel director Bert Farrimond, and Mr. James Corfe, the marketing director.

Tricia and Anne meet at a ball

TWO princesses met last night for the first time, at an exclusive young people's ball in London.

One was 18-year-old Princess Anne.

The other was Tricia Nixon, 23-year-old daughter of the US President —and known to her secret service guard by the code name of "The Little Princess."

About 100 young people arrived at Claridge's for the ball — on the eve of American Independence Day.

It was held in Miss Nixon's honour at the end of her eight-day visit to Britain.

It gave her a chance at last, to meet a member of the Royal Family.

She was to have had tea with the Queen yesterday, but the Queen was still ill with a cold.

Although she went to Tuesday's investiture, Miss Nixon did not meet Prince Charles.

Tricia Nixon at the ball.

A BATTLE broke out last night between two nations which have been feuding over the World Cup.

The clash came on the border between El Salvador and Honduras.

The two Central American countries broke off diplomatic relations following riots over Soccer matches leading up to next year's World Cup tournament in Mexico.

El Salvador's Foreign Ministry said a lone Honduran plane attacked the border post at El Poy and that troops returned the fire.

No casualties were reported.

First reports by the El Salvador Government said that a town had been bombed.

Chase

Later, the ministry said, two other Honduran planes flew over the area but were chased off by Salvadorean Air Force planes.

Meanwhile, border troops on both sides of the frontier exchanged fire for twenty minutes, the Foreign Ministry added.

There was no confirmation of the clash from Honduras.

The El Salvador Foreign Ministry said it had sent a letter to the Organisation of American States accusing Honduras of "aggressions."

Honduras and El Salvador broke relations after a simmering territorial dispute that came to a climax last month over the qualifying World Cup matches.

In a three-game play-off, Honduras won the first game in her capital and El Salvador won the second one, playing at home. Rioting followed both matches.

El Salvador won the third game 3—2 after extra

time on neutral ground in Mexico.

But before that match started, El Salvador had threatened to suspend diplomatic relations — and Honduras beat her by actually severing them.

Behind the Soccer episode exists a long-standing territorial conflict between the two neighbouring nations.

Honduras has five times as much territory as El Salvador and less than half the population.

As a result, land-hungry peasants from El Salvador have streamed into Honduras.

About 300,000 Salvadoreans have gone to live in Honduras, but about 14,000 have returned in recent months complaining of discrimination and ill treatment.

In some Honduran towns, the refugees claimed, mobs forced the Salvadoreans to flee for their lives.

TORIES JEER BARBARA ON STRIKE BILL

By DAVID THOMPSON

BARBARA CASTLE infuriated Tory MPs last night by accusing them of wanting wildcat strikes.

"They will have a vested interest in the increase in strikes . . . they want the TUC to fail," Mrs. Castle shouted when she wound up a bitter Commons debate on strike curbs.

Against a barrage of jeers she declared: "The Opposition have demonstrated to every trade unionist in the country the contempt in which they hold the trade unions."

The debate was on a Tory censure motion condemning the Government for dropping its Bill to reform the trade unions in exchange for a TUC undertaking to tackle unofficial strikes.

The motion was defeated by 301 votes to 242 — a Government majority of 59. Most of the six-hour debate was a bitter Party slanging match, although it was given a cool start by Mr. Robert Carr, the Tory spokesman on labour affairs.

Mr. Carr welcomed the TUC's commitment, but claimed that it was "not the equivalent of the legislative measures which the Government said were necessary, and promised to implement."

The noise began to mount when Premier Harold Wilson denounced the Tory industrial record.

Mr. Heath was cheered by the Tories when he declared that trade unions "cannot be outside the law."

A strike blackout threat to TV

By ALAN LAW
Industrial Correspondent

POST OFFICE engineers decided yesterday to hold a national one-day strike on Monday week over a pay claim.

Television programmes could be blacked out. ITV would be hit harder than BBC because it uses more Post Office engineers to relay programmes between its regions.

The strike is planned for July 11 in Northern Ireland and on July 14 in the rest of Britain.

The engineers would not carry out repairs or installations during the strike —the first national stoppage called by their union in eighty years.

The union wants a 10 per cent. pay rise. But the Post Office is offering less than half of this.

In the Liverpool dock strike, hopes for peace rose last night after union leaders and employers agreed peace terms.

The proposals will be put to a mass meeting of Liverpool dockers this morning.

Mr. Jack Jones, leader of the dockers' union, the Transport and General Workers, said last night that he was "very hopeful."

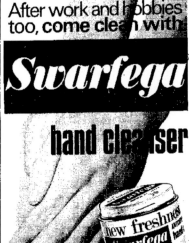
Printed and Published by DAILY MIRROR NEWSPAPERS, Ltd (01-353 0246) at, and for IPC Newspapers, Ltd., Holborn Circus, London, E.C.1. Friday, July 4, 1969.

© Daily Mirror Newspapers, Ltd., 1969.

4th July 1969

TWO NATIONS IN CUP ROW OPEN FIRE

After the Soccer riots ... 'One of our towns has been bombed: Our Army hit back'

A BATTLE broke out last night between two nations which have been feuding over the World Cup.

The clash came on the border between El Salvador and Honduras.

The two Central American countries broke off diplomatic relations following riots over Soccer matches leading up to next year's World Cup tournament in Mexico.

El Salvador's Foreign Ministry said a lone Honduran plane attacked the border post at El Poy and that troops returned the fire.

No casualties were reported.

First reports by the El Salvador Government said that a town had been bombed.

Chase

Later, the ministry said, two other Honduran planes flew over the area but were chased off by Salvadorean Air Force planes.

Meanwhile, border troops on both sides of the frontier exchanged fire for twenty minutes, the Foreign Ministry added.

There was no confirmation of the clash from Honduras.

The El Salvador Foreign Ministry said it had sent a letter to the Organisation of American States accusing Honduras of "aggressions."

Honduras and El Salvador broke relations after a simmering territorial dispute that came to a climax last month over the qualifying World Cup matches.

In a three-game play-off Honduras won the first game in her capital and El Salvador won the second one, playing at home.

Rioting followed both matches.

El Salvador won the third game 3–2 after extra time on neutral ground in Mexico.

But before that match started, El Salvador had threatened to suspend diplomatic relations – and Honduras beat her by actually severing them.

Behind the Soccer episode exists a long-standing territorial conflict between the two neighbouring nations.

Honduras has five times as much territory as El Salvador and less than half the population.

As a result, land-hungry peasants from El Salvador have streamed into Honduras.

About 300,000 Salvadoreans have gone to live in Honduras, but about 14,000 have returned in recent months complaining of discrimination and ill treatment.

In some Honduran towns, the refugees claimed, mobs forced the Salvadoreans to flee for their lives.

16th July 1969

Hopes of a ceasefire in a major flare-up between two small Central American countries –Honduras and El Salvador – rose last night.

Both countries indicated that they were willing to stop the fighting after the Organisation of American States intervened.

The organisation is sending a seven-man peace team to the warring nations which have both claimed that they have been invaded.

Earlier, Honduras had announced bombing raids on military targets in El Salvador in retaliation for what the Hondurans described as a 'Pearl Harbour attack'.

This, it was claimed, was a massive attack by Salvadorean planes and troops.

But Salvadorean officials alleged that 1,000 Honduran troops had crossed the border and aircraft had carried out widespread bombing.

17th July 1969

Troops from El Salvador were last night thrusting deep into Honduras territory in the mini-war between the two Central American States.

The Salvadorians were continuing the fighting although Honduras announced agreement to a ceasefire.

El Salvador demanded that the Honduran forces should "surrender or be destroyed on the battlefield."

Meanwhile, a peace team from the Organisation of American States was trying to halt the fighting in which both sides claimed their cities had been bombed.

Honduran Foreign Minister Carias Castillo reported more than 1,000 Hondurans killed.

He also alleged invasion by hundreds of Salvadorian paratroops.

BACKSTORY

While the short-lived battle between Honduras and El Salvador was dubbed the "soccer war", the reality was that on-field rivalry was merely one of the triggers behind a more deep-seated conflict.

Salvadorean troops eventually withdrew in August, though no treaty between the two countries was signed until 1980.

DAILY Mirror

5d.   Monday, April 6, 1970   +   +   +   No. 20,612

THE WAGES EXPLOSION:

Why the politicians are saying nowt

THE subject today is the £ in your pocket and the extra pounds that seem to be flying into everybody else's pockets.

■ Tune in—every wage-earner who would like to have a fatter pay packet.

Lend an ear—every hard-pressed housewife who would like more money for the housekeeping.

Here's a proposition nobody would disagree with—

● There are low-paid workers in this country who **NEED** more money to bring them up to a living wage.

● There are workers whose pay has lagged behind or been outstripped by the cost of living over the years.

● There are workers who can honestly justify wage increases by toil and productivity.

But what is now happening on the Wages Front, 1970,

MIRROR PAGE ONE COMMENT

has little to do with giving a leg-up to the needy or rewarding the industrious. What is happening is a Wages Grab by the strong, a Wages Surrender by the Government — and a threat to the real living standards of everybody who is fool enough to believe that higher wages automatically mean greater personal wealth.

The Mirror gives the warning which the politicians know to be true. It is this:

Higher wages will buy less and less, not more and more, unless they are earned by increased national productivity.

Britain's hard-won prosperity is still precarious. Ask

Continued on Page Two

'DRUNK' IS RESCUED FROM MORTUARY

David Wallis yesterday after his narrow escape from a mortuary. "I wasn't dead—only dead drunk," he said. "The whole thing is incredible."

By MIRROR REPORTER

A DRUNKEN man was driven to a mortuary in an undertaker's van yesterday after a telephone call from a party.

As the man—at first mistaken for a corpse—was about to be put in a refrigerator, the undertaker saw him breathe.

He immediately drove the man, David Wallis, 25, to hospital.

Doctors examined Mr. Wallis and discovered that he was only in a drunken sleep.

Brandy

Mr. Wallis, a garage proprietor who lives with his wife at Springfield-road, New Southgate, London, said yesterday: "I remember nothing about being 'dead.' Only opening my eyes in hospital.

"A doctor said, 'He's the healthiest-looking corpse I've ever seen.'"

Mr. Wallis went on: "The whole thing is incredible. I'd had a skin-

Undertaker saw him breathing

ful. I started off on draught lager and had a few Scotches. Then we went back to a pal's house, where we cracked a couple of bottles of champagne and drank them, mixed with brandy.

"I don't know who the undertaker was, but I'm glad he saw me breathe.

"My friends told me that two people had phoned him saying that someone had died.

"I wasn't dead—just dead drunk."

An official of North Middlesex Hospital, where Mr. Wallis was taken, said: "A man was brought into the hospital in an undertaker's van and presumed to be dead.

"He was examined and found not to be dead. The police were informed."

6th April 1970

'DRUNK' IS RESCUED FROM A MORTUARY

Undertaker saw him breathing

By Mirror Reporter

A DRUNKEN man was driven to a mortuary in an undertaker's van yesterday after a telephone call from a party.

As the man – at first mistaken for a corpse – was about to be put in a refrigerator, the undertaker saw him breathe.

He immediately drove the man, David Wallis, 25, to hospital.

Doctors examined Mr. Wallis and discovered that he was only in a drunken sleep.

Brandy

Mr. Wallis, a garage proprietor who lives with his wife at Springfield-road, New Southgate, London, said yesterday: "I remember nothing about being 'dead'. Only opening my eyes in hospital.

"A doctor said, 'He's the healthiest-looking corpse I've ever seen'."

Mr. Wallis went on: "The whole thing is incredible. I'd had a skinful.

"I started off on draught lager and had a few Scotches. Then we went back to a pal's house, where we cracked a couple of bottles of champagne and drank them, mixed with brandy.

"I don't know who the undertaker was, but I'm glad he saw me breathe.

"My friends told me that two people had phoned him saying that someone had died.

"I wasn't dead – just dead drunk."

An official of North Middlesex Hospital, where Mr. Wallis was taken, said: "A man was brought into the hospital in an undertaker's van and presumed to be dead.

"He was examined and found not to be dead. The police were informed."

7th April 1970

MORTUARY DRUNK WAS VICTIM OF HOAX

A drunken man who was taken to a mortuary in mistake for a corpse was the victim of a hoax, a friend admitted yesterday.

The friend, 39-year-old David Morgan, said he arranged the hoax during a birthday party at his home in Harlech-road, New Southgate, London.

Club

He and seven other party-goers – including his "victim," 25-year-old garage owner David Wallis – returned to the house early on Sunday after drinking heavily at a club.

When Mr. Wallis fell asleep on a couch, his face was blackened with burnt cork and a daffodil was put on his chest.

Then Mr. Morgan, a market worker, telephoned an all-night funeral parlour to arrange for the "body" to be picked up.

Three undertakers arrived in a van and put the sleeping man inside a canvas bag.

A girl pretending to be his widow screamed: "Don't take him away please!"

After Mr. Wallis had been bundled off, his friends realised that they had gone too far.

They hurriedly telephoned the undertakers to explain.

But Mr. Wallis was safe – because someone at the mortuary saw him breathing as he was about to be put into a refrigerator.

BACKSTORY

David Wallis's lucky escape from the mortuary slab provided a laugh for *Mirror* readers – and brought to mind the story of the Birmingham pub that was once a morgue.

"Could you drink a pint in what was once a morgue?" ran the story in May 1959. "At the Acorn Inn – one end in Wilton Street, Lozells, Birmingham, the other in Wheeler Street and the two joined by a long passage called Memory Lane – the regulars don't mind. In this bar which used to be a mortuary Mrs Valerie Fortnum, wife of the licensee, passes a glass to one of her customers while Mr Harrington reads the newspaper."

Daily Mirror

BRITAIN'S BIGGEST DAILY SALE

3p   Tuesday, February 1, 1972   No. 21,168

BASHER BERNADETTE!

—Was there a blunder?

By JOHN BEAVAN

MORE than once I have made the tragic pilgrimage to Northern Ireland. I have questioned everyone until dawn has broken and the Jameson's has run dry.

I have listened to every argument, every cause and plea in that ravaged land. Everybody has a case; they are all right.

They are all right—all these victims of history—whether they are hard-faced Orangemen like Faulkner's extremist supporters, good liberals like Terence O'Neill, or way-out republican Socialists like Bernadette Devlin.

I went to the Commons yesterday, as a British citizen with the deaths of thirteen people on my conscience.

I saw Bernadette cross the floor of the House and physically assault Mr. Maudling, the Home Secretary, with calculated anger.

Restraint

Her attack followed Mr. Maudling's cold, brief, perfunctory account of Sunday's tragedy. It was not the Maudling we know, that I heard, not the warm-hearted humane Reginald Maudling.

Not a word of sympathy for the thirteen Londonderry dead. No deep feeling for the tragedy, no indication that the honour of the British Army is impugned.

It is an Army which has had a golden record. No troops in the world have ever stood up with such restraint to the daily insults and the cowardly snipers and bombers.

Of course there have been deplorable isolated incidents. A few innocents may have been caught up in their fire. The troops may have handled people roughly in their searches. And they may have treated the people they interned

Continued on Page Two.

EXIT DEVLIN THE DEFIANT

A defiant thumbs-up sign from Bernadette Devlin as, white-faced, she leaves the Commons after her attack
Picture : ALISDAIR MACDONALD.

Murder! she screams—then hits Maudling

A PUNCHING and screaming Bernadette Devlin hurled herself on Reginald Maudling in the Commons yesterday during clashes over the Londonderry shootings.

Shouting "You murdering bastard," she showered blows on the Home Secretary's head and face as he sat next to Premier Edward Heath.

Seconds later, during a furious scrum on the floor of the Commons with Tory whips who were trying to restrain her, Miss Devlin punched one of the whips, Mr. Oscar Murton in the face.

Then, swinging punches, Labour MP Hugh Delargy raced to Miss Devlin, who was being held in the grip of Tory Chief Whip Francis Pym and Mr. Murton.

Mr. Delargy thumped Mr. Murton hard on the shoulder. He also hit Mr. Trevor Skeet, Tory MP for Bedford, who had intervened.

Removed

As she was dragged off, Miss Devlin held on for a moment to Mr. Maudling's hair with one hand and kept on punching him in the face with the other.

Finally, Labour Chief Whip Bob Mellish and Ulster Independent MP Frank McManus succeeded in partly calming down Miss Devlin. Mr. Mellish half-dragged, half-persuaded her to leave the Chamber.

As fists flew downstairs in the Chamber, about thirty demon-

By DAVID THOMPSON

strators were removed from the back of the public gallery.

They shouted: "Bloody hypocrites!" "Murderers!" "Killers!" and "Bastard Black and Tans!"

Miss Devlin had been protesting that Mr. Maudling told what she called "lies" in a statement he made on the Londonderry shootings.

Mr. Maudling said that the paratroopers involved opened fire only after they had been fired on.

Miss Devlin and dozens of Labour MPs were also angered because Speaker Selwyn Lloyd did not call her to put a question to Mr. Maudling.

Accused

Miss Devlin accused Mr. Maudling of "lying"—itself a breach of Parliamentary rules.

Afterwards, outside the Commons, Miss Devlin, the MP for Mid-Ulster, said: "I could cheerfully have strangled him."

Referring to the shootings, she said: "He didn't even say he was sorry."

Mr. Maudling, who went bright pink during the assaults, said: "As far as the physical assault is concerned, I regularly get my hair pulled by my grandchildren.

"As far as Miss Devlin is concerned, I recognise how deep and genuine her feelings are on this

☐ Continued on Page Two

Was the Army to blame for Bloody Sunday? —SEE CENTRE PAGES

1st February 1972

BASHER BERNADETTE!

Murder! She screams – then hits Maudling

By David Thompson

A PUNCHING and screaming Bernadette Devlin hurled herself on Reginald Maudling in the Commons yesterday during clashes over the Londonderry shootings.

Shouting "You murdering bastard," she showered blows on the Home Secretary's head and face as he sat next to Premier Edward Heath.

Seconds later, during a furious scrum on the floor of the Commons with Tory whips who were trying to restrain her, Miss Devlin punched one of the whips, Mr. Oscar Murton, in the face.

Then, swinging punches, Labour MP Hugh Delargy raced to Miss Devlin, who was being held in the grip of Tory Chief Whip Francis Pym and Mr. Murton.

Mr. Delargy thumped Mr. Murton hard on the shoulder. He also hit Mr. Trevor Skeet, Tory MP for Bedford, who had intervened.

Removed

As she was dragged off, Miss Devlin held on for a moment to Mr. Maudling's hair with one hand and kept on punching him in the face with the other.

Finally, Labour Chief Whip Bob Mellish and Ulster Independent MP Frank McManus succeeded in partly calming down Miss Devlin.

Mr. Mellish half-dragged, half-persuaded her to leave the Chamber.

As fists flew downstairs in the Chamber, about thirty demonstrators were removed from the back of the public gallery.

They shouted: "Bloody hypocrites! Murderers! Killers" and "Bastard Black and Tans!"

Miss Devlin had been protesting that Mr. Maudling told what she called "lies" in a statement he made on the Londonderry shootings.

Mr. Maudling said that the paratroopers involved opened fire only after they had been fired on.

Miss Devlin and dozens of Labour MPs were also angered because Speaker Selwyn Lloyd did not call her to put a question to Mr. Maudling.

Accused

Miss Devlin accused Mr. Maudling of "lying" – itself a breach of Parliamentary rule.

Afterwards, outside the Commons, Miss Devlin, the MP for Mid-Ulster, said: "I could cheerfully have strangled him."

Referring to the shootings, she said: "He didn't even say he was sorry."

Mr. Maudling, who went bright pink during the assaults, said: "As far as the physical assault is concerned, I regularly get my hair pulled by my grandchildren.

"As far as Miss Devlin is concerned, I recognise how deep and genuine her feelings are on this matter however much I do not share them."

A bid by Mr. Peter Rees, the Tory MP for Dover, to complain that Miss Devlin had committed a breach of Parliamentary privilege was ruled out of order because he made it too late.

An independent inquiry is to probe Ulster's "Bloody Sunday" shootings, and the Commons is to hold a three-hour emergency debate today.

Mr. Maudling said it was right to have an inquiry in view of public statements disputing that the troops fired only after they had been fired on.

The inquiry, he said, would investigate the circumstances of the march, and the incidents leading-up to the casualties.

Both Labour and Liberals demanded that the inquiry should be international. But Mr. Maudling said it would be a poor reflection on Britain if we could not find enough independent people at home.

BACKSTORY

Voters today often criticize the slanging matches that take place in the House of Commons. But the extraordinary scenes in February 1972 took parliamentary exchanges to entirely new levels. MP Bernadette Devlin reacted furiously to Home Secretary Reginald Maudling's statement to the House in the immediate aftermath of the "Bloody Sunday" massacre. Devlin was temporarily suspended from Parliament as a result.

Devlin had made her name as an activist in Northern Ireland and by becoming the youngest-ever female MP when she won a 1969 by-election at the age of just 21.

Bernadette Devlin leaving court in December 1969. Soon after being elected, she was convicted and jailed for incitement to riot in the Battle of the Bogside, a milestone in the conflict that spilled out into the violence of the Troubles and which plagued Northern Ireland and beyond for 30 years. Devlin herself and her husband Michael McAliskey, survived an assassination attempt in 1981.

They're streaking here, they're streaking there, they're streaking everywhere

STREAKOUT!

Ooh—la-la! France gets a glimpse of how things are running ▶

STREAKING is still streaking ahead as the fastest-growing fad since the heady days of those other great crazes, the yoyo and hula hoop. The number of people seized by sudden urges to nip around naked in public is increasing almost as rapidly as the rate of inflation. Everybody who can't think of anything they'd rather do is doing it. And the new sport started by American students — campus bums, presumably—has extended across the Atlantic. The picture above, for instance, was taken in Paris yester-day when a group of young American men raced past the Eiffel Tower in the altogether with letters painted on their backs to spell out "Illinois." The sophisticated French took it all in their stride of course. But the movement has barely begun . . . and who knows where the streakers are going to strike next?

STREAKERS' CORNER

What a riot..

A GOOD-HUMOURED streak turned into a riot at Newark in Delaware. A dozen students —men and girls—streaked down the main street, watched by a crowd of 1,000. Then students and police clashed in a wild melee. Police claimed that students threw bottles, stones and, in one incident, acid. Eleven policemen were injured and twelve students arrested.

WHAT A CHEEK..

STREAKING will not be tolerated in Bourne-mouth. That was the stern warning from Police superintendent Peter Hoper in the digni-fied resort yesterday. His announcement came too late to stop an anonymous blonde making a traffic-stopping 50-yard streak along Westover Road. But from now on, it is emphasised, the town's streakers face prosecution, fines and even jail.

What a crowd..

THE mass streak has been seen in its full glory at Georgia's state university in Athens. There, 1,500 students of both sexes ran naked through the campus and claimed a world record. The streakers were outnumbered only by the specta-tors. A school patrolman estimated that more than 20,000 people watched the event.

◀ ### What the well-dressed streaker is wearing

THIS is what the best-dressed streakers are wearing, if that's not a contra-diction in terms. Model Sue Paul shows what a pretty lace Malyard hat and high-heeled peeptoe shoes, by Terry de Havilland, can do for any enthusiastic streaker—except, maybe, a man.
Picture: DOREEN SPOONER

9th March 1974

STREAKOUT!

Ooh-la-la! France gets a glimpse of how things are running

STREAKING is still streaking ahead as the fastest-growing fad since the heady days of those other great crazes, the yoyo and hula hoop.

The number of people seized by sudden urges to nip around naked in public is increasing almost as rapidly as the rate of inflation. Everybody who can't think of anything they'd rather do is doing it.

And the new sport started by American students – campus bums, presumably – has extended across the Atlantic. The picture above [left], for instance, was taken in Paris yesterday when a group of young American men raced past the Eiffel Tower in the altogether with letters painted on their backs to spell out "Illinois."

The sophisticated French took it all in their stride of course. But the movement has barely begun . . . and who knows where the streakers are going to strike next?

STREAKERS' CORNER

What a riot...
A GOOD-HUMOURED streak turned into a riot at Newark in Delaware. A dozen students – men and girls – streaked down the main street watched by a crowd of 1,000. Then students and police clashed in a wild melee. Police claimed that students threw bottles, stones and in one incident, acid. Eleven policemen were injured and twelve students arrested.

WHAT A CHEEK...
STREAKING will not be tolerated in Bournemouth. That was the stern warning from Police superintendent Peter Hoper in the dignified resort yesterday. His announcement came too late to stop an anonymous blonde making a traffic-stopping 50-yard streak along Westover Road. But from now on, it is emphasised, the town's streakers face prosecution, fines and even jail.

What a crowd...
THE mass streak has been seen in its full glory at Georgia's state university in Athens. There, 1,500 students of both sexes ran naked through the campus and claimed a world record. The streakers were outnumbered only by the spectators. A school patrolman estimated that more than 20,000 people watched the event.

BACKSTORY

For a period during the 1970s streaking was a phenomenon that was either simply about people having fun, or the end of civilization as we knew it. Spreading from the US where it had been enthusiastically practiced on college campuses, the craze swept the UK, with sports events in particular becoming the 'go-to' place for people who wanted to – well, let it all hang out.

Among the most famous of these was Michael O'Brien (above), who ran across the pitch naked during a rugby match at Twickenham in 1974. PC Bruce Perry strategically placed his helmet.

Eight years later Erica Roe (right) made an even more impressive impact at the same stadium during a match between England and Australia.

STOP PRESS – STREAK LATEST

BRITISH streakers, not to be outdone by their American cousins, took to the roads last night. They flung caution to the chill winds with a series of spectacular nude dashes.

Claiming to be Britain's first male streaker was 28-year-old pop singer Chris Buckley. He flashed down a busy street in Hanwell, West London, to the cheers of an appreciative crowd.

Two Wolverhampton trail-blazers also successfully played hide-and-streak with the law. And girl streakers were reported seen in Regent Street and outside the Houses of Parliament.

Monsieur Crazy steps out 1,350 ft above Manhattan

OOOOOH-LA-LA!

HIGHLIFE: Philippe Petit during the tightrope act that made New York look up.

The sexy secret of TV curfew

By RACHEL HEBDITCH

BRITAIN faces a baby boom—all because television shut down early last winter, say family planning experts.

Maternity bookings have soared . . . exactly nine months after the start of the TV curfew imposed during the fuel crisis.

Thousands of expectant mums are due to have their babies at the end of September and early in October.

Hospitals all over Britain are preparing for the birth boom.

At the Royal Gwent Hospital in Newport, Mon, a spokesman said: "Our bookings have gone up for the time of year. In fact it is quite a peak."

Slap

It is a slap in the face for the Family Planning Association, who appealed to couples to take precautions.

The association feared that the early TV shutdown, which began in December, and the three-day working week were a dangerous combination.

A spokesman said last night: "People have lost the art of entertaining themselves. When ready-made entertainment fails, they resort to the oldest form of recreation."

BOB'S GOLDEN CATCH

CRICKET - MAD Bob Webb sighed with relief yesterday when he got a pools-win cheque for £295,000.

For Bob, a building site foreman, had thrown away his Littlewoods pools coupon without checking it.

When he heard about the win Bob, who has played for the Essex team at North Stifford for seventeen years, fished the torn-up coupon out of a rubbish bin.

The pools people, learning of Bob's love for cricket, arranged for England cricket captain Mike Denness to hand over the cheque.

Bat

Bob, of Horndon-on-the-Hill, Essex, shares the cheque with his friend Bill Claridge, of Corringham, Essex.

He says that he has already decided what to buy first with the win—a new cricket bat.

Bob, who is married with two young daughters, explained: "I've not had too bad a season as a bowler.

"With a new bat, I might finish the season in a blaze of glory."

TRAIN VICTIM NAMED

Police yesterday named a woman who fell to her death from a Euston - Wolverhampton express on Tuesday as Mrs. Felicity Grimes, 23, of Dublin.

HIGHSPOT: Where the daredevil walked.

STUNTMAN Philippe Petit hit the highspots of New York yesterday, with a tightrope walk in the sky.

The French daredevil walked twice across a 150ft.-long cable stretched between the 1,350ft.-high twin towers of Manhattan's World Trade Centre.

As Petit, 25, started his first walk, balancing himself with a long pole, crowds gathered in the streets below. Traffic stopped.

Police headquarters got a call: "There's some nut walking between the Trade Centre towers."

Emergency squads, with sirens screaming, converged on the area. Some officers headed for the top of the building, the world's second-tallest.

Chasm

Meanwhile Petit was still strolling across the concrete chasm. At one point he even hung by his legs.

Eventually, police made contact with the stuntman. Come off it, they said.

And he did — to be cheered by the crowds as he was put into a patrol car and taken to a hospital's psychiatric ward.

A police spokesman said: "We're treating this as a psycho case at the moment."

Later, hospital director

Geoffrey High offered a second opinion on Petit and his aide, fellow Frenchman Jean Heckel, who had helped to set up the tightrope.

"They seem like perfectly normal human beings," Mr. High said. "But anyone who does this 110 stories up can't be entirely right."

Petit and Heckel had hidden overnight in the Trade Centre.

The star of the show had previously staged his balancing act atop Notre Dame cathedral in Paris and on the Sydney Harbour Bridge.

But the Manhattan display was his top achievement yet. The police did not approve, though.

The adventurous pair were charged with criminal trespass and disorderly conduct.

Hospital director High couldn't resist the final word: "I guess they'll go on to higher things," he said.

Why girls are down at heel

By MARGARET JONES

ONE in seven women had trouble with the last pair of shoes they bought—either because they were uncomfortable or because they fell apart, says a Consumers' Association report.

And one in five found shops unhelpful when they took the shoes back to complain.

The report, in the magazine Which?, says that the most common problem was discomfort, then soles and uppers parting, uppers splitting and heels falling off.

The survey, made among 1,763 women members, showed that smaller shops were more helpful than average in dealing with complaints and were also rated well overall.

Trouble

A quarter of the women questioned, who had bought shoes most recently from Dolcis, said the shoes had given trouble.

Only one in ten who had bought shoes from K shops, Marks and Spencer and department stores reported problems.

A spokesman for the British Shoe Corporation, which owns Dolcis and other top names, declined to comment on the report yesterday.

DRINK THIEF RAIDS COPS

A THIRSTY thief has made a poteen raid . . . on a police station.

He stole twenty bottles of the famous illicit Irish liquor—and equipment to make more.

The raid was on the police station at Borrisokane, Co. Tipperary.

The poteen and equipment had been seized in a police raid on a house two months ago.

A police spokesman said: "No arrests have yet been made. The station is unoccupied at night while the sergeant is on border duty."

154

8ᵗʰ August 1974

OOOOH-LA-LA!

Monsieur Crazy steps out 1,350ft above Manhattan

From Gordon Gregor in New York

STUNTMAN Philippe Petit hit the highspots of New York yesterday, with a tightrope walk in the sky.

The French daredevil walked twice across a 160ft.-long cable stretched between the l,350ft.-high twin towers of Manhattan's World Trade Centre.

As Petit, 25, started his first walk, balancing himself with a long pole, crowds gathered in the streets below. Traffic stopped.

Police headquarters got a call: "There's some nut walking between the Trade Centre towers."

Emergency squads, with sirens screaming, converged on the area. Some officers headed for the top of the building, the world's second-tallest.

Chasm

Meanwhile Petit was still strolling across the concrete chasm. At one point he even hung by his legs.

Eventually, police made contact with the stuntman. Come off it, they said.

And he did – to be cheered by the crowds as he was put into a patrol car and taken to a hospital's psychiatric ward.

A police spokesman said: "We're treating this as a psycho case at the moment."

Later, hospital director Geoffrey High offered a second opinion on Petit and his aide, fellow Frenchman Jean Heckel, who had helped to set up the tightrope.

"They seem like perfectly normal human beings," Mr. High said.

"But anyone who does this 110 metres up can't be entirely right."

Petit and Heckel had hidden overnight in the Trade Centre.

The star of the show had previously staged his balancing act atop Notre Dame cathedral in Paris and on the Sydney Harbour Bridge.

But the Manhattan display was his top achievement yet. The police did not approve, though.

The adventurous pair were charged with criminal trespass and disorderly conduct.

Hospital director High couldn't resist the final word: "I guess they'll go on to higher things," he said.

BACKSTORY

The daring – not to say vertigo-inducing – exploits of Philippe Petit astonished up to 100,000 transfixed New Yorkers when he made his death-defying walk between the twin towers of the World Trade Center. It earned him fame and, in order for the charges to be dropped, an agreement to perform a show for children, which Petit gave in Central Park.

The Frenchman, meeting musician Sting in Newcastle in 2000 (left) continued his high-wire adventures, and in 2008 his crossing of New York's Twin Towers was turned into an Oscar-winning documentary called *Man on Wire*.

The 2001 destruction of the World Trade Center at the hands of terrorists made Petit's walk all the more poignant. From the devastated site of the attack however, a soaring new Freedom Tower would take shape (above).

Daily Mirror

EUROPE'S BIGGEST DAILY SALE

5p Wednesday, November 27, 1974 No. 22,037

Drama as row over baby ends her reign of 4 days

MISS WORLD QUITS

Where is the missing MP?

MYSTERY DEEPENS AS WIFE SAYS: I'M STILL WAITING AND HOPING

EVENING OUT: Mr. Stonehouse and his wife at a ball in 1968, when he was Postmaster-General.

MP's wife Barbara Stonehouse was "waiting and hoping" in Britain last night as the mystery of her vanishing husband deepened.

While FBI agents investigated the disappearance of businessman John Stonehouse from his hotel in Miami Beach, Florida, it was learned in London that four directors have quit his City organisation.

Clothes

Legal proceedings have been started over one of the resignations.

It was just a week ago that Mr. Stonehouse, who was in America on a business trip, vanished after saying that he was going to take a swim. He left his clothes with a beach club secretary.

But no one appeared to have seen him on his hotel's private beach.

And a massive air and sea search failed to find his body.

The beach club's girl secretary spoke yesterday of his "strange" behaviour just before his disappearance.

She said that in asking her twice to look after his clothes he had made it "pretty obvious" that she would remember him.

And two lifeguards on the beach said that they saw no one go into the water.

If Mr. Stonehouse had been drowned in the area, they said, his body would have been washed up.

The former Minister was known to be a strong swimmer.

His wife said last night: "He would always take a dip in the sea, no matter what time of the year it was."

Memory

Mrs. Stonehouse added: "I'm sitting here waiting and hoping."

No clues to Mr. Stonehouse's disappearance have been found.

One possibility, police believe, is that he may be alive and suffering from loss of memory.

● The missing MP—See Pages 4 and 5.

UNMARRIED mother Helen Morgan last night quit as Miss World after a reign of just four days.

Her dramatic decision followed a day of new controversy over her baby son Richard.

The climax was an announcement by nightclub dancer Linda Lovegrove that she planned to name Helen—pictured with Richard on the right—as the "other woman" in a divorce action.

Weeping

The 22-year-old beauty queen wept as she renounced the title that last Friday earned her £3,000 and the chance of £50,000 in "extras". She said: "This morning I felt on top of the world, but now that world has collapsed around me.

"I feel absolutely shocked and numb. I can't believe that my happiness has so suddenly turned to sadness and confusion. I was so looking forward to a wonderful year as Miss World. Now all my dreams are shattered."

Officials of Mecca, who stage the Miss World contest, were believed to have questioned Helen's family yesterday about her former boy friends.

Then contest organiser Mrs. Julia Morley spoke to the weeping girl on the telephone. Mrs. Morley said late last night:

● We had a lengthy discussion about allegations today — including a certain one concerning a possible divorce action.

The indication from her was that, due to the upsetting nature of certain allegations, she felt she had no alternative but to resign.

It is up to her to talk about the stories, not us.

She was very distressed, but we have no alternative but to reluctantly accept her ● decision.

Earlier, 28-year-old Mrs. Lovegrove said she would see solicitors about the break-up of her marriage to nightclub worker Raymond Lovegrove, 29.

By TERRY O'HANLON and PETER KANE

She claimed that Helen was responsible.

"My husband has left me," she said.

Raymond Lovegrove said: "My wife forced my hand. I want to start a new life, but there will be no chance of my seeing Helen.

Nightclub

"She moves in a completely different world now."

Mr. Lovegrove added: "I was a professional disc-jockey in Wales three years ago when I met Helen at a Cardiff nightclub."

Helen refused to talk about her friendship with Mr. Lovegrove . . . but she admitted she knew of his wife's divorce plans to "name" her.

● I want to talk the whole matter over with Mrs. Morley. It is only right and proper that she should hear my version of the rumours that are flying about concerning my private life.

All I would like to say about these allegations at the moment is that they are far removed from the truth. ●

Mecca officials will let Helen keep her £3,000 prize.

She shared a house in Barry, Glamorgan, with

● Continued on Page Three.

THE ROYAL RIB-TICKLER Centre Pages

27th November **1974**

WHERE IS THE MISSING MP?

MYSTERY DEEPENS AS WIFE SAYS: I'M STILL WAITING AND HOPING

MP's wife Barbara Stonehouse was "waiting and hoping" in Britain last night as the mystery of her vanishing husband deepened.

While FBI agents investigated the disappearance of businessman John Stonehouse from his hotel in Miami Beach, Florida, it was learned in London that four directors have quit his City organisation.

Clothes

Legal proceedings have been started over one of the resignations.

It was just a week ago that Mr. Stonehouse, who was in America on a business trip, vanished after saying that he was going to take a swim. He left his clothes with a beach club secretary.

The secretary spoke yesterday of [Stonehouse's] "strange" behaviour just before his disappearance.

She said that in asking her twice to look after his clothes he had made it "pretty obvious" that she would remember him.

And two lifeguards on the beach said that they saw no one go into the water.

If Mr. Stonehouse had been drowned in the area, they said, his body would have been washed up.

The former Minister was known to be a strong swimmer.

His wife said last night: "He would always take a dip in the sea no matter what time of the year it was."

No clues to Mr. Stonehouse's disappearance have been found.

One possibility, police believe, is that he may be alive and suffering from loss of memory.

27th December **1974**

THE FUGITIVE

Face to face ... but runaway MP will
only talk about the cricket
From Richard Stott in Melbourne

John Stonehouse had a tearful reunion with his wife last night – under guard in a Melbourne detention centre.

They met after the MP had pleaded in court to be allowed to stay in Australia.

Mr. Stonehouse threw his arms around his wife Barbara.

And later Mrs. Stonehouse told friends "If John is allowed to stay here, then I'll be staying with him."

Mr. Stonehouse – who staged his own disappearance more than a month ago from Miami, Florida – has been refused bail by the Melbourne court.

Climax

The magistrate ordered him to be detained for a week pending a Ministerial decision on whether he should be deported.

The reunion in the detention centre on the outskirts of Melbourne was the emotional climax of a tense two days in the astonishing Stonehouse affair.

Mr. Stonehouse entered Australia on a passport under the name of a dead man – Joseph Arthur Markham.

Melbourne police picked him up on Christmas Eve as a suspected illegal immigrant.

He was then using the name Donald Clive Mildoon.

Yesterday the packed Melbourne courtroom heard a statement giving the 49-year-old MP's reasons for fleeing.

The statement said he was under "a great deal of business and political pressure" and was being blackmailed.

It was a different John Stonehouse from the suave, sophisticated MP known in Britain for his flamboyance and business flair.

He was wearing a crumpled lightweight tropical jacket.

Daze

The shoes were old and tatty, the hair was wispy and out of place.

At times he seemed to be in a daze as the proceedings droned on around him.

At one stage some of the old cockiness reappeared as Mr. Stonehouse insisted on going around the court and shaking hands with every reporter.

He would not answer questions about his disappearance, and all he would say to me was "Nice weather for the Test match. Do you think you'll be going to see some of it?"

Later he asked me: "Did you have a good Christmas dinner?"

During the hearing, Mr. Stonehouse admitted that he "may have committed a technical offence in Britain" over the passport.

But he added: "I am not a criminal in the strict sense of the word."

After the case came the reunion with Mrs. Stonehouse, who had flown to Australia.

Their emotional greeting was watched by embarrassed guards and detectives at the detention centre.

Mr. Stonehouse said: "This is the best Christmas present I could possibly have had."

Mr. Stonehouse will spend his time in custody, with a couple of seamen who have jumped ship.

BACKSTORY

John Stonehouse's disappearance had every element required for a political sensation. Crime, rumours of spies, sexual intrigue and a spectacular fall from grace for a wealthy and powerful former minister turned Stonehouse into ready-made headline material.

He had faked his own death as part of an elaborate plot to set up a new life down under with his former secretary Sheila Buckley.

The plan soon unravelled, however, and once deported back to Britain in 1976 he was found guilty of theft, deception and fraud relating to a series of dodgy business deals.

Sentenced to seven years in prison, he suffered from heart attacks and was released after three years, before marrying Buckley in 1981. Stonehouse passed away in 1988 – the man who had "died" twice.

CHAPTER FIVE

OH, GOD. PLEASE HELP ME

"Blonde bombshell" Joyce McKinney pleads her innocence as she is bundled into a prison van after being charged with kidnap in one of the most bizarre stories of the 1970s (see page 172).

Daily Mirror

EUROPE'S BIGGEST DAILY SALE

5p Saturday, January 4, 1975 No. 22,067

MEET MAX AND THE MISSUS...

He earns up to £400 a week, lives in a £50,000 house, drives a £6,000 Lotus and relaxes with the wife in a bath that has gold-plated taps. SO HOW DOES MAX DO IT?

See Page Three

WILSON CRACKS THE WHIP

PREMIER Harold Wilson last night warned workers in Britain's strike-ridden motor industry that unless they did a fair day's work for a fair day's pay many of them would lose their jobs.

It was the harshest warning ever delivered by a Labour Prime Minister to a particular section of British workers.

Mr. Wilson's theme was that although the Government might bale out a firm in difficulties, it would not toss in public money to save jobs when workers were causing avoidable losses.

Appealed

He singled out British Leyland, the giant car firm which appealed for Government money last month in order to remain a major producer.

"Parts of British Leyland are profitable,

By TERENCE LANCASTER
Mirror Political Editor

others are not," Mr. Wilson said.

"But public investment and participation cannot be justified on the basis of continued avoidable loss-making."

Then came the key sentence:

"Our intervention cannot be based on a policy of turning a private liability into a public liability." Even as Mr. Wilson was delivering this warning in his constituency of Huyton, Liverpool, 250 engine-turners at the British Leyland works at Cowley, Oxford, started a strike which resulted in the company laying off 12,000 workers.

The Prime Minister was also speaking on the day when another vehicle manufacturer—

Fodens, the lorry firm—appealed for Government money to guarantee an increase in their overdraft.

Mr. Wilson said the Government could not justify to Parliament, or the taxpayer, the subsidising of large factories which **COULD** pay their way—but are failing to do so because of manifestly avoidable stoppages of production."

It was on British Leyland that he concentrated most during the 1,000-word speech.

This firm, Mr. Wilson said, could survive and prosper as a much smaller unit.

Promised

But a costly investment and modernisation programme would be required if it were to be maintained as a major producer, exporter and employer.

The Prime Minister promised urgent action to put the company on a secure and profitable basis.

Then came what amounted to an ultimatum to the workers:

"The achievement of that aim does not depend on the action of the Government alone.

"The success of public intervention to fight the threat of unemployment means a full contribution, a fair day's work for a fair day's pay, by everyone for whose security we are fighting."

Mr. Wilson blamed strikers for hampering British car production, so helping to boost imported car sales.

He stressed that what happened from now on depended on "the wider and wholehearted participation" of those whose future rested on the success of the Government's decisions.

In other words he was saying: You are at liberty to strike and strike again. But don't blame us if you land up on the dole.

● **Rescue for lorry giant . . . Car men strike: See Page Two.**

4th January 1975

MEET MAX AND THE MISSUS

He earns up to £400 a week, lives in a £50,000 house, drives a £6,000 Lotus and relaxes with the wife in a bath that has gold-plated taps.

SO HOW DOES MAX DO IT?

THIS IS HOW MAX DOES IT IN THREE LITTLE WORDS:

BLOODY HARD WORK!

By Edward Laxton

THE secret of success for Max Quartermain is . . . sheer hard work.

Max, a plasterer's mate, earns up to £400 for a normal 40-hour week.

He has a seven-bedroomed house worth £50,000, a £6,000 Lotus Elite sports car and a £1,000 Mini for his wife.

Pride of place in the expensively furnished house at Burnham, Bucks, goes to a £600 sunken bath with gold-plated taps.

Luxuries

"I wanted the luxuries of life," said 33-year-old Max. But I haven't got brains: O levels and things.

"So I soon realised that the answer was hard work."

Max's massive earnings are based on a super-hod, which holds up to 1½cwt. of plaster and is almost twice the size of a normal hod.

Max carries it on the run to a job and does not need to return as often to fill it.

So he can spend less time mixing the plaster and more time getting on with the job.

He added: "In my best week I took home £411. It's a disaster if my pay drops below £160. My average is more than £200 a week."

Max and his 32-year-old wife Eileen have three children, Lee, eleven, Angeline, ten and Emma, five.

Eileen said: "Max is tired when he gets home but he is never in a bad mood."

12th August 1976

MIGHTY MAX JUST KEEPS ROLLS-ING ALONG

SUPERCAR TREAT FOR BIRTHDAY SUPERHOD

IT'S SUPER-HOD – astride the bonnet of his new supercar.

He's buying himself the £19,500 Rolls for his 35th birthday. "I usually get socks or a handkerchief as a birthday present," said Superhod, alias plasterer's mate Max Quartermain.

"But I decided that this year I would have something slightly different."

Naturally Max, who claims that his giant hod helps him to carry more plaster than anyone else in his trade, has had to put in a bit of overtime to buy the Rolls.

In a normal week he has to scrape by on around £250. "But recently I've been working a seventy-hour week," he said, "taking home £350 to £400."

So he'll be paying cash for the supercar, which he is due to pick up from the local Rolls dealer on Sunday.

It will go well with his other symbols of success, like his £50,000 home in Burnham, Bucks, his £400 television set and his £600 round bath with gold taps.

Max, who is married with four children, said: "The only way a working man like me can buy a car like this – besides robbing a bank – is to work and work and work.

"It has been tough going, but it will all be worthwhile when I drive it home on Sunday."

BACKSTORY

Max Quartermain regularly featured in the pages of the *Mirror*, his wage-earning exploits coming at a time of economic worries providing curiosity and no little admiration. During his tabloid coverage heyday "Superhod" was said to be earning more than then Prime Minister Harold Wilson.

Daily Mirror

EUROPE'S BIGGEST DAILY SALE

6p   Friday, January 30, 1976   No. 22,396

Thorpe's MPs rally round on his day of trouble

THESE WILD SEX CLAIMS

By SYDNEY YOUNG, DOUGLAS SLIGHT and CHRISTOPHER BUCKLAND

LIBERAL leader Jeremy Thorpe hit back yesterday at "wild allegations" that he had been caught up in a sex scandal.

His denial came as Liberal M.Ps rallied to support his leadership.

At the same time Mr. Thorpe was shaken by a critical report on a collapsed fringe bank —London and County Securities— with which he was linked.

He admitted an "error of judgment" over his part in the bank affair.

The "sex scandal" claim was made during a court case at Barnstaple, North Devon.

In an astonishing outburst from the dock, 35-year-old author Norman Scott said: "I am being hounded by people the whole time just because of my sexual relationship with Jeremy Thorpe.

Sorry

"The whole thing gets worse and worse. I am sorry, but I must say it.

"I am so tired, and this is why all this has happened."

Scott, of Castle Street, Combe Martin, near Barnstaple, was put on probation for two years for a Post Office fiddle.

His claims were denied in a terse statement issued in London by Mr. Thorpe. It said:

"It is well over twelve years since I last saw or spoke to Mr. Scott. There is no truth in Mr. Scott's wild allegations.

The Liberal leader got immediate support from the twelve other Liberal M Ps.

The Party's Chief Whip, Cyril Smith, declared: "His parliamentary colleagues consider that the thing is ludicrous and totally irrelevant."

In the court case, Scott admitted obtaining £29·20 from the Post Office by misusing a supplementary benefits book.

His outburst came when the magistrates' chairman, Mr. Edward Stanbury, asked if he wanted the case to be adjourned so that a probation officer's report could be prepared.

Wilson papers swoop

By JOHN PENROSE

DETECTIVES hunting for Premier Harold Wilson's stolen tax papers carried out a series of lightning raids yesterday.

They questioned nine people—seven men and two women—after swooping on homes throughout London during the early hours.

Three men and both women later returned home.

One of the men questioned was 34-year-old antique dealer Terry Nichols, who last month handed police a batch of other documents stolen from Mr. Wilson.

He and his wife Janet were woken by police at their flat in Chalk Farm and taken to Cannon Row police station.

Mr. Nichols, also known as Nicky Emmett, revealed in the Mirror last week that he paid £2,500 for a champagne carton packed with Mr. Wilson's papers, tape recordings and photographs.

He refused to say who sold him the papers and denied any involvement in the robbery.

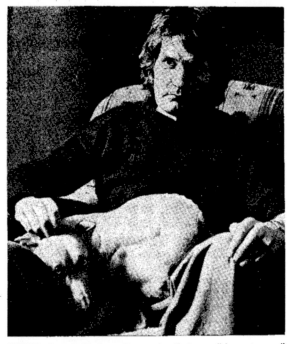

AUTHOR. Scott at his home. He was described as a "desperate man."

Writer in court outburst

assured a report can be prepared in a short time."

Scott went on: "It is just becoming so sick."

He then burst into tears as he made his claim about Mr. Thorpe.

The court clerk told him to be quiet.

Scott, visibly upset, shot ti: "This means a continuation of the whole thing which really is becoming so bizarre."

His solicitor, Mr. Jeremy Ferguson, said: "I am

"He is a man who sometimes breaks the rules. . . .

"He needs very great assistance, not punishment. He needs understanding."

Liberal M Ps have been aware for some time of what might emerge at the court hearing.

On Wednesday night, at

the regular weekly meeting of Liberal members, the issue was put on the agenda at Mr. Thorpe's insistence— and he got unanimous backing.

Among all parties at Westminster the whole business was being regarded with distaste.

Mr. Ferguson, Scott's solicitor, described his client as being "excitable and anxious."

Mr. Ferguson went on:

The bank blunder—See Page Two

30th January 1976

THESE WILD SEX CLAIMS

Thorpe's MPs rally round on his day of trouble

By Sydney Young, Douglas Slight and Christopher Buckland

LIBERAL leader Jeremy Thorpe hit back yesterday at "wild allegations" that he had been caught up in a sex scandal.

His denial came as Liberal MPs rallied to support his leadership. . . .

At the same time Mr. Thorpe was shaken by a critical report on a collapsed fringe bank – London and County Securities – with which he was linked.

He admitted an "error of judgment" over his part in the bank affair.

The "sex scandal" claim was made during a court case at Barnstaple, North Devon.

In an astonishing outburst from the dock, 35-year-old author Norman Scott said: "I am being hounded by people the whole time just because of my sexual relationship with Jeremy Thorpe."

Sorry

"The whole thing gets worse and worse, I am sorry, but I must say it.

"I am so tired, and this is why all this has happened."

Scott, of Castle Street, Combe Martin near Barnstaple was put on probation for two years for a Post Office fiddle.

His claims were denied in a terse statement issued in London by Mr. Thorpe. It said:

"It is well over twelve years since I last saw or spoke to Mr. Scott. There is no truth in Mr. A Scott's wild allegations."

The Liberal leader got immediate support from the twelve other Liberal MPs.

The Party's Chief Whip, Cyril Smith, declared: "His parliamentary colleagues consider that the thing is ludicrous and totally irrelevant."

In the court case, Scott admitted obtaining £29-20 from the Post Office by misusing a supplementary benefits book.

His outburst came when the magistrates' chairman, Mr. Edward Stanbury, asked if he wanted the case to be adjourned so that a probation officer's report could be prepared.

Scott, visibly upset, shouted: "This means a continuation of the whole thing which really is becoming so bizarre."

His solicitor, Mr. Jeremy Ferguson, said: "I am assured a report can be prepared in a short time."

Scott went on: "It is just becoming so sick."

He then burst into tears as he made his claim about Mr. Thorpe. The court clerk told him to be quiet.

Mr. Ferguson, Scott's solicitor, described his client as being "excitable and anxious."

Mr. Ferguson went on:

"He is a man who sometimes breaks the rules. He needs very great assistance, not punishment. He needs understanding."

Liberal MPs have been aware for some time of what might emerge at the court hearing.

On Wednesday night, at the regular weekly meeting of Liberal members, the issue was put on the agenda at Mr. Thorpe's insistence – and he got unanimous backing.

Among all parties at Westminster the whole business was being regarded with distaste.

BACKSTORY

Rumours of secret affairs, money, shadowy characters, high-stakes politics, a conspiracy cover-up, a dead dog and an alleged plot to kill: the Jeremy Thorpe–Norman Scott saga had the lot, and held the nation riveted during the mid- to late 1970s.

It was a complex story that hinged on the allegation that Jeremy Thorpe, the charismatic leader of the Liberal Party, had had a homosexual affair in the early 1960s with stable lad Scott. This would have been illegal at the time, and any potential exposure would be politically disastrous. Scott's outburst in the unlikely surroundings of a court case into a benefits fiddle set the story off. As it began to unravel, there were tales and allegations of compromising letters, hush money and conspiracies, drawing in an ever-more bewildering cast of political colleagues and assorted characters.

Thorpe resigned as party leader later in 1976, but matters turned far more serious when there was a bungled attempt to kill Scott and his pet Great Dane Rinka on a lonely stretch of Dartmoor. The dog was killed but the gun jammed and Scott survived.

After the gunman was convicted and served time in prison, he claimed he had been hired to kill. In 1979 Thorpe and three others were charged with conspiracy to murder. On 22nd June all of them were cleared. A flamboyant character who even met Jimi Hendrix backstage in 1967 (below), Thorpe faded away from public life, and was later diagnosed with Parkinson's disease.

Daily Mirror

EUROPE'S BIGGEST DAILY SALE

6p   Wednesday, May 12, 1976   ✦ ✦ ✦   No. 22,483

THANK GOD FOR MY LOVELY ROSIE!

JUBILANT George Davis walked to freedom and a joyous reunion with his wife last night.

And as she wept happily in his arms, George said: "Thank God for my lovely little Rosie. Thank God for my friends. Thank God for the Daily Mirror.

"Without them all, I would be behind bars for another fifteen years."

George, who had earlier been released from jail on the Isle of Wight, had just arrived at London's Waterloo Station.

I stood by his side as dark-eyed Rosie ran screaming with joy down the platform to fling her arms round him. Her tears of joy splashed my lapels as she hugged and squeezed the man she had battled so hard to free.

Cuddle

Calmly, East Ender George said: "Well, it's nice to be home again, Rosie.

"Give us a kiss and a cuddle and we'll go down to Bow for some nice pie and mash. I'm starved."

Rosie, crying on his shoulder, told me: "I just can't believe I have got my man back. I just can't believe it.

"I knew they had locked up an innocent man. But we never, never gave up hope.

"The odds against us were heartbreaking at times, but we had to carry on for George's sake.

"Doesn't it show you what faith can do—even if you have to wait for it? And my George is certainly worth waiting for."

Davis's release was ordered by Home Secretary Roy Jenkins just fourteen days after a Government report threw doubt on convictions obtained on only identification evidence.

George, 35, had been serving seventeen years for allegedly taking part in an armed robbery at Ilford, Essex.

Yesterday, as I rode with him on the train to freedom, he told of the fantastic fight to free him.

Wearing a striped jacket and blue jeans he drank tea from a cardboard cup and told me: "It will be hours before I come to earth. I just can't believe I'm free.

"I would have served two years this Sunday and I just felt like a caged animal in Cell 49 at Albany.

"I had to keep a grip on myself or I would have gone mad."

George, prisoner No. 131890, added: "Every night in my cell I used to sit down and write letters going over the case point by point, advising Rosie and the lawyers to pursue this point and pursue that point.

"I'm not really a religious man, but I

By ALAN GORDON

knelt every night and prayed."

George then hit out at identification parades.

"I was convicted only on the evidence of identification—all by police officers. The law just has to be changed."

Last August the Mirror called for a probe into the Davis case.

George had some surprise company on his journey home — none other than Charlie Kray, who had been visiting his twin brothers in Parkhurst Jail.

● What the Mirror Says — Page Two.
● Battle for freedom —Centre Pages.

FREE AT LAST: George hugs wife Rose and daughter Deana.   Picture: ALISDAIR MACDONALD

The Bessell tapes

Legal row looms over BBC deal

By GORDON GREGOR in **Los Angeles** and **JOHN PENROSE** in **London**

JEREMY THORPE'S anguish over the public exposure of his private life is far from over.

For the fallen Liberal Leader may face a "trial by television," with old friend Peter Bessell as chief witness.

The "trial" would be held either on the public screen or in a private viewing room with top Liberals as a "jury."

Runaway ex-Liberal MP Bessell has told everything he knows about the Norman Scott affair in a ninety-minute BBC TV interview recorded in California last weekend.

He did so, he claimed yesterday, after striking a remarkable deal with the BBC.

If the BBC makes cuts in the interview for a public screening, he wants a full, untouched version to be shown to senior Liberals.

In London last night, a BBC spokesman said: "The BBC here do not know of any such request by Mr. Bessell, but it is possible that something was said in America."

If the deal has been struck, it will inevitably spark off a round of legal headaches.

Apart from the BBC's problems in screening the full version, Mr. Scott will call for a copy or transcript for use in his libel action against Mr. Thorpe.

Protect

Lord Goodman, Mr. Thorpe's legal adviser, would also be expected to ask the BBC for a viewing.

In his interview, Bessell talked about the lies he told to protect Mr. Thorpe's reputation:

His own association and financial dealings with Scott;

Mr. Thorpe's friendship with Scott—which Bessell is understood to have described as much stronger and complex than Thorpe had indicated;

And the case of Scott's shot dog.

As a result of the interview police inquiries into the case, which led to a man being jailed at Exeter in March, are to be re-opened.

30th January 1976

THANK GOD FOR MY LOVELY ROSIE!

George Davis is okay, OK

By Alan Gordon

JUBILANT George Davis walked to freedom and a joyous reunion with his wife last night.

And as she wept happily in his arms, George said: "Thank God for my lovely little Rosie. Thank God for my friends. Thank God for the *Daily Mirror*.

"Without them all, I would be behind bars for another fifteen years."

George, who had earlier been released from jail on the Isle of Wight, had just arrived at London's Waterloo Station.

I stood by his side as dark-eyed Rosie ran screaming with joy down the platform to fling her arms round him. Her tears of joy splashed my lapels as she hugged and squeezed the man she had battled so hard to free.

Calmly, East Ender George said: "Well, it's nice to be home again, Rosie.

"Give us a kiss and a cuddle and we'll go down to Bow for some nice pie and mash. I'm starved."

Rosie, crying on his shoulder, told me: "I just can't believe I have got my man back. I just can't believe it."

"I knew they had locked up an innocent man. But we never, never gave up hope.

"The odds against us were heartbreaking at times, but we had to carry on for George's sake.

"Doesn't it show you what faith can do – even if you have to wait for it? And my George is certainly worth waiting for."

Davis's release was ordered by Home Secretary Roy Jenkins just fourteen days after a Government report threw doubt on convictions obtained on only identification evidence.

The George Davis story was one of the most famous of all crime sagas of the 1970s. In an era infamous for armed robbery, gangland rivalries, supergrasses and bent coppers, Davis' case seemed to be one straight out of the scriptbook of *The Sweeney*, the popular police drama of the period.

Davis was a mini-cab driver with a criminal record. He was arrested over a wages robbery at the London Electricity Board in Ilford, Essex, which ended in a shoot-out and the wounding of a policeman. Davis was accused of involvement by an informer and picked out by police officers in an identity parade. Despite a lack of apparent evidence, Davis was found guilty and sentenced to 20 years in prison.

This prompted an extraordinary campaign by his family and friends to prove Davis' innocence, leading to a string of protests, a supportive song recorded by the punk band Sham 69 and graffiti appearing all over London. "George Davis is innocent ok" became one the most recognizable phrases of the time.

The most remarkable stunt came when Davis' supporters dug up the pitch for the Third Test between England and Australia, forcing the contest to be abandoned, much to the consternation of England captain Tony Grieg (below) and his Aussie counterpart Ian Chappell.

The pressure told, however, and Davis was eventually pardoned and released, though not formally declared innocent. Things soon turned sour, however. The Davis marriage broke up and he was later convicted of other robberies. Davis' Ilford robbery conviction was eventually quashed in 2011.

George, 35, had been serving seventeen years for allegedly taking part in an armed robbery at Ilford.

Yesterday, as I rode with him on the train to freedom, he told of the fantastic fight to free him.

Wearing a striped jacket and blue jeans he drank tea from a cardboard cup and told me: "It will be hours before I come to earth, I just can't believe I'm free.

"I would say I served two years this Sunday and I just felt like a caged animal in Cell 49 at Albany.

"I had to keep a grip on myself or I would have gone mad."

George, prisoner No. 131890, added: "Every night in my cell I used to sit down and write letters going over the case point by point, advising Rosie and the lawyers to pursue this point and pursue that point.

"I'm not really a religious man, but I knelt every night and prayed."

George then hit out at identification parades.

"I was convicted only on the evidence of identification – all by police officers. The law just has to be changed."

Last August the *Mirror* called for a probe into the Davis case.

George had some surprise company on his journey home . . . none other than Charlie Kray, who had been visiting his twin brothers in Parkhurst Jail.

Daily Mirror

£££££££ **SAVE !** £££££££

SEE PAGE 23

Daily Mirror **DIAMOND DISCOUNT**

EUROPE'S BIGGEST DAILY SALE

6p   Monday, May 24, 1976   ✦   ✦   ✦   No. 22,493

ALI OOPS!

Romark's spell floors champ

SPELL: Hypnotist Romark puts his curse on Muhammad Ali.

From JOHN JACKSON in Munich

CURSES! That man Romark has struck again.

The British hypnotist put a spell on world heavyweight champion Muhammad Ali yesterday.

And an hour later Ali fell through the floor when a stage collapsed.

The incident happened at the weigh-in for Ali's title fight against Britain's Richard Dunn in Munich early tomorrow.

Before the weigh-in Romark told Ali how he had put a spell on the Crystal Palace football team, who failed to gain promotion, and their manager Malcolm Allison, who has now left the club.

"I have put the same curse on you, Muhammad Ali-son," said Romark.

Ali raised his arms in the air with a grin and did his famous shuffle. But the man who floats like a butterfly soon sank like a stone.

Just after he had stepped off the scales at the weigh-in the floorboards caved in with a loud crack.

There were screams as Ali and a dozen other people fell into a hole five feet deep.

Ali was pinned to the ground by floorboards. One woman was knocked out and several other people were injured. But the champion was pulled out unscathed.

Shaken

His trainer, Angelo Dundee, said later: "Ali was a bit shaken. He could have broken his leg."

Romark, who had left the stage only seconds earlier, commented: "I told you so."

WEIGHT NOTE: Ali weighed in at 15st. 10lb., which is 10lb. lighter than he was for his widely criticised fight against Jimmy Young last month. Dunn weighed 14st. 10½lb.

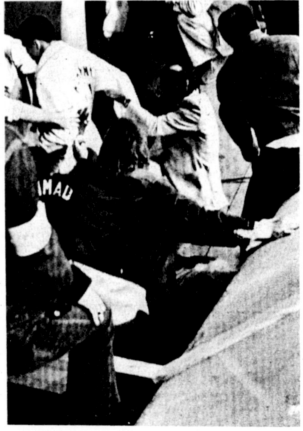

PLUNGE: The champ is helped to his feet after falling through the stage.

Coma girl 'lives on' as plug is pulled

From MARK DOWDNEY in New York

COMA girl Karen Anne Quinlan has been taken off her life-saving respirator, it was reported last night.

But, it is understood, she continues to live on unaided.

The 22-year-old girl has survived for at least three days—and perhaps as long as six—according to a newspaper in her home town of Morristown, New Jersey.

Battle

Karen went into a coma 13 months ago after mixing pills with alcohol. Doctors described her as "a vegetable."

A long court battle started after her parents decided they wanted her to die "with dignity." Hospital doctors refused to turn off the respirator.

Finally, New Jersey's Supreme Court ruled that the machine could be disconnected if doctors agreed there was no hope of recovery.

Neither the hospital nor lawyers connected with the case would confirm or deny last night that the plug had been pulled from the machine keeping Karen alive.

Survived

The lawyer for the Quinlans said the family regarded that whatever happened to Karen now was "sacredly private."

But it is believed that Karen has been moved from the intensive care unit to a private room. Medical sources have already confirmed that she had successfully survived periods of up to 24 hours off the respirator.

27th March 1976

CURSE YOU BIG MAL!

Hypnotist puts Palace under his spell

By Simon Dowling and Nigel Clarke

CURSES! An angry hypnotist has put the boot into Malcolm Allison's Crystal Palace.

Hypnotist Romark says he has put a curse on the team – because Big Mal snubbed him.

And it means Palace will CRUMBLE in their FA Cup semi-final clash with Southampton, and FLOP in their bid for promotion to the Second Division.

Romark – real name Ronald Markham – claimed yesterday that Palace's success this season was all in the mind . . . HIS mind.

"Up till now they have had a lot of luck in their games because I have been rooting for them," he said.

"I concentrated on making Palace win."

Romark now says he will reverse the team's winning streak – in a trance.

He will be concentrating on making the other side win.

Romark says he fell out with Big Mal because the manager broke an appointment at his office near Harley Street.

"That sort of thing makes me very angry," he said.

The curse is due to start today when Palace meet Bury in the Third Division.

"But I will save its full power until next Saturday when they play Southampton in the Cup," said Romark.

"Southampton will destroy them."

But Big Mal quickly countered Romark's tactics.

"Romark? Who does he play for?" he asked.

What did he think about the curse?

"A load of old rubbish," said Big Mal.

24th May 1976

ALI OOPS!

From John Jackson in Munich

CURSES! That man Romark has struck again.

The British hypnotist put a spell on world heavyweight champion Muhammad Ali yesterday.

And an hour later Ali fell through the floor when a stage collapsed.

The incident happened at the weigh-in for Ali's title fight against Britain's Richard Dunn in Munich early tomorrow.

Before the weigh-in Romark told Ali how he had put a spell on the Crystal Palace football team, who failed to gain promotion, and their manager Malcolm Allison, who has now left the club.

"I have put the same curse on you, Muhammad Ali-son," said Romark.

Ali raised his arms in the air with a grin and did his famous shuffle.

But the man who floats like a butterfly soon sank like a stone.

Just after he had stepped off the scales and the weigh-in the floorboards caved in with a loud crack.

There were screams as Ali and a dozen other people fell into a hole five feet deep.

Ali was pinned to the ground by floorboards. One woman was knocked out and several other people were injured. But the champion was pulled out unscathed.

⬆ Romark cheers on Palace's opponents Southampton, while wearing a 'Saints' halo.

His trainer, Angelo Dundee, said later: "Ali was a bit shaken. He could have broken his leg."

Romark, who had left the stage only seconds earlier, commented: "I told you so."

13th October 1977

CRUNCH

By John Jackson

HYPNOTIST Romark's blind faith in his amazing powers was dented yesterday – by the back of a Black Maria.

And he had to admit . . . he didn't see it coming!

For at crunch time his vision was obscured – by two lumps of dough, a couple of 10p pieces and a blindfold.

The brief encounter came when Romark chose the busy main street of Ilford, Essex, to prove that driving blindfold is just a question of mind over matter.

He cruised confidently along for 20 yards – then ran straight into the parked police van.

"It was in a place where logic told me it would not be," he protested.

"I appreciate that a police vehicle should give a person a sense of security – but not parked there!"

But seeing is believing . . . and the sergeant with pencil poised was not impressed.

"You're nicked," he said.

Now Romark has other matters on his mind. Like a summons alleging reckless driving and a £200 bill for car repairs.

BACKSTORY

The career of the hypnotist Romark provided an object lesson in how imaginative stunts could generate wonderful publicity.

Romark's promise to cause an astonishing upset by putting a spell on Muhammad Ali ahead of his fight against the brave but unpromising challenger, Britain's Richard Dunn, seemed it might be working when the champ took a tumble. But the collapse of the platform that sent Ali crashing through the floor was down to the sheer weight of Ali's massive entourage. And of course Ali promptly won the fight.

Romark's fairytales seemed to be made of merely mortal stuff, and his own life did not have a happy ending. He was jailed for embezzlement and died in 1982 after suffering a stroke.

Daily Mirror

BRITAIN'S BIGGEST DAILY SALE

6p   Friday, August 20, 1976   No. 22,569

DRIP, DRIP, DRIP..
Britain drains away on a Hampstead golf course

Shock alert over danger plugs

By MARGARET JONES

A NEW "danger" alert over electric plugs went out last night to thousands of householders.

The suspect plugs are on 600,000 domestic appliances made by Hotpoint and Morphy Richards since last October.

They were moulded to the leads for safety and convenience. But they could be dangerous.

So the appliances will now be sold without plugs.

And people who have already bought the appliances are being warned to get the plugs changed without delay.

The danger products include irons, toasters, hair dries, washing machines and fridges.

Check

The warning also applies to the Electra Twin Tub washing machine (model 1465) sold by electricity boards.

The trouble came to light after a customer in Hertford bought an iron and found a wire poking through the plug moulding.

A warning was published in newspapers last week, asking people to check their plugs.

Then a second faulty plug was found — this time on a hair drier.

Dr. Michael Moorcroft, quality director of Hotpoint, said last night: "We thought the iron was an isolated occurrence. But we've now had the trouble in two products and have discovered how it can occur in the manufacturing process.

"We don't intend to take any chances."

People who have bought the appliances should get in touch with the manufacturers' service departments, the retailers, or — in the case of the Electra washing machine — the electricity board.

WHAT DROUGHT?

THIS was the scene at an exclusive golf club in drought-stricken Britain yesterday.

A woman golfer clutches her dress to protect it from the gushing water spraying a green at the Hampstead club in London.

Story: JOHN JACKSON
Picture: IAN CUTLER

At Epsom racecourse, a battery of sprinklers were in full flow again last night to ensure that the horses will start racing on schedule . . . NEXT SPRING.

And fast bowlers at Hayes cricket club, in Middlesex talked of the lively time they would give the opposing batsmen this weekend—thanks to the newly-watered wicket.

All this, while millions of people struggled down from their bathrooms with buckets of dirty water to make sure their flowers and vegetables survive.

They have been banned by law from using hosepipes and sprinklers on their gardens and cars. The Mirror was flooded with calls yesterday from people incensed about the privileged sports centres.

But the Thames Water Authority said: "We have no powers to act at present. It is very unfortunate and anti-social, but our hands are tied."

Water authorities have used up their legal powers by banning domestic hoses and sprinklers.

The situation will not change until Environment Minister puts his signature on a Government Order imposing tougher curbs on waterwasters.

AT HAMPSTEAD, one woman on the golf course complained: "I wish they'd turn the damned water off! The area round the hole is soaked, and I get wet."

Another woman summed up

● Turn to Page Two

FORD PICKS HIS No 2—See Page Two

20th August 1976

WHAT DROUGHT?

DRIP, DRIP, DRIP. Britain drains away on a Hampstead golf course

John Jackson

THIS was the scene at an exclusive golf club in drought-stricken Britain yesterday.

A woman golfer clutches her dress to protect it from the gushing water spraying a green at the Hampstead club in London.

At Epsom racecourse, a battery of sprinklers were in full flow again last night to ensure that the horses will start racing on schedule . . . NEXT SPRING.

And fast bowlers at Hayes cricket club, in Middlesex, talked of the lively time they would give the opposing batsmen this weekend – thanks to the newly-watered wicket.

All this, while millions of people struggled down from their bathrooms with buckets of dirty water to make sure their flowers and vegetables survive.

They have been banned by law from using hosepipes and sprinklers on their gardens and cars. The *Mirror* was flooded with calls yesterday from people incensed about the privileged sports centres.

But the Thames Water Authority said: "We have no powers to act at present. It is very unfortunate and antisocial, but our hands are tied."

Water authorities have used up their legal powers by banning domestic hoses and sprinklers.

The situation will not change until [the] Environment Minister puts his signature on a Government Order imposing tougher curbs on water-wasters.

AT HAMPSTEAD, one woman on the course complained: "I wish they'd turn the damned water off. The area round the hole is soaked, and I get wet."

Another woman summed up the situation with the remark: "It isn't illegal – so piss off!"

A club official said: "We phone the Thames Water Authority every morning and ask permission to use sprinklers.

"They have to say yes at the moment, but soon we may have to stop like everyone else to save water."

AT EPSOM, a racecourse steward said that permission had been given for the sprinklers "because the course is in such a state that if we leave it too long, it could be ruined for next year."

AT HAYES a local water official said "There is nothing we can do about the watering of cricket pitches – yet."

An Environment Department spokesman said: "Many water authorities have applied for drought orders, and they are now going through the period for objections to be lodged."

14th September 1976

Roger Todd

DRIED-UP Britain got a welcome soaking yesterday.

Some parts of the country had their heaviest rainfall since the beginning of summer.

In London, the umbrellas mushroomed as commuters splashed their way through a real old-fashioned Monday morning downpour.

And heavy rain in the North has given Yorkshire folk a reprieve from water rationing.

Street standpipes were planned for this week in Huddersfield, Wakefield and Halifax.

But between two and six inches of rain fell in Yorkshire at the weekend, adding about 5 per cent to reservoir levels.

The West of England was not so lucky and householders in Devon face water cuts next Wednesday.

There will be no let-up, either, in South-East Wales, where a 17-hour daily turn-off will continue.

While the rain teemed down yesterday, weather forecasters were under a cloud for getting their predictions wrong.

BACKSTORY

The long hot summer of 1976 gave Britain a taste of the Mediterranean, but led to severe drought and all kinds of bans on water usage – for some, at least.

With families having to queue for water at standpipes and people living under all kinds of restrictions, the sight of golf courses using sprinklers caused tempers to soar, just like the temperatures.

From 22nd June until 26th August there was a period of nine weeks that was constantly dry and hot. Rivers, lakes and reservoirs ran dry across the country – to such an extent that camels from Longleat Safari Park felt well at home on the parched Penhow Reservoir in Monmouthshire.

DAILY Mirror

'Five hundred' are killed in collision at holiday island

JUMBO JETS IN AIRPORT DISASTER

CAROL: Wedding wrecked.

Beauty queen bride jilted at church

NO EXPENSE was spared to make beauty queen Carol Brown's wedding a perfect day.

There were six bridesmaids and a lavish reception had been laid on for 100 guests.

But happiness turned to heartbreak when the bridegroom, ex-Coldstream Guardsman Fred Lloyd, went AWOL—and left Carol waiting at the church.

The wedding had to be called off.

Carol, 20, sobbed at her home in Shildon, Co. Durham, and said: "I never want to see him again. Everything is finished."

Friends believe Fred, 22, of Bradford, Yorks, was upset because he had been refused a mortgage.

MORE than five hundred people were killed yesterday when two jumbo jets collided at a holiday island airport.

The planes, both Boeing 747 s collided on a fog-shrouded runway at Santa Cruz airport on Tenerife in the Canary Islands.

Hopeless

Both burst into flames, and the airport was closed as emergency services began a hopeless battle to save the passengers.

Tragically, neither airliner should have been at Santa Cruz. Both were diverted from nearby Las

By MIRROR REPORTERS

Palmas after a terrorist bomb blast near the departure lounge.

When Las Palmas was declared open again one jumbo, a Pan-American 747, was given permission to take off from Santa Cruz.

But as it taxied for take-off, the other jumbo, owned by the Dutch national airline KLM, was converging from another runway.

There was a shattering collision. Some reports said it was on the ground, others that it happened just after the Pan-Am jumbo took off.

But in the dense fog, the first most people knew of the disaster was a deafening roar which rocked airport buildings.

Then the tiny airstrip was lit up by a terrible glare as both planes caught fire. And a dense pall of choking black smoke drifted over the airport.

According to official figures released last night, 563 people died in the crash and 29 were injured.

Worst

Most were holidaymakers — from Los Angeles and New York on the Pan-Am plane, and from Amsterdam on the KLM airliner.

The grim death toll makes last night's crash the worst in aviation history.

Before that, the worst air disaster was in March 1974, when a Turkish Airlines DC-10 came down near Paris, killing all 346 people aboard.

The world's worst mid-air collision was between a British Airways Trident and a Yugoslav DC-9 over Yugoslavia last September.

Eight air traffic controllers at Zagreb airport are now awaiting trial accused of causing the crash, in which 176 people were killed.

MR BIG DODGES DRUG ROUNDUP

A "MR. BIG" dodged the huge drugs swoop at the weekend.

But police chiefs are sure he is the only leading suspect missed in Britain's biggest round-up.

They are delighted at the way the nationwide series of raids went.

The target was an

By SYDNEY YOUNG and EDWARD LAXTON

LSD racket worth millions of pounds.

The dawn swoops on Saturday followed a two-year investigation codenamed Operation Julie after one of the girl detectives involved.

Eight hundred detec-

tives from sixteen forces took part.

There were ninety arrests. Thirty people were still being questioned yesterday — most of them at Swindon, Wilts.

The rest were given

police bail. One senior detective described Operation Julie as "a huge success."

The "Mr. Big" who got away is an American who is believed to be the main importer of LSD into the United States.

● The monster drug— See Centre Pages.

28th March 1977

JUMBO JETS IN AIRPORT DISASTER

'Five hundred' are killed in collision at holiday island

MORE than five hundred people were killed yesterday when two jumbo jets collided at a holiday island airport.

The planes, both Boeing 747s, collided on a fog-shrouded runway at Santa Cruz airport on Tenerife in the Canary Islands.

Hopeless

Both burst into flames, and the airport was closed as emergency services began a hopeless battle to save the passengers.

Tragically, neither airliner should have been at Santa Cruz.

Both were diverted from nearby Las Palmas after a terrorist bomb blast near the departure lounge.

When Las Palmas was declared open again one jumbo, a Pan-American 747, was given permission to take off from Santa Cruz.

But as it taxied for take-off, the other jumbo, owned by the Dutch national airline KLM, was converging from another runway.

There was a shattering collision. Some reports said it was on the ground, others that it happened just after the Pan-Am jumbo took off.

But in the dense fog, the first most people knew of the disaster was a deafening roar which rocked airport buildings.

Then the tiny airstrip was lit up by a terrible glare as both planes caught fire. And a dense pall of choking black smoke drifted over the airport.

According to official figures released last night, 563 people died in the crash and 29 were injured.

Worst

Most were holidaymakers – from Los Angeles and New York on the Pan-Am plane, and from Amsterdam on the KLM airliner.

The grim death toll makes last night's crash the worst in aviation history.

Before that, the worst air disaster was in March 1974, when a Turkish Airlines DC-10 came down near Paris, killing all 346 people aboard.

The world's worst midair collision was between a British Airways Trident and a Yugoslav DC-9 over Yugoslavia last September.

Eight air traffic controllers at Zagreb airport are now awaiting trial accused of causing the crash, in which 176 people were killed.

29th March 1977

By Stuart Grieg

THE stark skeleton of a burnt-out jumbo marks the scene of the world's worst air disaster.

As the sun came up on Tenerife yesterday it revealed the remains of [the] KLM jet and a second jumbo – a Pan-Am – strewn across the holiday island's airport at Santa Cruz.

Experts began sifting the blackened remains as an international row blew up over the cause of the two-jet collision, which left 576 people dead.

Helped by the black box flight recorders recovered from the wreckage, the Dutch, American and Spanish investigators hope to discover where the blame lies.

Miraculously, nearly 70 people, including the only Briton on board either jet, escaped from the Pan-Am jumbo.

The shells of the stricken giants provided a grim backdrop as the hundreds of bodies were put in rows for identification . . .

ENGINEER Joñ Cooper, the only Briton on board either jet, told yesterday how he was hurled to safety.

Mr. Cooper, who works for Pan-Am and was on their jumbo, said: "I reckon I am the luckiest man on this earth.

"I didn't see the other plane until there was a hell of a bang.

"Next thing I knew I was tumbling out. I was dazed, but when I looked back at the plane I heard a roar and saw the flames licking up the body as people screamed and were trying to get out."

BACKSTORY

The Tenerife crash was the worst disaster in aviation history, claiming 583 lives. The sheer horror of the day shocked readers around the world. Graphic accounts of the scene, where there were lines of charred bodies, brought home the terrifying reality of what had happened to hundreds of holidaymakers.

No one in the KLM jumbo survived. Sixty-one on the Pan Am jumbo, including five flightcrew, lived. While there were a whole series of causes and effects, responsibility for the accident was eventually placed on the highly experienced KLM pilot who had not checked that he had been cleared for take-off.

The terrorist bomb that had diverted the plane to the small Los Rodeos airstrip had been placed by Canary Island separatists.

DAILY Mirror

BRITAIN'S BIGGEST DAILY SALE   7p   Wednesday, November 30, 1977
★★

IN YOUR SUPER NORTHERN MIRROR

| Ker-ikey! Now it's Kermit on ice.. —Page 3 | AMIN'S SQUAD OF KILLERS —Page 11 | Men on the pill.. a special report —Page 7 |

MY MORMON LOVER MADE MY HEART FLIP FLOP

Little Miss Perfect tells of the day they first met

JOYCE McKINNEY — "He pulled me into the bed and said: 'My precious little virgin.'"

BY MIRROR REPORTER

FORMER beauty queen Joyce McKinney's story of the day she met a young Mormon missionary was revealed yesterday.

Kirk Anderson, 21, whom she is accused of kidnapping, made her heart go "sort of flip flop," a statement read out in court at Epsom said.

She claimed that during their romance:

● He refused to have sexual intercourse at first — but "teased me and kissed me until I was out of my mind."

● Then one day, after he'd had a bad day with the Bishop, she "wanted to make it better for him, as any wife would do."

● She went into his bedroom. "I took a shower and when I came back he was under the covers nude — so you know who did the seducing." she said.

● He pulled her into bed and said. "My precious little virgin — I am so glad you waited for me."

● Later, she claimed, he said she was not worthy of him.

She said that when she first joined the Mormon Church, she was put in a room with three girls who were drunkards. They called her "little Miss Perfect" she said.

Then she met Anderson. "I will never forget the quiver when he first looked at me," Miss McKinney, 27, said.

She claimed that after she had followed him from the USA to England, when their romance had ended, and taken him to a lonely Dartmoor cottage, they played "bondage games"

Full story—centre pages

£52m ship order is switched

By JOHN GILBERT

SHIPYARD rebels ignored appeals from their shocked union leaders yesterday and lost the Tyne its £52 million share of a huge Polish shipping order.

And the affair threatened to lead to a political storm about details of the order being "shrouded in secrecy."

The deal was lost to the Tyne despite a last-ditch appeal by union leaders and the management of the Swan Hunter yards to the State-owned negotiators British Shipbuilders. After existing contracts have been completed, there are only two more ships on order for the five Tyne yards and the loss of the seven bulk-carriers they would have built for the Poles could herald a return to the idle gloom of the Twenties.

British Shipbuilders insisted that the ships would have to go to other yards in view of a refusal by 1,700 Swan Hunter outfitters to call off their overtime ban.

The outfitters are demanding

Turn to Page 2

Feuding soccer fans in M-way terror

By HARRY KING

RAMPAGING soccer fans terrorised a motorway service station last night.

Customers fled from the cafeteria and eight young waitresses dashed into the kitchens for safety as rival gangs of supporters flung cups and plates at each other.

The fans also overturned tables and chairs.

And despite police patrol crews being called, punch-ups outside on the coach park continued on-and-off for two hours.

Several hundred youths were involved in the violence at the Sandbach service station on the M6 in Cheshire.

The battles were between Coventry City and West Bromwich Albion followers travelling from the Midlands to League Cup games in Lancashire.

A service station spokesman said: "It was all hell let loose.

"The floor is littered with broken crockery and our poor waitresses were frightened out of their wits."

Coachloads

He added: "Fifteen coachloads of supporters arrived at regular intervals and for two hours there were fights throughout the service station area."

"At least eight supporters' coaches had their windscreens smashed. A mini-coach was nearly wrecked and the passengers beaten up.

About forty customers left their meals and ran outside when the battling began.

And motorists driving into the station took only quick glances at the fighting before driving off again.

The Coventry fans were on their way to Anfield for the fourth-round match at Liverpool.

And the West Bromwich supporters were heading for Gigg Lane for the tie with Bury.

A police spokesman said there was also trouble at the Knutsford service station as well as at Burtonwood on the M62.

But he added there were no arrests.

And only one fan had been taken to hospital, he said.

172

14th October 1977

PASSION, KIDNAP AND THE BEAUTY QUEEN

Blonde used handcuffs and shackles, say police

Garth Gibbs and Stuart Greig

LOVESICK beauty queen Joyce McKinney turned kidnapper after a romance broke up, it was claimed yesterday.

She went after her ex-boyfriend with leg shackles, handcuffs, chloroform and dummy guns, a court heard.

The target of her passion was 21-year-old Mormon missionary Kirk Anderson, police said. He was snatched near London and held prisoner at a lonely farm in Devon, magistrates were told at Epsom.

Joyce, a 27-year-old blonde American stood in the dock with fellow-American Keith May, 24. Reporting restrictions were lifted.

They were accused of abducting, assaulting and imprisoning Kirk. Detective Chief Superintendent Bill Hucklesby said the pair entered Britain on false passports. He claimed Joyce had confessed that she planned to kidnap Kirk Anderson.

He was held at a farm in Lower Halstock, Okehampton.

Defence lawyer Stuart Elgrod's plea for bail was turned down after police objections.

Mr. Elgrod said: "At no stage was any violence offered or rendered to Kirk Anderson. Anything that took place while he and Miss McKinney were together was not only with his active consent but, on occasion, at his instigation."

After Joyce and May were remanded in custody for a week, the girl wrestled with prison officers outside the court and called out: "Oh, God. Please help me."

Last night she was in Holloway jail on remand.

30th November 1977

MY MORMON LOVER MADE MY HEART FLIP FLOP

Little Miss Perfect tells of the day they first met

FORMER beauty queen Joyce McKinney's story of the day she met a young Mormon missionary was revealed yesterday.

Kirk Anderson, 21, whom she is accused of kidnapping, made her heart go "sort of flip flop," a statement read out in court at Epsom said.

She claimed that during their romance:

- He refused to have sexual intercourse at first – but "teased me and kissed me until I was out of my mind."

- Then one day, after he'd had a bad day with the Bishop, she "wanted to make it better for him, as any wife would do."

- She went into his bedroom. "I took a shower and when I came back he was under the covers nude – so you know who did the seducing," she said.

- He pulled her into bed and said. "My precious little virgin – I am so glad you waited for me."

- Later, she claimed, he said she was not worthy of him.

She said that when she first joined the Mormon Church, she was put in a room with three girls who were drunkards. They called her "little Miss Perfect" she said.

Then she met Anderson. "I will never forget the quiver when he first looked at me," Miss McKinney, 27, said.

She claimed that after she had followed him from the USA to England, when their romance had ended, and taken him to a lonely Dartmoor cottage, they played "bondage games".

BACKSTORY

British newspapers had long relished the familiar tabloid fodder of lustful encounters involving randy vicars and stunning blondes – but the case of Joyce McKinney was something else altogether.

McKinney was a former Miss Wyoming beauty queen who became a media darling after she was accused of abducting a former lover – a young Mormon missionary called Kirk Anderson – and taking him to a remote Devon cottage. There, McKinney was said to have chained Anderson to the bed and forced him to have frequent sex.

McKinney and her accomplice Keith May were arrested and charged but jumped bail and fled to the US in disguise. Pursued and wooed by the British press desperate to gain every detail of the sensational story, they were eventually caught by the FBI and given suspended sentences related to passport offences.

The lurid details of McKinney's life had in the meantime been entertainingly revealed, with various reports portraying her as a former nude model (below), how she tore off Anderson's special Mormon "chastity underwear", and as a fantasist with a penchant for outrageous disguises and dressing up (above).

But the story didn't quite end there. In 2008, McKinney resurfaced as the owner of the first commercially cloned dog, in South Korea.

GHOST STORY

BRYAN RIMMER investigates a mystery that has scientists guessing

SCIENTISTS from all over the world are now attending a conference on psychic phenomena at Cambridge University — and one subject on the agenda was a haunted council house in North London. The incredible story of one of the most fascinating ghost hunts of modern times is told here, just as it happened. But we have disguised the name of the family involved to save them further stress.

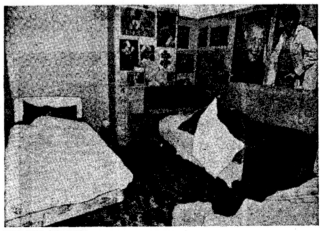

PILLOW FLIGHT   THIS pic shows one girl's pillow apparently flying of its own accord while her sister looks on.

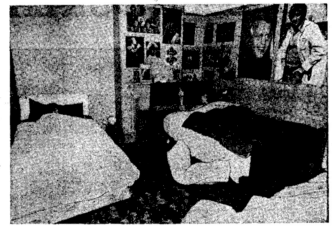

PILLOW FLIGHT   THE pillow is folding about 1ft off the floor. The girl reacts by raising a hand in alarm.

ONE hot August evening a chest of drawers took off across the floor of Peggy H's sitting room.

This started an eerie chain of events that have terrified the family, amazed police and journalists and baffled scientists, doctors and researchers.

For the mystery of the moving chest has been followed by other amazing goings-on in the North London council house — flying objects that seem to be propelled by a supernatural force, a dancing teapot and a spine-chilling voice, apparently from the grave.

Perhaps the voice was the most frightening of all the sinister happenings that have surrounded the family of five.

It started in mid-December . . . and it was no ghostly shriek heard only by members of the family. It was a rich, deep male voice.

Since then, I have spent hours chatting with it — and so have the baffled boffins.

Usually the voice speaks through Mrs. H's daughters, aged 12 and

The strange case of the dancing teapot

13½, though often their lips do not move.

It chats to them as they lie in bed at night, wishes each of the family "Good morning" and often asks for dance music to be played.

It also gives itself a variety of names: Andrew Garner, Stewart Certain and Dirty Dick.

The Daily Mirror has spent weeks investigating this amazing story and talked to many people who claim to have seen mysterious happenings in the house.

Spent

Psychic investigator Maurice Grosse has spent more than 1,000 hours watching the story unfold.

Grosse, a level-headed middle-aged businessman has made a signed, typewritten statement to the Mirror.

These are the astonishing events he claims to have witnessed:

● Marbles and plastic blocks flying across a room — after apparently materialising from walls and windows.

● A teapot dancing on a kitchen cabinet top.

● The shade on a bedlamp tilting 45 degrees, then straightening up.

● The lavatory door opening and closing when there was no one near it.

● A cardboard box full of cushions thrown at him while he was trying to communicate with the entity by knocking.

● A slipper thrown at him across a bedroom.

● A settee thrown up in the air and overturned when he was standing no more than a foot from it.

● Hearing footsteps walking across the ceiling when there was no one upstairs.

Says Grosse: "I have studied psychic phenomena for 40 years and this is the most exciting case I have come across or even read about. And I believe it will be the best documented poltergeist case in history.

"Much of what is going on here is unique and the tests carried out are the most exhaustive in the history of psychic research.

"The family are going through a period of tremendous stress because of what happened."

Grosse remains convinced, despite the fact that in a harrowing scene in the family kitchen one of the girls tearfully confessed to TV ventriloquist Ray Allen that the whole voice episode was a hoax.

Ray, better known as the sidekick of dummy Lord Charles was called in by the Mirror to use his special knowledge to find out if the voice was a spoof.

The younger girl admitted to him, in my presence, that she and her sister had invented the voices to keep attention centred on them.

The next day the girl retracted her admission.

But even if her retraction were not valid, it still does not account for the other odd events in the house.

Sad

The sisters knew nothing about the moving furniture and flying objects, but Dirty Dick and Andrew Garner were products of their imagination.

Ray Alan said later: "It's very sad, but these little girls obviously loved all the attention they got when objects were mysteriously moved around the house and they decided to keep the whole thing going by inventing the voices.

"But it got too big for them and they didn't know how to stop what they had started."

Many people, however, as well as Grosse, feel certain that the manifestations are genuine.

AND BUMPS THAT BAFFLE BOFFINS

MAURICE GROSSE was not the first person to witness things going bump in the North London night.

Before he was called in by the Society for Psychical Research, other independent witnesses had been amazed by what they saw. They were:

THE POLICEWOMAN: WPC Carolyn Heeps, one of the first outsiders called to the house, could scarcely believe her eyes as an armchair moved across the living room, apparently of its own accord.

THE AUTHOR: Guy Lyon Playfair, has spent countless days and nights observing the case. He has written two books on supernatural activity and spent four years observing ghostly goings on in Brasil.

He says: "This is my fifth poltergeist case and by far the most interesting. I, personally, have witnessed five incidents for which no reasonable normal explanation has yet been suggested. Each was recorded on tape.

On one occasion, as the younger girl got out of a heavy armchair, Playfair saw it slide forward and then overturn backwards. Next, while he was watching the girl, a table overturned in the kitchen.

"One morning I saw a red slipper go over the top of the door of the bedroom opposite mine. I went into the room at once. There was only one place the slipper could be and it wasn't there. Only the elder girl was in the room.

"When we went downstairs, there was the slipper on the doormat. Either it went round a corner on its own, or it went through the wall."

Other incidents included a flying book that turned corners, a short conversation with "the voice" by means of rapping, and recording tapes and cables that mysteriously snapped.

THE HYPNOTIST: Ian Fletcher is a surgeon, a hypnotist and a member of the Magic Circle—and it was in this role that he made two visits to the "haunted" house.

Visited

Happenings in that house are very strongly suggestive of paranormal phenomena.

"I hypnotised the younger girl, and from what she told me and from what other observers have said, I feel there is a poltergeist presence in the house."

THE ENGINEER: David Annette, product manager of Pye's business communications closed circuit television, and four other Pye technical experts visited the house with highly sophisticated camera equipment.

They set it up in the main bedroom where the girls were sleeping. But the camera jammed and they found the film had come out of the cassette and got entangled with the drive mechanism—so tightly that it would have taken the force of a sledgehammer to get it there.

David says "There's definitely something odd which I can't explain."

THE RESEARCHER: David Robertson is assistant to Professor John Hastead, head of physics at London University's Birkbeck College, who is supervising a series of tests on the girls.

He has heard knockings from empty rooms — one that he locked himself.

He says: "Once I saw a sideboard lift up at an angle and fall face down on the floor. Many strange things are unexplained."

THE PHYSICIST: Dr. Bernard Carr, Fellow of Trinity College, Cambridge, said that many odd things happened while he was there, but he did not see anything that was obviously paranormal.

The girls were being thrown out of bed and there were terrified cries from them—but always after he had left the room.

THE MAGICIAN: Milbourne Christopher is one of the world's most skilled magicians. He is also chairman of the Occult Investigation Committee of the Society of American Magicians.

He believes the only spirits responsible for the events are high spirits of the girls.

WILL APPEAR TOMORROW
WOW

30th March 1978

GHOST STORY

The strange case of the dancing teapot

Bryan Rimmer

SCIENTISTS from all over the world are now attending a conference on psychic phenomena at Cambridge University – and one subject on the agenda was a haunted council house in North London.

The incredible story of one of the most fascinating ghost hunts of modern times is told here, just as it happened. But we have disguised the name of the family involved to save them further stress.

ONE hot August evening a chest of drawers took off across the floor of Peggy H's sitting room.

This started an eerie chain of events that have terrified the family, amazed police and journalists and baffled scientists, doctors and researchers.

For the mystery of the moving chest has been followed by other amazing goings-on in the North London council house – flying objects that seem to be propelled by a supernatural force, a dancing teapot and a spine-chilling voice, apparently from the grave.

Perhaps the voice was the most frightening of all the sinister happenings that have surrounded the family of five.

It started in mid-December . . . and it was no ghostly shriek heard only by members of the family. It was a rich, deep male voice.

Since then, I have spent hours chatting with it – and so have the baffled boffins.

Usually the voice speaks through Mrs. H's daughters, aged 12 and 13, though often their lips do not move.

It chats to them as they lie in bed at night, wishes each of the family "Good-morning" and often asks for dance music to be played.

It also gives itself a variety of names: Andrew Garner, Stewart Certain and Dirty Dick.

The *Daily Mirror* has spent weeks investigating this amazing story and talked to many people who claim to have seen mysterious happenings in the house.

Spent

Psychic investigator Maurice Grosse has spent more than 1,000 hours watching the story unfold.

Grosse, a level-headed middle-aged businessman has made a signed, typewritten statement to the *Mirror*.

➡ This image supposedly captures the moment a pillow flew across the Hodgson sisters' bedroom – seemingly without anyone touching it.

These are the astonishing events he claims to have witnessed:

- Marbles and plastic blocks flying across a room – after apparently materialising from walls and windows.

- A teapot dancing on a kitchen cabinet top.

- The shade on a bedlamp tilting 45 degrees, then straightening up.

- The lavatory door opening and closing when there was no one near it.

- A cardboard box full of cushions thrown at him while he was trying to communicate with the entity by knocking.

- A slipper thrown at him across a bedroom.

- A settee thrown up in the air and overturned when he was standing no more than a foot from it.

- Hearing footsteps walking across the ceiling when there was no one upstairs.

Says Grosse: "I have studied psychic phenomena for 40 years and this is the most exciting case I have come across or even read about. And I believe it will be the best documented poltergeist case in history.

"Much of what is going on here is unique and the tests carried out are the most exhaustive in the history of psychic research.

"The family are going through a period of tremendous stress because of what happened."

Grosse remains convinced, despite the fact that in a harrowing scene in the family kitchen one of the girls tearfully confessed to TV ventriloquist Ray Allen that the whole voice episode was a hoax.

Ray, better known as the sidekick of dummy Lord Charles, was called in by the *Mirror* to use his special knowledge to find out if the voice was a spoof.

The younger girl admitted to him, in my presence, that she and her sister had invented the voices to keep attention centred on them.

The next day the girl retracted her admission.

But even if her retraction were not valid, it still does not account for the other odd events in the house.

BACKSTORY

Genuine haunting or just a hoax? The debate over the "Enfield Poltergeist" continues, four decades after it was covered in the *Mirror*.

The two sisters involved, Janet and Margaret Hodgson, were the subject of intense scrutiny. Janet would talk in a rasping man's voice which was said to be the spirit of Bill Wilkins, a man who had died of a stroke in the house many years before.

Investigator Maurice Grosse made a detailed study and was convinced there was paranormal activity at play. The girls later admitted that some of the incidents were faked, but the whole experience left its mark on the family, and Janet has since spoken about the trauma and stress it caused.

Subsequent residents of the house have also reported strange noises and sightings.

DAILY Mirror

Wednesday, May 10, 1978   7p

Italy mourns for Moro
DEATH OF A STATESMAN

THIS was how a life dedicated to democracy ended yesterday for Aldo Moro.

Until his capture by Red Brigades terrorists fifty-four days ago, he had seemed destined to be the next President of Italy.

But his kidnappers killed him. Moro's body was found, riddled by eleven machine gun bullets, in a stolen car in Rome.

Italy was plunged into anguish. And there was also fear . . . that democracy in Italy may have died a little, too.

President Jimmy Carter sent his sympathy to Italy with these words: ❝ His murder is a contemptible and cowardly act. He stood for civilisation and the rule of law, principles which always outlive the terrorism that seeks to destroy them. ❞

An epitaph for a statesman—from a statesman.

A nation cries revenge — Pages 2 and 3

10th May 1978
DEATH OF A STATESMAN

Italy mourns for Moro

THIS was how a life dedicated to democracy ended yesterday for Aldo Moro.

Until his capture by Red Brigades terrorists fifty-four days ago, he had seemed destined to be the next President of Italy.

But his kidnappers killed him. Moro's body was found, riddled by eleven machine gun bullets, in a stolen car in Rome.

Italy was plunged into anguish. And there was also fear . . . that democracy in Italy may have died a little, too.

President Jimmy Carter sent his sympathy to Italy with these words: "His murder is a contemptible and cowardly act. He stood for civilisation and the rule of law – principles which always outlive the terrorism that seeks to destroy them."

AN EPITAPH FOR A STATESMAN – FROM A STATESMAN

By John Penrose

A wave of helpless fury swept across Italy yesterday as a stunned nation learned of the brutal murder of Aldo Moro.

Thousands of Romans jammed the streets near the spot where the former Premier's body was found dumped in the back of a Renault estate car.

Many screamed "Death to the Red Brigades" – the terrorist gang which kidnapped him.

One black-clothed woman, her tear-stained face contorted with rage, yelled over and over again, "Assassins! They should be shot to death!"

The entire city came to a horror-stricken halt as people poured into the streets to express their grief.

They were appalled at the viciousness of the murder – eleven bullets from a big-calibre machine-pistol had smashed into Moro's head and heart.

Final

And Rome was horrified at the seeming ease with which, despite police roadblocks and a 50,000 strong manhunt, the terrorists were able to drive their victim's body right into the very heart of the capital.

This was the final slap in the face to the authorities who have been searching frantically for the 61-year-old since he was kidnapped on March 16.

A flurry of "communiques" from the gang, threatening his "execution" and then confirming it, and later denying it, served only to emphasise the helplessness of the police.

Then at 2 p.m. yesterday came the final callous phone call direct to the family home in Rome where Moro lived with his wife, Elenora.

Police intercepted the call, raced to the parked Renault, and found Moro – dirty, unshaven, bloodstained.

Police helicopters chattered over the thronging streets as the body was taken to the mortuary in an empty show of hunting for the killers.

There Elenora and four red-eyed children went to identify the body and pray over the man they had loved.

When they emerged, it was to release a bitter statement forbidding any public show of grief by the government which resolutely refused to negotiate with Moro's captors.

Silence

It said: "The family desires that the precise will of Aldo Moro be fully respected by the authorities of the state and of the Christian Democrat party. This means: no public demonstration or ceremony or speech, no national mourning nor state funeral nor commemorative medal.

"The family locks itself up in silence and demands silence. History will pass judgement on the life and death of Aldo Moro."

Then followed tributes and expressions of sympathy from many world leaders, including the Pope and the Queen.

But on the hushed streets of Rome last night, it was the arrogance and invincibility of the Red Brigade which struck fear into people's hearts.

A shop owner summed it up in an awed whisper. "I am real scared, now," he said. "The Red Brigade are striking at will. How will they be stopped?"

BACKSTORY

The activity of the Red Brigade was curtailed, if not wholly stopped, by a police offensive in the early 1980s, amid a tumultuous and dangerous period in Italian politics.

Economic troubles, corruption and political instability gave rise to increasingly extremist groups from both the left and the right, who waged a series of terrorist campaigns. The abduction and murder of Aldo Moro, Italy's Prime Minister for much of the 1960s, sent shockwaves through the country and added to a climate of fear and suspicion. There were claims – furiously denied – that the Moro murder was in fact a plot involving the Italian secret services.

Far-right atrocities, such as the Bologna bombing of 1980 that killed 84 people, and ongoing kidnappings and assassinations threatened democracy and the ability of the state to govern. Meanwhile, the grip of organized crime on the economy and political power tightened.

The story of Italy's complex and often deadly secret world of power was given a macabre twist with the death of the banker Roberto Calvi, found hanging underneath London's Blackfriars Bridge in 1982.

The man dubbed "God's banker" (above) for his connections with the Vatican, was implicated in illegal financial transactions, and the failure of Banco Ambrosiano, which Calvi headed. The Mafia and other shadowy interests, including the P2 masonic group, also had stakes in the bank.

The official verdict on Calvi's death was suicide, which was later overturned and ruled as murder. In 2012, a senior Mafioso confirmed to the *Sunday Mirror* that the banker had indeed been murdered.

DAILY Mirror

Monday, November 20, 1978   8p

SUICIDE SECT MASSACRE

DEAD: Congressman Ryan

MODEL Joanna yesterday. Picture by BUNNY ATKINS

By ANTHONY DELANO

TROOPS stormed into the remote jungle outpost of a weird American cult last night after five people, including a US congressman, were murdered.

As they hunted down the killers, there were reports that 200 of the religious sect's members had taken part in a mass suicide.

The congressman, Leo Ryan, 53, had

Five shot dead in jungle

been shot dead while leading a probe into the sect's activities in the South American republic of Guyana.

Three of the people killed with him were journalists who were reporting the investigation.

The party—twenty-five in all—had spent Friday night at Jonestown, a 27,000-acre estate run by members of the People's Temple. The estate is named after the cult's leader 46-year-old father of seven Jim Jones.

The following day, the party drove to an airstrip at nearby Port Kaituma with several members of the sect who said they wanted to go home.

Signal

After they had all boarded two planes to take them to Guyana's capital of Georgetown, 300 miles away, one defector brought out a pistol and began firing.

This appeared to be a signal for a tractor to pull alongside the planes.

Other members of the sect on the tractor joined in the shooting.

TV reporter Don Harris, 42, cameraman Robert Brown, 36, and newspaper photographer Greg Robinson, 27, were killed with Ryan. The fifth victim was an 18-year-old girl member of the sect.

Eight other people were

wounded and several were still listed as missing early today.

The plane was wrecked by the gunfire but some survivors scrambled aboard the other aircraft which took off leaving the dead and most of the wounded behind.

The government of the former British colony immediately airlifted police and a company of troops to Jonestown.

Police said that one woman sect member had killed herself and her three children.

But the reports of mass suicides were unconfirmed.

Beaten

Police were last night keeping a close watch on the sect's members in California as a result of the suicide reports.

Ryan's investigation into the sect in Guyana followed complaints that members were beaten, forced into parting with their money and property and held prisoner.

LEADER: Jones

Man behind the cult

THE REV Jim Jones, 46, founded the People's Temple in Indiana 15 years ago with the declared intention of ending oppression and breaking down class barriers.

He set up his HQ in San Francisco in 1971 and became a political force there, eventually becoming head of the city's housing department.

But after allegations of brutality and extortion, he resigned in June last year and took 1,200 of his members to settle in Guyana.

Although Jones is white, most of his following—which he claims is 20,000 strong—is black.

According to one defector, Jones has heavily armed guards.

FAKE PICTURES PROBE

By GEORGE FALLOWS

POLICE are investigating the origin of fake Victorian "urchin" photographs shown at a London exhibition.

The "urchin" is, in fact, child model Joanna Sheffield, of Twickenham.

Detectives are also concerned over an entirely separate series of alleged Victorian prints showing children in erotic poses.

The photos of Joanna dressed in rags, were taken four years ago, when she was only eleven, and were exhibited at the National

Portrait Gallery. They were said to date from the 1840s and be the work of a previously unknown photographer named Francis Hetling.

In fact, they were taken by advertising photographer Howard Grey, 36, of Stormont Road, Clapham.

The gallery believed them to be genuine.

But Grey said yesterday: "Hetling was invented."

He said he gave the black-and-white prints to a friend two months before the exhibition in 1974. Then, he claims,

unknown to him they were reprinted in sepia to make them look old, and exhibited without his consent.

The friend is publisher and Victorian art expert Graham Ovenden, who lives in a castle in Bodmin Moor, Cornwall. His telephone was out of order yesterday and he could not be contacted.

Mr. Ovenden has published a book called "Victorian Children," which contains photographs of girls described as child prostitutes.

He has denied that any of these photographs are fakes.

Last night Mr. Grey

Howard Grey

said he loathed and detested pornography.

He said he went to Scotland Yard on Friday and asked for an interview with the Arts and Antiques Squad.

QUEUES FOR THORPE CASE—See Page Three

20ᵗʰ November 1978

SUICIDE SECT MASSACRE

Five shot dead in jungle

By Anthony Delano

TROOPS stormed into the remote jungle outpost of a weird American cult last night after five people, including a US congressman, were murdered.

As they hunted down the killers, there were reports that 200 of the religious sect's members had taken part in a mass suicide.

The congressman, Leo Ryan, 53, had been shot dead while leading a probe into the sect's activities in the South American republic of Guyana.

Three of the people killed with him were journalists who were reporting the investigation.

The party – twenty-five in all – had spent Friday night at Jonestown, a 27,000-acre estate run by members of the People's Temple. The estate is named after the cult's leader, 46-year-old father of seven Jim Jones.

The following day, the party drove to an airstrip at nearby Port Kaituma with several members of the sect who said they wanted to go home.

Signal

After they had all boarded two planes to take them to Guyana's capital of Georgetown, 300 miles away, one defector brought out a pistol and began firing.

This appeared to be a signal for a tractor to pull alongside the planes.

Other members of the sect on the tractor joined in the shooting.

TV reporter Don Harris, 42, cameraman Robert Brown, 36, and newspaper photographer Greg Robinson, 27, were killed with Ryan. The fifth victim was an 18-year-old girl member of the sect.

Eight other people were wounded and several were still listed as missing early today.

The plane was wrecked by the gunfire but some survivors scrambled aboard the other aircraft which took off leaving the dead and most of the wounded behind.

The government of the former British colony immediately airlifted police and a company of troops to Jonestown.

Police said that one woman sect member had killed herself and her three children.

But the reports of mass suicides were unconfirmed.

Beaten

Police were last night keeping a close watch on the sect's members in California as a result of the suicide reports.

Ryan's investigation into the sect in Guyana followed complaints that members were beaten, forced into parting with their money and property and held prisoner.

MAN BEHIND THE CULT

THE REV Jim Jones, 46, founded the People's Temple in Indiana 15 years ago with the declared intention of ending oppression and breaking down class barriers.

He set up his HQ in San Francisco in 1971 and became a political force there, eventually becoming head of the city's housing department.

But after allegations of brutality and extortion, he resigned in June last year and took 1,200 of his members to settle in Guyana.

Although Jones is white, most of his following – which he claims is 20,000 strong – is black.

According to one defector, Jones has heavily armed guards.

BACKSTORY

Hopes that the story of mass suicide at Jonestown would be just a rumour were dashed when the full horror of what took place was revealed.

Jim Jones had been a political operator in America before establishing a muddled quasi-religious "communist" cult, funded by its predominantly poor followers. Fleeing to Guyana amid suspicions that he was about to be exposed, Jones set up a remote camp in thick jungle, drawing hundreds of his cult followers with him.

US representative Leo Ryan went to the camp with a number of journalists to investigate. While attempting to rescue several members who had indicated they wanted to leave, Ryan's party was attacked.

The mass killings of 909 cult members and their families then took place. Not all of the deaths were, by any means, suicide. Over 200 children were murdered, poisoned by a fruit drink laced with cyanide. Jones himself died from gunshot wounds, though it is unclear if these were self-inflicted.

Birdman bikes it over the Channel

SUCCESS: Bryan after his triumph yesterday.
Pictures: Alisdair MacDonald

FEAT FIRST

BIRDMAN Bryan Allen flew into the record books yesterday—by cycling across the English Channel.

The saddle - sore Californian pedalled his magnificent machine over in less than three hours to make the first non-powered flight to France.

It was worth every muscle tugging minute. For the historic flight earned Bryan a £100,000 prize offered as a challenge by British industrialist Henry Kremer. Bryan, 26, achieved his extraordinary feat on an amazing collection of tubes, glue, tape and a monster 96ft. wingspan christened Gossamer Albatross.

In perfect windless conditions he skimmed at seven miles an hour ten feet above the 22 miles of water separating Folkestone from Cap Gris Nez.

At the end the exhausted cyclist — who two years ago made the first man-powered flight over a figure of eight course—said:

"I couldn't go another ten feet . . . but I feel marvellous."

Mr. Kremer said: "I couldn't feel happier about paying out the prize money."

Secret jet in mystery sea crash

A TOP-SECRET Tornado warplane crashed on a test flight yesterday.

The £9 million jet plunged into the Irish Sea soon after taking off from the British Aerospace works at Warton, Lancs.

A massive air-sea hunt was launched within minutes for the wreckage and the pilot.

He was thought to be 34-year-old Russell Pengelly, of Lytham, Lancs. —one of a team of ace pilots recruited by British Aerospace.

A second man, believed to be a Nato official, was also feared dead in the crash.

BROWNED-OFF MISS FRYER BURNS HER HOUSE DOWN

ALL Yvonne Fryer wanted was a blazing summer's day and a scorching model-girl tan.

Yesterday the pretty typist got both. The tan came from her sun-lamp—and the blazing day burnt down her house.

And last night Yvonne and her family were well and truly browned off.

Trouble started after Yvonne, 20, had an early morning session under the sun-ray lamp in her bedroom at Sandall Park Drive, Wheatley Hills, Doncaster.

She unplugged the lamp and went downstairs. But:

PHEW! The lamp fell against the bed, setting fire to the covers.

PHEW! Her Dad, Ken Fryer, smelled burning while he was soaking in the bath, and

PHEW! Firemen battled to beat the flaming June fiasco, which caused £7,000 worth of damage.

By MIRROR REPORTER

Mr. Fryer said: "I was in the bath and finished up doing a bit of streaking to call the fire brigade.

"I thought something was burning on the stove.

"But flames were coming across the landing as I ran out of the bathroom.

"Yvonne had been trying to get a tan before going to work.

"It's just one of those fads girls have about looking brown."

Kennedy son 'to marry'

TWO top families in Britain and America may be linked soon by marriage. Bobby Kennedy, 24-year-old son of assassinated politician Robert Kennedy, is about to marry Rebecca Fraser, according to reports in New York. Rebecca, 22, is the daughter of Tory MP Hugh Fraser and his estranged wife Lady Antonia Fraser. Bobby spent a lot of time with Rebecca while he was studying in London last year.

13th June 1979
FEAT FIRST

Birdman bikes it over the Channel

BIRDMAN Bryan Allen flew into the record books yesterday – by cycling across the English Channel.

The saddle-sore Californian pedalled his magnificent machine over in less than three hours to make the first ever non-powered flight to France.

It was worth every muscle tugging minute. For the historic flight earned Bryan a £100,000 prize offered as a challenge by British industrialist Henry Kremer.

Bryan, 26, achieved his extraordinary feat on an amazing collection of tubes, glue, tape and a monster 96ft. wingspan christened Gossamer Albatross.

In perfect windless conditions he skimmed at seven miles an hour ten feet above the 22 miles of water separating Folkestone from Cap Gris Nez.

At the end the exhausted cyclist – who two years ago made the first man-powered flight over a figure of eight course said:

"I couldn't go another ten feet . . . but I feel marvellous."

Mr. Kremer said: "I couldn't feel happier about paying out the prize."

BACKSTORY

Man-powered flight had been the dream of humans since ancient times and Bryan Allen achieved the feat in 1979 with his wonderful crossing of the English Channel.

The Gossamer Albatross was built by American aeronautical engineer Dr. Paul B. MacCready (on the right of the picture below), and weighed just 70lbs. Amateur cyclist Allen made the crossing (bottom) under his own steam in 2 hours, 49 minutes.

DAILY Mirror

Tuesday, February 24, 1981   12p   ◆ ◆ ◆

SPAIN: CIVIL WAR ALERT

350 MPs held at gunpoint

SEALED OFF: The parliament building in the centre of Madrid.

REBEL LEADER: Fanatical right-wing Colonel Tejero

MOVING IN: Armed police block a road crossing near the parliament.

ALOOF: Juan Carlos

TROOPS stormed Spain's Parliament last night with machine guns and held 350 M Ps at gunpoint.

Millions of Spaniards heard the drama live over their radios.

Two hundred members of the para-military Civil Guard, led by right-wing National

By CHRISTOPHER BUCKLAND, Foreign Editor

Guard Colonel Antonio Tejero, burst into the chamber just as the deputies were about to elect a new Prime Minister.

M Ps cowered under their benches—including the man just about to become Premier, Leopaldo Calvo Sotelo—as the rebels pointed their guns at the head of the outgoing premier, Adolfo Suarez.

They threatened to shoot TV and radio commentators unless they went off the air and then smashed their equipment.

But radio listeners throughout Spain heard a Parliamentary reporter describe the scene. He said: "A Lieutenant Colonel of the Civil Guard is right now walking up to the podium. He is pointing with a pistol.

"Police and more police are coming in. They have submachine-guns and pistols. We can transmit no more because they are pointing at us."

In the background unidentified voices said: "Calm, everybody. Nothing is happening. We are not pointing at anyone."

A burst of machine-gun fire ended the broadcast and Radio Madrid began playing classical music.

Three hours after the
● Turn to Page Two

182

24ᵗʰ February **1981**

SPAIN CIVIL WAR ALERT

350 MPs held at gunpoint

By Christopher Buckland, Foreign Editor

TROOPS stormed Spain's Parliament last night with machine guns and held 350 MPs at gunpoint.

Millions of Spaniards heard the drama live over their radios.

Two hundred members of the paramilitary Civil Guard, led by right-wing National Guard Colonel Antonio Tejero, burst into the chamber just as the deputies were about to elect a new Prime Minister.

MPs cowered under their benches – including the man just about to become Premier, Leopaldo Calvo Sotelo – as the rebels pointed their guns at the head of the outgoing premier, Adolfo Suarez.

They threatened to shoot TV and radio commentators unless they went off the air and then smashed their equipment.

But radio listeners throughout Spain heard a Parliamentary reporter describe the scene. He said: "A Lieutenant Colonel of the Civil Guard is right now walking up to the podium. He is pointing with a pistol.

"Police and more police are coming in. They have sub-machine-guns and pistols. We can transmit no more because they are pointing at us."

In the background unidentified voices said: "Calm, everybody. Nothing is happening. We are not pointing at anyone."

A burst of machine-gun fire ended the broadcast and Radio Madrid began playing classical music.

Three hours after the troops stormed in, many of the country's leaders were driven away to a mystery destination in military vehicles.

Soon afterwards King Juan Carlos, commander-in-chief of the armed forces and head of State, issued a statement saying he "firmly rejected the action carried out this afternoon in Parliament."

The king is probably the one man who can prevent the mutiny spreading.

Colonel Tejero, the leader of the rebels, tried to storm the Prime Minister's office two years ago when the cabinet was in session and hold it hostage until a military government was set up.

SPAIN has been walking on thin ice, ever since the death of the great dictator, General Franco, in 1976.

For almost forty years his iron hand had guided the nation while the police and the para-military Civil Guard were given a free hand to track down opponents of the regime.

And when the newly enthroned King Juan Carlos gradually edged the country towards democracy with a skill that astonished even his enemies, there were still people who hankered for the good old days of privilege and order.

Unemployment rose, girlie magazines appeared on the bookstalls to shock the deeply Catholic Spaniards and petty crime rose sharply.

But the democratic experiment seemed to be succeeding despite all the setbacks when last night's daring coup attempt presented the biggest challenge yet to the democrats.

The apparent leader of the revolt is Civil Guard Colonel Antonio Tejero, a crazy fanatic who once before, in 1979, plotted to kidnap the cabinet until a military government was set up.

The civil guard lost most prestige and power when Franco died. They have been the main target of Basque separatist guerrillas, who killed 100 people last year alone.

The visit of King Juan Carlos to the Basque country earlier this month was thought to be the final straw for the Francoists.

There the young monarch met Basques and was treated to a bitter show of hostility.

Later senior police chiefs resigned following the arrests of officers accused of being involved in the torture and death of a suspected Basque terrorist.

Then, last Thursday night, Basque terrorists snatched three consuls from their homes and held them to ransom.

They said their captives would be freed only if a 1980 Amnesty International report on police violence in Spain was broadcast on national TV and radio and published in all the big newspapers.

They also wanted pictures of the battered body of the terrorist suspect who died in jail to be shown on television.

The latest demands infuriated many of the old guard militarists, who favour a policy of no compromise or even discussion with the guerrillas.

All now depends on how the army behaves throughout the country. And it may rest on the shoulders of King Juan Carlos to prevent another devastating civil war in Spain.

BACKSTORY

Fears of another Spanish civil war turned out to be misplaced. Just 22 hours after Colonel Tejero and his supporters had stormed the parliament, and following a denouncement of their actions by the King Juan Carlos (below), the coup leaders surrendered.

Further plotting against the democratic government would persist, but Spain made a largely successful transition to democracy following the years of dictatorship under Franco.

CHAPTER SIX

SORRY, MA'AM

An artist's impression of the moment Michael Fagan supposedly shared a bedside chat with the Queen (see page 188).

DAILY Mirror

Monday, December 21, 1981   14p   ★

In 70 minutes, the lives of these eight brave men . .
SHATTERED

LOST: Doomed crew at practice.   Picture: ANDREW BESLEY.

By GEOFFREY LAKEMAN

THESE eight men of courage set off in their lifeboat to rescue survivors of a shipwreck.

Within 70 minutes the men were lost, their boat smashed to matchwood in the raging seas.

Eight people from the stricken ship the Union Star—including a woman and two teenage girls—also lost their lives.

The Penlee boat was launched from the Cornish village of Mousehole at exactly 8.12 on Saturday night after the freighter Union Star sent out a distress call.

At 9.22 coxswain Trevelyan Richards radioed that he had managed to get four people aboard. Then there was silence.

Last night all hope had been abandoned for the lifeboatmen and the eight people from the freighter.

Seventeen-year-old lifeboatman Neil Brockman, whose father was one of the victims, escaped death because the coxswain refused to have two members of one family aboard.

Blasted

The Union Star, on its maiden voyage, lay capsized and shattered at the foot of cliffs at Tater Du, just along the coast from Mousehole.

Divers who blasted their way into the hull found some cabins were still bone dry.

They said that if the crew had stayed where they were they might have survived.

When the ship first reported it was in difficulties on its way from Holland to Ireland, a Dutch tug offered to take it in tow.

But Captain Henry Morton from Essex refused to accept an open contract for salvage without referring to the ship's owners, Union Transport of London.

Trinity House pilot Mike Sutherland listened in to the

● Turn to Page Two

WRECKED: Splintered wood on the beach was all that remained of the Penlee lifeboat.   Picture: GEORGE PHILLIPS.

186

21st December 1981

IN 70 MINUTES, THE LIVES OF THESE EIGHT BRAVE MEN... SHATTERED

By Geoffrey Lakeman

THESE eight men of courage set off in their lifeboat to rescue survivors of a shipwreck.

Within 70 minutes the men were lost, their boat smashed to matchwood in the raging seas.

Eight people from the stricken ship the Union Star – including a woman and two teenage girls – also lost their lives.

The Penlee boat was launched from the Cornish village of Mousehole at exactly 8.12 on Saturday night after the freighter Union Star sent out a distress call.

At 9.22 coxswain Trevelyan Richards radioed that he had managed to get four people aboard. Then there was silence.

Last night all hope had been abandoned for the lifeboatmen and the eight people from the freighter.

Seventeen-year-old lifeboatman Neil Brockman, whose father was one of the victims, escaped death because the coxwain refused to have two members of one family aboard.

Blasted

The Union Star, on its maiden voyage, lay capsized and shattered at the foot of cliffs at Tater Du, just along the coast from Mousehole.

Divers who blasted their way into the hull found some cabins were still bone dry.

They said that if the crew had stayed where they were they might have survived.

When the ship first reported it was in difficulties on its way from Holland to Ireland, a Dutch tug offered to take it in tow.

But Captain Henry Morton from Essex refused to accept an open contract for salvage without referring to the ship's owners, Union Transport of London.

Trinity House pilot Mike Sutherland listened in to the exchange between the tug and Captain Morton.

He said: "It's possible from that if he had accepted the tow this tragedy could have been averted."

All day long wreckage from the lifeboat Solomon Browne was being washed up along the Cornish coast.

Fishermen's sweaters were found, hats, boots and shattered planks from the 21-year-old lifeboat itself.

Groups of mourners clustered on the quay at Mousehole talking quietly of the tragedy that left ten children in the village fatherless . . .

Many messages of sympathy arrived at the village – among them telegrams from the Queen and Prince Philip and from Prince Charles . . .

Last night, as a disaster fund reached £12,000, a relief lifeboat was heading for Mousehole.

4th January 1982

PENLEE: CASH DONORS SHUN THE OFFICIAL FUND

By Geoffrey Lakeman

MANY people are boycotting the official Penlee Disaster Fund.

Instead they are travelling long distances to make sure their donations reach the bereaved families of Mousehole, Cornwall, or sending their money direct.

Their action follows the legal wrangle over how much the families should receive from the fund, now nearing £2 million.

Lifeboat crew spokesman Mike Sutherland said yesterday: "Two lads from the Midlands came to Mousehole by train and plonked £500 in cash in front of the postmaster.

"There is a chain reaction all over the country.

"Lifeboatmen everywhere are sending us cash and asking that it go directly to the dependants."

Mary Greenhaugh, landlady of the Ship Inn, whose husband Charles was among the eight men lost, has received many letters and cheques.

"Some cheques were made out to me personally," she said. "I passed everything to the lifeboat committee."

◀ The new Penlee lifeboat, launched in February 1982.

BACKSTORY

The tragic loss of the *Solomon Browne* moved the nation and led to an outcry when it appeared that grieving relatives would be taxed on the donations they received from the fund.

Then Attorney-General Sir Michael Havers (father of actor Nigel) announced that the government would waive the bulk of any tax.

Thirty years later, Luke Brockman, the grandson of one of the heroic lifeboatmen who died in the disaster, Neil Brockman, joined the crew of the Penlee lifeboat, now sailing out of Newlyn.

Luke's own father Neil would have been on the *Solomon Burke* himself had the coxswain Trevelyan Richards not refused to take more than one member from the same family.

DAILY Mirror

Fury over Royal security

Tuesday, July 13, 1982   16p   *

HOW could a man break into the Palace . . . TWICE?

WHY did police take thirty minutes to arrive?

The questions facing Home Secretary Whitelaw and Yard chief McNee

SEE PAGES TWO, THREE, THIRTEEN, FOURTEEN and FIFTEEN

13th July 1982

HOW COULD A MAN BREAK INTO THE PALACE . . . TWICE?

WHY DID THE POLICE TAKE 30 MINUTES TO ARRIVE?

The questions facing Home Secretary Whitelaw and Yard chief McNee

By John Desborough

PREMIER Margaret Thatcher went to Buckingham Palace yesterday to say "Sorry, Ma'am" to the Queen.

Her apology followed an appalling security blunder which allowed an intruder to get into the Queen's bedroom while she was alone on Friday.

The intruder, revealed yesterday as 30-year-old Michael Fagan, sat on the Queen's bed for ten minutes and chatted to her.

He was arrested after he asked for a cigarette, which enabled the Queen to call a footman.

After questioning, it emerged that Fagan had also got into Buckingham Palace early last month.

On Saturday he was remanded in custody at London's Bow Street court accused of stealing half a bottle of wine from the Palace in June.

Serious

Mrs Thatcher went to see the Queen yesterday after Home Secretary William Whitelaw made a Commons statement about the "most serious failure" of security at the Palace.

Mr. Whitelaw spoke of extra security measures at the Palace in recent years.

Amid jeers from Labour MPs he added: "But this latest incident shows that the position is still not satisfactory and that more needs to be done."

He said that on Friday the Metropolitan Police chief, Sir David McNee, had appointed Assistant Commissioner John Dellow to make an urgent inquiry and security was strengthened at the Palace on that day.

Labour's Shadow Home Secretary Roy Hattersley attacked the statement for being "bland".

He asked whether steps were taken to improve Palace security after the first incident involving the intruder.

Mr. Whitelaw replied that they "most certainly had".

GROSS NEGLIGENCE

Police are blasted after Palace raid

By George Webber and Jack McEachran

SCOTLAND Yard chief Sir David McNee is urgently investigating claims that policemen assigned to protecting the Royal Family at Buckingham Palace were grossly negligent.

He has called for a full report on the officers scheduled for duty at the time the intruder got into the Queen's bedroom.

The prowler was seen climbing over the Palace wall.

Fifteen minutes later a chambermaid spotted him walking through the Queen's apartments. But another 15 minutes passed before police replied to the alert . . .

It became known yesterday that the intruder who entered the Queen's room spent some time in a room nearby.

Blood

He previously roamed through several floors of the Palace trying door knobs before finding the door to the Queen's bedchambers unlocked.

It was also revealed that he dripped blood on the royal carpet from a hand wound he suffered when climbing over the spike-topped Palace wall.

A wire mesh guard outside a first-floor window was found wrenched from its fixture, and marks on a drainpipe revealed how the intruder gained entry.

14th July 1982

By John Jackson

THOUGH the Queen remained calm, she faced a situation of frightening uncertainty in her bedroom before help arrived.

Until yesterday only she and the intruder, 31-year-old Michael Fagan, knew what was discussed. Now it can be revealed that they chatted about the things closest to both their hearts – their children.

Fagan told the Queen about his four youngsters and went on to discuss his personal problems.

An astonishing series of blunders will be revealed by the inquiry ordered into the security failure at the Palace . . .

It has been reported that the police even switched off an alarm in the Queen's bedroom apparently believing it to be faulty . . .

BACKSTORY

Little did Michael Fagan know that his Buckingham Palace adventure would cause one of the great security rows of the 20th century.

Slightly worse for wear, in the midst of a split from his wife, and excited by the prospect of sneaking into Britain's most illustrious address, Fagan accomplished his aim for the SECOND time, having already done so a month before.

While the papers were dominated by a series of exposures of lax palace security, Fagan became something of a star and even recorded a version of the Sex Pistols' 'God Save The Queen' (above).

Fagan was not charged with trespass as it was a civil offence, but with theft of a bottle of wine, though this charge was dropped when he was sent for psychiatric evaluation. Fagan has denied that the famous bedside conversation with the Queen ever took place.

DAILY Mirror

Saturday, January 15, 1983

16p

POLICE SHOOT DOWN THE WRONG MAN

Ambush victim hit by hail of bullets

AMBUSHED: The Mini damaged by bullets stands behind a police cordon.

By KEVIN O'LONE, JOHN PEACOCK, GEORGINA WALSH and JACK McEACHRAN

ARMED police trying to ambush a dangerous escaper gunned down the wrong man last night.

They surrounded his car in a busy London street and shot at him 14 times.

The man, Stephen Waldorf, was seriously ill in hospital after an operation lasting three and a half hours. He was in intensive care.

Two senior Scotland Yard officers were investigating how the horrifying mistake occurred.

A police source said it looked like a case of mistaken identity involving nervous, trigger-happy officers.

Police were acting on a tip that an escaped prisoner would be in the area.

Some of them were staking out addresses in the area. One officer in plain clothes thought he recognised a fugitive.

When they approached and challenged the man, he leaned forward—and that was when police opened fire.

The man the police were hunting is 35-year-old gunman David Martin. A master of disguise, he escaped from a cell at Marlborough Street Court on Christmas Eve.

Mr Waldorf, 26, was in a yellow mini with another man and a woman when police attacked. The others were unhurt and the man ran off. He was being sought by police early today.

Their car was caught in a rush-hour traffic jam at Pembroke Road, Kensington.

Baroness Helen de Westenholz, 52, whose flat overlooks the scene, described what happened. She said:

❝I heard three sharp cracks which I thought might be a pistol. Then on the far side of the road I saw a Mini.

Behind it there was a white van and a man on a motorcycle, whom I thought was a policeman putting his bike against the van as if to get out of the line of fire.

Suddenly, from behind the van I noticed four or five men running from the pavement.

They crouched really low around the Mini,

Hunt for 'Houdini'

THE HUNT for David Martin, the 35-year-old escaped gunman police describe as "a vicious Houdini," has been going on since Christmas Eve. That was when Martin fled across the roof of the London Palladium and down the fire escapes after breaking out of a cell at Marlborough Street Court.

He had been charged with the attempted murder of a policeman, firearms offences, bank robbery and burglary.

Martin, 5ft 10in tall with long blond hair, was trapped by police last September. He pulled a gun and was shot in the shoulder before he could be arrested.

MARTIN: Broke out of cell

☐ Turn to Page 2

190

15th January 1983

POLICE SHOOT DOWN THE WRONG MAN

Ambush victim hit by hail of bullets

By Kevin Clone, John Peacock, Georgina Walsh and Jack McEachran

ARMED police trying to ambush a dangerous escapee gunned down the wrong man last night.

They surrounded his car in a busy London street and shot at him 14 times.

The man, Stephen Waldorf, was seriously ill in hospital after an operation lasting three and a half hours. He was in intensive care.

Two senior Scotland Yard officers were investigating how the horrifying mistake occurred.

A police source said it looked like a case of mistaken identity involving nervous, trigger-happy officers.

Police were acting on a tip that an escaped prisoner would be in the area.

Some of them were staking out addresses in the area. One officer in plain clothes thought he recognised a fugitive.

When they approached and challenged the man, he leaned forward – and that was when police opened fire.

The man the police were hunting is 35-year-old gunman David Martin. A master of disguise, he escaped from a cell at Marlborough Street Court on Christmas Eve.

Mr Waldorf, 26, was in a yellow mini with another man and a woman when police attacked. The others were unhurt and the man ran off.

He was being sought by police early today.

Their car was caught in a rush-hour traffic jam at Pembroke Road, Kensington.

Baroness Helen de Westenholz, 52, whose flat overlooks the scene, described what happened. She said:

"I heard three sharp cracks which I thought might be a pistol.

"Then on the far side of the road I saw a mini. Behind it there was a white van and a man on a motorcycle, whom I thought was a policeman putting his bike against the van as if to get out of the line of fire.

"Suddenly, from behind the van I noticed four or five men running from the pavement.

"They crouched really low around the mini, completely surrounding it.

"They were all wearing padded jackets and at least one looked as if he had a pistol. I heard one or two more cracks.

"It was like a scene from a film. All the traffic was stopped. One or two pedestrians were walking along the far side of the road, either not interested or they could not see what was happening because of the car lights."

The Baroness said she thought the police must have caught up with terrorists. She went to dial 999.

"By the time I got back to the window," she said, "two big white police vans with flashing lights and full of about 40 policemen had driven along the road against the traffic.

"They were so quick it couldn't have been as a result of my call.

"A man, the driver of the mini, was falling out of the car on to the road."

Chances

"It seemed a long time before an ambulance came and he was got on to a stretcher."

As the man was carried from the car, Baroness de Westenholz noticed a woman standing in the middle of the road wearing a long fur coat and talking to a policewoman.

"Suddenly the policewoman started pulling her coat up at the back as if she was searching her," she said.

The woman walked into the ambulance and appeared to have her hands handcuffed behind her back.

"It is very strange," said the Baroness . . .

A neighbour in Pembroke Road who refused to give his name said he heard seven or eight shots.

He said: "The man just sat in the driver's seat when he was surrounded. But the men with guns weren't taking any chances.

"They kept firing at him as his body slumped out of the car to the ground."

Secretary Jane Lamerill, 25, was one of the first to arrive at the scene.

Jane, a trained nurse, said: "I saw a man waving what looked like a gun and ran to my car to get my first aid kit.

"I saw a man lying on the ground. He was writhing around in pain saying, 'My God it hurts'.

"I was reassuring him and holding his hand. I held a dressing on a chest wound to keep it airtight." . . .

The Scotland Yard investigation is being carried out by Commander Mike Taylor and Detective Chief Superintendent Neil Dickens.

All the Yard would say was that the police were on a "special operation."

BACKSTORY

While Stephen Waldorf's parents later backed the police, with his mother Beryl saying "I still think our bobbies are wonderful," her son's mistaken shooting added to a climate of rising concerns over violent crime and how it was tackled with lethal force.

Waldorf (left) did not have a direct relationship with David Martin, but police suspected a female passenger in the car that night, Susan Stephens, did. Waldorf made a miraculous recovery and two police officers, John Jardine and Peter Finch, stood trial for attempted murder. They were cleared of all charges in October of that year. Waldorf received £150,000 in compensation.

Martin was recaptured and later found hanged in his cell.

Story of a Mafia boss who became the victim of bloody ambition

THE 12-year reign of Mafia godfather Paulo "Big Paul" Castellano ended in a hail of bullets on Monday night.

Castellano, 70, was shot dead as he stepped from his Lincoln Continental limousine at Sparks Steak House on New York's 46th Street.

Three men in trench coats and fedora hats sauntered over, drew semi-automatics, and pumped six bullets into Castellano and his heir-apparent, Thomas Bilotti, at point-blank range.

It was a classic Mafia killing and ended a story that began in Sicily . . .

by NICHOLAS DAVIES
Foreign Editor
and JOHN McSHANE

Killing of the Godfather

THE BOSS: "Big Paul" Castellano in his hey-day as a Mafia don.

PAULO Castellano was born into poverty a few years after his penniless parents arrived in New York.

Sixty years later he had reached the height of his ambition and became Capo di Tutti Capi—the boss of all bosses of the Mafia.

He had achieved the American Dream—Sicilian-fashion.

Paulo lived in a two million dollar mansion, a copy of the White House in the most exclusive part of New York.

Television cameras guard every entrance and sophisticated burglar alarms protect the house and grounds.

The 70-foot living room is littered with antiques and priceless paintings. There is a large indoor swimming pool.

It was from this lavish mansion, staffed by six armed guards, that Big Paulo ran the Mafia.

The key to his success was family.

Carlo Gambino, model for the film The Godfather, was his cousin and Paulo married

THE HEIR: Aspiring Mafia boss Thomas Bilotti, gunned down in a New York Street.

Gambino's elder sister Caterina.

In 1929 Paulo became an apprentice butcher.

During the next ten years, backed by the might of the Mafia, he rose to be the biggest meat and poultry wholesaler in North America.

Butcher

During Prohibition days Paulo rode shotgun for his cousin on illicit alcohol deliveries.

He quickly learned to butcher the victims his cousin selected—and became the perfect Mafia man.

Paulo came to prominence as a potential Mafia leader in 1957 when he was among 100 gangsters caught in a New York police swoop on a crime convention.

Six years later Big Paulo had risen to the rank of an under-boss in the Gambino family.

In 1976 he was snapped in a controversial picture, with Frank Sinatra backstage at a theatre. Castellano, and the singing star who had always denied links with organised crime, were shown surrounded by underworld figures.

Shark

That year Gambino died of a heart attack . . . and time began to run out for "Big Paulo," robbed of his protector.

Within two years Castellano was indicted as mastermind of a loan shark syndicate.

In 1980 Castellano's son-in-law disappeared and "Big Paulo" was suspected because the missing man had two-timed on Castellano's daughter.

Castellano was later indicted for murder but promptly released on three million dollar bail.

For the next four years Castellano went into retreat and masterminded his vast empire from his lavish mansion.

He continued to run the meat trade as well as a big slice of New York's construction industry, road haulage, property and the city's garment trade.

According to police, he also continued the Gambino family's illegal activities—loan sharking, protection, pornography and drug trafficking.

Murder

Big Paulo and his cohorts also found the time to carry out 25 gangland killings.

But the law's net was closing.

Last February, Castellano and the heads of the other four New York Mafia families were charged with operating a "board of directors" for organised crime.

Castellano was also awaiting trial for murder.

But Mafia justice got to him first.

How his fate was sealed

CASTELLANO'S fate may have been sealed by the death on December 2 of his one-time rival in the Gambino family, Aniello Dellacroce.

The 71-year-old Dellacroce, a sadistic murderer, who liked to look into the eyes of his victims at the moment of death, died in his sleep in a New York hospital of heart disease.

Dellacroce had a reputation for being the peacemaker between Castellano and other members of the Gambino family.

"Big-Paul had designated his trusted lieutenant, bodyguard and chauffeur, Thomas Bilotti, to be his heir," said FBI spokesman Thomas Sheer.

"When they hit Paul they rubbed out Bilotti as well . . . and removed the two top men at one go."

Castellano caused a storm in crime circles by not appearing at Dellacroce's funeral in New York two weeks ago.

An FBI man said: "The absence created a great deal of comment among the Gambino family. Castellano let it be known he didn't go because there were too many rats in the family.

The mob killings are believed to signal a power takeover bid by younger members of the Gambino family.

THE MIXER: Castellano (left) with Sinatra and Mafia bosses.

THE RETREAT: Castellano's palatial hideaway.

Research by Stuart Dixon in New York and Paul House in Rome

18th December **1985**

KILLING OF THE GODFATHER

Story of a Mafia boss who became the victim of bloody ambition

By Nicholas Davies and John McShane

THE 12-year reign of Mafia godfather Paulo "Big Paul" Castellano ended in a hail of bullets on Monday night.

Castellano, 70, was shot dead as he stepped from his limousine at Sparks Steak House on New York's 46th Street.

Three men in trench coats and fedora hats sauntered over, drew semi-automatics and pumped six bullets into Castellano and his heir-apparent Thomas Bilotti, at point-blank range.

It was a classic Mafia killing and ended a story that began in Sicily . . .

PAULO Castellano was born into poverty a few years after his penniless parents arrived in New York.

Sixty years later, he had reached the height of his ambition and became Capo di Tutti Capi – the boss of all bosses – of the Mafia.

He had achieved the American Dream – Sicilian-fashion.

Paulo lived in a two million dollar mansion, a copy of the White House in the most exclusive part of New York.

Television cameras guard every entrance and sophisticated burglar alarms protect the house and grounds.

The 70-foot living room is littered with antiques and priceless paintings. There is a large indoor swimming pool.

It was from this lavish mansion, staffed by armed guards, that Big Paulo ran the Mafia. The key to his success was family.

Carlo Gambino, model for the film The Godfather, was his cousin after Paulo married Gambino's elder sister Caterina.

In 1929 Paulo became an apprentice butcher. During the next ten years, backed by the might of the Mafia, he rose to be the biggest meat and poultry wholesaler in North America.

Butcher

During prohibition days Paulo rode shotgun for his cousin on illicit alcohol deliveries.

He quickly learned to butcher the victims his cousin selected, and became the perfect Mafia man.

Paulo came to prominence as a potential Mafia leader in 1957 when he was among 100 gangsters caught in a New York police swoop on a crime convention. Six years later Big Paulo had risen to the rank of an under-boss in the Gambino family.

In 1976 he was snapped in a controversial picture, with Frank Sinatra backstage at a theatre. Castellano, and the singing star who had always denied links with organised crime, were shown surrounded by underworld figures.

Shark

That year Gambino died of a heart attack . . . and time began to run out for "Big Paulo," robbed of his protector.

Within two years Castellano was indicted as mastermind of a loan shark syndicate.

In 1980 Castellano's son-in-law disappeared and "Big Paulo" was suspected because the missing man had two-timed on Castellano's daughter. Castellano was later indicted for murder but promptly released on three million dollar bail.

For the next four years Castellano went into retreat and masterminded his vast empire from his lavish mansion.

He continued to run the meat trade as well as a big slice of New York's construction industry, road haulage, property and the city's garment trade. According to police, he also continued the Gambino family's illegal activities – loan sharking, protection, pornography and drug trafficking.

Murder

Big Paulo and his cohorts also found the time to carry out 25 gangland killings.

But the law's net was closing.

Last February, Castellano and the heads of the other four New York Mafia families were charged with operating a "board of directors" for organised crime.

Castellano was also awaiting trial for murder.

But Mafia justice got to him first.

HOW HIS FATE WAS SEALED

CASTELLANO'S fate may have been sealed by the death on December 2 of his one-time rival in the Gambino family, Aniello Dellacroce.

The 71-year-old Dellacroce, a sadistic murderer, who liked to look into the eyes of his victims at the moment of death, died in his sleep in a New York hospital of heart disease.

Dellacroce had a reputation for being the peacemaker between Castellano and other members of the Gambino family.

"Big Paul had designated his trusted lieutenant, bodyguard and chauffeur, Thomas Bilotti, to be his heir", said FBI spokesman Thomas Sheer.

"When they hit Paul they rubbed out Bilotti as well . . . and removed two top men at one go."

Castellano caused a storm in crime circles by not appearing at Dellacroce's funeral in New York two weeks ago.

An FBI man said: "The absence created a great deal of comment among the Gambino family. Castellano let it be known he didn't go because there were too many rats in the family."

The mob killings are believed to signal a power takeover by young members of the Gambino family.

Research by Stuart Dixon in New York and Paul House in Rome

BACKSTORY

Less than a decade after the hit *Godfather* movies turned Mafia gangsters into cult heroes, New York's brutal mob war of succession laid bare the savage reality of organized crime.

Big Paul Castellano's public slaying was the decisive move in a long-running battle for control of one of New York's pre-eminent crime dynasties. John Gotti emerged as the new Gambino boss. A capo from Dellacroce's side of the family, he made his move to kill Castellano before he was murdered himself, and then took over the whole operation.

Gotti was a high-profile mob boss who courted publicity. His smart suits earned him the nickname "The Dapper Don" and his ability to avoid conviction the "Teflon Don", but this image belied his extreme violence. Eventually betrayed by close associate, Sammy "The Bull" Gravano, Gotti was convicted of numerous offences, including five murders, and died in prison in 2001.

BLACK LEGS!

Store colour ban on shop girls' tights

By MURRAY DAVIES

SUPERMARKET giant Sainsbury's have slapped an amazing colour bar on their checkout girls.

They threatened to sack Geraldine O'Sullivan for turning up to work in black stockings.

Then they issued a bizarre decree.

WHITE women workers must wear only fawn tights or stockings.

But BLACK female staff must wear black ones.

Geraldine was furious, and so were all the 250 women staff at the Sainsbury's branch. The union threatened action unless bosses backed down.

Unfair

Geraldine's husband, Thomas, 38, who works as a warehouseman at the same store in Lewisham, South London, said: "My wife always wears stockings and I especially like the sexy black ones."

He added: "It's an outrageous ban. God knows what they expect the Asian girls to wear."

Geraldine, who has five children and has worked at the supermarket five years, said: "It's just not fair."

The Daily Mirror repeatedly asked Sainsbury's head office in London about the ruling and a statement was issued. It said:

"When people are employed by us, they are made fully aware of the standards of dress that we require as part of the conditions of service."

Swedish police comb the capital for assassin

PREMIER SHOT DEAD IN STREET

MURDERED: Olof Palme

Wife wounded as they leave a restaurant

By ROSEMARY COLLINS and TED OLIVER

AN ASSASSIN armed with a pistol shot dead the Prime Minister of Sweden in a street ambush late last night.

Olof Palme, 59, was gunned down shortly before midnight.

His wife Lisbeth was also shot in the back and was seriosly ill in hospital early today.

Palme was leaving a restaurant in Stockholm with Lisbeth when a man in his late 30s appeared.

He was shot at least twice in the chest and died half an hour later after being rushed to hospital.

Early this morning police were reported to be involved in a high speed chase after a man driving a Volkswagen car.

The social democrat premier, who was serving his second term, believed in open Government and shunned tight security.

He and his wife were not under guard when they were attacked in the city centre.

Deputy Prime Minister Ingvar Carlsstrom arrived at the Government House

to head a Crisis meeting with other Cabinet members at 1 a.m.

"We have asked all those we could get to come over here. It is terrible. I just got to know it 30 minutes ago," Carlsstrom told reporters.

A preliminary Police report said there were at least four witnesses to the Prime Minister's death.

Two young girls who were sitting in a car close to the scene of the shooting tried to help Palme.

They said he seemed to have been hit by two bullets.

Palme was a special Peace representative to the UN and agitated for peace in the Iran/Iraq war.

1st March 1986

PREMIER SHOT DEAD IN STREET

Swedish police comb the capital for assassin

WIFE WOUNDED AS THEY LEAVE A RESTAURANT

By Rosemary Collins and Ted Oliver

AN ASSASSIN armed with a pistol shot dead the Prime Minister of Sweden in a street ambush late last night.

Olof Palme, 59, was gunned down shortly before midnight.

His wife Lisbet was also shot in the back and was seriously ill in hospital early today.

Palme was leaving a restaurant in Stockholm with Lisbet when a man in his late 30s appeared.

He was shot at least twice in the chest and died half an hour later after being rushed to hospital.

Early this morning, police were reported to be involved in a high-speed chase after a man driving a Volkswagen car.

The social democrat premier, who was serving his second term, believed in open Government and shunned tight security.

Deputy Prime Minister Ingvar Carlsson arrived at the Government House to head a crisis meeting with other cabinet members at 1am.

"We have asked all those we could get to come over here. It is horrible. I just got to know it 30 minutes ago," Carlsson told reporters.

A preliminary Police report said there were at least four witnesses to the Prime Minister's death.

Two young girls who were sitting in a car close to the scene of the shooting tried to help Palme.

They said he seemed to have been hit by two bullets.

Palme was a special peace representative to the UN and agitated for peace in the Iran-Iraq war.

THE KILLING OF THE DOVE

Sweden mourns the leader who hated violence

By Nicholas Davies
Foreign Editor in Stockholm

HUNDREDS of red roses cover the blood stains on Stockholm's main street. The old and the young have come in their hundreds to place them at the spot where Olof Palme was gunned down by an unknown assassin.

But no one speaks. The old, protected from the bitter cold in their fur coats and hats, the young in their jeans and brightly-coloured scarves, just stand and stare at the spot.

Sweden has been stunned by the seemingly motiveless murder of its Prime Minister on Friday night.

For more than anyone else he typified the spirit of a nation that abhors violence.

"It couldn't happen here, it just couldn't," was the only comment as people looked at the ground, too distressed, and too embarrassed to speak openly.

Such violence seems unthinkable in Sweden – a nation of peace and tranquillity in a world of war, bombings and shootings.

Safe

The Swedes have not fought a war since 1813. Their soldiers frequently act as peace-makers in the world's trouble spots, and the sky blue of the national flag – which matches that of the United Nations flag – symbolises peace.

The streets of Stockholm are safe. A woman can walk alone in the early hours of the morning without fear.

Old people have no worries about being mugged or having their handbags stolen.

Sweden's police carry guns. But, as the public know, they are more for show than for use.

Palme was determined that Sweden's reputation should be used to further world harmony.

He first leapt on the international stage when he took an active part in anti-American demonstrations against the Vietnam war.

He was often seen talking and smiling with his Socialist friends around the world – people like Fidel Castro of Cuba, Yasser Arafat of the Palestine Liberation Organisation and Daniel Ortega of Nicaragua.

He worked tirelessly on the international scene, trying to bring peace in the Iran-Iraq conflict, trying to find a homeland for the Palestinians and always defending the weaker, third-world nations from the superpowers.

Palme became Prime Minister in 1962 when only 42. After seven years he was defeated by the opposition coalition but regained power in 1982.

Fluent in seven languages, he stomped the world, preaching peaceful coexistence.

Back home he practised what he preached. He was determined to live the same as any other citizen.

He shunned bodyguards and always went unaccompanied during his off-duty hours.

Every morning, alone, he would walk the half-mile from his unpretentious flat in the old town to the Prime Minister's office.

For the past twenty years he spent his holidays working on a farm in Southern Sweden – never with a bodyguard and never with a gun.

Time and again security chiefs tried to persuade him to have full, round-the-clock protection, but he would not listen.

Palme told them: "If someone is determined nothing will stop them. In any case, this is Sweden."

Palme insisted on having a private, family life.

He wanted to be able to walk the streets, talk to people, go shopping alone, go to the cinema and the theatre and attend private dinners.

BACKSTORY

The slaying of Olof Palme remains one of the great unsolved crimes. A small-time criminal, Christer Pettersson, was convicted of the murder but this was overturned on appeal.

Since then a number of suspects have been put forward, from secret service agents to foreign spies.

The late novelist Stieg Larsson had investigated the assassination and left boxes of evidence, among which was a claim that the alibi of one suspect was false.

★★

RED BARON BUZZES THE KREMLIN

Joyride German beats Russia's mighty radar

HIJINKS: Pilot Rust

MISSION IMPOSSIBLE: The Cessna in the shadow of the Kremlin

THE Kremlin went on red alert as an unidentified aircraft swooped low over Moscow.

There was even more alarm when the plane buzzed Lenin's mausoleum . . . and landed in historic Red Square.

The daredevil pilot, 19-year-old West German Mathias Rust, coolly stepped out of the four-seater Cessna and started signing autographs.

Police quickly whisked the joyrider away.

And last night embarrassed Soviet officials were trying to find out how the plane dodged sophisticated air defence systems to fly to the heart of the Russian capital.

One senior Western observer said: "The implications for Soviet defences, and for the whole debate on how a war could start by mistake, are astounding."

Bet

Rust's amazing 560-mile flight began in Helsinki. He was thought to be heading for Sweden, but vanished from Finnish radar screens and was not heard of again until his landing in Moscow.

Planes are banned from flying over the city Crowds watched in astonishment as the little Cessna taxied over the cobblestones to park by buses lined up near the Kremlin wall.

The young Hamburg pilot, in hiking boots and a red flight suit, chatted to children and a group of German tourists.

Giggled

British nanny Juliet Butler, who was in Red Square, said: "At first the police seemed relaxed and just giggled.

"Then some higher officers came in big cars and the square was sealed off."

Russian artist, Ilya Anosov, 21, said: "All we could think was that he was drunk and made a bet that he could fly to Red Square."

The Cessna was carted off on a truck and Rust was still being questioned last night.

In Hamburg his flying instructor said: "We'll paint a red star on the plane when it returns."

Cleaned out

THE contents of 17th century Great Tew Park manor house in Oxfordshire fetched £2.6 million in a three-day auction.

WARNING: Tuffin

50,000 facing job axe

THEFTS PROBE SHUTS MORGUE

A MORTUARY has been shut while police probe alleged thefts from dead bodies.

One official at Southwark morgue has been suspended by the council after complaints that possessions had gone missing in the building.

Bodies which the mortuary would normally have handled are being transferred to Westminster.

Police said: "When a body arrives all possessions are logged, but it seems some have disappeared. The superintendent is not under investigation."

A man and a woman have been interviewed in connection with three thefts and are on bail.

STAR'S WIFE MISSING

THE wife of TV Honeymonster star Peter Jackson has gone missing.

Eve, 47, left home four days ago in her husband's Porsche, abandoning it for a rented Peugeot.

Peter, who plays the Honeymonster in a cereal ad called in police when she failed to return to their luxury home at Saffron Walden, Essex.

Police said: "We are concerned for her safety. She has been depressed."

HEART-SWAP MAN IN CELL DRAMA

A HEART-SWAP man collapsed in police cells yesterday minutes after magistrates' rejected his life-or-death bail plea.

Musician and songwriter Terrence Cox, 42, who was given a new heart a year ago, was carried from London's Marylebone court to an ambulance.

Last night, after hospital treatment, he was in the medical wing of Brixton jail.

Cox, of Bayswater, West London — ex husband of glamour model Flanigan —faces various drugs charges.

His solicitor said he could die unless he received regular treatment.

Cox was remanded in custody for a week.

UPSET: Freddie

Silent Starr quits show

ZANY comic Freddie Starr cancelled a sell-out concert in Sheffield last night after losing his voice.

Freddie had visited four towns on the tour, before his voice gave out on stage at Wolverhampton.

The tour promoters said: "Freddie is very upset about letting his fans down."

30th May 1987

RED BARON BUZZES THE KREMLIN

Joyride German beats Russia's mighty radar

The Kremlin went on red alert as an unidentified aircraft swooped low over Moscow.

There was even more alarm when the plane buzzed Lenin's mausoleum . . . and landed in historic Red Square.

The daredevil pilot, 19-year-old West German Mathias Rust, coolly stepped out of the four-seater Cessna and started signing autographs.

Police quickly whisked the joyrider away.

And last night embarrassed Soviet officials were trying to find out how the plane dodged sophisticated air defence systems to fly to the heart of the Russian capital.

One senior Western observer said: "The implications for Soviet defences, and for the whole debate on how a war could start by mistake, are astounding."

Bet

Rust's amazing 560-mile flight began in Helsinki.

He was thought to be heading for Sweden, but vanished from Finnish radar screens and was not heard of again until his landing in Moscow.

Planes are banned from flying over the city.

Crowds watched in astonishment as the little Cessna taxied over the cobblestones to park by buses lined up near the Kremlin wall.

The young Hamburg pilot, in hiking boots and a red flight suit, chatted to children and a group of German tourists.

Giggled

British nanny Juliet Butler, who was in Red Square, said: "At first the police seemed relaxed and just giggled.

"Then some higher officers came in big cars and the square was sealed off."

Russian artist, Ilya Anosov, 21, said: "All we could think was that he was drunk and made a bet that he could fly to Red Square."

The Cessna was carted off on a truck and Rust was still being questioned last night.

In Hamburg his flying instructor said: "We'll paint a red star on the plane when it returns."

5th September 1987

RED BARON BOY GETS FOUR YEARS

DAREDEVIL pilot Mathias Rust learned the price yesterday of making fools of the Soviet air defence brass-hats – four years' hard labour.

That is the penalty he must pay for his cheeky flight below Russian radar surveillance which ended with his historic landing in Moscow's Red Square last May.

Rust, dubbed the Red Baron after the infamous First World War German fighter pilot, was sentenced to four years for "malicious hooliganism," three years for violating international flight rules and two years for illegally crossing the border. All the sentences will run concurrently.

Rust, 19, showed no emotion when the sentence was announced and was escorted out of the courtroom by two guards.

Later his mother said she was "upset." But she would not say whether there would be an appeal against the verdict.

Rust's defence was that he had flown to Moscow to talk to Soviet leader Mikhail Gorbachev about world peace.

His defence lawyer told the Moscow court that he was "naïve".

But the judge cited the written testimony of a West German tour guide, who quoted Rust as telling him he had flown to Red Square "as a joke".

Threat

Judge Robert Tikhomirnov said: "This leads to the conclusion that Rust was motivated above all by adventurism."

Rust, making a final statement before the judge pronounced the verdict and sentence, told the court:

"I am very sorry ... I would like to appeal to you. I can guarantee that if you give me a mild punishment I will not betray your trust."

But the judge ignored the young West German's plea – and gave much weight to witnesses who said that he had flown dangerously low over the Kremlin wall and had posed a threat to people.

BACKSTORY

Mathias Rust had actually landed on a bridge and taxied into Red Square. A stomach bug would later stop him being sent to a Soviet labour camp. He served 432 days in all, before being freed to return to Germany as a sign of goodwill during East–West peace talks.

Rust later stabbed a nurse colleague in a Hamburg hospital. He has since worked as a financial analyst and yoga instructor.

The fallout for Soviet security officers was mass sackings and fury that the country's radar system had been penetrated.

DAILY Mirror

Wednesday, March 23, 1988   FORWARD WITH BRITAIN   ★   20p

EXCLUSIVE

Full story of the child brought up by a dog

SHOCKING: Little Horst Werner Reinhard

'We were stopped from saving soldiers'

MIRROR EXCLUSIVE
by HARRY KING

AN ARMY patrol could have saved the two British soldiers murdered by the Belfast funeral mob, a young serviceman told the Mirror last night.

But as they watched the pair being confronted by their executioners, they were told to pull out.

The soldier said:

❝ I was one of eight troops who saw them being strip-searched in Casement Park. We each had automatic rifles and could have dispersed the mob by firing over their heads.

But as we watched in horror, we were ordered over our radio to withdraw.

We had asked for instructions and the reply was: 'Don't interfere'. ❞

The soldier, from a Scottish regiment, declined to give his name.

Dragged

He said: "I am calling the Mirror to correct statements by the Northern Ireland Secretary, and others in authority, that there were no troops 'on the ground' at this funeral.

"There were 16 soldiers and two RUC men in the area. I was one of them."

The Army denied his claims last night, claiming the patrol on checkpoint duties was ordered to stay put because other soldiers were already on their way to the scene.

●TV Chiefs In Ulster Storm — See Page 2

WEIRD WORLD OF PUPPY BOY

COMING ALONG NICELY

Picture: MIKE MALONEY

RADIANT Fergie stepped out in the spring sunshine yesterday and showed the world she is blossoming steadily into motherhood.

Unusually, though, no one mentioned the baby due in August when

the Duchess visited a hospital for the mentally handicapped at Leavesden, Herts. Hospital sister Molly Sheppard explained: "We didn't talk too much in advance about the baby because we were afraid one of the patients might pat her tummy."

THE appalling life of a little boy brought up by the family dog shocked the world.

Now the Daily Mirror can reveal the whole horrifying story of three-year-old Horst Werner Reinhard.

As little Horst begins life as a human in a clinic, we report on how alsatian Asta, deprived of her own litter of puppies, turned her affection to the neglected baby and raised him as her own.

She shared her food with him and licked him clean.

She even kept him warm at night, curled up against her tummy.

And Horst, knowing nothing about human behaviour, learned everything from her.

Left alone with Asta day after day, little Horst grew into the puppy boy.

●Full story — Page 5

CHANGE YOUR LIFE TODAY ▸ YOU'RE ALL AT IT!
— *See Page 25*

23rd March 1988

WEIRD WORLD OF PUPPY BOY

Full story of the child brought up by a dog

THE appalling life of a little boy brought up by the family dog shocked the world.

Now the Daily Mirror can reveal the whole horrifying story of three-year-old Horst Werner Reinhard.

As little Horst begins life as a human in a clinic, we report on how Alsatian Asta, deprived of her own litter of puppies, turned her affection to the neglected baby and raised him as her own.

She shared her food with him and licked him.

And Horst, knowing nothing about human behaviours, learned everything from her.

Left alone with Asta day after day, little Horst grew into the puppy boy.

By Dennis Newson and Roger Todd

PUPPY boy Horst is three years and four months old – and just beginning his life as a human being.

He is the child raised by a devoted pet Alsatian called Asta while his parents went out drinking.

He became so like a dog that he didn't know how to use a toilet – and cocked his leg instead.

Now, as Horst gradually learns the behaviour of a normal little boy, the full shocking story of his lost babyhood is slowly being unravelled.

Alsatian Asta had a litter of eight puppies just before Horst was born in November 1984 and they were taken from her.

Pining for her brood, the dog turned her affections to the new baby.

Asta nuzzled him, licked his hands, face and bottom clean, kept him warm in a furry blanket under her tummy.

Horst's grandmother Elisabeth said: "I saw how the dog's mothering instinct was transferred to the boy. She never left his side and growled when anyone came near."

And the caretaker at the flats in Mettmann, West Germany, said: "They touched and stroked each other. The dog was the only one who gave him anything like love."

Meanwhile the parents left them in squalor. They gave Asta meat and water. They put bananas, milk and porridge out for Horst.

Growled

It seems they didn't notice that their son was growing more and more like a dog.

He whimpered and growled instead of talked. He preferred crawling to walking. He slept curled up like a puppy, his head between his "paws".

One day Horst, dressed only in pyjamas, was found tottering in the road.

Asta was nudging him with her nose to help him stand.

As a result, Horst's father took the handles off the doors to stop him escaping again.

Horst and Asta were confined to one room. They were eventually discovered there, sharing a raw chicken. The wallpaper was clawed into tatters.

There was a kennel stench. Scraps of old food were scattered round.

Horst's cot was unused, covered with a film of grime. There were no toys save a squeaky rubber rabbit.

Now Horst Werner Reinhard is in a clinic in Wuppertal being reborn.

He can keep down hot food – which he had never had – and he has added weight to his feeble frame, a third underweight.

A Hamburg psychologist said: "These 'wolf children' are emotional cripples. Their souls are lifeless."

But there is hope for Horst.

The staff are talking to him, slowly teaching him about cuddles, smiles, toys and encouraging him to explore his new world.

And he's learning that humans can be loving too.

DAILY Mirror

Friday, June 3, 1988   FORWARD WITH BRITAIN   ★ 20p

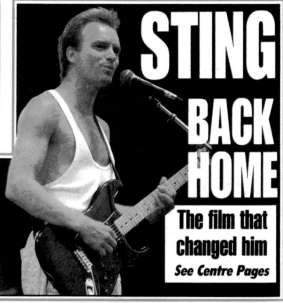

STING BACK HOME

The film that changed him

See Centre Pages

Colour Special
WHAT MADE THE QUEEN GIGGLE
Pages 2 and 3

'Greedy airlines putting lives in peril'

By ROGER TODD

THE Daily Mirror's shock revelations that greedy charter companies are forcing pilots to fly beyond their limits were backed yesterday by the TUC.

In a hard-hitting report, it said pilots are flying when exhausted because they fear the sack.

And a top expert with the pilots' union BALPA, Air Commodore Freddie Yetman, said one pilot had finally rebelled against his bosses.

Courage

He revealed: "One captain who was coming up to retirement landed at Bournemouth rather than continue to his destination, Manchester.

"But it takes a lot of courage to do that.

"Some of the younger pilots feel very vulnerable."

The report, launched by TUC general secretary Norman Willis and other unions, also accused the greedy charter airlines of neglecting safety maintenance for profit.

I LAUGHED MY HEAD OFF

(...but the docs have stuck it back on again)

By BRIAN CROWTHER

LUCKY John Font has made medical history . . by being the first man to literally laugh his head off.

Poker player John was so excited when he was dealt a winning hand that the pressure split open an old fracture in his skull, left from a fall when he was six.

His astonished workmates called an ambulance and an hour later surgeons stuck his skull back together with glue then stitched him up.

And still the happy-go-lucky council workman managed to raise a smile.

"He hasn't lost his sense of humour," his wife Sandra said yesterday. "I must admit I didn't know whether to laugh or cry."

She added:"The doctors were really surprised — I don't think they had seen anything like it before.

"They said his skull had been weakened by the accident when he was a lad and fell off a bridge."

John, 32, of Wallasey, Merseyside, has headaches and has twice suffered meningitis because

● Turn to Page 2

IN STITCHES: Laughing John Font after his op.

3rd June 1988

I LAUGHED MY HEAD OFF

(BUT THE DOCS HAVE STUCK IT BACK ON AGAIN)

By Brian Crowther

LUCKY John Font has made medical history . . . by being the first man to literally laugh his head off.

Poker player John was so excited when he was dealt a winning hand that the pressure split open an old fracture in his skull, left from a fall when he was six.

His astonished workmates called an ambulance and an hour later surgeons stuck his skull back together with glue then stitched him up.

And still the happy-go-lucky council workman managed to raise a smile.

"He hasn't lost his sense of humour," his wife Sandra said yesterday. "I must admit I didn't know whether to laugh or cry."

She added: "The doctors were really surprised – I don't think they had seen anything like it before.

"They said his skull had been weakened by the accident when he was a lad and fell off a bridge."

John, 32, of Wallasey, Merseyside, has headaches and has twice suffered meningitis because of the childhood accident.

He and his workmates at Wirral Borough Council were playing for 25p stakes when he came up with a full house to sweep the pot.

He threw back his head to roar with delight at his rare stroke of good luck.

John said from his bed in the neurological ward at Liverpool's Walton Hospital: "I didn't think much of it at first."

John will be off work for six weeks and may not be able to do heavy work again. But he doesn't even mind his family and friends laughing at his bald head after being shaved for the operation.

However, he won't be laughing when he next plays cards.

He'll keep a poker face – and his head on.

BACKSTORY

John Font's laughing fit and its dire consequences brought to mind the unfortunate story of Alex Mitchell.

In 1975, Mitchell, a 50-year-old bricklayer from King's Lynn, was watching an episode of *The Goodies* on television. The pivotal scene came when Bill Oddie, playing an expert in the Lancastrian martial art of "ecky thump", attacked Tim Brooke-Taylor, portraying a bagpipe-playing Scotsman.

Mitchell laughed so hard he collapsed and died. It was later discovered that he had a heart condition in which an attack could be triggered by sudden exertion. So Mr Mitchell literally did die laughing.

His wife Nessie later wrote to The Goodies (below) to thank them for making her husband die very happy.

DAILY Mirror

Tuesday, May 24, 1988   FORWARD WITH BRITAIN   ★   20p

'One dead' as fire hits cargo ferry

By CHRISTIAN GYSIN

FIREMEN were airlifted by helicopter to a Sealink cargo ferry in mid-Channel early today after fire swept through the ship.

A tug also set out from the Belgian port of Ostend to join in the dramatic rescue operation.

One crewman is feared dead.

The blaze broke out in the engine room shortly before 10pm as the vessel, Seafreight Freeway, headed for Zeebrugge from Dover.

The 5,088-ton ship — a roll-on roll-off lorry ferry loaded with trucks and containers — was 28 miles due east of Ramsgate.

Doctor

There were 32 crew on board and 45 lorry drivers.

Lifeboats from Dover and Ramsgate set off to help the stricken ship and a helicopter, carrying a doctor, flew from Manston, Kent.

A coastguard spokesman said last night: "One member of the crew is unaccounted for and we are still double-checking on figures.

"One crew member who has been badly burned has been taken off the ship by helicopter."

The engine room was evacuated and at one stage there were reports that the crew and passengers were set to abandon ship.

Last night it was reported that the ferry was carrying a dangerous cargo and the Dover lifeboat was keeping one mile away from the burning ship.

Here is The Six O'Clock News . .

BEEB MAN SITS ON LESBIAN

By JOHN PEACOCK and GRAHAM BARNES

FOUR lesbian demonstrators burst into a TV studio last night 'as Sue Lawley started to present the BBC Six O'Clock News.

In the chaos, co-presenter Nicholas Witchell 'swiftly SAT on one who had handcuffed herself to a desk beside Sue.

He put his hand over her mouth to silence her shouted slogans.

Another lesbian locked herself to a TV camera . . . but Sue kept her cool and pressed ahead.

As millions of viewers heard muffled shouting and the picture shook on their screens, Sue said calmly: "We have rather been invaded."

The commotion went on for four minutes during the bulletin before BBC staff managed to drag the women away.

The four lesbians came within feet of getting "on camera" to protest about the Government's law banning local authorities from promoting homosexuality, which came into effect at midnight.

Last night a major security investigation was underway at the BBC over the lesbians' raid on the Shepherd's Bush studios in West London.

Attack

Security was tightened last year after a gang of robbers squirted ammonia into the face of Jan Leeming as she was preparing to read the Ten O'Clock News.

A BBC man said last night: "Clearly, something has gone very wrong when this sort of thing can happen."

Ron Neil, the BBC's deputy director of news and current affairs, praised the actions of the Lawley-Witchell team.

He said: "Presenting

..while Sue reads on with woman chained to her desk

WITCHELL: Gagged shouting lesbian

LAWLEY: Stayed calm during drama

● Turn to Page 2

202

24th May 1988

BEEB MAN SITS ON LESBIAN

Here is the Six O'Clock News
By John Peacock and Graham Barnes

FOUR lesbian demonstrators burst into a TV studio last night as Sue Lawley started to present the BBC Six O'Clock News.

In the chaos, co-presenter Nicholas Witchell swiftly SAT on one who had handcuffed herself to a desk beside Sue.

He put his hand over her mouth to silence her shouted slogans.

Another lesbian locked herself to a TV camera . . . but Sue kept her cool and pressed ahead.

As millions of viewers heard muffled shouting and the picture shook on their screens, Sue said calmly: "We have rather been invaded."

The commotion went on for four minutes during the bulletin before BBC staff managed to drag the women away.

The four lesbians came within feet of getting "on camera" to protest about the Government's law banning local authorities from promoting homosexuality, which came into effect at midnight.

Last night a major security investigation was underway at the BBC over the lesbians' raid on the Shepherd's Bush studios in West London.

Attack

Security was tightened last year after a gang of robbers squirted ammonia into the face of Jan Leeming as she was preparing to read the Ten O'Clock News.

A BBC man said last night: "Clearly, something has gone very wrong when this sort of thing can happen."

Ron Neil, the BBC's deputy director of news and current affairs, praised the actions of the Lawley–Witchell team.

He said: "Presenting the news which is live is the most difficult of tasks in normal conditions.

"To carry on through that kind of unnerving and unpredicted invasion shows a superb level of professionalism."

Even cool, calm Sue admitted: "It was a very alarming experience."

Nicholas Witchell said: "I found one woman had handcuffed herself to Sue's desk so I sat on her and put my hand over her mouth.

"I thought we would be taken off air.

"But Sue, very calmly, kept running through the introduction to the first piece."

The four women detained by BBC security men were handed over to police.

But Scotland Yard said that no allegations of criminal offences had been made against them and they were released.

The leader of the lesbian raid, 25-year-old Sarah Ponsonby, told how they swung into action. She said:

"The second we got inside the news room a pal and I handcuffed ourselves to a desk. I was within a foot of Sue Lawley, but she just kept her cool and carried on reading the news as if nothing had happened.

"But within seconds I was flattened as a man with ginger hair – who I later discovered was Nicholas Witchell – jumped on top of me.

"He kept his hand over my mouth and hissed in my ear repeatedly, 'Keep your effing mouth shut'.

"I couldn't believe his language, especially someone from the BBC. It seemed so out of character – and in my opinion so unnecessary. I mean, I could hardly breathe, let alone speak.

"His grip was so tight during the incident my right arm has been left grazed and it's red raw. Amazingly, the police told me I could still be charged with assault – but it's him who should be charged with assault. He just flipped."

Annie Fields, who handcuffed herself to the camera, said: "Sue Lawley acted superbly and handled the situation very coolly.

"Nicholas Witchell, in contrast, just panicked."

How did the lesbian protestors get through the security at the BBC studios?

"It's like walking into Woolworth's – as simple as that," said leader Sarah Ponsonby.

◀ Newsreader Nicholas Witchell in less familiar guise, dressed up as Danny from *Grease*, for a Children in Need routine, along with colleague Jennie Bond.

BACKSTORY

The campaign against Section 28, banning promotion of homosexuality, was the cause behind the remarkable invasion of the BBC news studio. The section, part of the Local Government Act of 1988, led to waves of protest and its eventual repeal in 2003.

LOOK OUT COMRADE, THE ALIENS HAVE LANDED . .

Flying saucer drops into a Russian park!

By NICHOLAS DAVIES, Foreign Editor

IT'S OFFICIAL comrades! Aliens have landed their spaceship in a Russian park.

In a typically-deadpan announcement, the Soviet news agency Tass revealed that the visitors from outer space were up to 12ft tall and had little heads.

They went for a short walk, but didn't stay long. And the three strangers had a small robot-like creature with them.

Shining

Tass says the extra-terrestrial tourists dropped in on the Soviet city of Voronezh, 300 miles south of Moscow.

"Scientists have confirmed that an unidentified flying object landed in a park," Tass disclosed.

"They have identified the site and found traces of aliens who made a short promenade around the park." The visitors arrived and left in a large, shining ball or disc which hovered over the park.

Onlookers, said Tass, were overwhelmed by fear that gripped them for days.

Experts at the scene found a 60ft depression in the grass, four deep dents and two bits of unidentified red rock which "cannot be found on earth"

They apparently proved the story was true by a method of tracking which they called "biolocation"

Excitement

But Tass did not explain what on earth "biolocation" means.

Residents of Voronezh also reported recent sightings of a banana-shaped object.

The arrival of the lanky pea-heads has caused almost as much excitement as a previous story concerning a milkmaid and an alien in Perm in central Russia.

She swore that she met a man who was "taller than average, with short legs and had only a small knob instead of a head"

Last toll

BELL-RINGER Wilf Horwell, 63, died in the church tower at Newton Abbot, Devon, during a wedding service.

RED ALERT: He came from outer space..

Tragic angel on TV

MURDERED drug "angel" Liz Page-Alucard helped Esther Rantzen to launch a TV crusade against drugs, it was revealed yesterday.

Reformed addict Liz, 41, appeared with Esther on the Drugwatch programme on BBC three years ago.

Liz was found

BATTERED: Liz

battered to death on Saturday in a drug advice centre run by the Turning Point charity in Worcester.

Police hunting her killer said three-times married Liz changed her name to Page-Alucard –Dracula backwards – after jail terms for prostitution and theft.

TOGETHERNESS: Jane and boyfriend Lorenzo arrive for the premiere

JANE'S FAMILY MOVIE

IF a film's that good, take the family. And actress Jane Fonda was obviously pleased with her latest film, Old Gringo.

When it was premiered in New York, Jane made it a real family outing. She took along boyfriend Lorenzo Caccialanza . . . and her daughter Vanessa Vadim, her brother Peter Fonda and his wife and Shirlee Fonda, wife of Jane's late father Henry.

Which just goes to prove how Fonda each other they all are.

NEWS ‡ NEWS ‡ NEWS ‡ NEWS ‡ NEWS ‡ NEWS ‡ NEWS

PHEW! YOU ARE NICKED

JAIL escaper Kevin Halford, 22, was caught – because his feet smell.

He took off his shoes and ran when he was spotted in Dudley, West Midlands – and the pong led police dogs to him.

Tank crew calls RAC

RAC patrolman Tony Curtis wasn't up to the job when he answered a breakdown call – and found a TANK.

Three stranded soldiers who had phoned for the RAC, meaning the Royal Armoured Corps, got the Royal Automobile Club instead.

Tony, who found the eight-ton Scorpion tank near Wimborne, Dorset, said: "I was going to tow it but I couldn't move the thing."

LITTLE MONKEY.

CATS LIKE FELIX LIKE felix

10ᵗʰ October **1989**

LOOK OUT COMRADE, THE ALIENS HAVE LANDED

Flying saucer drops into a Russian park!

By Nicholas Davies, Foreign Editor

IT'S OFFICIAL, comrades! Aliens have landed their spaceship in a Russian park.

In a typically deadpan announcement, the Soviet news agency Tass revealed that the visitors from outer space were up to 12ft tall and had little heads.

They went for a short walk but didn't stay long. And the three strangers had a small, robot-like creature with them.

Shining

Tass says the extra-terrestrial tourists dropped in on the Soviet city of Voronezh, 300 miles south of Moscow.

"Scientists have confirmed that an unidentified flying object landed in a park," Tass disclosed.

"They have identified the site and found traces of aliens who made a short promenade around the park."

The visitors arrived and left in a large, shining ball or disc, which hovered over the park.

Onlookers, said Tass, were overwhelmed by fear that gripped them for days.

Experts at the scene found a 60ft depression in the grass, four deep dents, and two bits of unidentified red rock which "cannot be found on Earth."

They apparently proved the story was true by a method of tracking which they called "bilocation".

Excitement

But Tass did not explain what on Earth "bilocation" means.

Residents of Voronezh also reported recent sightings of a banana-shaped object.

The arrival of the lanky pea-heads has caused as much excitement as a previous story concerning a milk maid and an alien in Perm in central Russia.

She swore that she met a man who was "taller than average, with short legs and had only a small knob instead of a head."

BACKSTORY

The Voronezh UFO sighting remains one of the strangest cases of supposed alien encounters. There was widespread belief that Tass had greatly exaggerated the story. Other reports, however, said eyewitness accounts corroborated the supposed details – including that the aliens made children momentarily disappear and that they had three eyes.

Whatever the truth of the yarn, it was perhaps a sign of changing political times. The era of Glasnost in the Soviet Union under Mikhail Gorbachev (below, meeting John Major) marked a thaw in East–West relations and ultimately to the break-up of the Soviet Union and the collapse of communism in Eastern Europe.

DAILY Mirror

Friday, March 30, 1990 COLOUR NEWSPAPER OF THE YEAR Average daily sale w/e March 24: 3,916,303 (INCORPORATING THE DAILY RECORD) 22p

EXECUTED

KILLED: Arms dealer Bull

Man who could have blown nuke sting shot dead

EVIL: Iraqi tyrant Hussein

White couple keep Asian child

By ROD CHAYTOR

A WHITE couple last night celebrated a court ruling which allows them to keep the Asian foster child they have cared for almost since birth.

England's top family judge said the foster parents CAN adopt the three-year-old girl.

The Birmingham case was hailed as a major step towards ending the scandal of children being snatched from loving foster homes.

And it followed the Daily Mirror's "torn apart" campaign which highlighted the heartbreak caused by official opposition to mixed-race fostering.

Natural

The foster parents launched a legal battle last October to stop Birmingham social workers from placing the girl with an Asian family.

She has been with them since she was six days old and calls them Mummy and Daddy.

But social workers wanted her brought up with foster parents from the same cultural background as her natural parents.

In his ruling yesterday, Sir Stephen Brown, president of the High Court family division, said the child's welfare was "paramount."

The couple hope to adopt the youngster – who can't be named – within three months.

A friend said last night: "They are overjoyed."

COCKNEY comic Jim Davidson cuddled his stunning wife Tracie last night and asked: "How do you like her nose job?" Ex-model Tracie, 24, sported a bandage across her hooter, altered by plastic surgery.

"Nick Nick" Davidson, 36, was back filming a TV series in London 24 hours after police quizzed him over an alleged assault on his son's nanny. But his problems weren't over.

He was confronted outside the Royalty Theatre by an angry crowd protesting against his "racist" jokes on television.

Picture: TONY BOLDER

SHE NOSE, YOU KNOW

EXCLUSIVE

AN arms smuggler who could have blown the "sting" against Iraqi nuclear smugglers was shot dead just days before the trap was sprung.

Canadian-born Dr Gerry Bull, who was on the Iraqi payroll, had been due to check 40 A-bomb triggers being smuggled through Heathrow to Baghdad.

By TED OLIVER and RONALD PAYNE

He was the only person who could have spotted that agents had swapped the triggers for identical dummies after an 18-month undercover stake-out.

But before he could see the "merchandise," Bull was shot twice in the neck with a silenced 7.65mm automatic at his Brussels apartment on Saturday.

Killers

His wallet, containing £16,000, was untouched.

Last night, the list of his possible killers included:

● Britain's MI6 or the American CIA, to stop the 62-year-old weapons expert revealing the "sting."

● Iraq, which may have become suspicious of his links with arch-enemy Iran, who also used Bull.

● The Israeli secret service, Mossad, which will stop at nothing to prevent Iraqi tyrant Saddam Hussein developing nuclear weapons.

● Shady arms dealers who may have thought Bull was trying to double-cross them.

Security sources believe Bull was deeply involved in the trigger plot masterminded by Omar Latif, snared in Wednesday's swoop at Heathrow.

Latif, who is also believed to have been involved in a second plot to smuggle acoustic mine detonators from Britain to Iraq, will be deported today.

At least two more plotters are expected to be arrested as they fly in from North Africa.

Dr Bull, who would work for anyone if the price was right, was a ballistics genius.

He invented a system for the US to fire shells into space.

He produced a howitzer for South Africa.

And he helped China develop their Silkworm missile used in the Gulf war.

He was a man with many masters. Last night the big question was, which one killed him?

Thatcher sends atom bomber home: Page 2

30th March 1990
EXECUTED

Man who could have blown nuke sting shot dead
By Ted Oliver and Ronald Payne

AN arms smuggler who could have blown the "sting" against Iraqi nuclear smugglers was shot dead just days before the trap was sprung.

Canadian-born Dr Gerry Bull, who was on the Iraqi payroll, had been due to check 40 A-bomb triggers being smuggled through Heathrow to Baghdad.

He was the only person who could have spotted that agents had swapped the triggers for identical dummies after an 18-month undercover stake-out.

But before he could see the "merchandise", Bull was shot twice in the neck with a silenced 7.65-automatic at his Brussels apartment on Saturday.

Killers

His wallet, containing £16,000, was untouched.

Last night, the list of his possible killers included:

• Britain's MI6 or the American CIA, to stop the 62-year-old weapons expert revealing the "sting."

• Iraq, which may have become suspicious of his links with arch-enemy Iran, who also used Bull.

• The Israeli secret service, Mossad, which will stop at nothing to prevent Iraqi tyrant Saddam Hussein developing nuclear weapons.

• Shady arms dealers who may have thought Bull was trying to double-cross them.

Security sources believe Bull was deeply involved in the trigger plot masterminded by Omar Latif, snared in Wednesday's swoop at Heathrow.

Latif, who is also believed to have been involved in a second plot to smuggle acoustic mine detonators from Britain to Iraq, will be deported today.

At least two more plotters are expected to be arrested as they fly from North Africa.

Dr Bull, who would work for anyone if the price was right, was a ballistics genius.

He invented a system for the US to fire shells into space.

He produced a howitzer for South Africa.

And he helped China develop their Silkworm missile used in the Gulf War.

He was a man with many masters. Last night the question was, which one killed him?

12th April 1990
IRAQ'S NUKE SUPER GUN IS SEIZED

By Bill Akass

BRITISH Customs men yesterday foiled a bid to smuggle the world's biggest gun – capable of firing a nuclear shell – to Iran

The mighty "Big Bertha" cannon, with a 130ft barrel, could blast a nuclear or chemical shell several hundred miles into Iran or Israel.

And last night the Daily Mirror learned that it was designed by international arms dealer Dr Gerald Bull who was shot dead in Belgium last month.

The seizure at a British port came only a fortnight after Customs revealed that 40 nuclear bomb triggers bound for Iraq had been grabbed at Heathrow airport.

It raised new fears that the brutal regime of Saddam Hussein is building up forces to strike a devastating blow against its enemies.

BACKSTORY

With the First Gulf War that would put British troops into the firing line just nine months away, the story of Dr Gerald Bull provided one of the most mysterious and sinister aspects of the conflict. The Canadian's assassination in the midst of an operation to stop nuclear weapons parts heading for Iraq was just one chapter in a complex and extraordinary story.

The supergun that could terrorize and devastate Saddam's enemies at great distances was part of Project Babylon, a plan devised by Bull. Barrels, tubes and components were to be built by a number of companies around Europe.

At the time there was an arms embargo banning weapons sales to Iraq still supposedly in place. Arrests were made of personnel working for British companies, but the charges were dropped, amid claims from the companies that they had been duped, and later allegations of links to a wider arms-to-Iraq affair that reached right to the heart of the British government.

And what of the guns themselves? Tests had shown the concept was feasible, but the actual superguns were never completed nor fired in anger. Some of the material used in the construction was destroyed after the First Gulf War, while some of the barrel sections were assembled at the Royal Artillery Museum in Woolwich, South London.

Bull's murder was never solved. Saddam Hussein was toppled in the Second Gulf War.